DYNASTY

DYNASTY

SCANDALS, TRIUMPH, TURMOIL
AND SUCCESSION AT THE HEART OF
DUNNES STORES

MATT COOPER

eriu

First published in the UK in 2025 by Eriu
An imprint of Bonnier Books UK
5th Floor, HYLO, 105 Bunhill Row,
London, EC1Y 8LZ

A CIP catalogue record for this book is available from the British Library.

Hardback ISBN: 978-1-80418-898-9

Also available as an ebook and audiobook

1 3 5 7 9 10 8 6 4 2

Typeset by IDSUK (Data Connection) Ltd
Printed and bound in Great Britain by Clays Ltd, Elcograf S.p.A.

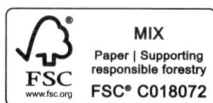

The authorised representative in the EEA is
Bonnier Books UK (Ireland) Limited.
Registered office address: Floor 3, Block 3, Miesian Plaza,
Dublin 2, D02 Y754, Ireland
compliance@bonnierbooks.ie
www.bonnierbooks.co.uk

Contents

Prologue: From The Chief to The Custodian   1

**Part 1 The Founding Father – the life and times of
Ben Dunne Snr: 1940s–1960s**

1. Dunn, not yet Dunne   7
2. The first shop   13
3. After The Emergency   17
4. Swinging through the sixties   21
5. The big new thing   27
6. Changing tastes   31
7. A display of power and justice   37
8. The last word   45
9. Keeping it all secret   51

Part 2 Bloodline: 1971–1981

10. The Dunnes juggernaut   59
11. Frank's reluctant ascent   65
12. The next Ben rises   73
13. The kidnapping   79
14. The rescue   89

Part 3 A New Era: 1980s

15. Death of the patriarch   99
16. Price wars and their casualties   109
17. The dark horse   117
18. Apartheid   125
19. The bread wars   133
20. Ruthless winners   141

Part 4 The Blowout and the Fallout: 1990–1994

21. Crossing the Rubicon   153
22. Weathering the storm   165

23. Seeking forgiveness 171
24. The war of the siblings 175
25. The coup 183
26. The slow unravelling 191
27. Bad blood 199
28. Courtroom drama 205

Part 5 Power Plays: 1995–1999

29. More tragedy, more conflict 215
30. Zealous custodian and guardian 227
31. The Lowry affair 237
32. Investigating hidden payments 243
33. The McCracken Tribunal and its revelations 249
34. Haughey's evidence 257
35. Lowry's skewed perception of reality 265
36. Desperate people and desperate things – the
    Moriarty Tribunal 271

Part 6 New roles for Ben and Margaret: 2000s–2020s

37. Rivals 283
38. Legal combat 291
39. The Great Recession 297
40. Fitness test 305
41. Attention-seeking 313
42. Frank's legacy 321
43. Ben's death 325

Part 7 The 21st-century Dunnes Stores

44. At your service 333
45. Simply better 339
46. Market leader 347

Epilogue: The dynasty endures for now . . . 351
Sources cited 359
Acknowledgements 361
Index 363

Prologue: From The Chief to The Custodian

THE STORY OF DUNNES STORES – of both the company and the family that owns it – is simply better than any other business saga in the history of the Irish State. It is a story of success, scandal, and schisms, tragedy, disaster and disgrace, with big personalities, both male and female, taking centre-stage in a battle for leadership and legacy. The corporate and the personal are essentially as one, the company and family being everything to each other, identities deeply entwined. It is a story of wealth and power and the use of both.

It also tells us much about how Ireland has developed over more than 80 years, economically and culturally. It describes how we spend our money and our changed and changing tastes. It reminds us how once it was the men who held sway, with sons expected to take control because that's what sons did – and what daughters did not do. But the story of late 20th-century and 21st-century Dunnes Stores is of strong women coming to the fore and displacing the men.

The significance and importance of the Dunnes and their company is clear. What other Irish family corporate dynasties have endured so successfully and for so long? A claim could be made for the Guinness family, but not a particularly strong one. Arthur Guinness created what we now call a 'brand' centuries ago – giving his name to a stout, the country's most famous alcohol product to this day – but ownership and control of the creation passed from his family to others generations ago. Dunnes Stores is not an international brand, admittedly – although that is by choice, having wisely retreated from its foray into Britain – but its name is recognised by almost everyone living in Ireland. It is one of our best-known companies, visible in our streets and shopping centres, part of the fabric of Irish life since the 1940s. On a weekly basis, at least €1 in every €5 spent in our supermarkets goes into its tills. It has clothed generations at prices affordable to them. It was and remains a significant employer, although the pay and conditions for workers have often been contentious; and it was and remains crucial to the financial wellbeing of many suppliers, although again this has led to controversy, sometimes recounted in court battles.

Dunnes has seen off various local and international competitors and is in active contest with those who remain or arrive to challenge it for market share and profitability. It has over 130 outlets across the 32 counties of the island of Ireland. It has not just survived in the internet shopping era but thrived; its directors, cautiously at first, have adapted to modern retailing. The improved quality of its stock, both in food and clothing, illustrates the evolving demands of the Irish consumer and Dunnes' willingness to know and follow its market. The Dunne family have created a 21st-century retailer that is dramatically different from what it was but has stayed true to the core principles of the founders.

Financial details of the company's performance are closely guarded – even from the top levels of management – but annual profits of over €300m may be achieved regularly, according to industry estimates. The overall value of the business, if it was ever sold, could be over €4bn, according to competitors, based on trading profitability and its vast property portfolio. Despite much speculation over the years that it would be sold, that proposition is unlikely to be put to the test for many years yet, for sentimental as much as financial reasons. The Dunnes are ruthless and hard-headed businesspeople, but not so much that they would sell the company to convert their wealth into hard cash; when it comes to that, the heart rules.

It's not just that the name will remain above the door, but that the family will own and run it, the shareholdings spread between offspring bearing the names Dunne, Heffernan and McMahon, but all from the Dunne bloodline. There are no shares or options for trusted advisers and management: they get paid generously according to performance but will never receive equity; family ownership will not be diluted. The Irish businessman Michael Smurfit once said 'equity is blood', but it is the Dunnes who have lived by that maxim, not him.

This success has created extraordinary wealth for the family to share, and yet money has not insulated them from the vicissitudes of everyday life and the experiences that mould all of us. It is a family that has been cursed at times by the impact of addiction, in particular to alcohol but also in one famous case to cocaine. The illness of alcoholism has caused tragic premature deaths. There have been many instances of serious ill-health, relationship disharmony and marital break-up. A plentiful bounty of money has provided a salve in some difficult situations but, equally, great wealth has been an accelerant of difficulties for others. Wealth came quickly, and perhaps too easily, even though the initial demand of the family was that every beneficiary had to work. In one generation there was no choice but to contribute because it was expected by the founders, no matter what ambitions were held by their children. In the next generation fewer children wanted to pitch in as their parents had, some were found wanting when it came to the necessary ability and were jettisoned. Others have detached themselves, choosing to do different things, cushioned by access to family money. In some cases personal identities have been dictated by service to the company, or rejection of it.

Many families have siblings who row, or children who disagree with their parents, but with bigger stakes at play this is a family that has often torn itself apart. At times, and in the public eye despite best efforts not to be there, it has become embroiled in argument and controversy, some of it caused by personal behaviour but more of it by anger at the perceived impact of personal failings on the all-important business.

A family that prizes its privacy has seen many of its stories played out in the public eye, partly because one member in particular sought the limelight. Ben Dunne Jnr – or Bernard, as his siblings called him, his given name – became one of Ireland's best-known figures, central to major public controversies that rivetted the nation and ruined the reputations of so-called important men. Ben was also the victim in a sensational kidnapping and ransom demand in the 1980s, a harrowing experience that affected him for the rest of his life. Interviews that I conducted with him over the years are central to this book.

Any company that takes so much of our money – willingly spent by its customers, it must be said – is bound to attract notice, no matter how much some of its members attempt to protect their privacy. The company largely shuns publicity, but with careful investigation information emerges that allows a picture to be painted. There are places we find the company engaging publicly, especially when it comes to fighting its corner – we see it in the courts with suppliers or customers, or with the staff, or with union representatives, or when there is interaction with politics, leading to public tribunals of inquiry. There is much silence, but there is also much to be discovered and told.

This is a story, too, of Ireland. The country has changed radically since the first Dunnes clothing store opened in 1944, by a husband and wife in their mid-thirties, Ben Snr and Nora Dunne. They gathered the money to start their business at a time of deep national economic trouble, alongside a friend who was later ditched. The business continued to grow, even during the periods when Ireland went into recession. Keeping the position of market leader has never been guaranteed and the desire not to fall by the wayside, as others have, has driven the family incessantly. This is a business that uses outsiders as counsellors and trusted confidants but ensures that control, its final decisions, are always made by family members, for good or bad.

Three figures dominate this book: Ben Snr, the founder, and two of his six children, Ben and Margaret. If Ben is the most widely known figure, Margaret is the woman who has quietly led the company for more than 30 years, thrust into the role when her brother failed spectacularly (for reasons stemming from the extraordinary experiences of his life, as set out here). Margaret arguably saved the business when Ben's actions undermined it. Margaret provided cohesion; Ben represented chaos. She was consistent when he was wildly inconsistent. Ben lived the fullest of lives, but not always the happiest of ones, and he did so publicly, often enjoying the gossip that comes from the company of journalists. Margaret seeks privacy as avidly as her father did before her and disdains the media. She did not reply to a letter and texts to her private phone number requesting an interview for this book.

Her father was known as The Chief, and now Margaret has become the custodian. In the last decade she has repositioned Dunnes with extraordinary guile, at an age when most people are retired. Margaret has determined the order of succession, picking the winners and dispatching the losers in a family race. She seems obsessed with many things – particularly control – but with a single overriding ambition: that Dunnes Stores remains a family-owned business for the generation that follows her, and possibly beyond. But for how much longer can they maintain that position? And when Margaret finally releases the reins, what happens then?

PART 1

The Founding Father – the life and times of Ben Dunne Snr

1940s–1960s

1.

Dunn, not yet Dunne

THE FIRST RETAILER in the Dunne family was Margaret Byrne, from Kilkenny. In the early years of the 20th century Margaret married Barney Dunn of Rostrevor, a seaside town on the shores of Carlingford Lough, below the Mourne Mountains in county Down. This was in the decades before Ireland was partitioned, when the whole island was under British rule. It was a time when most people lived frugally, often in poverty. Their first child, Annie, was born in 1906, followed by Bernard (known throughout this book as Ben Snr) on 19 May 1908, and the third and last child, Dennis, also known as John, was born a year later in 1909. Records suggest that Annie and Dennis were born in county Down, but that Bernard may have been born in Kilkenny, Margaret's homeplace.

Barney Dunn was reasonably well-off by the standards of the time, having inherited the Woodside Restaurant Temperance Refreshment Rooms, located in a prime position on the quay in Rostrevor. It was a popular destination for the limited tourism that took place in that era. He was also given possession of an auctioneering firm set up by his family in the late nineteenth century. He was described as 'a noted amateur entertainer' and poet. The Woodside provided his stage, and Margaret Byrne was one of the tourists who was captivated by his performances. Less attractive, as she would come to realise during years of marriage, was Barney's appetite for alcohol. It was a disease that would lead to his eventual death in a poorhouse in 1949, and it would wreak havoc among future generations of their offspring. Ben Snr was not considered particularly close to his father: perhaps he recoiled from his father's drinking and associated behaviours, and the loss of money it brought about and the pressure it put on his mother to keep the ship at home on an even keel.

What is known of Ben Snr's childhood and youth has come mainly from the recollections of Ireland's most famous public servant of the 20th century, Thomas Kenneth Whitaker, known as either TK or Ken. He was brought daily to St Mary's national school in Rostrevor by his neighbour and fellow pupil, Ben: 'He was a few years older than me and would take me by the hand to school, passing his mother's little drapery shop on the way.'

It was the start of an enduring friendship between the two men, of which Ken was very proud. They would both have a major influence on the economic development of the Irish Republic in the twentieth century, after independence and partition. Whitaker moved through the ranks of the civil service of the new southern State and became secretary of the Department of Finance in 1956. There, he wrote what became a famous blueprint for progressive economic development, the *First Programme for Economic Expansion*, which advocated increased private sector competition and the end of protectionism. In the same period Ben Snr would become the major Irish retailer of his generation, first selling clothing, later food and drink, at usually cheaper prices than his competitors, providing exactly the benefits of competition that Whitaker espoused.

Out of necessity Margaret took hold of the Dunn family finances, opening a small one-shop drapery business and setting up a shipping agency that organised passage for Irish emigrants to Australia and New Zealand. She encouraged her son's early entrepreneurship. As a child, Ben Snr was given a corner of her shop where he repaired bicycles and mended punctures. He also built a small income from selling berries that he and Dennis picked in the local fields. He left school at the age of fourteen and got his first job as a 'bootboy'. The selection of this role seems to have been due to a combination of his father's influence and pressing financial need. Barney contacted Johnny Parr, described as a farm manager with the Rosses of Bladensberg, a local family of landed gentry, and young Ben was assigned his role, which was the lowest form of male household servant. His job was to clean, polish and care for the family's boots and shoes and perform other menial tasks. This suggested that money was tight in the Dunn household, despite his mother's business endeavours, much of the income presumably being spent by the reckless Barney.

Using the savings he had accumulated repairing bicycles and selling berries, Ben Snr bought five sheep from Parr and kept them on a hill with Parr's existing flock. But it wasn't enough to sate his ambitions. Whitaker later told many times, and with pride, how his father, Edward, had persuaded an 18-year-old Ben Snr to give up on a plan to emigrate to America. Instead, Edward used his contacts to get him a job with Anderson's, the biggest drapery shop in Drogheda, where he spent five or six years. 'Ben later regarded this as a turning point in his life, but it probably diverted him from achieving even greater success on a bigger stage,' wrote Whitaker in Ben Snr's obituary for *The Irish Times* in 1983. Somewhat surprisingly given what Ben Snr achieved in Ireland, Whitaker believed America might have provided a better outlet for him as he was 'a dynamic proactive fellow always wanting to be in the thick of things and later such a shrewd businessman ... it seems likely that it would have been something substantial.'

Ben became a draper's apprentice, although Whitaker described him as a 'bachelor assistant behind the men's counter'. He 'lived-in' overhead the shop on West Street, as was the convention of the time, getting his food and lodgings and going unpaid for the first three months before earning a low wage. There may have been the opportunity for a little extra money subsequently through commission on sales. He usually worked a five-and-a-half or six-day week. Whitaker said that the work was 'unexciting' and gave Ben little opportunity to exhibit 'the dynamism that broke through later'. Ben himself saw it as an opportunity to save, and when promotion gave him a weekly income of 50 shillings, he saw to it that he saved 12 shillings a week. 'People who work to spend have nothing, people who work to save have something,' was a motto of the Anderson's bosses that he came to share. He spent his leisure time playing football, although the available records do not make clear if it was Gaelic Football or soccer. For reasons that have never been explained outside of the family, he added a letter to his surname, Dunn becoming Dunne. Perhaps he wanted to distinguish himself from any embarrassment caused by his father?

Many years later Dunnes would purchase Anderson's and rename the shop, but first Ben Snr went on his travels around Ireland. He moved to Cameron's drapery shop in Longford town, although little is known about his time there. In the mid-1930s he moved to Cork to take up a job with Roches Stores as a buyer in the menswear department.

Roches Stores was unusual in its time in that it offered a significant provisions and grocery department in the years before supermarkets emerged. Otherwise, it was a conventional department store of the era, catering for the relatively small number of wealthier people in Cork city and environs. These upmarket shops were formal places where the floor staff dressed in morning suits and ushered customers to relevant departments. Samples of stock were often placed in glass display cabinets or kept in closed drawers from which they were taken to display to shoppers. Sales assistants fetched cloth and discussed the merits of the desired product and took measurements to tailor the item to the desired size. There were no ready-to-wear racks. There were drapery stores for the less well-off that stocked hosiery, white goods and fabrics, but similar principles of service applied.

It was at Roches Stores that Ben Snr met the woman who would become both his wife and partner in developing the business they would set up together. Nora Maloney was a butcher's daughter, born in 1912 in the tiny North Cork village of Meelin, just a few miles from the Limerick border. Her father, Pat, had moved to Meelin from Abbeyfeale in county Limerick and settled there when he married local farmer's daughter Mary Ellen Broderick. After they married the Maloneys set up in the retail business beside the post office. Mary Ellen ran a women's drapery shop at the front of their building and Pat had the butcher's shop at the back. Unfortunately, Meelin was not big enough to sustain a living in retailing. The nearby limestone quarries had once supplied the stonecutting sector and had benefited greatly from the mass construction of churches around the country in the 19th century. In the 20th century this construction boom waned, and Meelin's fortunes with it. The Maloneys, now with four daughters, moved to seek a better standard of living.

They went first to Doneraile, also in North Cork, in the early 1920s and then to Midleton in East Cork as Nora entered her teens. They were regarded locally as blow-ins, and poor ones at that. Nora's father rented one of the four small units under the Town Hall on the Main Street to run his butcher's stall and the family lived in a flat over a shop on the other side of the street. Nora went to school at the local Presentation Convent. She got her first job in retailing in Cork city, travelling to work by bus with her sisters each day. Nora was regarded as good-looking and vivacious and at Roches Stores became a millinery buyer.

Ben and Nora had plenty in common, which explains the mutual attraction: they had both experienced want and were ambitious. They married in September 1939, the month in which the Second World War started, which in Ireland was called The Emergency. Children came quickly: Margaret was born in March 1942, Frank in May 1943, Anne in July 1944, Elizabeth in January 1947, Bernard (Ben) – the fourth Bernard in the family going back to 1835 – in March 1949 and finally Therese in October 1950. Two of the children were born when Ben Snr was in the employment of Roches Stores; all were born in Cork.

In 1944, Ben Snr left Roches Stores. There are several versions of his leaving the established company: one is that he quit after a manager complained that he was earning more in commission than his salary; another that he decided he should be profiting more personally from his acquired skills as a buyer. Another was that he was expected to accept extra responsibility but wasn't offered a matching pay rise, on the basis that if he got what he sought, he would be paid more than the directors. 'Am I not worth it?,' he asked, allegedly. Whatever the case, he left and set up, in partnership with a friend called Des Darrer, a business that was to bear Ben's name despite the other man's input: Dunnes Stores.

2.

The first shop

ON 31 MARCH 1944 the Gardaí intervened at the opening of a new shop on St Patrick's Street in Cork. The opening had attracted hordes of people, all eager to buy the 'better value' clothing promised. The press of people was so great, a window was pushed in and smashed. But nothing could deter the crowd from getting their first glimpse of this new way of shopping, under the name 'Dunnes Stores'.

A newspaper advert was the first call to attention – but newspapers were small because of the rationing of newsprint, so the impact was limited. Nonetheless, word went around Cork city and the people gathered. The new shop was opposite Roches Stores, but it wouldn't follow its traditional approach. An advertisement in Cork's *Evening Echo* on 30 March promised: 'Luke Burke's Stock to be Cleared' – a retail draper in the city had failed and Ben Snr had purchased its stock cheaply, allowing him to offer it at very low prices.

When those waiting impatiently finally got into the very first Dunnes Stores, they were met by 'a long-roomed tunnel of a place', as Ben Snr later described it. Everywhere they looked, cheap clothing was piled high, people picked items up themselves and brought them to the cash registers. Crucially, Ben Snr insisted on cash: there was no store credit, no instalment payments. The model would provide Dunnes with cash flow and profit almost immediately, especially as payments to suppliers for those goods were delayed. Costs were kept as low as possible: few staff were on hand to serve customers. The self-service model may be ubiquitous now, but it was very unusual, indeed novel, then.

That Ben Snr was able to open a shop was remarkable. Even though he had saved money from his employment, and had been earning higher than normal amounts, it seems unlikely that the

35-year-old would have had enough savings to allow him to rent a commercial premises, fit it, purchase stock in advance and pay employees. It is most unlikely that a bank would have regarded him or Darrer as good credit risks, unless Darrer had access to some capital. Darrer was born in Belfast and had arrived in Cork only in 1935. He and Ben Snr were Catholic in a country where Protestant shopkeeping was still pre-eminent, albeit less so than in previous generations. There was a perception that Irish Catholics were not very good entrepreneurs.

Ben Snr and Darrer's timing was remarkable, too. The country was in the depths of The Emergency and Ireland had become even poorer because of it. 'The whole economy was deeply affected by wartime conditions,' wrote Professor John A. Murphy. 'Keeping things going rather than making progress was the economic keynote of the war years. Many raw materials were almost completely cut-off and there was a heavy fall in industrial production and employment.'

Jobs were scarce and often poorly paid and people worked long, unsocial hours. Most had little or no disposable income. Poverty was rife. The cost of living was high, and rationing was in place. Even if clothing was an essential, much of it was handed down between children, mended to make do. The repair of clothes was part of the domestic chore, almost inevitably carried out by the women who were taught the necessary skills at home. People had 'good clothes', brought out only for special occasions. Few people could afford to follow 'fashion', and even those who could worked within a very tight budget. The Irish were conditioned to accept frugality.

During this era Ireland had a significant drapery trade. Clothes and shoes were manufactured, not imported, providing work for tens of thousands of people. The country had a wide variety of shirt, clothing and hosiery factories, none of which exported and all of which operated on a small scale, leading to higher prices. Ben Snr's opening of his first store was a rare show of optimism for the period. This was months before the Allied Forces counterattacked the Germans (in June 1944) and more than a year before continental Europe was liberated from the Nazis. Then, as now, most of the country's relative wealth was concentrated in the Dublin area. Cork city was not particularly prosperous. Agricultural parts of county Cork were relatively so, depending on prices available for food output, which were inconsistent. However, farming families did not travel into the cities often, getting most of what they needed in town shops. Cash was often in short supply, but credit was available from local shops, allowing people to settle their bills once or twice a year, often at harvest time.

But that doesn't answer the question as to how Dunne financed the premises and stock. A hint comes from the property developer Johnny Ronan. Somewhat surprisingly, given that they were close in age, he told me that he never knew the younger Ben but he did know Ben Snr through his own father: 'In 1944 auld Ben asked my grandfather John for advice about setting up on his own and they went to look at the first shop on Patrick's Street in Cork. My grandfather gave him the courage to lease it, and I know that because auld Ben told me that himself.' Courage is one thing, but it doesn't pay bills. It's quite likely that Ronan's grandfather provided financial help or guarantees as he was one of the most prosperous businesspeople in Munster at the time, thanks to a large and successful tannery business in Tipperary.

Ronan came to know Ben Snr because when he was a young man, starting out in business, he and his father arranged to meet with Ben Snr in Dublin in 1972. 'We ended up meeting him every Wednesday evening in the Shelbourne and then later the Berkeley Court for a drink. Ben drank champagne, which amused my father. This went on for about ten years before he died. He'd say to me, "I'm not a grocer, Johnny, I'm a banker".'

That was only partially true – because there were many other elements that Ben Snr applied ruthlessly to the growth of the business – but cash management was central to the swift growth of Dunnes Stores. Much would be made over the years of buying as cheaply as possible and in volume, then selling at just a little bit more, the prices low enough to ensure every item sold, as a key business principle, but Ben Snr's comments to Ronan about being a banker emphasised that with scale came complication . . . and opportunity.

3.

After The Emergency

IRELAND'S ECONOMIC CONDITION IMPROVED once The Emergency ended in 1945. The national cumulative savings doubled between 1938 and 1945 because of the lack of consumer goods to buy. The end of the war meant more production of consumer goods – and a wider variety available – and these savings were spent between 1945 and 1948, with a huge surge in imported goods, now including from America.

'Once the war was over, people wanted to return as quickly as possible to pre-war normality,' wrote Dublin retailer Alex Findlater. 'In 1946 it seemed for a moment as if this was going to happen, with trade routes reopening and luxuries such as bananas and nylons reappearing in the shops.' The availability of nylon stockings for women was largely due to Ben Snr, who somehow secured a supply of ladies' stockings from an international source, something that was almost unbelievable given the level of demand in post-war Europe. He kept the name of the source and country of origin secret in case others would try to steal his supply; it was a secret that died with him. Ben Snr could find things people wouldn't get elsewhere and sell them at affordable prices.

The national consumer boom didn't last for too long. A very wet summer in 1946, which impacted on grain production, was followed by an extremely severe winter in 1946/7 with continual gales and heavy snowstorms, which hit farmers badly. In 1947 bread and coal rationing was reintroduced and gas and electricity were limited to two hours a day per household. Passenger rail traffic stopped running again. Wages were controlled and exports fell. In 1948 the government increased taxes on beer, spirits, tobacco, entertainment, and petrol. Inflation went up again.

However, economist Brendan Walsh estimated that the volume of personal spending went up by about one-quarter between 1945 and 1950. Some of that must have been on clothes because Dunnes thrived. The first store outside of Cork was opened in Waterford, on Cathedral Street, on 8 August 1946. Expansion came relatively quickly. Another shop was opened on North Main Street in Cork city, a 10-minute walk from St Patrick's Street, in 1947 and another in Mallow, in north county Cork, about 30 miles from the city. Mallow was a relatively prosperous town, benefiting from the extensive dairy farming in the area and from Irish Sugar locating one of its four manufacturing plants there. In 1954 the fifth store was opened on O'Connell Street in Limerick and the sixth in Wexford in 1955. Crowds like those seen in Cork in 1944 attended the opening of the first Dublin store in 1957, on Henry Street.

This was all achieved by following the same principles Ben Snr had established in the first shop: pile the goods high, sell them as cheaply as possible. This allowed Dunnes to use wisely and profitably the time between being paid by the buyers in their shops and paying the manufacturers for the supply of goods. As Ben Snr had told Ronan, he used the cash flow to get interest from the bank on his deposits. That implied that bank borrowing was kept low, or was almost non-existent, because the interest paid on any loans would have been higher than the interest earned on deposits.

TK Whitaker acknowledged his friend's business methods in his obituary for Ben Snr: 'Coupled with perceived toughness towards employees, his business model earned him notoriety because he depended on pushing his credit terms with suppliers to the limit to make the profits he sought. With ninety days to pay, he could bank his cash at generous terms and pocket the interest before discharging his invoices.'

Ben Snr was highly conscious of what his customers could afford to pay. He gave them little choice but guaranteed 'better value'. There was a much-quoted business legend from the time, how Henry Ford told buyers of his first mass-produced motor cars that they 'could have any colour that they wanted, as long as it was black'. In other words, if your priority was a good price, you weren't going to be afforded choice into the bargain.

Ben Snr insisted that the suppliers stocked the shelves upon delivery, reducing his staff costs. He demanded supplies in high volume but drove down the price for the bulk purchase as much as possible, allowing him to reduce his selling price for each individual item below what retail competitors, buying more expensively, could offer. If any products were found to be flawed, then further discounts would be applied when the invoice was being paid – long after the goods had been sold. Ben Snr was a hard negotiator but struggling manufacturers needed the business and had to put up with it. Telling his suppliers that they needed to be 'efficient', Ben Snr believed it was up to them to sort out their own costs to make sure they made their own profits.

'Despite the criticism of his dealings with suppliers, the demands he made for high quality at low prices made many Irish manufacturers more competitive on international markets than they had previously been,' Whitaker wrote. In doing Dunne's bidding, they drove down their own costs, improved their quality and sold into foreign markets. The Irish market was very small, exports limited, and the country was held back by an inefficient, highly protected manufacturing sector: factories employed few, had small plants, limited products and short production runs. That meant consumers overpaid for low-quality products. Government-imposed price controls distorted the market and arguably increased inefficiencies. Ben Snr's approach modernised Irish clothes manufacturing production and opened new potential for all businesses, even if he was doing it for personal rather than patriotic reasons.

Ben Snr and Darrer's partnership was dissolved in 1952. Darrer became the sole owner of the Waterford store, which traded under the name Dunnes Stores for some years before being renamed Darrers in 1966. The reasons behind the rupture are not clear, but Darrer was able to open stores in Dungarvan and Tramore in county Waterford and in Carlow town. He was quicker than Dunne to expand beyond clothing into offering a food supermarket. (Des Darrer died unexpectedly in Cork in December 1967, when only in his late fifties. His family continued with the business but the last shop closed in 2007.)

The dissolving of his business partnership didn't slow Ben Snr's ambition or achievements. He was keenly aware of the value of branding and advertising. Dunnes Stores' first own-brand item was a lady's lumber jacket available in just one colour: London tan. It sold in its own box for a penny short of a pound and was made by Sunbeam, a textiles company in Cork.

Ben and his staff travelled overseas to anticipate fashion trends. They copied what they decided the Irish population would want to wear, influenced by what was seen in the imported movies they watched in cinemas, or in popular magazines. When they bought cloth to bring back to Ireland, they already had designs and colours chosen and specifications for the manufacturers to follow. Ben Snr developed a reputation for knowing what his customers wanted to purchase, usually before they knew it themselves.

Things did not improve overall economically in Ireland during the 1950s. Many books detailing the history of the period regularly reference a widespread feeling that Ireland had become a 'failed state', and a collective gloom and depression took hold. This failure couldn't be blamed on colonial misgovernment or wartime restrictions: it was down to us now. Between 1901 and 1961 the birth rate halved, and an estimated 1.72 million people emigrated, with the 1950s being the worst of all decades. There was also a drift from rural Ireland towards the cities, particularly Dublin. 'Economic growth was nonexistent,' wrote Professor Tom Garvin. 'Even some who were securely employed threw up their jobs to seek a new life and countries which held up brighter prospects for the future of their families.' In a 21st-century appraisal of how post-1950 Ireland was a notable failure, economic historians Cormac O'Grada and Kevin Hjortshøj O'Rourke called it a 'lost decade', when Ireland underperformed almost every other European economy. It meant there were fewer customers with money in hand to enter Irish shops, and yet Dunnes' shops thrived, a tribute to a particular type of business genius.

This stagnant landscape needed a tectonic shift to forge a new economic vision for the future. The economic and social crisis of the decade forced a fundamental rethinking of Irish economic policies and the cosy federation of monopolies. The late 1950s brought about a turning-point in attitudes and actions, especially after Seán Lemass became Taoiseach and made economic progress his priority. Whitaker wrote the template for progress that the politicians now followed, becoming the most important civil servant in influencing economic change. As Irish society and business moved towards a new, wider horizon, Ben Snr was one of the local businesspeople who benefited most.

4.

Swinging through the sixties

IN THE LATE 1950S Ireland finally entered a period of economic growth. Despite the reluctance of the State to invest heavily in roads – something that didn't happen until the early 1990s – car sales began to rise and were 40% higher in 1960 than in 1959, continuing this upward trend for many years to follow. After the mass emigration of the 1950s, net emigration was lower between 1961 and 1966 than during any inter-census period since Independence. There were jobs to be had, money to be earned, and for Ben Snr that meant a market to be mined and expanded.

Ireland was partly swept along by the rapid growth in demand from its trading partners, particularly the UK, but Lemass's commitment to trade liberalisation gave a fillip to growth at home. The introduction of free second-level education was transformative, even if the full benefits would only be seen later, and an increasing number studied for third-level degrees. The inward-looking nature of the country's leaders was exposed by the arrival of television and the establishment of RTÉ as a public service monopoly broadcaster. Even if a degree of censorship was imposed on its programming, RTÉ provided a window to the world – something Ben Snr appreciated would be important to the clothes demanded by customers. From 1960 to 1967 the economy expanded at a rate of 4% per annum, a 'truly staggering acceleration by the admittedly dreary standards of Irish past performance,' noted Garvin. It could have been better. The country was still poor compared with the growth rates experienced elsewhere around the European periphery.

None of this bothered the ambitious Ben Snr, however. He travelled widely across western Europe, carefully observing the changes occurring in retailing in France, Germany and Italy, in particular.

His daughter, Margaret, often accompanied him, having been inducted into the process at a very early stage of her career, aged 14, and without completing secondary school at the Ursuline Convent in Cork. In early January 1962, with a teenaged Margaret alongside him, Ben Snr was part of a delegation of 16 members from the National Federation of Drapers and Allied Traders who attended the 51st annual convention of the National Retail Merchants Association of America (NRMAA) in New York, a meeting of over 5,000 delegates. Many of Ireland's leading manufacturers and retailers attended but none became as engaged with that US organisation as Ben Snr. In 1970 he received the award for the most outstanding retailer in the world by the NRMAA, which had 16,000 members globally.

It was on one of those American trips that an incident occurred – in 1968 – that would have resonance in the future. Charles Haughey – then a rising minister, son-in-law of retired Taoiseach Seán Lemass, and himself to become Taoiseach in 1979 – flew to New York to open a new office for the Irish tourist board, Bord Fáilte. While there, he launched an Irish trade fair at a Manhattan hotel. One of the most prominent stands was a Dunnes Stores' display, showcasing the latest trend: Bri-Nylon shirts.

Bri-Nylon was the brand-name for British Nylon, synthetic man-made fibres that provided clothes that were sometimes shiny and often mocked as cheap-looking. They needed less care and ironing – they would 'drip-dry' when hung on the clothes-line – but could be some-what uncomfortable to wear. In stark contrast, Haughey's elegantly tailored shirts, natural fibre, cotton, sometimes silk-mixed, were hand-made by Charvet at an exclusive outlet in Paris, where they kept a bust of him for precise measurements.

When Haughey saw the Dunnes display, he erupted in fury at such products representing Ireland. He rounded on Ben Snr. 'What do you think this is? The fucking Iveagh Market?' he is said to have roared. It was Ben Snr's turn to be furious when Haughey instructed officials from Bord Fáilte to dismantle the stand and get its cheap shirts out of sight. Margaret was incensed on her father's behalf and nursed a resentment towards Haughey that would last right up until her father's death and beyond.

By the 1960s Ben Snr's focus had switched from Munster to Dublin, which was the main centre of economic activity in the country, with a larger population who had more money to spend. In January 1957 he announced the purchase of a premises in Henry Street, Dublin, just off O'Connell Street. This brought him to the heart of the city centre, on one of the busiest shopping streets. In 1959 he bought Kelletts on George's Street, another Dublin retailing mainstay, and set to work changing the premises dramatically to create a HQ for Dunnes Stores, renaming it St Bernard House. The George's Street superstore opened that month, with entrances there and on Exchequer Street, promoted by a blitzkrieg advertising campaign. An *Irish Times* piece praised it: 'The layout of the store permits customers to see and handle the stock which includes fashion, knitwear, hosiery, shoes, men's and children's things, household goods, and canned and packaged goods as well as fruit and confectionery.'

The expansion continued apace. Ben Snr held a press conference on New Year's Eve 1963 at Jury's Hotel on Dame Street in Dublin to announce the purchase of Anderson's in Drogheda, where he had served his apprenticeship 37 years earlier. 'I have always had a special place in my heart for Drogheda and the Drogheda people,' he told reporters. 'Planning this latest Dunnes superstore in this progressive town gave me a particular pleasure. My career has come full circle and my wish is that this new venture of ours will do something to repay the debt that I owe to Drogheda for the hard constructive training I received.'

He revealed the purchase of a site for a building in Dundalk, and that in the next few years he intended to open 12 more stores across the country. He noted that all the capital for the firm was Irish – amounting to £500,000, all held by the family – and that over 85% of the goods handled by the firm was also Irish. He said he wished to state those facts as there had been reports that this was not so. He also emphasised that there were three joint managing directors, himself, wife Nora and son Frank, who at that stage seemed the designated heir apparent. His daughters Margaret, Anne and Elizabeth made up the board of directors. At this stage, Ben and Therese were too young to be directors.

In retrospect, Anne's inclusion is somewhat surprising as she played no part in the running of the business. A decision had been taken to institutionalise Anne at the age of 12 years because of ongoing health issues, the nature of which were kept private although there was speculation about epilepsy, which was treated differently in that era. She was known as 'the gentle child'.

In May 1964 Ben Snr announced the purchase of Rowes, a draper's store on North Earl Street, Dublin, for an undisclosed sum, and that Rowes would continue with its usual business for the time being. It wasn't long before it was subsumed into Dunnes Stores. Cork was not forgotten either. The building beside 105 St Patrick's Street was bought in 1964 to allow expansion into a far larger stand-alone building.

Twenty years after opening the first shop in Cork, Dunnes now had nine outlets in Dublin alone and an annual turnover of more than £6 million. On 19 November 1964 *The Irish Times*, in a paid-for feature, wrote that the successful expansion of the business was 'based on the realization that the girl who goes shopping for a bra or a sweater nowadays will be keenly aware from the intensive pressures of television and the press just what is fashionable and what is not – and that she will be on the lookout for clothes that meet the limited resources of her purse'.

Ben Snr was greatly influenced by the business methods and style of Marks & Spencer. It had put the brand-name *St Michael* on many of its products, and Ben Snr copied this by introducing the *St Bernard* label for products manufactured to his specifications. The use of his own Christian name suggested a degree of ego already on display with the use of his surname over the door of each of his shops and on the HQ offices. The St Bernard brand and its strict specifications on quality and cost control were the keys to sales volumes and value for money. It was affordably priced, but Ben Snr established a quality control panel that tested the merchandise, ensuring zips, buttons and overall quality were of a sufficiently high standard. He maintained that 99% of the clothes for the St Bernard label were made in Ireland and that Dunnes was proud that it was helping to employ many thousands of factory workers throughout the country.

The nominated factories had to produce St Bernard garments on a 'cut, make, and trim' (CMT) basis, which was personally supervised by Ben Snr and regarded within the industry as the best choice for a retailer seeking to establish new clothing lines. The first stage, 'the cut', was the most time-consuming process as detailed patterns were required. It was not easy to cut material to the exact specifications set down by Dunnes, but factories invested in the equipment to do large volumes at speed and to sufficiently good quality so there was very little waste. In 'the make' step, they stitched together the cut pieces of fabric to form the finished items. This was done by hand before machines took over the bulk of the work, although even then the final finish was often done by hand. 'The trim' process might be better described as checking for any problems, such as hanging threads, missing buttons, excess fabric, anything that might dissuade the buyer. The intention behind CMT was that it would create volumes of clothes without large capital investment on expensive equipment. The suppliers learnt quickly that any defects in finished products would mean the full payment would not be received.

Some suppliers found themselves becoming excessively dependent on Dunnes and therefore squeezed. As buyer, Dunnes liked to place large orders with small to medium-sized manufacturers who were more easily controlled. An order with Dunnes might represent an excess of 50% of its normal output and lead a factory to invest in new machinery. But that made it vulnerable if Dunnes decided to reduce the price on future contracts. The factory had little option but to cut its margin and often ended up only breaking even. Ben Snr is reputed to have once said: 'I don't get ulcers, I give them.' In business it is said that every good deal leaves profit for both sides: Ben Snr didn't care about leaving something for the other party. One unnamed supplier complained to *Business & Finance*: 'I don't know if they really accept that suppliers have to make a profit if they are to stay in business.'

Much of how Dunnes did its business was disclosed at public hearings of the Fair-Trade Commission in November 1961, over ten days. The Commission inquired into price trends and marketing influences for nylon stockings and hand knitting yarns. It interviewed twenty-eight witnesses, but Ben Snr's testimony was the most significant.

In his public evidence, Ben Snr said Dunnes was an entirely cash firm and did not give any credit or allow discounts to its suppliers. 'We want to give the people what they want at the price they want to pay for it,' he said. That required continuity of supplies, quantity and quality. If a manufacturer offered lower terms, they would not be considered unless the Dunnes quality requirements were guaranteed. 'The biggest risk in nylons is taken by ladies who buy them because they have no guarantee that a pair will last for longer than five minutes,' he said. He explained how Dunnes marketed its own brand of nylons and had never yet come across a case of competitors underselling them. Asked if the customers for nylons were more price-conscious than brand-conscious or both, he replied: 'I think if we changed our brand tomorrow it would not make any difference.'

It was a strange comment given the emphasis he increasingly placed on the St Bernard brand. But what was perhaps telling in it was that Ben Snr expected people to come to Dunnes to seek good quality products at cheap prices, whatever brand name was attached to the individual items. The most important name to drag in purchasers was the one over the door, the real brand winner, even if that was not the language of the time: Dunnes Stores.

5.

The big new thing

IN THE EARLY 1960s Ben Snr had his biggest idea yet, one that combined what he had learnt from his overseas trips with his innate understanding of how Irish consumer tastes would develop over the coming decades. Ben Snr noted the trend in the USA and Europe to provide shopping outside of the traditional city centres and in new types of stores. People wanted to shop relatively near to where they lived, but that would become more of a challenge as cities grew and the suburbs spread ever wider. Ben Snr, with Frank strongly encouraging him, decided on a flagship store of a different kind in the expanding Dublin commuter belt: he built Cornelscourt.

In the late 1940s a half-mile of dual carriageway was built between Galloping Green and Foxrock, south of what was then the outskirts of Dublin city, to expand the Donnybrook–Bray main road. Political infighting halted the further expansion of the project for decades. One lane of traffic in either direction was deemed to be more than enough for Irish needs, especially given the cost of road construction. The example of Europe, where motorways were an integral part of post-war reconstruction and economic development, was disdained. But Ben Snr and Frank realised that, whatever about the limitations of the road network, tens of thousands of houses were being built in the southern suburbs and they saw a ready market to serve and an opportunity to invest their rapidly increasing capital.

They needed a suitable location. Ben Snr went hunting for land with Frank, now aged 22. Indeed, some interviewees for this book believe Frank should get the bigger share of the credit for both the idea and the location, although it would never have happened had Ben Snr not been convinced of its merits. Journalist Sam Smyth described how one day in 1965 the two men waded through shoulder-high grass and weeds to inspect two disused factories at Cornelscourt. Stepping between piles of rubble beneath swooping gulls, Ben Snr apparently told Frank, 'If we can get those birds out and our birds in, we'll be in business' – slang from the era that referred to women as 'birds'. The 15-acre site was purchased for an undisclosed price and cleared, allowing construction of the biggest shopping development to date in the country to get underway.

Cornelscourt Shopping Centre was opened in October 1966 by Kathleen Lemass, wife of Taoiseach Seán Lemass. An advertisement feature in *The Irish Times* on 28 October 1966 promised that it 'marks the beginning of a new era in shopping systems in Ireland'. There may have been fawning puff in its content, but in retrospect it wasn't far wrong either and much of it is suitable for quoting nearly 60 years later because it lays out well the optimism and foresight of the business plan and the way in which Ben Snr and Frank correctly saw how Ireland was changing.

Frank was quoted directly, another example of how the family engaged with the media in that period, at least on its own terms. Frank said the family had paid attention to the new shopping centres in Germany, which were modified to suit Ireland with added American ideas. 'When it opens today there will only be the vast shopping area of a Dunnes Stores at over 25,000 sq.ft in completely pillarless open space. You will be able to buy from an extremely comprehensive range of foodstuffs, including fresh meat, fresh chickens, fresh fruit and vegetables to a large range of "soft goods", clothing for every member of the family bearing the famous Saint Bernard quality label.'

The article declared, presumably at the suggestion of the Dunnes: 'It may not be the biggest shopping center in the world but by the time all the "customer convenience" ideas are put into operation Cornelscourt will certainly rank with the leading shopping centres of the world, such as the Great Eastern in Long Island New York, the mid-island shopping center in New York and the centres of Hamburg and Frankfurt and, to a certain extent, Bullring Centre in Birmingham. The reason is simple. They all have one thing in common – to bring as many things as any family would need to buy, into the one area, so that one family – father, mother and even the children – could not only go shopping but enjoy the weekly outing as well.' It was one big ad, but still the article showed that the Dunnes were very ambitious – and somewhat boastful.

There was also a keen recognition of a changing Ireland. Dunnes promised different opening hours that would better suit the working hours of its customers, including opening later into the evening on some days of the week. This is normal today, but in the 1960s most shops opened on a strict 9am–6pm basis. 'Few housewives and almost no people who must go to work can get near a shop before 10:30am, whether it's for food, clothes or morning coffee. There's not much fun to be attached to lunch forgone or hurried. The entire idea, long overdue, is to turn hurried worried shopping into an enjoyable and practical outing.

'On top of all this is the location. No frustrations trying to park cars or scooters or bicycles, no tensions perhaps trying to get home with your parcels in the lunch or evening bus rush hour. Plenty of fresh country air all around and all kinds of amenities. There is little amusement for most mothers who have to cart on their parcels while perhaps the family car is parked in the city when father is at work. He just might be enticed to make a night out of it shopping over Friday night or a Saturday afternoon taking the whole family along.'

Dunnes had long since cut out the 'personal service' of old and this was touted as a convenient virtue: 'And obviously this makes sound sense for the customers concerned for the benefits in his pocket by the fact that he decides without pressure from the salesman what he wants or needs. It also means that the customer becomes more selective, more discerning and more adult in the shopping habits.'

The article promised that soon after its initial opening, an additional 8,000 sq.ft would display hardware goods and furniture. It also promised household appliances, including radios, televisions, and dishwashers. However, this movement into the electrical or home appliances market did not last very long because the profit margins proved too thin and people continued to prefer to rent or purchase with finance that Dunnes would not provide.

Crucially, the car park was even bigger than the store, allowing for more than 700 cars. This was prescient, as a boom in car sales was underway and would continue unabated. However, for those without cars there were special bus services laid on from Bray, Dún Laoghaire,

Blackrock and even central Dublin, advertised in the national daily and Dublin evening newspapers.

'Ben and Nora would often drive out to Cornelscourt on a Saturday, park the car and just watch the throng of customers coming and going without even going into the store,' wrote Smyth. It's not known if they ever popped in to pray thanks for their good fortune, but many members of the families referred over the years to their deep commitment to Catholicism. In 1970, the company built a temporary private oratory in an adjacent portacabin where staff could go for prayer and reflection and in 1974 this was turned into a permanent structure.

It may have been divine intervention that averted a near-disaster in early 1970. On 7 January a fire of unexplained origin broke out and within 30 minutes had burned most of the drapery and hardware building to the ground. Newspaper reports put the estimated losses at £500,000 and described how about thirty staff members and many customers 'fled as the flames spread through the building with intense ferocity'. Nobody was injured, and the cause of the fire, which started in the roof and caused explosions, remained undisclosed.

Ben, not yet 21 years old but working alongside his father now in Dublin, having moved from Cork in his late teens, arrived shortly after the outbreak and was confident enough to speak to reporters at the scene. He said that the store was the biggest of the seventeen operated by his father throughout Ireland and confirmed that the drapery and hardware departments had been destroyed. Luckily, the firemen and a favourable wind had prevented the fire from spreading to the adjoining supermarket and café, now arguably the more important parts of the business.

6.

Changing tastes

WITHIN JUST TWO DECADES Ben Snr had established Dunnes Stores as one of the most successful clothes retailers in Ireland, but he had also started experimenting with selling food. Dunnes was slightly later to the new food retailing business, but many of the same principles that applied to drapery could be used to sell food and homewares. He had discovered the markup on fruit and vegetables was very generous and introduced boxes of apples and oranges in St Patrick's Street in Cork in the 1950s. He introduced just one more food choice: cream crackers. He had them put in smaller packets and sold with a free portion of cheese. The response encouraged him to do more of the same across all his stores. By 1964, about 5% of turnover came from this activity. It was time for Dunnes Stores to dive deeper into this related form of business while continuing to do what it was already doing so well. Ben Snr decided to focus on the same income group as purchased his clothes; the food offering was also going to be 'pile them high and sell them cheap'.

The competition in the sector was tougher than in the drapery business, however. There were more new entrants with modern ideas. Pat Quinn from Leitrim, born in 1935 (and died in Canada in 2009), was a former store manager at Woolworth's in Limerick and he opened his first shop in Longford in 1958 with his uncle. It didn't last too long, before he headed to Canada to work as a music promoter with The Beach Boys, Johnny Cash, and The Supremes, among others. But in 1965 Quinn returned to become general manager of H. Williams, one of the major food retailers of the era. When it refused to open in the new Stillorgan shopping centre, he quit and set up the first branch of Quinnsworth at the centre in December 1966. Quinn invented the term 'yellow pack' for low-priced, non-branded items. He was one of the best-known and high-profile Irish business figures in the 1960s and 1970s. He did his own advertising, wearing a distinctive polo-neck jumper in his many TV appearances. Quinn opened six stores in Dublin and in Cork, Galway and Limerick and is believed to have made £6m profit within five years by selling to Galen Weston's Associated British Foods (ABF).

Power Supermarkets was established by Weston, a young man of English and Canadian heritage and extensive family wealth who used Ireland to develop his skills before being put to work in the larger family empire. He expanded Power by buying Quinnsworth and then rebranded the merged group under that acquired name. Galen's first outlet was located on South Great George's Street in Dublin, adjacent to Dunnes Stores, a premises he rented when he was still in his mid-twenties. 'Old Benji was looking at me through the window and I was looking back at him while he was having his lunch,' Weston recalled in an interview with Kathy Sheridan of *The Irish Times* in 2008. 'I learned a lot from Dunnes. I always say to Margaret that her dad was the greatest teacher I ever had. I was taking my trousers off at every turn,' he says with a roar of laughter. 'Every afternoon he'd have done something . . . It was fantastic. I was foreign; he was local. He used every trick in the book.'

By December 1971 Richard Keatinge of *The Irish Times* estimated that supermarkets accounted for about one-third of all the food sold in the country, and a far greater proportion in Dublin. The buying power of large chains enabled them to obtain goods cheaper than other retailers, making bigger profits or selling at lower prices to increase market share. The supermarkets stocked a larger number of lines and therefore offered a wider variety. Keatinge noted that 'supermarket chains have adopted modern marketing methods including national advertising merchandising and special promo-tions, and all this has generated excitement. Shoppers get the impression of constant change created by the promoting of new bargains every fortnight or so, coupled with special gimmicks.' He also noted how the total number of food shops had 'declined heavily over the past decade' and how 'the proportionate turnover now controlled by the chains is far greater than their share of the total number of retail shops'.

Once Pat Quinn had departed the scene, Feargal Quinn (no relation) became possibly the country's best-known retailer, actively courting media coverage. Feargal, whose family was also from county Down, anticipated great change in grocery retailing and 'determined to be among the leaders of that revolution in Ireland'. He set up his first supermarket, Quinn's, on Clanbrassil Street in Dundalk in 1960. He sold grocery staples at below-cost as loss-leaders to get customers in the door. He progressed slowly, moving first into Finglas and then into other so-called 'working class' areas of Dublin, like Coolock and Walkinstown. His rationale was that car-parking was increasing the cost of retail properties, so he bought sites in areas where people still did their shopping when travelling by bus.

Quinn's had a more expensive offering than Dunnes would have contemplated. The shops were renamed Superquinn in 1970, and Feargal decided that they would specialise in fresh food: staffed departments provided a very wide range of fresh fruit and vegetables, meat, bacon and seafood. Higher cost meant higher prices. It would be later, in the early 1970s, that he pioneered the idea of in-store bakeries and developed a range of in-store 'kitchens' that included customised pizza counters, salad bars and sausage-making, all designed to support the fresh-food ambience. He provided customer service counters within the stores and conducted customer panels for market research. But for all his 'crowning the customer', there was a ruthlessness to the way Quinn did his business. His use of so-called 'hello money' – upfront payments from suppliers for the use of shelf space – was a practice that had to be outlawed, but not before Dunnes Stores had made use of it too.

The competition was fierce, but once Ben Snr joined the supermarket sector, Dunnes muscled its way into prime position. The secret of how Dunnes made its profits in supermarket retailing were disclosed largely at a public inquiry in January 1971, set up by the Minister for Industry and Commerce, Paddy Lalor, to investigate a perceived need to regulate prices of essential items and led to the formation, in late 1971, of the National Prices Commission.

Frank gave evidence, much as his father had done in similar circumstances nearly a decade earlier when the drapery business was investigated. Before Frank put forward the Dunnes' position, he listened as Jack Travers, on behalf of an alliance of independent retailers, complained that supermarkets, and Dunnes in particular, were exercising their market power ruthlessly against smaller competition.

Travers stated that staff costs at Dunnes were only 1.75% compared with an average of 6% at other grocery stores and alleged this was because the company exploited the merchandising system as no one else did. Some supermarkets rented a permanent area of shelf space to manufacturers on an annual basis, with an additional rental charge for a sign over the area. Travers alleged that the position of this shelf was often influenced by the size of a personal cheque made to the supermarket owner. This was often dressed up as an advertising allowance, but Travers said it was a way of creating tax-free profit.

Travers also alleged that some manufacturers supplied large quantities of shelving free of charge – and tax-free – to the supermarket owners and that cash rebates and bonuses to the supermarkets were a 'rampant' practice: 'They are seldom if ever declared as profit and are cashed for personal use thus avoiding turnover tax, income tax or wholesale tax. Some of the tea companies are particularly active in this kind of practice.' Sometimes an extra case of goods would be delivered for free and not appear on the invoice. The supermarket could then sell it for clear profit.

The independent retailers complained that, while they had to accept single deliveries from their suppliers, the bigger multiples insisted on orders being broken up into many deliveries for different branches and in quantities suitable for immediate shelving. This eliminated the need for the retailer to have a warehouse, but forced extra costs on the supplier whose delivery staff had to load the goods on the shelves and put the prices on them. The alliance claimed that 'shelf loading has been recognised as an unfair trading practice and is estimated to be worth approximately a 5% discount. It is only available to multiples, and we feel that this practice constitutes discrimination against the independent retailer and that it should be either discontinued or else the independent retailers should be granted an extra 5% in lieu of same.' Dunnes at Cornelscourt had an average of fifty merchandiser shelf-loaders permanently present at the suppliers' expense.

The independent retailers complained that the sector would eventually be eliminated as the multiple was the only entity receiving these special terms and discounts, making it impossible for the independents to compete. Travers summed up the core problem: 'The net result of such a situation would be the total domination of the retail trade in Ireland by fewer and bigger multiple groups. These people would then be in a position to dictate to the Irish manufacturers. Indeed, they would have total power over them. They would also be in a better position to organise price rigging.'

Frank put the Dunnes case publicly in early February 1971. Dunnes operated eighteen outlets, five in the Dublin area, primarily drapery and textile outlets, but twelve including food sections, and in all twelve stores the margin of profit on food was lower than on clothing, but the turnover on the former was greater. The prices of foods and of clothing were the same in every store, irrespective of the income of people living in a locality.

Frank insisted that any advertising allowance received from the manufacturers was used for ads in national newspapers or for the purpose of reducing the price of goods in the shops. If the external shelf loading was eliminated, he might have to increase his staff numbers or pay existing staff overtime, which would lead to increased prices for his customers. Alternatively, he would seek lower prices from suppliers.

He agreed that in certain cases he used his power to negotiate the keenest prices he could get for his companies, and that on some occasions he decided not to carry certain goods when he did not get the terms he felt he should get. He admitted that Dunnes enjoyed a better service than other retailers. It had happened that manufacturers had approached him and asked him not to sell below-cost, but he believed he should run his business and they should run theirs. 'Competition is the life of trade,' he said. It was a mantra he had inherited from his father, almost certainly repeated at his absent father's insistence given that Ben Snr had not relinquished control and would have discussed with Frank what he would say.

Frank argued that below- or under-cost selling should not be abolished because it applied mainly to basic food lines and without it food prices overall would increase for the housewife. Below-cost selling was used to give better value to Dunnes' customers and it was a deliberate practice to pick certain items and sell them below-cost. These usually included basic items, like butter, sugar, or soup, which poorer families had to purchase. He agreed they were operating at a loss on these items but insisted they did this to gain 'better value for customers'. When asked if Dunnes charged more on other products to compensate for this practice, Frank replied that all supermarket price structures were geared to show a profit, but the housewife had a choice as to what items to buy. When it was put to him that the price of meat in his provincial stores was higher than in provincial butcher shops he said, 'I don't know the price charged by the butchers throughout the country.' He also outlined how turnover tax – the forerunner to Value Added Tax (VAT), introduced in 1972 – was not charged on the customer bills at the checkout but was still paid to the Revenue Commissioners. 'It is a big overhead and has to be taken care of somewhere along the line,' he said.

In response to the question about what he saw as the future of supermarket retailing, Frank said that car-parking facilities were going to be a bigger factor in future locations. 'In view of this, I think it's going to become uneconomic to trade in food lines in places like Henry Street,' he said of a major store that continues to sell food to this day. Correctly, though, he thought the future trend would be for food stores to move out to the city suburbs. 'Even in towns outside the cities it will become essential for car-parking amenities to be provided.'

Dunnes conducted the food side of its business on wafer-thin margins, but it provided a massive cash flow and attracted customers into the stores. Food suppliers were paid, on average, about eight weeks after the date of invoicing. This left Dunnes with a huge weekly cash flow from its food operations, running into millions of pounds. For suppliers, Dunnes was often a nightmare to deal with, demanding prices that could put an inefficient firm out of business. To that, Frank and Ben Snr simply argued that nobody was forced to do business with them, the choice was theirs. It was an easy stance to take when many of his suppliers were David to his corporate Goliath.

7.

A display of power and justice

TK WHITAKER ONCE REMARKED that Ben Snr was 'talking forever' about pilfering or thieving from his shops. One of Ken's sons recalled as a child listening with fascination to the famous retailer's explanation that 'shrinkage in the stores' referred to shoplifting, and that he made a 10% allowance for it in his budget calculations. Ben Snr was particularly worried about losses at his largest drapery outlet, South Great George's Street in Dublin. Its size led to big turnover and profits but also, he suspected, a significant loss of stock and therefore money. This was long before security tags were attached to clothes.

Ben Snr's apparent obsession with combating this 'shrinkage' brought him into the courts and into the public eye during two dramatic cases – one criminal, one civil – in the mid-1960s. It gave the public its first glimpse of Margaret Dunne, then in her early twenties but already a director of the company, as both she and her father were forced to give evidence in open court.

Dunnes employed a private security firm, K Security, to prevent shoplifting. When this private firm detained somebody suspected of theft, it called the Gardaí, who decided if making an arrest was appropriate. In July 1963, Ben Snr decided to employ the additional services of Sergeant Dennis Culloty. He was one of the Gardaí who came to the store from his station whenever K Security needed assistance. Culloty was in the shop one day, in Garda uniform, to remove some alleged shoplifters to the Garda station, and he approached Ben Snr on the shop floor. Culloty asked if there would be any work available in the shop during his off-duty hours, such as 'floor-walking'. He suggested this could help to reduce the amount of theft. 'I said to him if there was anything that could be done to protect unstored [sic] property and goods I would have no objection,' said Ben Snr in giving his evidence to one of the cases.

Margaret was present for this conversation, which she mentioned in her evidence: 'My father told him to see me the following week and that I would make arrangements with him.' Margaret agreed to pay Culloty seven shillings and six an hour. He could not work set hours because of his Garda duties and asked if he could bring in a colleague – Garda Jerry Molloy – to work on days when he was not available. Margaret told him their duties would entail walking around the stores and watching out for shoplifters. Culloty was to keep a note of the hours he worked, and she would pay him at the end of each week. Whichever off-duty Garda was working on the Saturday afternoon would take the pay for both for the week from Margaret, although both tried to be there to walk the floor during those busy hours.

The arrangement was focused on the customers, but the twenty-five or so staff members came under the microscope, too. It is not clear how their suspicions were raised, but the two Gardaí became convinced that some of the staff might be stealing. In early January 1964 they decided to act, with the knowledge of Ben Snr, Margaret and Frank, against six female employees they suspected of either taking clothes for themselves, applying discounts for others, or simply stealing cash.

Garda Molloy, now wearing his official Garda uniform, confronted the young women. Over two days he took each of them in turn to an office in the shop set aside for him by Margaret and Frank. There, he sought to extract confessions that would be used to bring criminal charges to the courts. It wasn't clear to the women whether they had been arrested, or could leave, or could refuse to answer questions. They had no legal or trade union representation with them in the office.

One of the women, Elizabeth (Betty) Dillon, a teenager at the time, subsequently alleged in court that she was detained for about two hours and questioned by Molloy and Culloty, apparently working in relay. Molloy told her he was sending her to Mountjoy Prison for six months if she did not admit to taking money from the shop. He accused her of 'getting something for nothing' and giving wrong discounts to people. She said she had never seen him in uniform in the store before that day and knew nothing about investigations being carried out in the store. Eventually, she signed a statement in which it appeared that she confessed to stealing goods and money belonging to the company, crimes of which she was subsequently found innocent.

At the end of the two hours Betty was taken to Ben Snr's office by Margaret and told she was suspended, in common with the five other women. Ben Snr asked her where she was going on her holidays that year and she told him Spain. In her evidence in court Dillon said that Ben Snr replied, 'No wonder you went to Italy last year on Dunnes Stores' expense . . . you're a great one for running to the unions. Your Mr Collins [a union representative] was here this evening, and he left a sad man. Let's see you run to your union now. You thought you were cute, but you were not clever.'

Within months the six women were facing criminal charges. They were charged first in Dublin District Court on 8 May 1964, with conspiracy, larceny and receiving stolen property on dates ranging from 1960 to 1964. It took nearly three years for the case to reach full trial, after it had already been in front of the courts for 66 days for various hearings. On one occasion, Margaret had been due to give evidence but did not attend because she had 'flu. After legal argument, the case was upgraded to the Dublin Circuit Criminal Court despite the objections of barristers for the six accused, who argued it was too serious an escalation for the level of charges being brought.

In December 1966, *The Irish Times* reported 'six young Dublin girls, former employees of Dunnes Stores, South Great George's Street, Dublin, who have pleaded not guilty to charges of larceny and receiving from the firm on dates between 1960 and 1964'. The charges involved stealing ladies' clothes, a sum of £5 in cash and some cosmetics. There were also several alternative charges against some of the 'girls', as all the newspapers consistently called the young women.

Barristers for the defendants argued that it was inappropriate for Garda Molloy to undertake a formal investigation on behalf of the Gardaí about allegations he was raising from his part-time, off-the-books role with a private employer. It would become a question, too, if anyone in Dunnes had used influence with An Garda Síochána to ensure that Culloty and Molloy were the Gardaí selected to lead the formal investigation that followed, and whether influence was brought to bear to ensure that prosecutions would result.

There was a difficult day for Ben Snr on 19 January 1967. The following day's headline in the *Irish Press* read: 'Dunne's managing director unwell in witness box'. Underneath was the subhead: *Unfair to call me a tyrant*. So difficult was the experience for 59-year-old Ben Snr that the criminal case was adjourned for about twenty minutes during the afternoon session when he complained of feeling unwell. He put it down to the fact that he had been travelling since 2pm on Wednesday, returning from the USA, to attend court on Thursday morning and was very tired.

In Ben Snr's evidence he claimed that Dillon had told him that 'her mother would kill her for what she had done' and that she had admitted to taking £5 'in silver' from the cash register. Ben Snr said that two days prior to confronting the six women, Garda Molloy had asked him for permission 'to interview' some of them in the store and he had consented. He had also allowed him to use one of the offices for that purpose. He denied that he had made efforts with more senior members of An Garda Síochána to ensure that Garda Molloy was officially assigned to investigate at the store. He said that the Garda also did security work for Dunnes did not strike him as unusual. He had hired the Garda originally to protect goods from being stolen by members of the public, with the aim of preventing theft, not to catch anybody. He had never instructed the Garda to watch staff members. The arrangement was that Molloy was to walk around the store, so that people coming in would know that a member of the Gardaí was present. (Although how they were to know this given he was not in uniform was not explained in the various court reports from the time.) When asked if Dunnes had tried to hide the fact that Culloty and Molloy were working in Dunnes Stores for payment, Ben Snr replied, 'I never suppressed it. I never denied that the two Garda officers were employed by the firm at any time.'

Ben Snr said it was not correct to say there were negotiations between him, the Chief State Solicitor, the Attorney General and the Commissioner of An Garda about the prosecutions. He could give no explanation why a directive from high authority to Superintendent Culhane should have led to Culloty and Molloy investigating the case. Asked if he was 'a person of very considerable influence who could ensure that Molloy was officially assigned to investigations in your store,' he replied, 'I don't agree with that point.' He said he thought his solicitor had written a letter to the Attorney General sometime around the District Court proceedings, but he did not know the contents of that letter. Such a letter would have been highly unusual, regarded as potential interference with due process.

Ben Snr bridled when asked if he knew anyone high up in the Gardaí personally. He answered that he had worked many years earlier in Anderson's in Drogheda with the now deputy commissioner Michael Wymes, but 'had not met the gentleman ten times since . . . You may as well ask me if I know the Taoiseach because I live in Cork' – a reference to Taoiseach Jack Lynch. Ben Snr did not enjoy many of the questions from the barristers for the defendants, especially one who said, 'Would I be right in saying that you are a very influential man, and you have all the power that comes from a man who's in high esteem, wealthy and successful in business?' Ben Snr was very direct in reply: 'Really, that's an embarrassing question. I want to lead a simple life. You were trying to say that I took privilege of my position, that I would never do. I know many people, rich and poor, but I would never use influence. I don't use my power. I started at the bottom and got to the top with common sense.'

He denied saying there were three or four troublemakers in the store and surprised many observers when he said he liked all his staff to be trade union members. He agreed that several staff grievances had been brought to his notice, but it was incorrect to say that he had advised staff not to bring their complaints to the trade unions but to come to management first. Ben Snr complained that the questions implied he was a tyrant. The defence barrister agreed that this was the impression he was trying to convey and added, 'but I'm also suggesting that you're both a tycoon and a tyrant'. Dunne replied, 'It suits you to say that.'

Eventually, all six women were acquitted, one on the direction of the judge prior to the case going to the jury, the others by verdict of the jury.

Worse was to come for the Dunne family. Dillon took the unusual decision to take a separate civil action against Dunnes Stores, against Ben Snr and Margaret by name, and against the two Gardaí. In November 1966, the courts opened an action in which she claimed damages for unlawful detention, false imprisonment, wrongful dismissal, defamation of character, injurious falsehood, and conspiracy to injure.

Dillon's case was a 15-day hearing held before a jury, with 28 witnesses giving evidence. After 95 minutes of deliberations the jury decided that Ben Snr, Margaret and the two Gardaí were involved in a conspiracy to imprison her, that she was unlawfully imprisoned by Sergeant Culloty and Garda Molloy, and that there had been an arrangement between Sergeant Culloty and Garda Molloy and the two Dunnes to unlawfully imprison her. The jury awarded Dillon €2,500 arising out of the conduct of Sergeant Culloty and the same amount arising out of the conduct of Molloy. These were very large sums at that time.

Ben Snr was horrified by this outcome. He, the company, Margaret and the two Gardaí appealed on thirty grounds, the principle one being that there was no evidence of any actionable conspiracy put to the jury. Their lawyers also argued to the Supreme Court that the findings of the jury were 'equivocal and uncertain', that the verdict was influenced by 'an inflammatory closing address' by Dillon's counsel, and that the damages were grossly excessive and unreasonable.

In October 1967 the Supreme Court heard an appeal against the award by the jury and the judgement of Mr Justice McLaughlin. The Dunne side, as defendants of the civil claim for damages, sought an order setting aside the findings and judgement and asked that cost be entered in their favour or alternatively that a new trial be directed. The appeal was heard by Chief Justice Cearbhall Ó Dálaigh.

Just four days before Christmas, Ben Snr and Margaret received the gift that the Supreme Court had upheld their appeal and gave judgement discharging them. In the case of the two Gardaí the court directed a new trial, confined to the issue of false imprisonment. The Chief Justice deemed the evidence against the Dunnes insufficient: 'We do not find any evidence that would warrant the jury holding that the Dunnes agreed with the Gardaí to falsely imprison Dillon . . . the court must therefore set aside the jury's findings that Ben and Margaret Dunne had so agreed.'

The next part of the Supreme Court appeal raised the question as to whether the Dunnes had agreed with the Gardaí to falsely imprison

Dillon, as the jury decided had happened. The Chief Justice again found in the Dunnes' favour on this count and a judgement was entered in their favour.

Both court cases garnered an extraordinary amount of press coverage, which may have influenced the family's subsequent distaste for publicity, but there was no comment in the newspapers about the case or the status of Dunnes as employers. That's not how the newspapers operated in those days, most especially with a big advertiser who might have withdrawn its spend for a period if criticised. Nonetheless, it also appears to have impacted on Margaret's approach to industrial relations and personnel matters, over which she took control subsequently. Like her father, she was determined to ensure that Dunnes Stores would not be ripped off, as they saw it, by its own staff.

8.

The last word

THE FAMILY MIGHT HAVE held strong opinions about the press based on their different experiences of being the story over the years, but contrary to the popular belief that he snubbed the press entirely, Ben Snr hosted various press conferences in the early decades of his career, usually to announce expansion by acquisition.

On 13 October 1966, the unnamed author of The Irishman's Diary column in *The Irish Times* asked Ben Snr at one of these press conference, 'What do you think of mini-skirts?' and noted that the question 'didn't halt him in his stride'. In typical style, Ben Snr took the retailer's view. '"Stockings," he replied, "the tops of stockings." Fashion, and even morals, he leaves to the good sense of Irishwomen, especially their mothers, but mini-skirts, to him, as he elaborated, meant that he had to get in a whole new stock of stockings.'

'"The trouble with the girls," Ben Snr went on, "is that they were inclined to wear the minis without changing their stocking lengths, and when their best friends told them, they made a dive for longer stockings. I anticipated them and I was ready."' He had already figured out that the rule of miniskirts was that the braid of the stocking mustn't show. He said that men like him, who ran women's clothing stores, didn't make the fashions but had to be a step ahead of the trend, so now he had a stock of 'minis and maxis' to sell. That meant, according to the diarist, Ben Snr had decided that the short skirts may have reached the point of no return. '"By that I don't mean the point at which they have gone up too far," Ben Snr said, "but the point from which they won't come back".'

The image of Ben Snr that later solidified was that he was gruff to the point of angry, not necessarily displaying happiness despite his great wealth and achievements. However, interviews conducted for this book suggest that, at least before he aged, he had a sense of humour and a quick wit that was known to his closer associates, albeit of quite a 'macho' demeanour. It is unlikely he would have formed connections and struck deals over the years unless he had the ability to communicate amiably with those with whom he did business.

John Bourke, a very well-known figure in Irish banking in the 1970s–1990s, knew Ben Snr when Bourke was a young man in the 1960s, working for EK O'Brien Ltd, a company that had the franchise in Ireland for the sale of DuPont Textiles products. Bourke and his partner, Conal O'Brien, used to sell Orlon – an acrylic fibre used as a wool substitute – to Ben Snr, which he then had spun into yarn and put into sweaters, particularly for children and women. It was spun by Tullamore Spinners and Sunbeam Wolsley in Cork on behalf of Dunnes. 'There are not enough sheep to give you all the wool you need,' Bourke told me. Acrylic on its own is warm, and warmer again when blended with cotton, but not as warm as something like wool or cotton. It is soft and has a wool-like feel, but could degrade quicker than natural fibres and did not allow for much breathability. It is also easily dyed with the very bright colours that became fashionable then. DuPont discontinued Orlon fibres in 1990.

John Bourke described his business relationship with Ben Snr:

'We used to meet for lunch once a week in the Hibernian Hotel on Dame Street. Either me or Conal O'Brien, whichever one of us was dealing with the account that week. He would always have one glass of champagne with lunch and there was a retired lawyer from Matheson Ormsby Prentice [Eddie Montgomery] who would often join us. When he switched it on, he was fascinating company, full of talk, great company, very likable. "Hear what I say," he would tell me, as he spoke about business, politics, world affairs, everything. We brought him to Holland once, to visit the Dupont factory, and we had great fun. He ate, drank and told stories.

'He was his own manager, his own buyer, and when I asked him who was in control of quality control he growled, "You're looking at him". He had a good eye and quality was very important to him. He copied Marks & Spencer in everything, the layout of the stores, the lines of clothes. He would buy their end-of-the-lines when he was allowed to, if he managed to secure the import licences, full lines from them too at times, at very cheap prices because otherwise they would have gone into the bin. M&S loved Dunnes too, as a repository for what it couldn't sell.

'The opening up of free trade in 1965 was wonderful for him. He brought Conal and I out to Cornelscourt to show us the factory he was going to demolish and replace with the big Dunnes Stores. We were thrilled by his idea and told him he had to go for it. We asked him for the rights to the first promotion when he opened and got it and he never did another promotion for another customer again.'

Ben Snr only gave one major interview in his life. It was conducted by Andrew Whittaker, then working on the business desk of *The Irish Times,* and published on 13 August 1971 under the headline: 'Ben Dunne airs his views on Irish management and the business structure'. It appears that this was not a formal sit-down interview but what's known in media as a 'doorstep', that Whittaker perhaps caught Ben Snr on the hop in an unexpected location and got him to talk without preparation. It is worth quoting at length because it provides an extraordinary insight into how the retailer's mind worked. Whittaker quoted him verbatim, which means some of Ben Snr's pronouncements seem rambling and contradictory and may need to be re-read to get the full gist of what he meant. But it also means that it's unusually entertaining for a business interview because it has little of the polish or PR spin of interviews given by businesspeople of the era . . . or indeed today.

'If there's one thing I hate, it's publicity,' Ben Snr declared, suggesting this was an unplanned and therefore unvarnished conversation. 'No one's allowed to write about Ben Dunne for anyone could have done what I did, but they didn't do it. I don't like the people who talk about what they've done and the people who talk about what they're going to do.' But he carried on with the interview nonetheless. 'For a business, for success you have to have three things: imagination, determination and common sense. If you don't have common sense, you won't have the other two. What's common sense to me could be all bull to you.'

'We used to go out to play football in my young days. I used to turn around and say to a fellow, "Do you want to get hurt?" The next thing I saw him lying down and he'd gone off to the pavilion. I did the team a good job because he was yellow [cowardly] but when I turned around and said to a fellow, "Do you want to get hurt?" and he said, "Do you want to get killed?" that was a good man on the opposition team. I tried to keep away from him.'

There was an element of humble-brag: 'No-one could have done what I did on their own. A good organization did it. I could see no reason why an Irishman couldn't do what was done in every other country. When people are looking at what you're doing, you're winning, you're ahead of them ... Give your job to somebody else if you're not working. People tell me that they work a 40-hour week, I often think that they're present for 40 hours but that they're not working. I think the only hobby I have is work. You can make a hobby out of work just the same as people make a habit out of worry. If I went away for a holiday, I'd never ring up to ask how they were doing.'

Asked about the role of company directors he said: 'I don't think there's any future for companies except they want to be making money. The day for having men on boards that won't take a personal interest and be there twenty-four hours a day has gone. To be on the main board of Dunnes Stores you've got to be on call twenty-four hours a day and seven days a week. I think the worst thing in this country is top personnel are not working. They're bringing in consultants to look at a company but the first thing you should look at in the company is the director.'

He carried on from there to discuss the role of management and repeated what he had apparently said to Galen Weston: 'I told Weston when I was speaking to him that I run my place like the Catholic Church. The Catholic Church is a very successful organization. I said you could have the parish priests, the bishops and the curates but you've got to get the Cardinals and the Pope before you get Dunnes Stores. When you tell me the Pope is infallible certainly, he's bloody well infallible. You know why? Because the Catholic Church runs the Pope not the Pope runs the Catholic Church. If he didn't do the job they'd fire him and the same in Dunnes Stores. I've always made it that Dunnes Stores is the boss, not me. When you build a company where any individual is the boss that company will disappear. There's no such thing as getting to the top, there's no top. When you get to the top you go down the other side. If a company goes wrong you've got to blame the top management. It's no good blaming anyone else.'

It was an era when Ireland was preparing for its entry to what was then the European Economic Community (EEC), now the European Union (EU). Ben Snr was far-sighted and optimistic even though many people feared, correctly, for the Irish clothing manufacturing sector in a less-protected environment. He saw it as a challenge to relish: 'I think there's no alternative. It's a challenge and Dunnes Stores must accept all challenges. I can't see any difference going into the common market from going into Northern Ireland. There are competitors just as smart as you are. There's nothing to be afraid of in this world only to be understood. When people talk about the economy in Ireland so little puts it wrong, so little puts it right. As far as we're concerned, we're a selling operation on the Irish market. I think the biggest obstacle here is to have enough retail outlets to sell Irish-made merchandise on the Irish market. I think Irish manufacturers are as good as in any other part of the world. . . . You can pass laws that put people out of business but you can't pass laws that keep bad people in business. When people say they have no chance they're putting their nails in their own coffin.'

More of his comments were a touch contradictory. 'People are more conscious now of money than they ever were before, of prices. The young generation has completely changed. In the old days they wanted something different from everybody else. Now they all want to be alike. Sheep all dressed together.' That comment ignored the much smaller range of goods of just a couple of decades earlier and how Dunnes offered buyers clothes in volumes that meant many people wore the same thing. The 'pile them high and sell them cheap' approach had created the clothing sense of this generation, so it seems a little rich from the proponent of that approach to call people 'sheep' and criticise them for it.

He was asked by Whittaker to look to future trends, and in comments that may have influenced later efforts by his daughters to diversify into different segments of the clothing market Ben Snr said, 'Boutiques, a great future for them if done properly. They've done a great job on the continent.' He drew an analogy with service in continental restaurants and bars. 'You've got to pay for service if you go to Italy and have a bottle of Coca-Cola. If you sit down the price is doubled.' But he used that to explain why Dunnes did things differently or, as others would have seen it, on the cheap, using an analogy based on service in the hospitality sector: 'Can you give me an explanation why in the one hotel you can get three different prices for the one glass of whiskey or the one bottle of stout? What is it only but snobbery that the people in the low bar are fighting to get into the second bar and the second bar fighting to pay the top price you get at the top bar and all you've got is a carpet there.' All this from a man who drank only champagne in the Berkeley Court.

He also said that 'why people read newspapers is that they have nothing else to do and they think it eases their tension, like drinking'.

The reference to tension and drinking was interesting: while seemingly referring to others, was it a conscious or unconscious moment of introspection or self-awareness? The interview mixed insight with cliché, suggested that he was becoming somewhat out of touch with changing trends – something of which he could not have been accused previously, being ahead of the curve for decades – and that great wealth had made him remote from the customers he served. Or maybe, as a habitual drinker, he'd had a few too many glasses of champagne when Whittaker pounced. Whatever the case, it suggested that success had led to a degree of egotism.

9.

Keeping it all secret

IN FEBRUARY 1949 Ben Snr returned to county Down to bury his father, Barney Dunn, who apparently had lived in Newry for 20 years and ended out his days living in the workhouse. The circumstances of how he came to be there are unclear, a family secret, but it is not unreasonable to assume that alcohol played a significant part. Ben Snr's mother, Margaret, had moved to Cork to live with his family until her death in the early 1950s.

As the business expanded, Ben Snr and Nora moved house on a few occasions. Their family first lived at Browingstown Park in Douglas, in a relatively modest four-bedroom house in a privately developed suburb. But quickly they moved to the more expensive and longer established Blackrock area, nearer the River Lee, at Barnstead. Blackrock was where some of the city's so-called emerging merchant princes now lived, on the south side of the River Lee and on the other side from the heights of Montenotte, the other location most favoured by Cork's old money. Barnstead was a fine house, built on several acres of land, where Frank kept a pony and the younger Dunnes, except Ben, developed a love of horses that would stay with them all their lives. It was just across the road from Saint Michael's Church, for whom the local Gaelic Football team was named, and not far from Constitution Rugby Club and Tennis Club.

Ben Snr and Nora wanted more. The family moved again, this time to Ringmahon House, a stately residence on a 100-acre farm near Blackrock. Legend has it that the Dunnes kept to themselves and were not interested in the social milieu of upper-crust Cork society, being the definition of 'nouveaux riche' in very class-conscious Cork. That might be exaggerated, though, as Margaret is known to have dated boys from some of the better-off families. What may be true is that the parents kept to themselves – busy either at work or at prayer – while the children, to varying degrees, integrated themselves into the social lives enjoyed by young people in the more prosperous parts of Cork.

Sam Smyth made the point that whatever the big new houses they bought, the family was really living above-the-shop, with both parents 'absorbed in the stores and family life was relegated to a neglected branch of the business'. Ben Snr and Nora both worked long hours in the early years of the business. Ben Snr left home on a Monday morning and didn't get back until Saturday night. Nora took charge of the Cork stores and was seldom available to her children.

Ben Snr was like many driven businesspeople before and since, choosing to devote most of his waking hours to his business while his relationships with his children were almost exclusively driven by what interest they took in it. This meant that relationships with them as young children were distant – partly because he was almost always away from home and attended to them only on Sundays – but that improved when they were teenagers or adults involved in the business. Nora may have been just as driven and as devoted to the business as her husband. Even if she did stay in Cork for many years when he was travelling to expand the burgeoning empire, she was rarely at home, spending her time in the Cork shops, overseeing things, with the assistance of the deeply trusted Dan Barrett, Ben's first employee.

Their drive and focus and business acumen saw them accumulate a personal fortune. The business still operated largely in cash and with no borrowings, so there was a huge well of money that kept getting deeper. In order to manage their wealth and their legacy, he and Nora created a trust to ensure the business remained in the family after they died. It was also designed to transfer their wealth in the most tax-efficient manner possible by legally reducing their inheritance taxes – although this would become very complicated and controversial in future times.

The control issue – and his desire to ensure the family worked for their inheritance – was best explained in the Andrew Whittaker interview. Ben Snr was asked about bringing Dunnes Stores to the stock market, or 'going public' as it was known because it involved selling shares to the public. This would have meant being accountable twice annually in public for the results earned over the previous six months, and holding an annual general meeting that would have been attended by the media. It would have provided the opportunity both to raise capital from those investors for further expansion and for the Dunne family to sell shares to raise cash for other uses.

'What percentage of companies went public here and have been successful?', Dunne asked Whittaker rhetorically. 'I can tell you that if Dunnes Stores went public tomorrow, do you think the whole six Dunnes family [members] would kill themselves working? Public companies are like the government. The government has one privilege: to spend the public's money foolishly. Public companies are no better.'

His response rambled somewhat before he got back to his core point: 'Ireland's for the Irish people and the sooner people realise that the better. Dunnes Stores has no call to go to the lists [as a public company] and will never go. It's a trust company and it can't be split up for 17 years. I don't want Dunnes to go public. I want to make the Dunne family work. In other words, the Dunnes will have to work for 17 years or go bankrupt, they're my own family.'

The mechanisms of the Dunnes' settlement Trust were complicated, and in retrospect possibly unnecessarily so. Settlements and trusts can be complex legal arrangements. One party, the settlor (in this case Ben Snr and Nora), transfers (or settles) assets on another party, the trustee, to hold and manage those assets for the benefit of a third party, the beneficiary (in this case the six children of the settlors). The usual objectives are wealth preservation and/or tax planning, which makes solicitors and tax consultants central to the drafting of the necessary documents, known as the deed, but privacy is also provided.

The trustee is given certain instructions in the deed as to how to perform its work, which must conform with the law. Done properly, the aims of the settlor will be clear and enforceable and the trust will be resilient and immune to legal challenge. They need to be reviewed and altered regularly to take changes in law into account. The trustees have a fiduciary duty to put their clients' best interests ahead of their own and act prudently with the money and assets. It is a relationship of trust and confidence, bound by legal and ethical considerations, which may include filing returns and other reporting requirements. Damages could be awarded to beneficiaries if a fiduciary fails to fulfil its duties appropriately. It was a mechanism that was used frequently by the wealthy as a form of legitimate tax-planning. It enabled income that would otherwise be subject to ordinary tax enjoy limited exposure to tax, so long as the income remained within the trust and was not distributed.

What seems clear is that Ben Snr did not regard his children as ready to take control of the company. The Trust he established was a discretionary trust, which gave no immediate benefit to the beneficiary. Its life was 21 years, to run until 1985. The 'subject matter' of the Trust was the shares in the overall Dunnes Holding Company. In other words, the Trust took ownership of all the assets in the Holding Company. Dunnes was an unlimited company, which meant it did not have to file full annual returns and make its profitability visible to the public – but it also left the owners personally liable for all losses in the unlikely event that the business crashed. Each of the Dunnes trading companies – and there were many – was a wholly owned subsidiary of the Dunnes Holding Company. This essentially meant that the entire ownership of all the trading companies was held through the Dunnes Holding Company, in turn owned by the Trust and subject to the terms of the Trust.

Ben Snr and Nora were named among the trustees, as was allowed by law. They were joined by John Dunne (Ben Snr's brother) and by Dunnes company secretary John Spillane. The beneficiaries were their six children, although 'provisions' were also made for grandchildren. The trustees were permitted 'in their absolute discretion' to apply both the income and the capital of the Trust for the benefit of the beneficiaries. The trustees controlled the money paid to the beneficiaries and decided the size and type of the investments made by the Trust. Beneficiaries of a discretionary trust are not entitled to receive anything as of right. Instead, they enjoy the potential to receive money and the right to ask the trustees to give it to them at the appointed time. The trustees decide when and how much funds can be distributed to the beneficiaries. It made the adult children dependent on the generosity of the trustees, even after they took control of management of the business.

Nobody in the Dunne family was left out in the initial construction, but that didn't guarantee there wouldn't be issues over the lifetime of the Trust. The idea would no doubt have disturbed Ben Snr, but the trustees could ignore the settlor's wishes, especially after death. Whatever their decisions, trustees must agree unanimously on any course of action; they cannot decide by a majority vote. Most pertinently, trusts can cause problems when they reach their expiry date and the trustees are faced with new decisions, usually without the input of the original settlor.

Ben Snr set up the Trust from a desire to exert control and will and to ensure his offspring were hardworking and worthy beneficiaries, but maintaining control from beyond the grave is an egotistical illusion. There was so much that would happen in his children's lives that he could never have foreseen, and all of it would impact the Trust, his legacy, their sibling relationships, and the future of Dunnes Stores. In one way, a trust is an excellent financial mechanism to protect family wealth; in another way, it's a ticking timebomb.

PART 2

Bloodline

1971–1981

10.

The Dunnes juggernaut

THE 1970S WAS A DECADE in which the people of the 26-county Republic of Ireland watched anxiously in case what was known as 'The Troubles' in the north spread into the south – which tragically it did in 1974 when loyalist terrorists bombed Dublin and Monaghan on the one day, to murderous effect, killing 34 people. There were other occasions when firebombs were placed in Dublin stores, including Dunnes at North Earl Street in 1972, but they were defused and thankfully no more lives were lost.

It was a brave time for a Catholic business from the Republic to open in the north, but then Ben Snr didn't see borders as an obstacle to making profit. Ben Snr achieved what his family has since described as 'a major business ambition' when Dunnes opened at Bangor, in county Down, near his first home, in July 1971. The near-civil war in the north was just two years old then, the British Army having moved in to protect the Catholic population initially before essentially turning against it to protect the unionist majority. Terrorists of all denominations liked the mayhem of bombing commercial premises, most especially shopping stores, because they could gain easy access to them. Sometimes no warnings were given to allow for evacuation of shoppers and staff, and even if warnings were given the bombs often still went off, causing considerable damage. Commericial insurance may have been unobtainable, but government compensation covered those bills if and as they arose.

But war or no war, people still needed to shop for their weekly groceries and Ben Snr ploughed on. He was now entering what would be regarded as his retirement years, owner of 17 increasingly valuable stores that provided the cash for further expansion, and his ambition didn't dim. He acted as chairman and joint managing director (with Frank) and all the children, except Anne, had executive titles, with support from managers external to the family.

It took time, though, for Dunnes to expand its initial footprint. In 1976 Frank, more and more the face of the company, said publicly he would open eight new retail outlets in the north over the following twelve months, saying 'all the initial groundwork' had been laid. He delivered on this, even opening in unionist strongholds such as Portadown, all to suit his father's ambitions, which it was assumed the rest of the family shared.

Dunnes faced well-established competition in the north from, once again, Associated British Foods (ABF). Galen Weston's business had purchased the Stewarts supermarket business, Stewarts Cash Stores, the market leader in the six counties. At its peak it had 65 stores, making it by far the largest player. Many people didn't care where they bought their food as long as they could afford it, but some chose to shop along sectarian lines and Dunnes Stores, even if it did not say so publicly, benefited when people preferred a 'Catholic' shop. And yet it also bucked that trend: in March 1980 Dunnes opened in Lisburn, widely regarded as a loyalist stronghold. It was all about money, not politics, for Ben Snr.

Competition from Weston was something Ben Snr was used to combating by now. Weston was also interested in clothes retailing, a passion he had inherited but now shared with his new Irish wife Hilary Freyne, a former model. She made her own mark in Irish retail – she ran the CMT operations that stocked the first Penneys store in Dublin's Mary Street. Penneys was on its way to becoming what Dunnes arguably could have been with more ambition: a genuine international clothes retailing brand. It had been established in 1968 when 28-year-old Arthur Ryan, one of Ben Snr's executives at Cornelscourt, quit in frustration at what he perceived as a lack of ambition at Dunnes. Ryan proved to be dynamic and succeeded, backed by Weston's capital, in serving the same lower end of the market as Dunnes, with many of the same business principles. Ben Snr's loss was the consumers' gain and Penneys is now an iconic home-grown brand, employing 80,000 people across 460 stores in 17 countries, although known as Primark outside of Ireland, all managed from Mary Street in Dublin 1.

In 1970, Weston bought Brown Thomas on Grafton Street, property included, when closure threatened, for just £300,000. Similarly, in 1971 a failing Switzers department store, which had a presence on Grafton Street since 1838, was taken over by a subsidiary of the UK retailer House of Fraser. Brown Thomas moved to the Switzers building (and Weston later sold its premises to Marks & Spencer in the early 1990s), and Weston invested heavily in Brown Thomas to make it the high-end luxury goods department store it is today, although now in Asian ownership since his death in 2021. Ben Snr had no interest in taking on upmarket properties and businesses like Brown Thomas and Switzers, although Dunnes did buy property at the other end of Grafton Street, nearer to St Stephen's Green.

In a prelude to what has been said every decade since, from the late 1960s onwards there was a narrative of doom and gloom about the future of shopping in Dublin city centre. Department stores were particularly written off in this scenario, despite increased prosperity. None of the stores offered parking facilities, although this would change over the coming decades. Increased car ownership gave consumers greater mobility, but traffic congestion and parking diffi-culties affected sentiment about travelling into the city centre. Rising incomes and changing lifestyles shifted the emphasis from value and service to rapidly changing fashion. Small fashion boutiques offering fast-changing styles sprang up around the city and competed strongly.

Ben Snr sought an acceptable compromise, seeking to develop a clothes retailer that didn't just concentrate on the lowest price end of the market, while still adhering to the cost disciplines. He was partic-ularly busy in 1972, first buying the Bolger Stores Group, with branches in North Earl Street, at Stillorgan Shopping Centre, in Limerick city and the family's original store in Enniscorthy, county Wexford, employing about 300 people. A press release promised that the stores would continue to operate as a fashion group under its original name and 'will be expanded to make it the largest group "of its kind" in the country'. Bolgers was an old-style, traditional general draper, with a high emphasis on personal service, the type of business Ben Snr had rejected in building Dunnes Stores. Jeanne Bolger, whose father John owned the business, remembers how Bolgers had a big business in shoes, especially for children. 'We had a designated person from Clark's, the biggest shoe company in those days, in each store, who fitted the children for their shoes,' she recalled. 'It was also a significant player in ladies fashion, at a higher price point to Dunnes and Penneys but cheaper than what was available at Switzers and Brown Thomas.'

But her father John, who had been forced by his own parents to take on the business, wanted to sell. 'It happened so often in family businesses, the expectation being to take on what the parents provided even if it wasn't what they might have been best suited to doing,' Jeanne said. 'My father would have been suited to being an actuary or accountant.' Weston made the higher offer, but Bolger decided he wanted an Irish buyer. Jeanne recalls the Dunne family coming to her family home on Shrewsbury Road in Dublin 4 with bottles of champagne to celebrate the transaction. 'I remember Ben being there, about twenty years old or so, and Ben Snr being this small, wiry little man,' she said.

Within weeks Ben Snr also bought the entire share capital of the House of Cassidy, which had four stores in Dublin and one in Cork. Whereas the Bolger management was retained initially, the Cassidy board resigned immediately, allowing Dunnes to take full control. The purchase, for undisclosed sums, enhanced Dunnes' position as the largest drapery retailer in the country. The Cassidy chain of women's-wear shops had its own factory where some of the goods were manufactured. It remained under that name, giving Dunnes ownership of a somewhat more upmarket brand with different service levels.

Bolger then accepted an invitation from Ben Snr to run Cassidy's on behalf of Dunnes, although he would only do so for a couple of years. Jeanne remembers being brought as a teenager with her parents to foreign trade shows, especially in Italy, and being particularly impressed by the verve of Therese Dunne. 'My parents thought, and I did too, that Therese was the brains of the clothing operation. Margaret may have been the one who drove the pricing and production of the product, but Therese was very innovative, with a brilliant eye for things. She would have sourced the emerging collections. It was so sad what happened to her.'

Dunnes was now positioned to cover a somewhat wider market, reflecting greater disparity in incomes. Journalist Fintan O'Toole acknowledged that Dunnes 'became brilliantly adept at imitation' during that period, producing affordable versions of the latest fashions in its shops apparently within weeks of them appearing in Britain: 'I remember my sisters as they came into their teenage years always looking great when they were going out because there was enough money to buy them stuff that looked new and up to date. There was a world of difference between a knockoff and a hand-me-down. Young Irish people quite liked the idea that what they were wearing was a native imitation. If you were wearing something nice and someone asked where you got it you would say *donez* in a mock French accent, the joke both deflecting shame and claiming pride.'

The 1970s saw successive governments effectively make a dash for economic growth, but it was an era of double-digit inflation, pay increases that more than matched that to settle regular strikes, and rows over the rates of personal taxation at a time when many of the better-off evaded their responsibilities by hiding money from the taxman. As historian Diarmaid Ferriter noted, 'Looking at the decade, the economy continued to grow at 4% a year, similar to the 1960s, and the free trade involved in EEC membership proved beneficial overall. Irish industrial wages rose to about equal UK levels by the end of the decade. But Irish consumer prices rose by 13.8% a year from 1970 to 1977, 4% above the EEC average.'

Fianna Fáil was out of power between 1973 and 1977 but returned to office in 1977 with promises of an economic giveaway. In a mini version of what would later be the Celtic Tiger, consumers bought new houses, new cars and went on foreign holidays as employment numbers boomed. From August 1977 to August 1978 'personal borrowings from the banks increased by an extra 45%. It was the year of the big spenders.' However, a second oil crisis of the decade – when prices soared, and home heating and petrol became prohibitively expensive – meant that the boom soon turned to bust. Whitaker, now governor of the Central Bank, had warned it would happen, being deeply worried by the growth in public expenditure. He was the first to use the phrase that as a community 'we are at present living vastly beyond our means', which was repeated by Charles Haughey in an infamous televised address to the nation in early 1980, not long before he started tapping up donors for cash to fund his own overspending.

Whitaker's take was prescient – the country paid dearly for its profligacy as personal and business spending contracted. And yet Dunnes seemed impervious to the vicissitudes of the economy. As it had since the 1940s, the Dunnes juggernaut rolled on, sweeping up opportunities, driving hard bargains, always expanding. But age was catching up with Ben Snr. The handing over of responsibility within this family business was coming, and despite the presence of three strong women, it was the two boys who would get first opportunity to succeed him. But they were different from their father.

11.

Frank's reluctant ascent

DUNNES STORES ENDED the 1970s on a high note with 61 shops, having started the decade with 17 – an admirable feat given that so many businesses failed to keep step with the changing times and economic circumstances and closed.

The 1970s started with the purchase of two premises in Limerick for approximately £200,000. In April 1973 it opened a new 6,000 sq.ft. branch at Main Street, Killarney, about two-thirds of the store devoted to drapery and the balance to food. Back in Cork, the thirty-ninth outlet in the chain was opened by Ben Snr and Nora together in 1976 at Bishopstown, a suburb in the south-west of the city, opening the west Cork hinterland. Another store opened in Mayfield, a rapidly expanding estate of public and private housing high on the hills of the north-east of the city. In January 1978, Dunnes paid more than £2m for the 107,000 sq.ft Crumlin Shopping Centre on the former Moracrete industrial site, beside Sundrive Road Garda Station. Dunnes would be the anchor unit, the main draw at each of these sites, the other tenants a secondary attraction.

The commercial property and business pages of the newspapers regularly carried details of the Dunnes expansion, often where major new housing developments were under construction. In 1976 it bought land from the controversial builders Brennan and McGowan at Kilnamanagh, near Greenhills Road in Dublin, to build its own 70,000 sq.ft complex next to a large new housing estate. *The Irish Times* reported how Dunnes decided to buy and develop the site itself 'rather than follow the usual retail pattern and become tenants of a development company'. Half of the space would be given over to Dunnes Stores, with the remainder let to 25 or so tenants, making Dunnes the landlord. It was to be an 'enclosed centre, with air-conditioned malls for all-weather shopping comfort. And there will be parking for 650 cars.' Frank had been best man at Joe McGowan's wedding and McGowan later confirmed that Dunnes paid £250,000 for the land.

In March 1976 a further report showed architect Brian O'Halloran's impression of the £1m development: 'The project marks the entry of Dunnes Stores to the purpose-built shopping centre market as major retail-space developers in their own right.' It described how pedestrian malls would link Dunnes with the smaller shop units and provide four entry points on each side of the complex. The housing estate, which was to host 1,500 homes, was part of the biggest single planning application granted by the local authorities in the era. The intended catchment area – with an estimated population of over 250,000 eventually – was to include Tallaght, Terenure, Templeogue, Rathfarnham and as far as Clondalkin and south county Dublin. 'It is a phenomenon relating to the motorised shopper that he/she will travel great distances in search of bargains. This, combined with a high-density local population, is the cornerstone of all shopping centre plans.'

The Irish Times noted how 'Dunnes Stores, under Mr Frank Dunne, is now in an expansionary phase and new moves now underway will augment the multiple's outlets throughout Ireland.' It also reported how 'Frank Dunne is considering a sophisticated form of unit mortgage, to provide long-term finance for the Kilnamanagh units, instead of the standard shopping centre lease with built-in rent reviews. Such a scheme will be sure to interest unit traders because many would prefer to buy their outlets, thereby avoiding the burden of rent reviews while at the same time building up a valuable asset.' Frank was apparently comfortable talking about property development to the media. He was being treated, at least in newspaper reports, as the boss of the company.

Later in the year *The Irish Times* quoted Irwin Druker, of the estate agent Fanning Druker and who would represent Dunnes for many decades more, who said that 'the drawing power of the Dunnes Stores name has made a retailing magnet of the previously almost unknown district of Cornelscourt, and there are parallels in the many other locations throughout Ireland where the group trades . . . The Tallaght shopping centre will complete the infrastructural mix in the Tallaght area, which will now move towards the planners' ideal of a self-sufficient town, complete with houses, industries, community and educational facilities.'

Dunnes was leading the field, but supermarket competition was intense. When Liptons went in to liquidation in 1976, there was no single buyer and the units were sold piecemeal. Isle of Man-based entrepreneur Albert Gubay established the 3 Guys supermarket chain in a blaze of publicity in 1977, but sold the chain to Tesco just two years later, unable to make a go of it. Gubay described it as a 'no frills warehouse with goods sold from manufacturers' boxes'. There were only 450 items, with only the most popular brands stocked, most of them variations on the 'essential ten': tea, sugar, coffee, margarine, butter, bread, beans, milk, washing power and toilet rolls. Ben Snr reacted furiously. He walked up to Gubay in the Royal Hibernian Hotel and snapped, 'So you're the man who's going to put us all out of business . . . we've seen your kind before,' before storming off. That implied threat – we've seen your kind before and they're nowhere to be seen now – should have rattled Gubay to his core. However, entrepreneurs like Gubay tend to be positive and rarely allow themselves to be put off by confrontation.

Later that same evening, Ben Jnr passed Gubay in a stairway at the hotel and said to him, 'You're costing me at least two Mercedes a week in trying to keep down to your prices.' But true to form, Dunnes dug deep and saw off Gubay by undercutting on price and offering a wider range of choice, the former being more important. Tesco struggled badly in the Irish market, too, and exited a few years later (to return much later). 'Dunnes Stores better value beats them all' wasn't just an advertising slogan aimed at customers: it was a declaration of war against competitors.

Possibly the most interesting local competition was provided by Five Star, which peaked with 35 outlets in the mid-1970s and emphasised range and convenience over price. But it was too small to compete once the other supermarkets moved beyond Dublin in the late 1970s and was sold to Quinnsworth for £5m in 1979.

All this competition didn't necessarily mean that the consumer was getting a great deal. In November 1973 the National Prices Commission published its monthly report in which it alleged that the average percentage markup on fruit and vegetables was two to three times higher than that of the best British multiple stores. It also said the higher Irish margins were generally associated with low-quality produce and that, since Irish prices were higher than British prices, the Irish margins in money terms were even higher by comparison than the percentage margins would indicate.

Promotional activity to attract shoppers became a major feature as the stores competed for every sliver of the market share. Dunnes avoided involvement in the Green Shield Stamps mania, which was the 1970s equivalent of a successful customer loyalty programme. The stamps were available in many petrol stations as well as supermarket groups like H Williams, Quinnsworth and Five Star. Back in the pre-decimal 1970s, for every 6d (six pence) a customer spent, they received a stamp to stick into a special collection book. Once full, books could be exchanged for goods that were showcased in specially printed catalogues. In 1972, for example, 100 books of stamps could be exchanged for a 20-inch Pye black-and-white television. Two books might allow the redemption of a kitchen utensil or a child's toy. The scheme ended in 1977 and its creator, Richard Tompkins, formed the catalogue retailer Argos instead. Dunnes concentrated on keeping prices down and advertising without adding what it regarded as gimmicks.

Dunnes noted how smaller independent shops competed by putting symbol group names over the door and buying from wholesalers. The Spar retail franchises became prominent throughout the country and the Mace and Londis symbol groups had begun to trade by the early 1970s. The plethora of independent wholesalers consolidated into four wholesale groupings, two of which, Musgrave and BWG, clearly emerged as highly profitable new industry leaders.

Frank wanted to compete as a wholesaler as well, showing a degree of initiative that contradicts the subsequent portrayal of him as averse to risk. In February 1976, *The Irish Times* reported on Frank's plans to open a cash-and-carry unit, a 35,000 sq.ft unit from which independent traders could buy goods, located close to the main arterial roads from Dublin to the south and west. Frank said that his many visits to major European cash-and-carry operations had 'convinced him that they are a good deal for the independent trader, because of the range of goods offered and the prices available'. He noted that his retail outlets differed in many respects from the independents, which had a special niche on account of their location, service flexibility and convenient and often extended hours. He denied that his move was intended to provoke a price war, but that 'it would certainly be strong enough to match price for price with anyone'. He said that the cash-and-carry market would be better filled by an Irish firm than by a multinational or foreign one.

More details came in April when Frank was interviewed by *Retail News*. He said the operation, to be opened in July, 'will combine the best of modern European methods, suitably adapted for the Irish market'. It never happened. Dunnes never entered the wholesale business because the rest of the family disagreed with the direction Frank wanted to take it. Whether anyone knew it then or not, Frank was starting to become unmoored from the family business.

He may have become the main face of Dunnes and have been working hard to grow the company, but the truth was that Frank had never really wanted to join the family business. His ambition had been to become a vet, his love of the company of animals, especially horses, being a defining feature of his personality. He was to say this constantly over the years, including to union officials during strike negotiations during the 1990s and to other businessmen, bemoaning that he was required by family to do something he really didn't want to do, even if he displayed the ability to do it.

Frank and the Dunne family quickly became established among the confident class of Irish entrepreneurs of the era, who socialised together in prominent locations. Property developer Joe McGowan was part of that set: 'Frank Dunne and the Dunne family were a huge help in introducing me to influential connections. Frank introduced me to Patrick Gallagher and his father Matt, who owned one of the largest property and house-building companies in Dublin. They often invited me to join them for lunch at their Mitchelstown stud farm outside Athboy, County Meath. The gossip at the time was that Frank Dunne was our financial backer. I did not confirm or deny those rumours. Frank Dunne has a great personality and is an astute businessman. To the outside world, he was the quiet man. Frank had great vision, and was saddened by the sudden death of one of his right-hand man, Denis Keane of Keane Mahony Smith Estate Agents. I used to meet them when Frank was competing with his showjumpers, Henry Street and Cornelscourt.'

Frank's drinking and partying became well-known in wealthy social circles in Dublin. 'The Horseshoe Bar in the Shelbourne Hotel was the social spot for the medical and legal profession, entrepreneurs and politicians. The clients included Mr and Mrs Ben Dunne senior; Frank Dunne; Margaret Dunne and her husband Dr Andrew Heffernan, a racing enthusiast; John Mulhern; Jim Gleeson; Jim Stafford, the merchant from County Wexford who dealt in property and fine art; David Austin, who worked with Jeff and Michael Smurfit.' However, Frank found it difficult to moderate his intake and was known to be far more boisterous in his behaviour when drunk, as if overcompensating for his relative quietness – and anxiousness – when sober.

McGowan provides the most reliable guide to Frank's socialising. Frank introduced McGowan to membership of the Galway Blazers, an elite group of riders who rode their horses, along with dogs, over the fields of Athenry in a hunt of foxes. McGowan described Frank as 'a very experienced showjump rider, bordering on international standard. When we went hunting people met socially. On one such occasion after a meet in Athenry, we were gathered in our hunting gear in a pub. The place was packed with locals, talking about lambing and cattle prices. Frank Dunne and John Mulhern ordered drinks for the house.' One of the locals told Mulhern 'that thing in your hand would make a fine handle for a spade', referring to his Havana cigar.

McGowan told of parties that included Senator Ted Kennedy, of the famous American political dynasty, which he and Frank attended at Dunguaire Castle in Kinvara, county Galway. 'They wore their Aran sweaters, and that set the tone for a cheerful and chatty evening. The Kennedy sisters were good company. Lord Hemphill and Frank Dunne discussed both Irish and American politics with Ted.'

Perhaps seeking some stability in his life, Frank decided to marry, to a Danish woman, Ann Achmann. Ben Snr and Nora not only disapproved but refused to attend his wedding in 1971, causing bitter resentment and further alienating Frank. If it was too late to become a veterinary surgeon, he could indulge his passion for horses by becoming involved in competition, as a trainer.

Frank's successes in horse-racing was limited. Having grown up in Cork with land for horses, he had taken possession of his parents' 300-acre Mitchelstown stud and made it his own home. He took out a training license and trained his own horses from 1982. He had early success with a horse called Stanerra, bred in Ireland by the Moyglare Stud. She had emerged unexpectedly as a five-year-old in 1983 as one of the leading middle-distance performers in Europe, winning a series of races in Ireland and the UK before becoming the first horse trained in Europe to win the prestigious Japan Cup.

If Frank thought he had found his calling, then this early success confirmed it for him. However, the horse had hit her peak and after one unsuccessful run in 1984 she was retired to stud but had no impact as a brood mare. It was to be Frank's last major success as a trainer, despite investing heavily in facilities at his stud, including what was apparently the country's first swimming pool and solarium for horses. A widely held view in the racing industry was that Frank overtrained some of his horses, that not all had the capacity for hard work that Stanerra displayed. Others, however, would later state that he was an innovator whose methods were successfully used by other trainers in subsequent decades.

'When he had Stanerra, he had a great team behind him, including Wally Swinburn and Chris Ryan, who would go on to be a leading huntsman,' said Peter Reynolds, manager of the Ballymacoll Stud. 'Frank was a great innovator. He had a treadmill before anyone else and put in superb gallops. He was a generous man and always good to his staff.' Among the best Frank bred were classic winner Night of Thunder and Group 1 winners Creachadoir and Youmzain.

Behind it all, though, alcohol was ruining his life. An unnamed friend told the *Sunday Independent* that 'there are two characters to Frank Dunne. When he is sober, he's very nice but when he was pissed he was a nightmare.' When he was with his horses, he was happy, so it suited him to be away from the family business on a day-to-day basis.

It was no surprise that Frank drifted more and more towards those other parts of his life. His more limited public appearances on behalf of Dunnes from the mid-1970s onwards may be attributed to difficulties beyond his alcoholism. He also had to deal with emotional distress of the breakdown of his marriage.

In a legal statement made in 1990, Ann outlined problems in the marriage in its early years. She said one of the most upsetting things was that she wanted but never had children. After a year of marriage, she attended at the Coombe, a maternity hospital in Dublin, and, in her own words, 'was found to be perfectly normal'. She blamed the 'intensive pressure' under which she and Frank lived for her failure to conceive, and while she didn't fully explain what she meant by that, it may have been the demands he was under as a director of the family business and his reliance on alcohol. 'We never really relaxed together, and this is the only reason that I know of as to why I did not become pregnant,' she swore.

Five years after they married, Ann said she became ill 'as a result of my unhappy marriage'. She said she suffered from 'depression, anxiety and a nervous state'. She left Frank, moving to England for a year and producing a doctor's certificate to say she suffered from 'severe nervous tension and insomnia'. Frank appears to have made efforts to save the marriage. 'My husband came over begging me to return and saying he couldn't live without me, and I eventually returned in September 1977,' she disclosed.

The reconciliation didn't last. On 18 May 1980, the couple signed deeds of separation. She received £150,000 in a settlement and went to live in London. It would not be the end, however, of contact, and of conflict, between the pair.

Frank was undoubtedly distracted and distressed by these unhappy events, which would have come between him and his work. This meant the way began to clear for his younger brother, more inclined to agree with Ben Snr's way of doing things, to take control of the family business.

12.

The next Ben rises

MARGARET SUFFERED A MAJOR disadvantage when it came to her father's thinking on succession: her sex. She was sufficiently deferential – she rarely contradicted her father – which meant he could have trusted her to continue to run the business according to the template and disciplines he had set down. Instead, when Frank failed to pass muster, the leadership baton was passed to the next son.

The younger brother was perhaps an unlikely future leader. Ben was sent to a private school, Presentation Brothers College (Pres), on the Western Road in Cork, one of two such schools in the city favoured by the well-to-do. Pres graded students according to perceived abilities and Ben was streamed into a class seen as weak academically. He didn't show an interest in or an aptitude for the most basic academic subjects. He would later discover that he was dyslexic, but in that era such a diagnosis was not easily or often made.

To his credit, there were no stories of him behaving in a spoilt fashion during his school years. He was not considered a troublemaker by teachers. He didn't make many close friends or socialise much. He didn't enjoy, despite his size, rugby, the sport upon which the school placed an enormous importance. Leaving school at the age of sixteen, without completing any state exams, was apparently a happy day for him.

He was happier at home, where he engaged in farm work enthusiastically, learning the skills of a dealer, buying and selling cattle and sheep in the mart. He worked out prices in his head rather than on paper, learnt how to talk with people. His hobby had been to build model airplanes during winter and to fly them in the summer holidays. He worked at the Patrick Street premises from an early age, conducting the floor tasks like any ordinary worker and getting paid the same rate for it. Ben's first car was a Ford Anglia that he drove to dances across Cork.

He was fortunate, perhaps, that his father scorned education, as was clear in an account by TK Whitaker: 'What is the secret of this outstanding success? Ben himself, being a self-made man, affected to scorn the utility of formal education. To send a youngster to college to do a commerce degree was, in his view, to spoil any innate talent he or she might have for business."

As is sometimes the case with business-obsessed parents, they were largely absent from their children's early lives, but Ben Snr bonded with teenaged Ben over a shared interest in business, perhaps one the son felt he had to grasp if he was to connect with his father. Even as a child, it was all he heard his father talk about during his Sundays at home: sales prices, turnover, competitors and how to beat them. As a 19-year-old Ben followed his father on working trips to Dublin, leaving Cork every Tuesday and returning home to Ringmahon on a Friday in his latest car, a Triumph 2000. Ben got to see how his father operated up close while Ben Snr explained his methods. They got on well, even if others might have found daily sermons of toughness, diligence and thrift to be somewhat wearying.

As an adult, Ben told friends that his father was 'firm but fair' or 'very kind, but tough and ruthless with a huge heart', and it seems he had to endure tough love before earning the right to move ahead. He also said his father had low self-esteem, which may have accounted for his brusque dismissal and suspicion of what he saw as snobbery in the manners and conventions of the middle class.

Fintan O'Toole wrote of having a summer job in 1972, working as an assistant in Dunnes Stores, and of spending a day working with 'young Ben as he was called then to distinguish him from his father'. This was when Dunnes had bought Cassidys on George's Street and 'I was ordered to help young Ben move stock . . . we spent hours just the two of us wheeling rail loads of dresses down the busy street dodging pedestrians and traffic. It seemed completely mad. There was easily a truckload of stock to be shifted. While they were not bothered to do so in the obvious way it also seemed very menial for the boss's son. He was 22 and heir to a dynasty and I was 14 and being paid 15 pence an hour. The task placed us both on the same level. He was not surly just taciturn and gruff. As we were constantly at the far ends of a rail from each other we were not able to talk much and even if we could we had nothing in common. I just wonder what was going on? Was young Ben being humiliated or taught a lesson to be kept in his place?'

O'Toole also wrote about how 'I would see old Ben around the store sometimes and he seemed stern and dour and quietly menacing. Once trying to impress a girl who worked on the shop floor I did a crude impression of old Ben for her. She laughed and told me that yes that was just like her grandfather. So maybe this was just the ritual of the family business that the prince would have to do the grunt work before he could inherit the throne.'

Ben Snr and Nora never bought a house in Dublin, even when it became the centre of the expanding empire's activities, and nor did they return to live in Cork. In June 1971 a public inquiry at City Hall in Cork heard of proposals by Cork Corporation for the development of Mahon peninsula for social housing. Over 200 objections by property-owners and occupiers were lodged against compulsory purchase orders made by the Corporation. Ben Snr, who was rarely in Cork, was one of the principal objectors. His deposition said he was the owner of Ringmahon House, Blackrock, comprising his dwelling house and lands used as a stud and to maintain a Friesian herd and Suffolk sheep. He said he thought that, as an Irishman, he should withdraw his objection to the acquisition of 80 acres on one side of the laneway in which he built his stud, but he also owned 40 acres on the other side, including a residence, and he wanted to keep that. He said it had taken him about 20 years to build his residence at Ringmahon House and while he and his wife did spend a lot of time in Dublin, Ringmahon was his home. He said he looked forward to his retirement there, when he could look after his stud farm. That never came to pass. The land was acquired and used for extensive public housing.

Disappointed, perhaps, by the acquisition of that part of his land in Cork, Ringmahon House was essentially abandoned. Over the years it fell into dereliction, until it was later gifted to the State and turned into a training centre in the early years of the 21st century.

Instead, Ben Snr and Nora moved into what was then Jury's Hotel on Dame Street in Dublin (now an office-block) and that, by default, became 'home' to the young adult children when they came to work in Dublin. It was an unusual living situation. It meant that when family members sat down to eat together, it was in the hotel restaurant, having made reservations, to be served by the staff. When they wanted to talk, they did so using the internal telephone service. Sam Smyth quoted one former member of staff who described the Dunnes as 'room service brats'. A businessman who remembered Ben when he first arrived in 1967 said it was sad to see a teenager living in an impersonal hotel, away from his friends in Cork. But his father wanted him and the others to be close to their place of work and Dublin had replaced Cork as the centre of activities.

In late 1972 Ben Snr and Nora were inconvenienced when Jury's decided to relocate to a brand-new hotel on a much larger site in Ballsbridge. Ben Snr decided that the two-mile walk to the city centre from Ballsbridge was too far, so he and Nora checked into the Shelbourne Hotel on St Stephen's Green, just a five-minute walk to the company's headquarters on South Great George's Street. That would remain their home for the next decade.

Ben was soon moved on from the menial tasks and given control of the footwear and men's-wear divisions. But there was a major issue that affected his relationship with his parents – one that echoed Frank's earlier experience. Ben had fallen in love and wanted to marry, even though still in his early twenties. His choice of life partner was Mary Godwin, two years older, from Kilkenny and working as an Aer Lingus flight attendant. They married in a Kildare church in April 1973 and their first child, Mark, arrived later that year, on 4 November. So it would seem that Mary's pregnancy was the reason why Ben Snr and Nora did not attend the wedding. Even by the strict social codes of the time, this very public act of disapproval was harsh and deeply hurtful to the couple. Father Dermod McCarthy, who was later to figure in times of crisis for the family, performed the marriage ceremony. Margaret, careful of her parents' displeasure, did not attend either. The newly-weds bought and moved into a large, detached modern home on five acres in Porterstown, near Castleknock. It would be their home for decades to come, upgraded significantly on occasions, extended to have eight bedrooms, a swimming pool and a putting green. They called it Winterwood.

It would be about six years before Ben Snr and Nora relented and asked to see their first two grandchildren and the home in which they lived, which was remarkable given that Ben Snr regularly met his son at work. They got a tour on the visit and Ben Snr, somewhat astonished and impressed by the opulence, asked his son how he could afford this. Ben couldn't resist. According to him, he responded, 'For God's sake, Dad, we've all been robbing you blind for years.'

Ben may not have had the initial blessing of his parents, but his life was well set now. He was a married man, he was managing divisions of the company, and the way had cleared – thanks to Frank's misfortunes – all the way to the throne. He was the youngest son, but he was now the favourite to take over. The future was very bright, the money was flowing, the potential was enormous. That is why what happened next sent deep shock reverberations through the whole family, through the company, and through the very fabric of Ben's life and sense of self.

13.

The kidnapping

THE DEFINING EVENT of Ben's life began on 16 October 1981. He was just 34 years of age, married and with two small children, when the IRA kidnapped him for ransom. He was held hostage for just under a week before he was freed, but he was imprisoned psychologically by the ordeal. The consequences of that trauma rolled on for years, affecting not just him but many others, and everyone he held dear.

The morning it happened, Ben was driving to Portadown to complete preparations for a new store opening. He was near the border at Killeen, on the Newry Road, when he was intercepted on the border's northern side. The story reported in the media initially was that he stopped to give assistance at a faked accident scene and when he did so was pulled from his distinctive black Mercedes car. But it was far more dramatic than that, as he described it to reporters after his release.

'I was travelling fairly quickly and a car heading towards me in a bunch of traffic cut across the road in front of me and I hit my brakes and swerved to avoid it. I went onto the side of the road, pulled my own car back and stopped. I said to myself: "That was a close one." I looked in the mirror and I could see smoke from my tyres I had hit the brakes so hard. I saw the car behind me turning and coming back after me. I thought he was coming up to apologise. So the next thing, what happened, I was confronted by four masked men with rifles and they ordered me to get out. I got out and I was in a daze. Time froze and one second became like an hour. One guy pushed me inside, saying "Get in". Their car was now facing towards the southern side of the border. I hesitated, waiting for traffic to come from Newry which didn't seem to happen. I got in and a guy got in either side of me and the two others were in the front.'

He was bundled quickly into their car which, according to witnesses who contacted the RUC, drove south across the border again. However, nobody knew whether the kidnappers continued south or turned back immediately into South Armagh. The border was (and is) not a straight line and was criss-crossed by many minor roads and footpaths, unmanned by security forces. The kidnappers moved off the main road quickly, into the forests and mountain land that provided excellent cover for an easy getaway, heading north.

The immediate assumption by the RUC and An Garda – who were quickly contacted by witnesses in other cars – was that the IRA was responsible. Nobody else would have been brave or mad enough to get involved in criminality in that area. South Armagh was the most dangerous area in Northern Ireland for RUC officers, British soldiers, Protestant farmers and anyone else regarded as targets by the Provisional IRA. The area, nicknamed Bandit Country, was arguably where the IRA was strongest. Committed Republicans intimidated anyone who might have provided information or assistance to the authorities. It was where Captain Robert Nairac of the British Intelligence Services had been abducted just four years earlier and held captive for a number of days before being murdered. His body was never found.

'Are you going to shoot me?' Ben asked, as he was told to put a hood over his own head. 'Keep your head down, don't ask questions and you won't be shot,' his abductors said. He was driven for what he thought was about twenty minutes, then taken out of the car to 'some sort of pigsty'. He recalled: 'I could feel mud under my feet and the stone walls and I was given some sort of crate to sit on. About ten minutes later they came to me and asked me for my wife's name and telephone number and my father's name and telephone number.' Ben said he knew it was a ransom they wanted. They said to him, 'What do you think you are worth?' to which he replied, 'Nothing, you will get nothing from me.'

'I was left in the hut. I think for about two hours, and then I was caught and dragged across the fields. I heard them make references to the fact that the Brits were close, or too close, and two of them caught me, one on either side, and started to run. I had to run with them blindfolded. I was exhausted. I said, "Take it easy, lads, go easy," but they kept running and dragging me over the ground.'

They finally stopped running when they reached a ditch and spent another couple of hours crouched, hiding. When they moved again he heard noises from passing cars on a road. At every noise the men would stick the muzzles of their guns into his neck or face or ribs, telling him to get his head down, warning him to cooperate 'or else'. Then he was bundled into the back seat of a car. They sat on him during a drive he thought lasted a half-hour before they stopped and moved him, still hooded, indoors.

Ben was forced to lie on a hard floor for most of each day of captivity, with a pillow for his head, which remained hooded. They helped him to a bed at night. 'They were certainly rough characters,' he said. 'You knew they meant business.' He was given food, but didn't each much. 'I had to lift up the hood to drink or eat and I was told, "if you see anything, you are going to be shot". I didn't look at anything, even if I had the opportunity. I wasn't worried about myself. I was worried about my wife and children and family. I was helpless and there was nothing I could do. If they wanted to take me out and shoot me, there was very little I could do.'

He said he didn't fear for his life after talking to his captives. 'I asked them three times whether they were going to kill me. On the fourth time, one of them turned around and said, "If we were going to kill you, we would have done it already." I have a fairly logical brain and that calmed me down.'

On the third day of the kidnapping, he asked for a beer. 'One of the men shouted out and said, "The big fellow is looking for a bottle of beer". The guy outside shouted back, "Give him what he wants, he's a paying guest." So even with serious situations like that, you have to see the funny side. They obviously thought I was worth more to them than the price of a bottle of beer.'

He had rosary beads in his pocket which he rubbed repeatedly as he prayed. 'The only thing I could do was talk to God, he was the only one left. I remember at the time thinking I had a direct link to him. One minute I would be giving out, the next I would be begging him to allow me see my wife and family again. Funnily enough, he kept talking back to me. It's been like that right through my life. I always thought he kept a watchful eye over me. I couldn't have been in so many scrapes over the years and come out the way

I am without the help of some people and some superior power, that being my God.'

While Ben spoke freely afterwards of his experiences, his extended family remained silent about how they found out about the kidnap, the trauma it caused, or their discussions around how to deal with it. Mary couldn't deal with this on her own. Immediately, security had to be provided for Ben's parents and siblings as they feared their own vulnerability to similar kidnapping, as well as being terrified for Ben's safety.

Accountant Noel Fox, a trustee for Dunnes and employed by Oliver Freaney & Co., was to become central to what transpired. On the evening of the kidnap he went to meet with leading trade union official Phil Flynn at Malahide Castle. Born in Dundalk in 1940, Flynn had been a senior member of Sinn Féin for many years and involved in republican activities since 1955, but successfully defeated charges of being a member of the IRA during the 1970s. It was well-known that Flynn was instrumental to securing the release, in June 1974, of 71-year-old John Hely-Hutchinson and his 67-year-old wife Dorothy after the pair – also known as the the Earl and Duchess of Donoughmore – were violently attacked and kidnapped from their home at Knocklofty House, Clonmel, county Tipperary. A year later Flynn negotiated the safe release of Dutch industrialist Tiede Herrema, who was kidnapped by Rose Dugdale and Eddie Gallagher on behalf of the IRA. It made Fox's approach entirely logical.

'Noel asked me to act as an intermediary to secure Ben's release, but I told him that I couldn't, that the Special Branch would be expecting that to happen and that I would be watched and couldn't act,' Flynn told me in a 2025 interview for this book, his first time disclosing his involvement. 'I told him not to worry too much, that I was highly confident that Ben wouldn't be killed because the IRA would not want to bring the amount of trouble on itself that his death would have caused it.'

Fox told Flynn that Ben Snr, who was not particularly active in the business anymore but still the patriarch and therefore would make the decision on this, was willing to pay a ransom. Flynn suggested a plan of action to Fox, one that appears to have been largely followed. He anticipated, correctly, that the two governments would do what they could to prevent the ransom payment. He told Fox that a formal process would have to be initiated, but also a secret, parallel one that would secure Ben's release. The formal process, which the Gardaí would notice and attempt to influence or stop, would involve the family and trusted advisors, such as Fox. The secret parallel process would involve a fellow accountant colleague of Fox's in Oliver Freaney and a middle manager in a branch of Dunnes, both of whom Flynn knew and trusted to be discreet. Flynn's reasoning was that Fox's colleague would have easy access to Fox without arousing suspicion, and that the middle manager would slip under the radar too. Flynn believed this is essentially what happened, although he said he had no further contact on the matter after the meeting with Fox. Flynn also advised that the money be sent with one of the men by train to either Dundalk or Newry, where it would be collected, and that this be done at the same time as the Gardaí were intercepting a more obvious payment attempt.

The Irish and British governments were alerted quickly and, as Flynn anticipated, did not want a ransom paid. This was considered a priority, particularly for the government in the Republic, as much as they wanted Ben back alive. Neither government wanted the IRA to receive the financial boost of a ransom and they didn't want to encourage it to see kidnapping as a lucrative source of future income. They didn't want to have to deal with the murder of a prominent businessman in such circumstances either. The memory of what had happened to Thomas Niedermayer in 1973 remained strong: he was the German managing director of the Grundig factory in Belfast, who was kidnapped in December 1973 by the Provisional IRA and murdered and buried before they could receive a ransom. Then Taoiseach Garret FitzGerald later recalled that 'a man's life was at stake and it's very difficult to tell a man's wife and his family that you're going to stop them from doing what they need to do in order to save his life. Balanced against that realisation was the fact that ransom money could be used to buy weaponry and that weaponry could kill many more people than an individual who had been kidnapped.'

The Gardaí appointed Senior Deputy Commissioner Larry Wren as the point man with both the family and the RUC. To the horror of the Dunnes, they realised Wren's power did not quite match his title and his authority was being undermined by a power struggle within An Garda Síochána. An empire was being built by Assistant Commissioner Joe Ainsworth, under the supposed supervision of Commissioner Patrick McLaughlin, one that essentially broke the established chain of command. Ainsworth ran the security task force based at Dublin Castle and its main function was to provide instant reaction to hijackings, kidnappings and other such events. He also controlled the Intelligence and Security Branch (ISB), which now became involved in the urgent search for Ben. Numerous telephones were tapped, locations were staked out and ISB men disguised as maintenance workers drove around Dundalk in a van trying to gather information.

Wren was not happy with the way in which Ainsworth's men did their work and neither was the Dunne family, especially when the Gardaí intercepted ransom couriers and prevented payment on four separate occasions. The Dunnes complained to McLaughlin and threatened to cease cooperation unless Wren was returned to command of the investigation. At the same time, the Dunnes continued their own back-channel connections with the kidnappers despite being under surveillance themselves now by An Garda.

The RUC and An Garda tried to follow international protocols on handling a kidnapping. Ideally, they would have imposed a news blackout to lead the kidnappers to believe that the family had not contacted the authorities and were arranging a ransom payment. The hope would have been that the hostage would develop a relationship with the kidnappers, so they would be sympathetic to him and less likely to inflict physical harm or death. A news blackout would also have given An Garda and RUC time to gather information as to who might be involved. However, that wasn't possible in this case because news of the kidnap emerged almost immediately, even in those days before the internet and mobile phones, because people had witnessed it and spoken about it to the RUC, Gardaí and journalists.

From the police point of view, care had to be taken to prevent the kidnappers from panicking and taking rash action, particularly if they feared being discovered. The family was told there was a risk in offering a ransom and not being able to deliver it. In high-profile cases in Italy the removal of body parts, such as a finger or ear, for delivery to the family had happened in retribution for non-payment. Another danger was the kidnappers might keep the ransom money and kill the hostage anyway for fear he had information that might lead to their identification.

The family was told not to offer a reward for information, but once the initial 48 hours had passed, public appeals to the kidnappers on behalf of the hostage were allowed. The idea was to put pressure on the kidnappers, but not so much as to panic them, to let them feel they had a good chance of both receiving the ransom and getting away safely. All the while An Garda and RUC continued their investigations, aided by the armies on both sides of the border.

The proposed intermediaries or negotiators were in a difficult position. They had to be calm and authoritative but also unthreatening, able to win the confidence of the kidnappers, but at the same time avoid provoking them or encouraging them or giving them an advantage in any way. Fr Dermod McCarthy, who had married Ben and Mary, was sent to the Fairways Hotel in Dundalk to make contact with the abductors, but he was authorised only to open communications, not to make decisions. Essentially, he was a decoy.

One of the failed attempts to pay the ransom, not reported at the time, involved multiple shots being fired, although not within Ben's earshot. Details of one of the ransom interceptions quickly became known: within 36 hours of the kidnap, on the Saturday evening, Gardaí swooped on a car travelling north near Dundalk and told the driver they would not permit the money to be handed over. They feared that if the car went over the border, the IRA would take the money and they would have no way of arresting the kidnappers or securing Ben's release. The car returned to Dublin as the British Special Air Service (SAS), Gardaí and Irish soldiers combed both sides of the border. Terrified that the IRA would respond by killing Ben, Mary issued a statement to say that the family had made every effort to fulfil the request of the abductors but had been stopped by the Gardaí. 'We at no time contacted the Gardaí, or advised them of what has happening. We will co-operate fully to secure Bernard's release,' she said.

The following evening, two vans were stopped by the RUC near Newry and found to have IR£500,000 in the back. Once again, the vehicles were turned back. Later that night, Fr McCarthy was arrested in the Republic, a move to prevent him facilitating the paying of a ransom.

Ben was allowed by his kidnappers to listen to the radio and so he knew by Saturday evening that the authorities were determined that the ransom not be paid, and that at least one effort to make the payment had been foiled. But then one of the gang came into him and read out a note from Fr McCarthy and, according to Ben, 'it was like manna from heaven'. They asked him who the priest was and Ben told them that he had officiated at his wedding and was a close friend.

After that came what Ben called the roughest moment. Another gang member came in and said, 'Listen, one of our fellows nearly got shot on account of you', ignoring the very obvious fact that nobody would have been nearly shot if they hadn't kidnapped Ben. They demanded the name of a new contact, other than McCarthy, and when he said he didn't have one, they told him that his life depended on it. 'That is when I resigned myself to the fact that the Gardaí have a job to do and if these people are going to shoot me, they are going to shoot me.'

Ben came to believe that the radio and television coverage, particularly the broadcast appeals, helped: 'I have no doubt that the appeal brought home to them that people were zooming in on all sides and now was the time to get out. There was dead silence around the place as they listened to it.' The appeal was made by Fr McCarthy on behalf of the Dunne family. It may have been that they were listening for a signal in the wording used that the ransom was to be paid, and in retrospect that may have come in Fr McCarthy's urging of the kidnappers to 'cut their losses and get out fast'. The kidnappers were preparing for a night in the fields on Wednesday, but about 30 minutes after the 9pm news on RTÉ, in which McCarthy's appeal was repeated, they told Ben: 'We have good news for you. You won't have to sleep in the fields. You're being released.'

'I didn't know what to make of it,' Ben later said, 'but I was glad to hear it. I wasn't asking any questions. I was playing the cards close to my chest.'

He was driven to St Michael's Church in Cullyhanna, a village of about 600 homes, scattered widely and, crucially, without an RUC station. It was just 10 miles from Dundalk but on the northern side of the border. 'I was more frightened then that at any stage because I knew they were bringing me to my freedom and I had the hidden fear we were going to be ambushed by the army or someone and have a shoot-out. We reached our destination, and I was told to turn my back. They took the hood off and they said, "Don't look at the number plate".' They told him somebody would pick him up in about twenty minutes.

To intimidate Ben further, the kidnappers gave him three bullets as a permanent reminder of his ordeal: one was for an Armalite rifle; another from the revolver they said had been used to guard him; the third was also for an Armalite and they told him to give it to Fr McCarthy. They told him the bullets would be used later if he didn't do as they had told him, which included not cooperating with An Garda.

His kidnappers had brought him to a graveyard. They took off his hood and told him not to look at the car or its number plate. He didn't try. After they gave him the bullets, they left him there and told him not to move for 20 minutes. It was dark and cold and silent but he wasn't going to disobey this last order, not with freedom apparently so close. But standing out there in the open, among the gravestones, was nerve-racking. In a macabre turn, a clearly terrified Dunne climbed into a waiting open grave, ready for a funeral the next day. He didn't want to be found by anybody before the 20 minutes was up and it seemed the best hiding spot. 'I looked up and I could see the stars in the sky. I thought, "Good God, they could shoot me and throw the earth back in", so I crawled out of that grave.' He waited, for who he didn't know.

14.

The rescue

EAMONN MALLIE, THE POLITICAL correspondent of Downtown
Radio in Belfast, lived about four miles from the graveyard. As Ben
waited in the cold silence, Mallie received an anonymous telephone
call, and the person on the other end said to him: 'The man who is
missing can be picked up at Cullyhanna Parochial House'. Mallie never
missed the opportunity to chase a story and, despite potential dangers
to his own safety, he got into his car immediately. He arrived at the
graveyard and looked about. After a few minutes, Ben revealed himself,
trusting that this was the man he had been told to expect. Ben remembers his first words as being, 'Jesus, I'm glad to see you.' Mallie
reported it slightly differently and in more detail: 'When he checked
who I was, he immediately embraced me. All he could say was, "Thank
God I am free. You don't know how glad I am".'

Mallie took Ben to the house of the local parish priest, Fr Hugh
O'Neill. Even though Mallie didn't know the priest – who was relatively new to the area – he instinctively trusted him because of his
position. O'Neill remembered that Dunne 'looked ashen-faced. Very
pale, and heavily unshaven, but still remarkably clean-looking. His
clothes looked okay, considering the six days. He looked so shook I
thought he might need a brandy, but he asked for a beer . . . He was
very anxious to get home to his wife and family, although he was quite
calm when he was in the house. Mr Dunne seemed to be concerned
in case there might be any delay in getting home if he was stopped
by the RUC or Gardaí.'

Mallie drove Ben to an emotional family reunion at his home in
Porterstown. 'You've no idea of the ecstasy, the excitement in that
house,' Mallie said. 'There were tears everywhere.' Fr McCarthy
said he was present when Mary got a call from Ben to say he was

free and almost home. He described how she broke down in tears when she heard her husband's voice and then, after she hung up and as they waited for Ben's arrival, they said a decade of the Rosary in thanks.

The following morning the reporters who had been camped outside the house awaiting news were invited inside to meet Ben. He spoke freely in the hope that once that was done, the media would have all it needed and leave them all alone. All the typically reticent Ben Snr said was, 'we thank God for this happy outcome of our ordeal'. He didn't mention the role of Mammon.

The Gardaí seemingly were not informed that Ben had been freed until he had arrived back at his home, hours after his release. This raised considerable speculation as to whether his release was due to a ransom payment and if he had been told to delay alerting the authorities to give the kidnappers more time to make their getaway.

On Friday, 23 October 1981, *The Irish Times* reported 'major discrepancies' about unexplained telephone calls that Ben apparently made around midnight on Wednesday from Cullyhanna parochial house. On the *Today Tonight* programme on RTÉ that Thursday, Fr McCarthy said that Ben had not contacted his family home until almost 3am, when he was within a half-hour's drive of his house. He had used a public telephone kiosk at the side of the road to make the call. However, Mallie emphasised that he had watched Ben use the telephone but had not overheard the conversation.

After the TV programme, Ben explained that there was no mystery. He said the call from the priest's house was to a very good friend, unnamed, in the Dublin area, who had been involved in trying to secure his release. He had asked this friend to break the news gently to his parents that he was free. He said he didn't phone Mary immediately because he feared he might be detained at one of the many roadblocks in the area. There was a certain logic to that: not unreasonably, a paranoid Ben feared he might be taken again by the IRA, or that those looking to rescue him might mistake him for one of the kidnappers and harm him accidentally in trying to free him. He said he decided to wait to tell Mary until he felt certain he would be able to get home. Presumably, the Gardaí knew then that he had been released, because the Dunne's home phone was tapped to intercept any possible contact from the kidnappers. There were also Gardaí on permanent sentry duty at the house.

Questions were raised, too, about the seemingly easy passage that Ben and Mallie enjoyed in the drive to Dublin from Cullyhanna, driving through several roadblocks without being questioned or recognised, amazing as that might seem. Newspaper reporters in county Louth said the Gardaí had lifted roadblocks at around 3am but did not know why they were told to do so. Ben had apparently not arrived home at that time and there were no suggestions that he telephoned the Gardaí before arriving in Porterstown. Nor does it explain why the journey to Dublin took so long, even in that pre-motorway era.

The Irish Times asked pointedly: 'Who was the friend who must have been unknown to the Gardaí and not under surveillance that he [Dunne] phoned from Cullyhanna and who and at what time eventually told the detectives that he was freed?' This increased the speculation that the Dunnes had used somebody else to pay a ransom after the Gardaí had stopped previous delivery efforts by Fr McCarthy. The name of property developer Patrick Gallagher subsequently surfaced and that, given his known closeness to Fianna Fáil leader Charles Haughey, led to speculation that the leader of the opposition was somehow involved. Gallagher claimed nearly 20 years later that he had supplied the ransom money, because the Dunne family was unable to access the cash while under surveillance, and that he was refunded subsequently. Few took the claim seriously. Gallagher, who died in 2006 aged 54, was a convicted fraudster who had served prison time and was something of a fantasist.

Ben subsequently told different stories as to whether a ransom was paid for his release. 'I genuinely don't know,' he insisted in a 2001 interview. 'The first person I went to when I got out was my father because I knew if someone paid it, it would have been him. He said there was none paid. I don't think about it because everything I have done in my life is involved in controversy. Some people believe it was paid, others believe it wasn't. I genuinely don't know.'

However, in a wide-ranging interview with Miriam O'Callaghan on RTÉ Radio in 2012, Ben revealed that a ransom was paid to secure his freedom, but he had no idea how much. 'I was never worth £1.5 million. I was never told how much it was. I asked my father and he wouldn't tell me.' He doubted that Gallagher or Haughey were involved. 'In my opinion, they had nothing to do with it and I think I would have an idea if they had.'

It may have been the case that, in addition to receiving the ransom, the IRA unit involved feared that the heightened presence of security forces suggested the British Army was closing in on them. It has been claimed that an informer within the IRA ranks – Freddie Scappaticci, known as 'Stakeknife' – was aware of details of the kidnap and let his handlers in the British Army know where to go. Some historians of the period have suggested that Ben owes his life to Scappaticci, while not forgetting many others died because of the Belfastman's actions on behalf of the IRA as the head of its infamous 'Nutting Squad', which tortured and killed informers. This version goes against Flynn's contention that Ben's life was never in danger.

Ben told O'Callaghan that he didn't co-operate with the Gardaí when he was released because he was intimidated after the kidnapping. Those unused bullets had a chilling effect on him. 'I was left in no uncertain terms that my kidnappers knew where my children went to school and where my wife shopped so I didn't co-operate.'

Nobody was ever charged with his kidnap, let alone convicted and jailed. A senior IRA figure at the time, who remains deeply involved with Sinn Féin in 2025 but in a non-elected capacity, was arrested and questioned by the RUC, but was released immediately on Ben's return home. There was never any evidence to link him to the crime, but the RUC was under pressure to be seen to do something and 'lifting' one of the most prominent IRA activists in the area would do as much to assuage the criticisms of inaction coming from FitzGerald in Dublin as it would to advance the investigation.

The Irish government was deeply relieved that Ben had been returned safely, but incorrectly and deliberately insisted that the IRA had not profited from its action. 'My belief is that no money has been paid,' said Minister for Justice Jim Mitchell. 'All Garda information is that no money was passed to the kidnappers. In the nature of things, one cannot be 100% certain. There are many ways of transferring money. Money can be exchanged outside this State, outside this island.' Yet, he said he had no reason to doubt the word of Fr McCarthy when he said no money had been handed over; this was true because

McCarthy hadn't been involved in the successful payment. 'I knew the decision not to allow any money to be paid could be putting Mr Dunne's life in further jeopardy,' claimed Mitchell. 'Saving his life was our first priority, but I also had to take into consideration the effects of allowing so much money to fall into the hands of subversives, how it could be used to kill people, and how it could open the floodgates to more kidnappings. On reflection, we took the only decision open to us. Happily, that decision has been vindicated by Mr Dunne's safe return. I prayed very hard every day – several times a day – that it would be the right decision.' Mitchell said it was 'natural and under-standable' that the Dunne family had wanted to pay the ransom. 'I fully understand their position. I must say that I very much admired their courage, particularly the courage of Mrs [Mary] Dunne.'

Ben returned to his desk at Dunnes Stores one day after his release. He did so at the insistence of his father. In 2024, Ben's son, Rob, remembered how his grandfather had behaved on the night of Ben's return. 'The only thing his dad said to him – and imagine his son has been gone for six nights, held by terrorists – and his only sentence is, "Benny, it's all over now. Keep your head down. I'll see you in the office in the morning". As much as my grandad did dote on his grandchildren, I do have resentment because I think my dad developed what we would now call PTSD and he needed counselling,' said Rob in an interview with Niamh Horan of the *Sunday Independent*. 'Although I recognise it was a very different time.'

The return to work was to show that he would not be cowed and would return to his old normality as quickly as possible. If only that had been possible. Ben received no counselling and later came to regret that – even if he also said that he didn't believe trauma from the kidnapping played any part in subsequent decisions he made in his life. He was somewhat contradictory in the many interviews he later gave, perhaps suffering from denial as well as PTSD: 'I'm not a fella who ever calls himself a victim. But I should have went and got professional help after being kidnapped. I didn't realise the scarring that took place in my brain. But I'm not blaming it for any of the things that happened in my life.'

In another interview he said: 'It was a frightening experience, and it was traumatic. But I recovered from it. I recovered without any professional help.' And in another: 'I had the right to go for counselling but I didn't go. I did mad things after the kidnapping but I don't blame it for that. It had nothing to do with it.' He also said: 'It's a bit like a heart attack. You keep it in your mind all the time. I know that I was kidnapped so I do watch myself.'

He wasn't the only one in the family who suffered the consequences of his ordeal. Rob recalled how the children were protected from what was going on during their father's captivity, but how everything would change after that: 'It was only me and my older brother Mark who were around. I was seven at the time, Mark was nine. I remember being taken to my mum's sister. We spent six or seven days there, and the rule was no newspapers and no news on TV. I was told school was cancelled and we were getting a holiday. Then I was taken home by my aunt. I remember arriving at the house and there was a melee of reporters down at the gate and I was thinking, What's all this?'

It was Ben who told them what had happened and Mary tried to explain it further. 'My mum put it very simply and gently,' Rob said. 'She said, "Rob, Mark, some bad men took your dad for a few days and we were very worried, but we got him back and he is safe and sound. All of this is just newspaper people who want to report on it in the news." He gave us a big hug, but it was kind of chaotic. He came in and sat with us and said, "It's been a crazy few days." At seven, I could just about comprehend bad men. The ransom and everything just wouldn't have been suitable to explain.'

All of their lives changed in the aftermath. 'We ended up having to regroup completely in terms of security measures,' said Rob. 'We had full-time 24/7 security [Garda and private security for a time, then just private] at our gate, very strange. They would drive us places and pick us up. It was really odd, and I felt very self-conscious about it, particularly at secondary school.'

His father's mood changed too, understandably. 'He became very jumpy. He became super-vigilant about his surroundings. He would want to sit in a certain area of a restaurant, for a vantage point. He would say, "I want that spot over there". He wouldn't go into why. He would be very wary, although he was always approachable and friendly. If a stranger came up, he would try to gauge the situation.'

The children adjusted their own approach to Ben. 'I might have messed around or jumped out of a closet before, whereas after the kidnapping I wouldn't, because I would scare the crap out of him and it was obviously extremely traumatic.'

It would only be later that Ben's family would come to realise the extent of the trauma he was going through, but they were focused on his behaviour rather than its causes. He turned to alcohol and, in time, to cocaine. During one long conversation in the mid-1990s, Ben identified to me the woman he claimed had introduced him to cocaine. He told me that he'd had an affair with her, despite her being the wife of one of his friends, a well-known entertainer of the time. He explained why he entered into this relationship with the woman – that there was an element of revenge involved – but two of his friends have told me that I was misled by Ben, that he entered into the relationship with her before he had any reason to fall out with her husband.

Two extraordinary events followed. Ben decided to go to Frank to unburden himself of his feelings of guilt. This was surprising as the two brothers were barely on speaking terms. Ben told Frank that he needed to see him, as his eldest brother, to discuss a serious personal matter. When Ben got to Frank's Meath estate, he broke down in tears. He confessed that he had been unfaithful to Mary and provided other information of a deeply personal nature. Expecting Frank to be sympathetic, he was horrified when Frank laughed and, as Ben felt, mocked him. Ben left quickly and the brothers did not speak again for many years.

Two highly reliable – both of whom spent many hours with Ben and in whom he confided regularly – sources have told me of a particularly incredible additional twist, one they say Ben told them. In an act of revenge, Ben arranged for three men to kidnap the entertainer on his way home from a late-night gig. The hired assailants dragged the man from his car and having hooded him they restrained him as they drove to the Dublin mountains. They took the man out of the car and told him this was his last chance, that if he ever offended Ben again, he would be taken back to this spot and killed. Both of the people to whom Ben confided this story were appalled at the action itself, but even more so that Ben would subject someone else to the same ordeal he had suffered. If ever anything demonstrated that Ben was losing control of himself, this was it, but there was far more to come. It was reckless of Ben to confess to criminality, and it is entirely possible he embellished the tale. However, he often needed to unburden himself and was trusting, sometimes naively so. In this case, his trust was not betrayed. The entertainer did not respond to requests for interview for this book.

PART 3

A New Era

1980s

15.

Death of the patriarch

BEN SNR DIED IN his seventy-sixth year after a very short illness. On 29 March 1983 *The Irish Times* carried a one-paragraph report that stated: 'Mr Ben Dunne, the supermarket owner, is seriously ill in St Vincent's Hospital, Dublin, where he is suffering from a coronary condition following an incident at the weekend when he was accosted by youths who were attempting to steal his car. Mr Dunne, a Dundalk-born businessman, was returning to his suite at the Shelbourne Hotel at the time.'

The report was disputed subsequently. One account had it that Ben Snr and Nora had returned to the Shelbourne from their nightly dinner at the Berkeley Court Hotel in Ballsbridge, but as Nora stepped out of their car, some youths had snatched her handbag. Ben Snr tried vainly to give chase. Exhausted and stressed by the sudden exertion he went to his room in the Shelbourne, where he had a stroke. He was removed to hospital, where he went into a coma. This was denied subsequently, too, with fresh reports stating there had been no such incident and he had fallen ill in the natural course of events.

Ben Snr had given an impromptu semi-interview only a few weeks before he fell ill. Frank Fitzgibbon, then a young reporter with *Business & Finance* but now retired after ending his career as Ireland editor of *The Sunday Times*, laughed at the idea that it was Ben Snr's 'final interview', as many were to portray it. 'I got a few quotes as he rejected my request for an interview, but we had enough from those to present it as an exclusive.'

Business & Finance had planned a cover story on an ongoing industrial dispute at Dunnes and its editor, Jim Dunne (no relation), dispatched Fitzgibbon to talk with the company's founder. The belief was that Ben Snr continued his involvement in the business, instructing his now adult children, making regular tours of his shops and, fore-armed with the recorded previous turnovers, checked the returns at each of the cash registers. These tours were unannounced and unex-pected. Long-serving staff would stiffen when they saw him arrive. He demanded and received the utmost deference from his staff, all of whom, even more senior employees, were required to address him as Mr Dunne. 'He was intensely disliked,' one unnamed Dunnes' veteran told Sam Smyth. 'We lived in fear of him. Anyone that worked with him would recall how he used to shout and roar. All he had was money. He had nothing else of value to offer.'

Some days the old man would wander from the Shelbourne to the company's headquarters for an hour or so. Fitzgibbon had not received a response to many phone calls seeking an interview, but he knew that Ben Snr dined each night at the Berkeley Court after first drinking champagne at a reserved table in the bar, with a driver who doubled as security in close proximity. On consecutive evenings Fitzgibbon watched this ritual before plucking up the courage to introduce himself as Ben Snr and Nora walked towards the restaurant. He asked Ben Snr if he was prepared to comment on an ongoing industrial dispute at the company. 'It has nothing to do with me,' Ben Snr responded. 'Talk to personnel about it.'

Fitzgibbon tried another tack, requesting a general interview, some-thing along the lines of 'the life and times of Ben Dunne'. Ben Snr responded: 'The *News of The World* offered me £10,000 for my story and I turned them down. Gay Byrne asked me on to *The Late Late Show* to talk about myself. I told him that if I went on the show, all I would say is "Dunnes Stores better value beats them all". He told me that I couldn't say that as it would be just advertising. I told him that "Dunnes Stores better value beats them all".' Few people in that era would have turned down the opportunity to appear on RTÉ's most highly watched television show, but Ben Snr was wily enough to doubt if his appearance would attract new business for the stores: if it wouldn't, then why bother?

Fitzgibbon asked if he would like to share the secret of his success with others. 'I hate people,' Ben Snr replied. 'The only people I like are Dunnes Stores customers. I am successful because Dunnes Stores better value beats them all. It's not that we are so good. It's that the others are so bad. Anybody could do what I did. Even you could do it.'

Fitzgibbon persisted, suggesting that somebody should record his story. 'Everybody wants to write my story. It will be written when I'm dead. The only successful people are dead people.' The last question from Fitzgibbon was to ask who would write it. 'My family will write it,' Ben Snr replied.

More than 40 years later Fitzgibbon recalled that Ben Snr, possibly because he had been drinking, was not particularly coherent and, in retrospect, he wondered if ill health had already taken hold. Fitzgibbon's interview – limited as it was – and background information that he wrote for *Business & Finance* were readily seized upon in the newspaper obituaries that would follow in April, after Ben Snr died in hospital.

Fitzgibbon had revealed how Ben Snr and Nora lived in a relatively ordinary £56 per night room at the Shelbourne and not, as might have been expected, in a more spacious suite. 'Theirs is the dullest room in the Shelbourne as redecoration is made impossible as Nora Dunne does not like the smell of paint,' wrote Fitzgibbon. 'Even in the Shelbourne, the couple has never been known to entertain and they spend Christmas there alone . . . Even though they are obviously fond of champagne, there is an unopened bottle in the bedroom. It is the bottle which they received as a present upon the successful return of their son Bernard following his kidnap.'

Fitzgibbon wrote that Nora tended to rise earlier than her husband and leave before 10.30am to whereabouts unknown, returning between 11am and 12 noon to collect Ben Snr before going out. From wherever they went, they would go to the Berkeley Court every evening for dinner, almost never anywhere else. Further details were supplied weeks later by Fr Dermod McCarthy, chief concelebrant at Ben Snr's funeral mass. He described Ben Snr as a man of deep religious conviction who recited the Stations of the Cross in Clarendon Street church every morning before starting work and who recited the Rosary with his wife Nora each evening.

Smyth wrote many years later that the Dunnes were not popular with staff at the Shelbourne, possibly because they rarely tipped. Every morning the couple ordered and shared a half-bottle of Lanson Champagne and two measures of Green Chartreuse, a syrupy herbal liqueur that is 55% alcohol. Their choice of the Berkeley Court for dinner might have been explained by Smyth's story of what happened one evening in the Shelbourne dining room. Ben Snr asked the waiter how the sole was cooked and was told it came in a white wine sauce with piped mashed potato and browned under a salamander. Ben Snr ordered it, but after the first mouthful he asked for tomato ketchup to be brought to the table.

Whatever the incident that led to his hospitalisation, Ben Sr spent weeks unconscious before his death on 18 April. The newspaper obituaries were generous, as they always were at that time for reasons of politeness. There would also have been an eye to their commercial relationships with Dunnes, which was a big advertiser for some papers. Therefore, a certain amount of reading between the lines was demanded of the reader.

Aengus Fanning, in the *Irish Independent* on the day after the announcement of Ben Snr's death, wrote that 'there were not many people who really knew Ben Dunne but then he didn't ask to be known or even liked, only to be allowed run his business as he saw fit and as only he knew how.' Fanning quoted an unnamed colleague who said: 'I believe he was a genius, but like many geniuses he had his eccentricities. There are not many people who had his money who would live in a hotel. He was obsessive about his privacy. This did not make him very popular but I'm certain he won't be judged as hard by God as by his fellow man.'

Fanning wrote that Ben Snr 'took little trouble to cultivate the gracious lifestyle that lay open to him if he had wanted it' despite estimated assets of well over £100 million, making him probably the wealthiest man in Ireland. 'Popularity or the lack of it did not bother him. To others he was dour or even colourless but to those he trusted he was often a witty lively companion who specialised in one-line quotes and equally loved to tell yarns.' He quoted an unnamed one-time associate who said: 'You don't become a millionaire the Ben Dunne way by being a nice guy. He fought fire with fire. But he was one of the funniest men I knew to tell a joke. He could see the humour in things. He could rant, he could rave, but he could laugh too. If you were in trouble, he was the first to ask you and you didn't have to ask.'

Fanning fell back on the old trope of the time, of how the country needed to be run by businessmen. He reported a 'commonly expressed consensus' that 'the country could do with a few more Ben Dunnes. He knew how to run his business and would make a better job of running the country than most politicians.' It was a theme expanded upon in an appreciation in *The Irish Times* signed by "PF": 'The debt of gratitude which this country has to Ben Dunne has never been recognised or appreciated. He did what political parties of every side promised: he lowered the cost of living and by doing so raised the standard of living for countless thousands of people. He employed over 3,000 people directly and through his suppliers gave direct employment and indirect employment to many thousands more. He was in the vanguard of the new commercial Ireland. He made Irish manufacturers realise that in many cases their standards and prices were not fit for international competition. Many people have found fault with him for this but there are companies successfully exporting now who learned standards in Dunnes Stores. He drove a hard but fair bargain and worked for small margins, and he expected his suppliers to do likewise. It was a source of constant annoyance to him that many Irish manufacturers would not supply his stores because they wanted to use their own brand name. To him the name Saint Bernard was of paramount importance. He felt right to the end that many firms would never have gone out of business in this country if they sold a certain percentage of their products to him.'

Fanning also described how Ben Snr 'liked to project a tough image, but it was his greatest self-protection. There are people close to him who speak of his kindness, warmth and charity, but he showed few signs of it to the public.' Years later Smyth wrote that 'he seemed to confuse kindness with weakness and would have hated to be thought of as an easy touch. On a more practical level old Ben believed he could be swamped with begging letters and hard luck stories if he got a reputation for generosity.'

TK Whitaker, in an obituary published after the funeral, wrote about his charitable nature: 'Ben Dunne may have been thought by many to be a "hard man" but those who knew him well saw his soft and charitable side. He preferred to do good by stealth – partly no doubt for the sound business reason that he did not want to invite too many wasps to his honey-pot. The causes he supported quietly and mostly anonymously were many and varied including cancer and other forms of medical research, boys football club, poor artists and even the making of Neville Presho's film on Tory Island. I had only to vouch for a good cause and he would almost let me write the cheque.'

As may have been appropriate in the circumstances of the immediate aftermath of his death, Whitaker made excuses for Ben Snr's way of doing business: 'He had the reputation of being tough in trade union negotiation, but he had been a trade unionist himself and knew how the game was played.' That game involved what Whitaker called 'a clear perception of the principles of management and of the need for vigilant financial control. He kept his management accounting system in his pocket, a day-to-day comparative table of purchases, sales and stocks under various heads at every store compared with corresponding figures for earlier dates.'

Another unnamed friend told Fanning: 'Ben Dunne was the hardest working man I've ever known. He didn't live the high life. He didn't like "yes men", he respected a man with an opinion of his own. He totally ran his own show, his own business the way he wanted to. Public opinion never worried him. If there are people who ridicule the apparent dullness of his lifestyle he ignored them. In this regard as most others Ben Dunne paid little heed to most people's opinions. His instinct was to follow his own instinct.'

In an appreciation published in the *Irish Press*, Joseph Charleton wrote: 'I would not claim to have been an intimate friend of the late Ben Dunne. It was just that in the way of business our paths are crossed and we discussed certain affinities ... Ben was all his life a good nationalist, in the most practical of ways, providing markets for struggling Irish industries particularly in the clothing trade. There was another tie between us. We have both grown up to maturity in the deep recession of the 20s and early 30s. Emigration appeared to be the only hope for the future. No one ever survived this temptation as magnificently as did Ben. I think my last meeting with him a few years back was at half seven in the morning in Dublin airport. I said to him: "Ben, have you forgotten our boyhood anthem? 'I don't work for a living'." "Not a bit," he said, and we both sang a few verses among the waiting outward-bounds. Perhaps they thought we were already drunk at that early hour. We were in fact celebrating survival which was a song born out of the Great Depression we had lived through in youth and early manhood. As always Ben Dunne was full of life and high spirits.'

Similarly, the appreciation in *The Irish Times* signed by "PF" said 'he has no time for people who talk instead of doing and could be harsh with them. On the other hand, when he found a person trying hard to get on, he helped in every way he could. Those of us privileged to meet Ben Dunne found there was a very soft heart under the gruff exterior and a tremendous sense of fun. With a perfectly straight face he could say something shocking, wait until the person was gone and then laugh uproariously and say, that fellow would have something to talk about now.'

Whitaker wrote that 'it is not often that a business version of the log cabin to White House story can be told in Ireland. Ben Dunne's is one of the most admirable. Ireland has greatly benefited from his unflagging enterprise and his loss is a national one as well as being a private grief to his wife and family with whom we deeply sympathize.'

As the cortege from St Vincent's hospital passed into the pro-cathedral, a group of Dunnes Stores checkout girls stood by. Undertaker Tom Stafford said he had never seen as many wreaths at a funeral. Many of those hundreds of wreaths were from voluntary and charitable bodies. The biggest wreath had *Dunnes Stores* traced in white flowers on a green background. The congregation overflowed onto the cathedral steps and footpath. Once the coffin and the vanload of wreaths had been set inside, the Dunne family took their pews.

The funeral report in *The Irish Times* said it was attended by the Taoiseach Dr Garret FitzGerald and former Taoiseach Jack Lynch. No mention was made of Charles Haughey. Rival supermarket bosses were there, including Feargal Quinn, MD of Superquinn, Dick Reeves, MD of Quinnsworth, and Pat Quinn, the founder of Power Supermarkets. The family was not there in its entirety: 'Mr. Dunne's widow Nora was unable to attend as she was not well.' No explanation was given as to her condition. His daughter Anne, described as 'an invalid', was not reported as being there either. Ben Snr's chief mourners were listed as Bernard, Frank, Therese, Margaret and Elizabeth. At Glasnevin cemetery, Ben spoke briefly of the father 'who believed in God and in himself'.

Margaret noted who was and wasn't at the funeral. She remembered the New York incident with Haughey in 1968 and Haughey's biographer Gary Murphy believes it led to 'simmering resentment' on the part of the Dunne family. He recounted how Margaret had apparently inquired as to Haughey's presence at her father's funeral. In February 1984 one of Haughey's personal assistants sent a letter to Margaret, to thank her for a donation of sheets for deprived children in Haughey's Dublin northside constituency. But the letter also said that Haughey had indeed attended her father's funeral, but had been unable to remain to sign the book of condolences as he had to go to a meeting. Murphy speculated that Margaret's inquiry was 'perhaps a further sign that the Dunne family felt slighted by Haughey over Ben Dunne senior, and she surely could not have been impressed by the delay in replying to her inquiry.'

When Ben Snr died, Dunnes Stores had 48 stores in the Republic, 10 in the Cassidy chain, another 18 stores in Northern Ireland and one in Spain, with a total annual turnover of around £300 million. When his probate was settled his address was given as Mitchelstown Stud Farm, Athboy, county Meath. He left a net estate of £1,320,570; the gross was £2,298,456. This indicated just how much of his wealth had been moved to the Trust he had set up for the benefit of his children.

Nora would live until 9 March 1986, when she died at St Vincent's Private Nursing Home, where she had spent the years since her husband's death. It seems that she did not return to the Shelbourne Hotel after his death, or that if it she did it was only for a short period. The hotel closed for a period during 1983 because of a strike, and when it was about to reopen its manager, Marcello Giobbe, gave an interview to *The Irish Times*. In it, he said he was looking forward to welcoming back the permanent residents of the hotel and mentioned Nora by name: 'Everyone loves Mrs Dunne here and we were just in the process of reconstructing an apartment for her, designed by herself and her daughters, when the strike happened.' In December he revealed that 'we're in the process of redesigning her suite' and 'she's due to return next week'. It's not clear if she ever did. While details of her illness remained private, she spent an extended period in a coma before she died, but the cause was not made public.

There were no obituaries for Nora, although all Dunnes Stores and Cassidys outlets closed for one day as a mark of respect. Reports about her death and funeral arrangements made up only a couple of paragraphs in the newspapers, although she was acknowledged as co-founder of the company. Ironically, the only published tribute to her came in one of her husband's obituaries, written by Whitaker: 'Her own great business acumen as well as her love and understanding were to be a never-failing support and encouragement to him in the years of development and innovation that followed their setting up their own business on their own in Cork.' It was somewhat typical in that era to assume that all the business direction came from the man in a family business, but Nora kept things ticking over in the shops in Cork while her husband expanded into Dublin. Her involvement was more than providing support.

With the patriarch dead and the matriarch in no position to assist before she died, a succession plan of sorts went into place at Dunnes. Ben became joint managing director with Frank, while sisters Margaret, Elizabeth and Therese were appointed directors. The joint managing position was somewhat of a fig leaf as Frank was still struggling with alcoholism. In effect, Ben was largely in charge, though he would come to resent that Frank drew the same salary for doing a fraction of the work. One era had ended, and a new one had begun.

16.

Price wars and their casualties

THE 1980S WAS A grim decade for Ireland. Much of the economic optimism of the 1960s and 1970s faded and, for some, evaporated. A combination of the Troubles, the political fallout from the 1981 hunger strikes and international recession meant that the improvements in material circumstances of the previous decades faltered. Unemployment soared and emigration returned in its biggest numbers since the 1950s. From 1981 grocery sales barely increased and between 1983 and 1984 they fell. Not only was there no growth in the market, the number of 'symbol group' shops increased, including SuperValu and ADM/Londis. This increased competition and for some stores lowered or even eliminated profit margins. In this landscape, a company could only grow by winning over another company's customers – a situation that led to the price wars.

Dunnes was in a strong position to endure. Ben embarked on business expansion with gusto, fully supported by his siblings. Ben kept control of the grocery business. Margaret oversaw personnel and women's underwear, Elizabeth took responsibility for womenswear, and Therese for childrenswear. Frank had his title but did little.

Ben boasted regularly of being a 'very aggressive' retailer when looking back at his time in charge of Dunnes Stores. He unashamedly sold some goods for less than they cost him to buy, but did it as a short-term tactic aimed at undermining his opposition, with a longer-term goal of eventually driving them out of business. One of his tricks was to require suppliers to engage in 'long-term agreements' (LTAs). He sold goods he purchased at the invoice price – theoretically for no profit – but Dunnes also pocketed 5% surcharges levied on the suppliers over the year and which came in as profit at year end.

At the time of his kidnapping, Dunnes Stores had an 8% share of the national grocery market, worth £1.4bn annually. By 1985 he had achieved a 21% share on a turnover estimated in the trade at £460 million. It was an extraordinarily rapid growth. The 1980s was his hey-day, working at the peak of his powers despite suffering PTSD and a developing addiction to alcohol and cocaine. His personal demons were largely hidden at the time or, if they were seen, they were largely ignored or indulged because wealthy and powerful people often behave in ways that wouldn't be accepted in the less prosperous and well-connected.

Ben saw off his competitors: one major international behemoth – Tesco – sold its Irish operations rather than continue against him; a snappy upstart – H Williams – failed despite its confident boasts; and his main rival – Quinnsworth – was kept at arm's length despite major and expensive efforts funded by one of the world's richest men. He overcame the loss of the company's head of food, Dick Reeves, who decamped for the biggest rival Quinnsworth. Over about a decade, despite tough economic conditions, Ben roughly tripled the size of Dunnes Stores and its profitability, making him one of the most successful Irish businesspeople of the decade, arguably the century. By 1990 the company commanded 24% of all national grocery sales.

When Tesco departed the Irish market in March 1986, it sold its 23 stores for £17m to H Williams, a noisy competitor under the control, since 1984, of a brash property developer, Finbarr Holland, also from Cork. Holland wanted to generate a level of cash flow that would secure his property empire, one that was coming under pressure in the recession-hit 1980s. As Richard Smyth, who was the H Williams chief executive for nearly three years, rued, 'the desire to extract cash for that purpose undermined the necessary investment in the business'. Holland embarked on advertising campaigns geared to improving the somewhat stodgy H Williams profile, but James Morrissey, a financial journalist with the *Irish Independent* who specialised in covering the sector, recalled that Holland's 'gung-ho attitude to his retailing rivals provided the supermarket scene with a degree of entertainment'.

Holland's ambition was to put H Williams into third place nationally, behind Dunnes and Quinnsworth, believing that the economies of scale would give greater efficiency and profits. He unveiled the new

H Williams slogan: *You'll notice the change*. But Morrissey wrote presciently: 'It is generally accepted that HW does not have the style of Superquinn, the professionalism of Quinnsworth or the low prices of Dunnes Stores. It has, certainly, a mix of ingredients that draws customer attention but is the mix strong enough to take on the rivals in the first division?' H Williams had a confused marketing offering. It tried to engage Dunnes by unveiling a gimmick called the 'half-price hooter'. When it sounded, the shopper at the checkout got all the groceries in their basket or trolley at half price. It worked at getting shoppers in for a while, but Ben responded by furiously cutting his prices for all customers.

In late August 1987, Holland resigned as a chairman and director and Bank of Ireland, fearful it would not recover its debts, put H Williams into receivership a month later, appointing Lawrence Crowley to recover as much money as possible for creditors, with the bank at the front of the queue. On his return from his holiday home in the Bahamas, Holland addressed reporters at Dublin Airport and focused his ire not on the bank – with whom he wanted to do a deal to release the personal guarantees – but on Ben. He told disgruntled employees that 'there is no necessity to picket the Bank of Ireland. The real enemy is Ben Dunne who said that he was going to put us out of business and pick up the assets cheap', referring to a discussion Ben had had with the new H Williams boss, Frank Dee. Holland claimed the government should create a situation 'where nobody can deliberately put someone out of business'. He detailed how Ben had strung him along on the completion of deals to buy individual stores to give him cash, but Ben was under no obligation to buy H Williams' assets and Holland was naïve if he thought Ben would do deals to save his competitor. Instead, Ben would be able to do later deals at an even better price.

An *Irish Times* editorial of September 1987 argued that 'the collapse of the H Williams supermarket chain is not in itself an event which will significantly alter the grocery trade in the state. It is, however, a direct consequence of the cutthroat competition in the business and it might accelerate a growing and undesirable trend, the dominance over too much of the trade by too few people. It was the exceptional nature of the competition which convinced Tesco to pull out and which encouraged the other UK grocery giants, notably Sainsbury, Fine Fair and Asda not to venture in at all. As a consequence, some 50% of the grocery trade is accounted for by just two companies. The demise of H Williams suggests that the dominance of the big two will become even more pronounced.'

This was when Noel Smyth entered Ben's life. Smyth, a solicitor who doubled as a property investor, Brendan Gilmore, a corporate finance specialist, and Paschal Taggart, an accountant, came together to form a company called Aviette. It paid the H Williams receiver £12.5m to take ownership of all its properties: 33 stores and a warehouse in Tallaght. No guarantee was obtained by the Department of Industry and Commerce from the receiver that no stores would be sold to Dunnes. Fine Gael spokesman Ivan Yates told Minister Seamus Brennan, 'You've been duped again'.

Taggart bought the stores with the intention of operating them under the franchises he was developing under the brand '8 to 12'. But offers that were too good to refuse quickly emerged. Four of the acquired stores were sold immediately to Quinnsworth. Then Taggart, Smyth and Gilmore were contacted by Ben via an intermediary and a meeting arranged. Taggart knew Ben from both being members of The Castle Golf Club in Rathfarnham in Dublin, which had been Ben's main club until he nominated a good friend for membership and the club rejected the application, leading a furious Ben to quit in protest. 'Ben was notorious for betting on the outcome of nearly every hole,' recalled Taggart, a man who liked a bet himself but who was more measured. He knew what to expect from Ben.

Ben brought the trio in for a meeting. 'He hardly let us speak,' Taggart recalled. 'It was all, "Fuck you, Paschal, you have what I want but you're selling them to me." He went through the nine stores one by one, setting a price and not letting us interrupt to put our position. In total it came to £9m for nine stores, no room for negotiation. Not that we cared. We came out of the room and did handstands. We had 20 stores left, almost for free. We went to a meeting to finalise it in the Berkeley Court over drinks, no solicitors, no accountants present. James Morrissey was there and he came over and congratulated me. I turned pale. Was he going to put it into the paper? He said no, that Ben had told him in confidence. I was afraid the Competition Authority would block the deal, that Albert Reynolds as minister would get them to do that. But he didn't and we sold another nine stores to SuperValu. We made a lot of money, but most of it went in tax. There was a capital gains tax rate of 60% at the time on short-term gains, something that Red Richie Ryan had brought in as a minister in the 1970s.'

Ben's method of completing the transaction would have ramifications some years later: he used a company called Ringmahon, named after the Dunnes' home area in Cork, to buy six of the stores, which put them beyond the Trust's reach. This meant Ben and his siblings could access and use those profits without informing or requiring the permission of the trustees. His siblings took equal shares in Ringmahon, but its assets – the acquired shops – traded under the Dunnes Stores name. It never became clear what the trustees thought of all this, but they did nothing about it.

Something else happened, never reported. 'Ben told me that he wanted me to look after Frank, to do something for him,' Taggart said. 'I went out to his stud to meet him and over the next couple of months a friendship with Frank formed. He was a brilliant guy, smoking 100 cigarettes a day, off the drink, but full of ideas. We had an idea of buying Green Property, which was not going well at the time, this was before it got the planning permission and finance to build its Blanchardstown shopping centre. We went to John Corcoran and struck a deal where we could buy Green for just £5 million. It would have been the deal of a lifetime. But Frank said the rest of the family had to be cut in. So, I went back to Ben and he said, "Fuck off, I told you to look after him, not to spend our money". It was typical family or sibling rivalry type of stuff. It was a great idea, but it wasn't Ben's idea, so he wouldn't do it. And then Frank wouldn't go ahead without him, said he couldn't do it without the rest of the family.' It was a huge, missed opportunity.

After everything, it was Quinnsworth that emerged as the main competitor to Dunnes. Quinnsworth chose its young and earnest marketing executive, Maurice Pratt, to be the face of its TV and press advertising. Dunnes didn't go the personality route, although Ben, with his outgoing personality, most probably was itching to do so and prevented only by the disapproval of his more reserved siblings.

'You had to have an enemy in business,' said Ben. 'And the enemy in those days was Quinnsworth because we were the biggest in terms of the number of stores.' Many business consultants would say not to give the competition any oxygen of publicity, not to create any awareness of what they are doing. Ben thought differently, believing he could bring the fight to Quinnsworth and convince its shoppers they could do better by switching to Dunnes. He targeted Pratt personally, as well as his employer, often through full-page advertisements that used cartoons of him, Reeves and Don Tidey, the Quinnsworth chief executive, to ridicule them. Pratt, still a significant figure in Irish business decades later, didn't take it personally: for him, too, it was just business.

Even if both sides liked to throw about the word 'war' to describe their business skirmishes, it wasn't going to be a case of mutually assured destruction; others would suffer the collateral damage instead. Pratt said decades later that Dunnes were 'unconventional and I used to think of them as being a tiger in the long grass. They didn't follow whatever the consensus was and because of that you had to expect the unexpected. When we were planning, we always had to think about how Dunnes would react and how we would react to the way Dunnes reacted. That was part of the engagement and part of the fun and the enjoyment, the rough and tumble.' Pratt believed that Dunnes fed and clothed a large part of the population for decades and did so at prices consumers could afford and should be remembered in Irish history for that.

Quinnsworth won a lot of new custom when it opened Crazy Prices in The Square in Tallaght, to Ben's vexation. One Friday morning Ben marched into the store and up to Pratt, and demanded to know if he knew how much 'effin money Dunnes Stores had taken that morning. Then he took a bunch of coins out of his pocket and threw them down before storming off. Pratt was highly amused by the performative element of it and didn't take offence; his company's new store was proving to be a big success and that was what mattered to him. It was reported at the time that Dunnes in Tallaght was taking only £100,000 a week in revenue, when it used to take £300,000. By that Sunday, Dunnes Stores had a full-page advertisement in the *Sunday Independent* as Ben introduced a 20% discount voucher initiative nationwide to try to win business back. Quinnsworth responded in kind. It was reckoned that the skirmishes cost the pair £1m each.

At the time, about 60% of the products in Dunnes supermarkets were labelled St Bernard. Before ABF brought Crazy Prices south of the border it decided that Quinnsworth had to respond with Yellow Pack products, a range of own-brand groceries available from the 1980s onwards. They did not always meet the approval of less price-conscious consumers. Their quality was sneered at, deemed as low as the prices, and 'yellow pack' became a national euphemism to describe going down-market, in jobs, products and lifestyles. Undeterred, Pratt continued with his TV adverts and his promise, 'Now, that's real value.'

Consumers won from all of this posturing, but only to an extent. They got cheaper prices on certain items but overall the big two retailers – Dunnes and Quinnsworth – were coining excellent profits, and Superquinn wasn't doing badly either. As to who won between Dunnes and Quinnsworth, it almost didn't matter, as they swapped top billing on a fairly regular basis. The desire to be number one – even if there were no prizes on offer for that – was what drove their competitive spirits and arguably made them better retailers. If there were short-term dips in profits as they spent, in the long term they made big money, and that essentially came from their customers, and at the expense of smaller competitors.

17.

The dark horse

IF BEN SNR HADN'T BEEN BLINDED by the prejudices of his time, which favoured sons over daughters in all matters of succession, he might well have nominated his daughter Margaret as his natural inheritor because she was essentially his 'right-hand man'. He should have seen that she was utterly loyal to her father's ways of doing things and to his desire that, whatever about getting assistance from others, Dunnes Stores was to be and to remain a family-owned and operated company. Margaret had worked in the business since she was a teenager, not going to third-level education even though she was clearly well able for it. Instead, she had taken on responsibilities very early in her Dunnes Stores career and shown herself well capable of meeting them. But all that evident hard work and ambition wasn't considered sufficient when Ben Snr was deciding on the company's future.

If Margaret believed that she was being blocked unfairly from doing what she was best able to do, she hid it well, continuing to serve loyally, not displaying any selfish ambition. Her official role was head of personnel and buyer for ladies' underwear, but she essentially ran the drapery business throughout the 1980s, when Therese's alcoholism made her progressively less effective in her role, even though the pair remained close. While Ben focused on the lower margin but much bigger volume supermarket side, Margaret's eye for reasonably priced clothes drove expansion. She inched the stores relatively more upmarket, towards a mid-price-range niche, buying in clothes of somewhat higher quality, the cheapest end of the market already being serviced at least as much by Penneys as by Dunnes.

Margaret worked 10- to 12-hour days in Dunnes Stores, but she also added other adjacent business interests. She became an investor in a franchise for the designer label Yves Saint Laurent, which she opened on Molesworth Street in central Dublin, near Grafton Street, and which relied upon the wealthiest of clients to buy the very expensive stock. But it didn't last long in the pre-Celtic Tiger era.

It was unusual during that era for a married woman with children to spend so much time at work. As a young woman in the 1960s, still in her early twenties, she had married Dr Andrew Heffernan, a consultant endocrinologist who worked between St Vincent's Hospital, the Blackrock Clinic and the Royal College of Surgeons. Heffernan was considered quiet but was popular and well regarded in medical circles. He was eight years older than Margaret but was regarded as a suitable match by Ben Snr and Nora, who bought the couple a spacious detached home in its own grounds in Stillorgan, not far from Cornelscourt. In the 1980s it became known to sections of the media as the epitome of modern flash, a 'Dallas-style' compound, complete with swimming pool and jacuzzi. It is still the family home.

The couple had four children, born between the late 1960s and into the 1970s. Anne, the eldest, qualified as a doctor at the Royal College of Surgeons Dublin before later joining Dunnes Stores. The boys, Michael, Andrew and Bernard, went to school either at St Michael's or Clongowes. Margaret had two housekeepers in place full-time to help her juggle child-rearing and business commitments. She drove a Mercedes sports car or station wagon, although in the years after Ben's kidnapping she often had a driver for added security. She dressed expensively, although often loudly in very brightly coloured clothes. She sported a year-round deep mahogany tan and always took a winter break in Barbados but also, more imaginatively, travelling to Japan and China before it became more popular to do so. She treated the upstairs reception areas of the Westbury Hotel – a five-minute walk from the company headquarters – almost as an extension of her office. She regularly frequented the most expensive restaurants in the city during the 1980s, such as Le Coq Hardi, Restaurant Patrick Guilbaud and The Lobster Pot. She enjoyed her wealth, but she gave up drinking alcohol at an early point in her adult life when she saw the impact it had on her siblings.

Margaret – known to many in business as 'H', but more commonly as Mrs Heffernan – did not always agree with Ben's decisions. He had strongly advocated for building a hypermarket in Fuengirola in southern Spain, which opened in the late 1970s. PV Doyle, the most famed Irish hotelier of the era and the man who hosted Ben Snr and Nora's nightly meals in the Berkeley Court Hotel, had a home in the same area and advised strongly against the idea, arguing that the market would be very difficult in a different culture for shopping. Ben ignored his advice. Margaret moved her family to the Costa for every school holiday but then spent most of her time at the premises, trying to make it work financially. Dunnes still has it, though, as well as two other Spanish locations subsequently opened by Margaret. Similarly, when Ben insisted on an ill-timed expansion into England in the mid-1980s, Margaret took it upon herself to travel to the stores there each week, frustrated to find that the supermarket operations were struggling to replicate the success in the domestic market. It would be later that Ben would admit they had failed, but a trend was emerging: Ben would bullishly progress an idea, then Margaret would pitch in to try to make it work profitably by being on site to see what was not working and why and then try to rectify it, not always successfully.

Outside of her working life, Margaret developed something of an obsession with horse-racing, a hobby she shared with her sisters and Frank; Ben showed no interest and threw himself into golf. She enjoyed the social scene connected to horse-racing enormously, as did her sister Therese. She socialised with people who had similar wealth, such as John and Susan Magnier of Coolmore Stud, and Michael Smurfit, then arguably the country's leading industrialist, and his wife Norma, although their marriage became strained and ended during the 1980s. Margaret became friendly with the sport's foremost trainer, Vincent O'Brien, and his son, Charles O'Brien, would later marry her daughter, Anne. Beef exporter Seamus Purcell was another in this circle, as was Ken Wall, the chief executive of Lombard and Ulster Bank and his wife, Nuala.

Margaret was one of the first purchasers of one of the sixteen luxurious panoramic suites built on top of the main grandstand in the Curragh racecourse in the 1980s, paying an annual rental of £8,800. The *Irish Independent* wrote of the 'splendid isolation from the hoi polloi' for private suite owners who had 'private bar and restaurant facilities, waiter service, close circuit and broadcast television, wall-to-wall carpeting and central heating. Telephones are available for those who need to keep in touch.' At the Phoenix Park Racecourse, before it closed in late 1990, the cost of an unfurnished bare room with balcony and a superb front view of the course was £10,000 annually. Margaret also took one of those. She visited the Prix de L'Arc de Triomphe – one of the most famous flat races of the international calendar – every October, staying at the Hotel George V in Paris, the most expensive location in France.

While her own stable of horses was nowhere as sizeable as her brother Frank's – she kept them with various trainers while he kept his on his own land as he became a trainer himself – she had one or two notable competitors and, because of her ownership of them, they probably got more coverage in the media than they deserved. Female owners were not the norm then, with few enough women having the independent means or interest in competing in the 'Sport of Kings', especially given the expense involved. Her most successful horse was called Fundraiser, while one called Latin Quarter was a winner at the Galway Races. Margaret accepted the invitation of Smurfit, as chair of the Racing Board, to become involved in its subsidiary, the Racing Promotions Group, and at one stage was mentioned as his potential successor. *Irish Independent* social diarist Angela Phelan wrote, more than somewhat doubtfully, that it is 'a title that not only carries a hell of a lot of prestige here at home but is indeed a title to be reckoned with when travelling abroad'. As with Dunnes Stores, the job went elsewhere.

Where she would have found the time for it was debatable. She was already an active charity fundraiser, particularly for St Vincent's Hospital, and her interests in horse-racing and charity overlapped sometimes. In May 1986, the Trevor Danker social diary column in the *Sunday Independent* carried an interview with Margaret about selling seats for a £25-per-head lunch at the Phoenix Park racecourse 'in the mammoth £300,000 fund-raising effort she is making for cancer research at St Vincent's Hospital'. It reported that Charles Haughey would be there. This probably resulted from Margaret's friendship with his daughter, Eimear Mulhern, now married to Frank's old friend John Mulhern.

'The one difficulty Margaret could face may be much closer to home,' Danker wrote. 'She wants her brother Ben Dunne to host a table – but that's asking for the near impossible. Not that Ben isn't just about the most charitable man around. I know he has done incredible charity work behind the scenes, very quietly, insisting on absolutely no publicity.' Margaret told me, wrote Danker: 'I know how he [Ben] feels about publicity. But St Vincent's is very close to us all. My mother was there for over two years in a coma. They looked after her marvellously and we want to do what we can for them. I hope Ben will host a table.'

The Danker interview demonstrated that Margaret was not always reticent about dealing with the media. She simply did it on her terms, with those she could rely upon to not ask awkward questions and when it did not directly involve Dunnes Stores. She was prepared to talk about her involvement with charities and horse-racing. Angela Phelan was a friend who mixed in her social circles and who had a son who went to school with Michael. Phelan wrote flatteringly about her in the *Irish Independent*, even about things such as Margaret and Andrew hosting the St Michael's debs' class of 1988 with their escorts and parents. She also wrote about Margaret having the nickname 'the corporate dentist' because of ability to extract donations from the wealthy. 'When I see Margaret coming, I cross to the other side of the road because I know if I meet her, she will get me to do something,' said one unnamed person in a Phelan profile. 'She has a great way of not letting people say no.'

Margaret's charity work in that decade was outstanding, not just in persuading others to contribute but in doing so herself. She bought Stephen Roche's bike, on which he won the Tour de France 1987, at auction for £28,000 and put it back in for resale, before buying it again. The money was put towards a £1m target for Our Lady's Hospice at Harold's Cross in Dublin.

In a conferring speech for Margaret in September 2007, on behalf of the National University of Ireland, UCC president Dr Michael Murphy praised her outstanding efforts on behalf of St Vincent's Hospital: 'In the early 1980s, three professors of medicine at UCD had a vision to establish a centre of education and research at St Vincent's Hospital. They approached Margaret, who not only supported the concept with a generous personal donation but also spearheaded the campaign to raise the necessary funding from a range of private donors. The Education and Research Centre was opened in the early 1990s with a mission to increase our understanding and treatment of important diseases, enhancing opportunities for the career development of Irish medical researchers, while, at the same time, facilitating improved care of patients in the hospital.'

He revealed that Margaret was also a key fundraiser for many years for the Diabetes Centre in St Vincent's and the funds that she raised allowed the hospital to employ specialist nurses essential to optimal care of diabetic patients: 'A personal donation enabled the restoration of the former chapel at UCD Smurfit Business School to become a state-of-the-art research library. The library houses a collection of 20,000 books, 5,000 theses and an extensive collection of reports and related items. It is the largest and most modern dedicated business library in Ireland.'

In 1988 she received a Lord Mayor's Millennium award for helping to raise more than £1m for the Hospice Foundation and, despite opposition from left-wing councillors still smarting at the treatment of the anti-apartheid workers at Dunnes Stores (see chapter 18), was one of the first awardees for Dublin's Lord Mayor's Award in 1989. In this she was in the company of Olympian runners Eamon Coghlan and Ronnie Delaney, and City Manager Frank Feely. They were chosen by Dublin City Council for their 'marvellous work in promoting and improving Dublin life', according to corporation spokesman Noel Carroll.

Heffernan became the driving force behind the creation of People in Need, a central fund to help charities that otherwise struggled to raise the money they needed. The charity sector was reckoned to be raising about €150m a year, but about 3,500 organisations with charitable status, not all of them registered, were competing for that money with various degrees of success. The high-profile charities had professional fundraising arms and got bigger shares of the available money, while smaller outfits struggled to raise enough to cover their costs. The ways of raising money had become predictable, although they are still very much in vogue in the 21st century: fundraising balls, dinners and fashion shows aimed at an unsurprising collection of so-called celebrities and the wealthy.

'People in Need will act as a central fund for a wide variety of worthwhile organisations; many of these lack a high public profile and do not have the capacity to raise sufficient funds, yet they provide an invaluable service in Irish society,' Margaret said in an interview with Phelan to promote the concept. The money collected was to be returned 'pro rata' to the regions where it was collected, and regional committees would be given a say in how it was distributed.

Margaret used her connection to Carmencita Hederman, Lord Mayor of Dublin during the 1988 Millennium celebrations, to get the fund going. Her first board was a mix of high-fliers and the ambitious in both private and semi-state businesses. It included Dermot Desmond, the founder of NCB Stockbrokers, Charles Kenny, a property developer, Noel Gilmore, the high-profile marketing manager of Bord Báinne, Paddy Wright, a senior executive at Jefferson Smurfit, Norman Kilroy, the boss of Grafton Group, and Matt McNulty, head of Bord Fáilte. She also put pressure on RTÉ to agree to staging a major live TV fundraiser, citing the success of Live Aid and Self Aid as templates. More accurately, the model was from the US, where telethons to raise cash had become a feature of television. In the pre-internet era, banks of volunteers at various locations would sit at phones and take calls from people who pledged donations, prompted to do so by what they were watching on TV.

The first seven-hour show, in 1989, was longer than RTÉ's general election coverage. Hosted by Gay Byrne, the country's leading broad-caster, it involved thirteen outside broadcast locations, including live coverage from RTÉ regional stations, coverage of two concerts – in Dublin and in Cork – and a slot from London hosted by Byrne's wife, Kathleen Watkins. Eddie Cochran's 1950s American hit 'Come On Everybody' was the theme tune for what was the first of nine such events between 1989 and 2007, raising more than €35m in total. Most of it was distributed in small amounts, of as little as £5,000, but with significant impact in local areas.

Those who worked with Margaret on People in Need described her as 'incredibly focused' but also pleasant to work with, realising that this wasn't Dunnes Stores and it wasn't a retailing exercise. 'As chair she did bring a business discipline to it, but she was collegiate and collaborative,' one of her directors, who asked not to be named, told me. 'She wasn't the boss, she was the chair of a group of people who had their own successes in different endeavours. She realised that she was working with partners. She was never overbearing, realising that success depended on everyone working together. She was chatty, never arrogant, and very interested in what was going in your life and more generally. She was totally on top of everything going on in the news. She never expressed her motives, but I don't think she was doing it as a way of promoting Dunnes Stores. It was her way of wanting to make a contribution and she was content to take a very low profile. You had to get used to her. She eyeballs you, her eyes demonstrating her focus and if you're not the type of person who can deal with that, then I can understand why you'd be intimidated. I don't know if she does it deliberately, this staring down of you.'

A friend of mine, who was hired to work on a major promotional event for the charity, described her as 'incredibly demanding, but you knew what was required of you and she was right more often than wrong'.

These charity events aside, her public profile was relatively low. She made a short speech at the Dublin premiere of the U2 concert movie *Rattle and Hum* in October 1988, having made a pitch to have People in Need be a charity partner. She also appeared briefly on screen on the first telethon night but said little.

'Even though she confesses to dreading public speaking Margaret made a really terrific speech on behalf of her worthwhile charity,' wrote the ever-laudatory Phelan of one event for People in Need. There was an interesting line in one of those articles from Phelan: 'Many feel she is the brains behind her brother Ben Dunne in the mega-successful family business. Her capacity for hard work is phenomenal.' Nobody doubted the latter, but the first part of that might have hinted at an ambition that had not yet registered publicly. It suggested that there was more to Margaret than might have been perceived at the time, that she had reasons to be concerned about Ben, that she was willing to work herself into the ground for the business, and that the 'mega-successful' business was her laser-focused priority. If all that was the case, Ben had more to contend with than he might have realised.

18.

Apartheid

THROUGHOUT BEN SNR'S YEARS in charge, Dunnes Stores gained a reputation for being an employer that liked to enforce control over its employees, everybody knowing their place and staying rigidly in it. This didn't change after his death. That reputation possibly reached its nadir in the mid-1980s: an industrial dispute brought Dunnes unwanted international attention and, in some quarters, opprobrium. Not that Dunnes or Ben seemed to care about reputational damage. For both, facing down those they regarded as telling them what to do was more important.

The most infamous strike, and one that is still celebrated by some, began on 19 July 1984 and ended two years and nine months later, in April 1987. It started when a 21-year-old check-out operator, Mary Manning, refused to handle or take payment for two pieces of South African fruit – Outspan grapefruits – in Dunnes on Henry Street in Dublin. She was complying with a directive from her union, IDATU (later renamed Mandate), not to handle any South African goods in protest against apartheid in that country. Against that, Dunnes management had issued a final warning to staff not to engage in any such protest. Manning now defied them. She was brought to her manager's office and suspended with immediate effect. In response, her shop steward, Karen Gearon, called a walkout and they were joined by young trade union colleagues, Liz Deasy, Michelle Gavin, Sandra Griffin, Theresa Mooney, Vonnie Munroe, Cathryn O'Reilly, Alma Russell and Tommy Davis. Some of them were friends, others barely known to her, and all were suspended.

The rest of the staff worked on, either not interested in the dispute or fearful of the financial consequences of striking; jobs were scarce in the recession-hit 1980s. The general attitude of both employers and workers in the retail sector would have been to pay lip service to the union mandate. It was a gesture of support that nobody expected anybody to act upon. South African goods were sold all over Ireland, and while the government said trade with the country was discouraged, no official sanctions were in place. Supermarkets routinely dealt in South African fruit and vegetables because seasonal supply meant there was few other sources for produce.

Manning may have been provoked too by a prevailing animosity between management and staff at the Henry Street store. As she and her colleagues saw it, management treated them disrespectfully, seeking to maintain a level of 'them and us' control over things as trivial, yet important, as toilet breaks. What she did was as much to show defiance on behalf of the staff as to stand up for the people of South Africa. Quickly, however, she and her colleagues learnt all about apartheid, a word that literally means 'apartness'. They were encouraged by regular visits to the picket by Nimrod Sejake, a South African exile who had been tried for treason alongside Nelson Mandela in 1962 but had managed to escape the country. A former teacher and trade unionist, he was now living in a Red Cross hostel four miles from Henry Street and for most of the strikers was the first black person they ever had met. He explained apartheid vividly to them. He held up his hand as if holding a glass and said, 'You have to imagine South Africa as a pint of Guinness – the vast majority of it is black and a tiny minority is white and, like a freshly poured pint, the white sits firmly on top of the black.'

In a 2019 celebration of the strike ICTU boss Patricia King said: 'They had to sustain a daily picket outside that store in the face of bitter recrimination from their employer and indeed colleague workers who didn't join the dispute. Their income was derived solely from the small weekly union strike-pay, which left them unable to meet their normal living expenses, including mortgage payments.' The strikers received £21 a week strike pay when the average weekly wage was £180 (although few at Dunnes below management earned as much). Brendan Archbold, a trade union activist and campaigner for social and human rights, who claimed the strike was 'the finest example of trade union solidarity ever', organised the strike for them from the outside. 'As the union organiser, I was paid at all times. It was the strikers, one of whom lost her house when she was unable to meet her mortgage payments, who made the sacrifices,' he said.

King recalled 'routine harassment by the Gardaí', which bizarrely included a visit by the Special Branch, which dealt with terrorism, to Manning's home. Other unions did not strike in support with them and Manning said they received abuse from members of the public and from their co-workers. Dunnes management refused to negotiate or meet with them on any basis. The strikers were marginalised, set apart.

'One letter after another arrived from other unions and companies that supplied Dunnes Stores, stating that while our action was a courageous one it could not be supported for various reasons,' wrote Manning later. 'Who were we? Ten working-class shopworkers, nine women and one man, in a recession-hit country, where most felt lucky even to have a job, striking about an issue that affected people in a country thousands of miles away.'

Yet, they endured. The strikers were invited to London to meet Bishop Desmond Tutu in 1985. He publicly endorsed the campaign and invited them to visit South Africa. They went, but when they arrived were denied entry at Johannesburg Airport and held under armed guard before being sent home, creating an international incident. They travelled to other countries for speaking arrangements, to picket some other branches of Dunnes Stores, and they marched through Dublin with thousands of supporters. They received support from high-profile names, such as singer Christy Moore (who wrote a song praising them), poet and future Nobel Laureate Seamus Heaney and, most notably of all, the still incarcerated Nelson Mandela, who later said the Dunnes strikers gave him comfort in the final years of his 27-year imprisonment. British firebrand trade unionist Arthur Scargill – at the time organising coal-miner strikes against Margaret Thatcher's assault on the industry – also appeared one day on the picket-line. That may have been counterproductive, though, as was a perception that Sinn Féin was involved behind the scenes.

The support of the Irish Anti-Apartheid Movement (IAAM), led by Kader and Louise Asmal, waned over time, according to PhD candidate Padraig Durnin in a 2024 thesis for Queen's University, which included the Dunnes strike as one of its chapters. Durnin revealed that Ben arrived unexpectedly at the IDATU head office in September 1984, demanding to meet with union officials despite giving no prior notice. While there were negotiations, there was no give in the Dunnes position and Asmal apparently went behind the back of the strikers and their union, writing to Ben to offer himself as a negotiator alongside Eamonn Casey, the Catholic Bishop of Galway and Chair of Trócaire. Asmal's letter to Ben said the IAAM had not started the dispute and 'did not desire its prolongation'. He expressed concern that a further lengthening of the dispute was ill-advised given the possibility of 'dangerous tendencies' to 'batten onto issues', making matters 'uncontrollable'. Durnin was unable to locate a response from Dunnes in the IAAM achieves.

Casey wrote to IDATU and called the strikers 'impertinent', particularly for their failure to consult with Trócaire before taking action. However, a group of nuns changed his position. On 1 February 1985, St Brigid's Day, members of the Brigidine order of religious sisters donned white masks and joined the strikers on the picket. Three weeks later, Casey endorsed the Dunnes' workers at the televised launch of Trócaire's Lenten campaign and said the strike deserved 'the respect and solidarity of the people of Ireland'.

The strikers also had a significant supporter in the coalition government. The Labour Party's Ruairi Quinn, a veteran anti-apartheid campaigner, was Minister for Labour with responsibility for industrial relations. He referred the dispute to the Labour Court, which recommended 'an agreement between the major supermarkets to voluntarily restrict their marketing of South African goods and a code of practice be put in place by the Department of Labour'. This was rejected by the importers and shop-owners, including Dunnes, who argued that as non-political organisations it was not part of their responsibilities to form codes of practice that would include bans on any produce.

The Labour Court then suggested that as normal industrial relations could not end the strike, a political move was the only way to break the stalemate. It was an implied recommendation of economic sanctions against South Africa. Fine Gael's Minister for Industry, Trade, Commerce and Tourism, John Bruton, responded: 'I have given much thought to this question and I am afraid all my instincts tell me that the Government should not become involved in any activity which is designed to restrict imports from South Africa.'

Quinn had to find another way. His officials examined international labour organisation conventions and found that imported goods and services that were the product of forced prison labour could be banned under international law. They confirmed that the prison authorities were hiring prisoners from South African jails to white farmers. Quinn proposed a ban on this basis. While some Fine Gael ministers still voted against, Taoiseach Garret FitzGerald, the party leader, voted along with Labour at cabinet to secure a majority. In 1987, Ireland became the first Western European state to ban South African imports.

Dunnes was not generous when it came to taking the strikers back. Durnin said that 'in an act reminiscent of the petty management style that had first sent them to the picket, Ben Dunne was not willing to let the strikers win and return to work without a final knock. On arriving back at Dunnes in January 1987, they were presented with a new contract that committed them to handling everything on sale, including the South African produce that remained.' They refused and went on strike again. When it officially ended on 12 April 1987, the ten had spent two years and nine months out of work.

As Margaret had responsibility for industrial relations at the time, and given what had happened in other disputes, it is almost certain that the decision was not Ben's alone. They were united in their desire to face down the strikers, even if they said little publicly. They regarded the boycott as a challenge to their authority and right to conduct their business as they saw fit. Ben, in one of his few public comments during the affair, said he would not allow the workers to have a say in 'what goods we sell and what not to sell'.

There was another curious twist in the whole affair in January 1987 when IDATU accused Dunnes of attempting to break South African sanctions in an entirely different manner. The union found a letter on Dunnes headed notepaper, signed by Fionnuala Maher, Margaret's secretary, addressed to Sister Attracta Whitaker at a post office number in Port Alfred, South Africa. It made reference to a supplier in Rome and said 'at present I do not see any difficulty for us in paying your supplier in Italy when the deal has been made. However, in view of the present political differences I would suggest that you inquire the position vis-à-vis sanctions between Italy and South Africa in case you have difficulty getting delivery.' The union believed that Dunnes was going to try to sell South African produce as Italian.

Within days the union had to withdraw this allegation. A furious Ken Whitaker entered the fray to defend the honour of his half-sister. 'Anyone less likely to be involved than this 88-year-old Assumption Order nun, who has given seventy years of service to the education of black and coloured children in South Africa would be hard to imagine,' he thundered. He outlined how she had requested help from Dunnes for the donation of new stations of the cross of a kind available only in Italy. They were to be set up in a cathedral in Port Alfred in honour of Nora Dunne. Whitaker revealed that 'the late Ben Dunne had, amongst many unadvertised good deeds, donated a holiday home for the Assumption Sisters and a tabernacle for Sister Assumpta's chapel some years ago. That is all there is to this absurd "sanction busting" allegation,' he concluded. The union backed down.

In 2008, Ben apologised on RTÉ Radio 1 to the strikers for how he handled the whole affair. 'I want to apologise unreservedly for the hardship, the hurt that I caused you all those many years ago and I hope you'll accept my apology,' he said to Mary Manning on *Liveline*. 'I mean it, and when I have an opportune time I'd like to go down and I'd like to see the two of us being photographed together at that plaque in Henry Street showing that you can mend bridges and there's life goes on, even though wrongs was done [*sic*], you know you can still overcome them and still can be friends; at the end of the day you regret what you did. I think, as I said it earlier on, you cannot defend the indefensible. I feel one thousand times better now having said this and if anybody else would like, if you want to send me numbers of any of the other strikers and I'll meet them, I will apologise to them personally.' Manning had not been told to expect the apology and was somewhat nonplussed, if generous, in her response.

Ben offered a more nuanced approach when interviewed by the *Irish Times* after the death of Nelson Mandela in 2013. He said he admired both Mandela and the Dunnes strikers, but that the attempts to boycott South African produce would have created a precedent of the 'tail wagging the dog': 'You have to admire the twelve people in Dunnes who took a stand. Unfortunately, I got caught up in it. It didn't escalate the way it should have done,' he said, before going on to deny that he would have done things differently if he could turn back time. 'Absolutely not. If you have ten thousand people working for you and ten or twelve go on strike on an issue, you think about the other ten thousand people who are working rather than the ten or twelve who are out on strike. I feel very proud for the people who took the stand that they took, but as a commercial man, you have to protect ten thousand jobs instead of twelve jobs.'

He said his decision to oppose the strikers was a 'commercial decision' rather than signalling support for the apartheid regime in South Africa: 'If it was South Africa and oranges one week, why could it not be British goods the next week? All of a sudden, you could have got yourself into a situation where people with secure jobs lose them and the place closes down. That is the only reason I took the business decision I took.'

He said the Irish government could have intervened and banned the importation of all South African fruit and vegetables, long before it eventually did so in August 1987. However, various government memos from the time indicated an official view that the strike could have been prevented if any degree of common sense had been shown by the supervisors at the Henry Street branch of Dunnes.

Manning emerged the hero from the episode. A street was named in her honour in Johannesburg and a plaque outside the Henry Street shop is dedicated to 'Mary Manning, a young Irish woman who led a strike against apartheid from 1984–1987'. To this day, Dunnes Stores as a corporate entity has said nothing on the matter.

19.

The bread wars

IN THE MID-1980S, people cottoned on that shopping in the Republic was more expensive than in Northern Ireland. Wages in the Republic were higher for employers, but higher personal tax rates took more from gross pay than in Northern Ireland. Take-home pay in the Republic was significantly lower and then people paid more Valued Added Tax (VAT, essentially a sales tax) on their purchases. The rate of VAT on goods varied depending on annual budgets, but usually came in at about 25% – compared to 15% in Northern Ireland.

Irish supermarket prices were 10–15% above those of Britain and Northern Ireland, but VAT wasn't the only element in that. A survey by RGDATA (the Retail Grocery Dairy & Allied Trades Association) found an overall difference between Dublin and northern prices of 10% and it accused the supermarket multiples of running a cosy monopoly in the food trade in the Republic. Over a range of 70 items the survey found Dunnes in Newry to be an average of 10% cheaper than Dunnes in Cornelscourt. Washing powder, toiletries, minerals and biscuits were among the things significantly cheaper in the north. A survey by the Consumers Association of Ireland showed Irish prices to be 14% higher on average than prices in an English provincial town. Why, it asked, should Kerrygold butter be dearer in Dunnes in central Dublin than in the two stores it surveyed in the English Midlands?

Once shoppers realised this, they voted with their feet. It became common practice for people to travel over the border to fill their bags with shopping. On the Saturday before Easter in 1986, for example, it was reckoned that 4,700 shoppers crossed the border, stockpiling the boots of their cars with alcohol, cigarettes and fuel. It was estimated that cross-border shopping was worth £340m a year to the Northern Ireland economy.

In April 1987 the Irish government acted to curb this significant outward flow of money. Minister for Finance Ray MacSharry imposed VAT to be paid in the Republic on all goods imported across the border, a confirmation of partition if ever anything was. This involved the abolition of what was called the '48-hour rule' of no import duties for those travelling outside the state for less than that period. The same survey conducted one year later, on the Saturday before Easter 1987, with the new laws in force, estimated only 400 shoppers crossed the border.

In the autumn of 1987, Minister for Industry and Commerce Albert Reynolds introduced legislation banning low-cost selling in the Republic, arguing that it did not benefit consumers. Reynolds was a businessman, rare enough in politics, who turned from promoting showbands to manufacturing and selling petfood. He claimed his decision was designed to protect consumers in the long run, that the supermarkets were only using below-cost selling to increase market share. The supermarkets believed, in turn, that the minister could not proceed with prosecutions against them until the legislation had passed. In the Dáil there was debate as to whether the laws would have retrospective effect and supermarkets appeared to be prepared to take a chance until it came into effect.

Bread was to be the new frontline in the price wars, as Ben reacted to government initiatives. The price of bread was important to those on limited incomes – the typical Dunnes shopper – and provided Ben with the opportunity to sell this essential item at cheaper prices as a way of getting customers into his stores during the depressed 1980s. 'The bread wars were where Ben showed his genius as a businessman,' said Rory Godson, a journalist who covered the story extensively during the 1980s. Dunnes Stores put up an effective challenge to the power of the government and the State in that era simply by dropping the price of a standard loaf of sliced pan by half, from 76p to 39p. It was a move that not only was of benefit to hard pressed shoppers but gained an enormous amount of media attention, creating the type of headlines that provided the type of publicity the Dunnes enjoyed.

Every major town in Ireland once had a distillery and often a brewery, but modern methods of production had brought about consolidation and smaller units were either bought or closed (before the resurgence of craft entities in the 21st century). Similar market forces affected the bread industry belatedly: there were too many bakeries, overstaffed, government-subsidised, and with a reluctance to introduce fully automated baking techniques.

Bread was considered so vital that its price was subsidised by government between 1975 and 1986, with manufacturers getting the equivalent of 15–17p per sliced pan, at a total cost to the State of £247m. The bread, biscuit, flour and confectionery industry employed 9,600 in 1975, but this number had fallen to 7,200 by 1986. The subsidies were to keep people employed, but instead resulted in profiteering and inefficiency, and the cash delayed the long overdue rationalisation of the industry, which operated as if it was still the early 20th century.

In the 1960s and 1970s bread was often delivered to the home door, just as milk was. Now people headed to the supermarkets instead. The manufacturers were price-takers instead of price-setters as Dunnes and other big retailers became the dominant vendors of both white and brown sliced pans, the most popular bread consumed in Ireland. Fintan O'Toole wrote in February 1989 that 'the Irish supermarket chains have been built on bread and circuses. Bread for the poor and circuses (space age shopping centres with lobster tanks and kumquats) for the better off. Now it has all come down to bread.'

The closure of bakeries was ongoing long before this. The loss of jobs began in the early 1980s but it accelerated in the mid- to late 1980s. Night-time baking was resisted by trade unions for years. Employees didn't want to work through the night, but for the customer it meant, for example, that bread bought on a Monday morning was probably baked on Friday. Rationalisation meant abandoning uneconomic lines and moving into niche markets, like rolls and buns, health breads and specialties – much as applies in the 21st century.

In 1987, 22 bakeries closed with hundreds of jobs lost. The trend continued into the following year, but about 250 mainly family-owned bakeries remained, the majority employing fewer than 12 people and with turnovers of less than £100,000. Most had no future. The closure by Odlums of the Johnston Mooney & O'Brien plant in Ballsbridge, Dublin 4, in February 1989 was arguably the highest profile change: 485 people lost their jobs as the company looked to build a new plant employing just 80. The move was largely a reaction to Ben's actions.

Ben established his own production line to produce a limited range of low-cost bread lines with minimal distribution costs. Ben's first cousins in Cork operated Neville's bakery in Macroom and he quietly and secretly took control of that business. The Cork bakery supplied Dunnes in the Munster region but, importantly, Ben financed the £3.5m construction of a brand-new branch of Neville's at Ballyfermot in Dublin 10, the country's most modern bakery. Both parties denied his involvement for years, insisting that Dunnes was merely a customer, albeit one with exclusive contracts that cut down its distribution costs. More pertinently, Ballyfermot had only 28 workers in a plant fully automated from the mixing to the wrapping stage. This allowed Dunnes to get loaves at 19p each, which Ben sold at 29p in the late eighties, far below the 55p at which branded bread sold. His competitors disputed the production costs, accusing him of selling at below cost, but the real issue was that cheap bread brought consumers into his shops, where they bought other items that were selling for far more than what they had cost Dunnes to buy.

Suppliers to Dunnes and its rival retailers feared that what had started as a bread war could become, as in the past, a potato, milk or fruit war. The Irish Farmers Association pointed out that a year previously Dunnes had started below-cost selling of potatoes, which had created a downward spiral effect from which the potato industry had not yet recovered.

Some of Ben's supermarket competitors responded by forcing bakeries to sell to them at prices that independent retailers could not demand. The independents tried to retaliate by banning bread from the offending bakeries, but that was self-defeating. If bakeries were asked to produce bread – and invoices – at a loss-making price for a few weeks a year, they had to do so or risk losing the business of the multiples entirely.

The bakeries demanded that government intervene to force Dunnes to increase its prices. Following an investigation by the Restrictive Practices Commission, which recommended banning below-cost selling, the government enacted legislation. The 1987 Restrictive Practices (Groceries) Act made it illegal to sell certain foodstuffs at less than the net invoice cost. But this simply presented a challenge for Ben to find new ways to sell as he wanted. Taking control of

Nevilles made it possible for him to control the price at which he was invoiced.

There was something of a lull in the bread wars in 1988, before Ben turned up the heat again in January 1989, after he dropped the price of a loaf by 20p to 35p. The Confederation of Irish Industries' Paddy Jordan claimed this was unequivocally below-cost because bread could not be baked, wrapped, and delivered to a store at 35p. He alleged, correctly, that Dunnes' bread was supplied by a bakery the company controlled. At this stage, most independent retailers paid a minimum of 60p for branded sliced pans, to be sold at around 76p. Others followed Dunnes in reducing bread prices, even though they struggled to get the bread as cheaply; Quinnsworth, Superquinn, Roches Stores and Musgrave/SuperValu were among those who were forced into the 'bread wars'.

It was claimed that Dunnes won £2–£3m worth of extra business with its price cut. A conviction for below-cost selling would have brought only a maximum fine of £16,000. 'I suppose we broke the law,' Ben told *Business & Finance* in 1989, referring to the prices order Dunnes had broken and which was scrapped after just 10 days by the minister.

Jordan said it was quite incredible that someone would be rewarded for breaking the law. He argued that unless immediate action was taken, irreparable damage, including further job losses, would occur. The CII stressed that the credibility of the Act introduced in 1987 was at a stake and claimed that the demise of H Williams was essentially due to uncontrolled competition and unfair pricing. The fear was expressed that any gain for the consumer could be short-lived while the job losses for the bakery industry would be permanent.

Ray Burke had replaced Reynolds as Minister for Industry and Commerce. He announced an order restoring bread prices to their pre-Christmas level because, he said, he didn't believe he was receiving sufficient co-operation from Dunnes and that the others were copying it, even though they wanted to revert to the old pricing models. He said he wanted to provide 'stability in the marketplace' amid fears more bakery and flour-milling jobs could be lost.

Ben was scathing about the minister: 'Then Ray Burke rang me and told me to stop selling cheap bread because I was killing the country's bakeries. He wanted us to prop up inefficient producers.' The prices went back up as Dunnes obeyed the order but then in February, surprisingly, Burke shifted his ground dramatically from a concern for jobs in the bakery industry to an alleged concern for the rights of consumers to enjoy the benefit of lower bread prices. He decided that he was not going to intervene, saying that jobs had to be viable and not supported by protectionism or state subsidies. 'It is my belief that much of the present difficulties have been brought about by a failure of some firms in the industry to make use of the most efficient means of production. I strongly urge those in the industry to modernize in their own long-term interests and that of employees.'

That was easier said than done, for reasons of getting capital and the competitive forces now at play, and it was never explained convincingly why Burke changed his position. What wasn't known at the time was that Haughey was on the take from Ben and that Burke was using his position to collect cash for personal use – euphemistically called political donations – from several sources, including Frank's close friend Joe McGowan. It has never been suggested that Burke took money from Ben, but it was never examined subsequently whether Haughey put pressure on Burke to revise his position.

If the jobs in Johnston Mooney & O'Brien could not be saved, Labour Party leader Dick Spring told the Dáil, 'Ray Burke will have to shoulder a large share of the responsibility and if he fails to act now the suspicion will inevitably arise that he is in collusion with Dunnes Stores, whose only interest in this matter appears to be the creation of monopoly in the bakery trade.' The Irish Bread Bakers Association accused the minister of sitting on the fence while job losses hit their trade. It was, it said, in favour of free competition provided it was fair competition, meaning fair prices for the consumer and fair margins for the baker.

It may have been an issue of basic politics, however. O'Toole wrote: 'If the government and particularly the department of industry and commerce has appeared to be on both sides of the argument it is precisely because both sides is the best place to be. On the one hand, the government cannot be seen to condone the market anarchy which will almost certainly put people out of work. On the other it cannot be seen to be robbing the working class of the only benefit the free rein of market forces has ever given them, however short lived that benefit may prove to be. The government has evolved a policy of masterly inconsistency, slapping on an order to control bread prices and then lifting it while making tough noises about the rule of law and then allowing the supermarket chains to make a proper ass of that law.'

One of Ben's previous critics from the apartheid issue, trade unionist Brendan Archbold, said the government was 'promoting the economic law of the jungle' and called Dunnes Stores 'the unacceptable face of Irish capitalism'.

Ben did not care and was talking freely to the media. He said what motivated him 'is the fear of failure. We are dealing with professional operators when we are dealing with the Quinnsworths of the world and if we don't continue to give the Irish housewife better value every day, she won't continue to support us.' He argued that if Dunnes Stores was 'squeezed out of the marketplace in the morning because our competitors were smarter, I would not blame our competitors, I would blame our management team for being weak'. The implication was that the bakeries only had themselves to blame for the outcome. Ben had clearly learnt from his father: the ruthless and unforgiving approach would not be diluted.

20.

Ruthless winners

BEN'S MAIN SKILLS WERE as a retailer, but he also fancied himself as a property developer, in which venture he was ably assisted by Irwin Druker, the family's commercial real estate agent of choice. Even if the future of shopping seemed to be outside of the city centres in all-under-one-roof shopping centres, and even if the overall economic situation remained dire, in 1984 Ben decided to take a significant gamble on the possible success of a major new shopping venue in Dublin, what was to become the Stephen's Green Shopping Centre. It would provide a very public example of his ruthless nature.

Planning permission for the major development was secured by the Cork dentist-turned-property developer Robin Power, who brought in British Land (BL) as a partner for the financing of the development. Power sold his company's interest in the development to BL, but not before cutting a deal with Ben, one that also involved Ben Snr's old lunch companion John Bourke, who now worked with Power. Instead of becoming a leaseholder, Dunnes would own the freehold of its portion of the centre and not pay annual rent. But it would pay its share of the building costs of the 375,000 sq.ft development and the fitting out of its own space, about £15m in total. Essentially, Dunnes would become a partner in the centre, even if it was to be formally owned by BL. It would not be treated as a tenant.

It was BL's responsibility to find tenants for the remainder of the centre but in late 1987, as it struggled to let space, it made an enormous mistake. It secretly approached Superquinn and offered it a lease on 12,000 sq.ft in the middle of the centre, right next to Dunnes. Ben got wind of the negotiations and was incensed. He maintained that his issue was the secrecy, not that the landlord was prepared to have a competitor open alongside him. He told BL that he would not open his giant store. The British company was disbelieving, but soon realised that Ben was not bluffing and had the financial resources to allow the space remain vacant for years. Without the anchor tenant open and trading, the remainder of the centre would be nearly impossible to rent to other tenants. The negotiations with Superquinn were quickly abandoned, but BL discovered to its horror that a huffing Ben still would not commit to opening his store. To persuade him to honour the commitment to open, BL had to give Dunnes Stores the 12,000 sq.ft earmarked for Superquinn, a donation estimated to be worth up to £4m.

It didn't end there. The Stephen's Green Centre was the biggest shopping centre ever built in Ireland, nearly half as large again as the ILAC on the north side of the river, but it wasn't ready for opening on its due date of 25 October 1988. When BL opened it on 1 November, there were only two of the 70 shops – Tie Rack and Tierney's Gifts – open for business, and a third later in the day.

Ben watched it from a balcony in the company of reporters and told them: 'You can see for yourself what the problems are.' He said he would not open Dunnes Stores until the whole centre was ready because it would be a 'customer disservice'. He had an estimated £2m of goods in his closed shop and he demanded that BL pay the wages of the 200 staff on his payroll since 25 October.

In response, BL tried its own bluff. 'I have no fight with Ben Dunne. If they want to look for money from us they can write to our solicitor,' BL boss Cyril Metliss said. 'They know their remedy. Ben Dunne has a shop stocked and ready to open. Maybe the fact he is not opened means he has an internal problem in his company.'

That wasn't the wisest of approaches. Ben responded emphatically: 'We are an £800m company. We are not in the business of playing games. We were promised a new experience in shopping and that's what we got – a £50m development with seventy shops and all you could buy was a tie or a vase.'

Metliss responded that it was quite usual for individual shop units to fail to get their act together in time, asking if anyone would have expected 70 shops on Grafton Street to open simultaneously. It was a weak riposte. The centre's management had to play 'Swan Lake' at full blast throughout the day to drown out the incessant noise of saws, drills and hammers as work continued at individual units. Opening day was for sightseeing rather than for shopping. It was rumoured that Ben had people going around with video cameras filming, either for posterity or perhaps for use in the courts.

A week later, Ben relented. Even though only 27 units were open, apparently his lawyers advised him to go ahead, telling him he had made his point. Later it would become clear that the Trust did not own the Dunnes unit in St Stephen's Green, but that Ringmahon did. Another jewel in the Dunnes crown was held solely and privately by the family, beyond the reach of the Trust.

When the discretionary trust was established in 1964, only some of Ben Snr and Nora's children were adults, and young ones at that. Ben Snr had told the trustees that he wanted the business to be in his family's ownership for at least 50 years after his death – and, if possible, that family members would manage the business, a desire that Margaret, in particular, would always be very concerned to honour. The Trust was designed to end on 15 March 1985 and the plan was that once 'expired' the shares in the Holding Company would then transfer to the Trust's six beneficiaries. That plan changed when Anne's health issues meant she was incapable of administering her own finances, and she was written out of the Trust.

When the Trust was established there was no such thing as capital gains tax (CGT) or capital acquisitions tax (CAT). Both were introduced by government in the 1970s to raise money for the Exchequer. The ending of the Trust was always going to present issues, especially after Ben Snr's death in 1983, but now the ending would also create two significant tax issues: the Trust itself would become liable for CGT; and the five beneficiaries would become liable for CAT on receipt of the shares. Tax advisers warned that the total tax bill could be as much as half of the value of the business, whatever that was deemed to be by the Revenue Commissioners. Dunnes Stores might have to raise money to pay these tax bills, either by selling shares to outsiders or by selling assets, or by borrowing from the banks. The family might even have to sell the entire business, an idea that was anathema to them.

By the mid-1980s new trustees were in place: accountants Oliver Freaney, Noel Fox, Frank Bowen and Bernard Uniacke, and Ben Snr's old lunch pal, the retired solicitor Edward Montgomery. After Ben Snr's death the trustees realised that if they didn't distribute the company shares before 15 March 1985, the shares would transfer automatically to the children, creating an as-yet-to-be-determined tax liability. Extending the life of the original trust deed was an option, but it wasn't clear if this could be achieved without triggering its own tax issues.

The trustees approached Revenue to see if they could agree a deal whereby the shares would be vested, but the CAT and CGT would be levied at an 'affordable' level. They had left it very late to ask. The rate of tax for CAT and CGT was fixed by law, but the variable would be the value placed on the shares by Revenue, to which the rate of tax would then be applied. The valuation of shares in a private company can only be determined accurately when there is a sale on the open market, otherwise it is an estimate. There would inevitably be a difference of opinion as to the value of the Trust, and that would require negotiation. Informal discussions were held with Revenue, which indicated that it had assessed the value of the Trust to be £120m. The tax due on this valuation would be £43m.

Horrified by the potential size of the tax bill, Bowen arranged for Ben to meet the Minister for Finance Alan Dukes. Just what they thought this would achieve was never satisfactorily explained when disclosed more than a decade later. Ben recalled later that Dukes was unsympathetic to the argument that the profits were used to redevelop the shops and said the tax bill would do little more than hamper that investment for a couple of years. Dukes subsequently rang Bowen and told him that Séamus Paircéir, the chair of the Revenue Commissioners, would contact him to arrange a meeting, but he stressed that he was not getting involved in any negotiations, and that what the Revenue decided was a matter for it and not for him.

A crucial meeting took place on 7 March 1985, just one week before the Trust was due to expire. It was attended on behalf of Revenue by Paircéir and some of his officials and on behalf of the trustees by Bowen, Fox, Uniacke, Montgomery and Liam Horgan, the latest addition to their ranks. The trustees suggested a value of £34m for the Trust – an extraordinarily low gambit – and argued that it was unlikely that the indigenous Irish company could sustain its current level of profits in the face of increasing foreign competition. The only good news for the Dunne family was that Paircéir conceded that the valuation of £120m put on the Trust by his officials was excessive. Bowen recalled Paircéir saying that he regretted this was 'the awfulness of the position', but he could not consider Dunnes Stores' contribution to the Irish economy and give it a valuation any lower than £80m. He said his obligation was to raise revenue for the State and he could not base the valuation on the economic arguments advanced by the trustees. Bowen responded that the amount sought was impossible, and that he was left with no alternative but to seek to extend the life of the Trust.

On 14 March 1985, a day before the deadline, the trustees appointed 100 preference shares between Margaret, Elizabeth and Therese, and 99,000 ordinary shares to the trustees of a new discretionary trust, to be divided into five equal parts and held for five of the six children of Ben Snr and Norah Dunne, and their children in turn. Anne was still excluded, essentially dependent on the charity of her siblings and whatever provisions her parents had put in place for her privately.

Revenue was unimpressed by the feint. It took the view that a CGT liability had been triggered. The trustees argued that a CAT liability arose from the deaths of Ben Snr and Nora as settlors, but that the new trust meant no CGT liability arose. A battle loomed, with further complications involved.

The Finance Act of 1984 provided for a new form of tax, a Discretionary Trust Tax (DTT). This involved an annual tax of 1% on the total value of the assets in any trust, but also a one-off 3% levy on the value of those assets upon the death of any settlor or disponer. From 1986 onwards, the trustees were liable for an annual charge to DTT of 1% of the value of the shares held by the trust, as well as the 3% charges on the deaths of Ben Snr and Nora.

On 8 September 1986, Revenue informed the trustees that the Trust was being valued at £100m and that DTT was due. The tax demand was appealed by the trustees to the Appeal Commissioners and was listed for hearing on 16 March 1987. After negotiations, a value of €82m was agreed and a payment of £3.56m was made to cover the time since the first claim was made. The separate discussions about CGT and CAT continued and it was agreed that the DTT valuation on the Trust would not apply for those taxes.

Revenue wrote to the trustees in November 1986, seeking a CGT payment of £38.8m based on its valuation of the Trust assets at £120 million. The trustees were aghast that Revenue stuck to its original valuation, especially as this was a far larger number than implied by the DTT settlement. Haughey, who was then Taoiseach, intervened and agreed with Paircéir that he should met with Ben and Noel Fox in April 1987.

Within Revenue, a senior official wrote a note for the files that described Haughey as 'acting' for Ben. Paircéir and other Revenue officials would have met with Ben's accountants as a matter of course, without the need for Haughey to arrange introductions, although there might have been some reluctance to meet with Ben personally rather than his representatives. Paircéir apparently held a 'series of intensive meetings' with Revenue officials to discuss whether the bill should be 'discounted'. Shortly afterwards, Revenue offered to revise the value of the Trust to £82m and the tax demand to £23.6m. Ben told Paircéir the money would be 'too much for him to pay now' and rejected the offer. There were further discussions about paying £16m over three years, an enormous reduction by Revenue on its opening position.

Ben wanted to have his cake and eat it: a declaration that essentially the Trust had never ended, even though its date for expiry had passed. He gambled and rejected the settlement suggestion from Revenue. Instead, he continued the Trust's appeal, confident in the advice from his trustees and accountants that no CGT liability would be found at the Appeals Commissioner because the asset had not been transferred, meaning there had not been a disposal by the Trust to trigger a tax bill. Ben's siblings were every bit as concerned as he was by the tax implications – which would suggest they would have enquired regularly as to what he was doing about it, and with whom, and would have endorsed his approach because it was so important to their finances.

Even after his efforts with Paircéir had failed to get the resolution he desired before the official retired, Ben had a meeting with his successor, Philip Curran, another Revenue boss who'd been subjected to a call from Haughey suggesting he meet with the supermarket boss. Ben and Curran met in the latter's Dublin Castle office on 21 March 1988, even though Curran felt that it was unusual to have a lay client (Ben) as well as professional agents dealing with the Revenue and that it should have been clarified as to who was acting for the trustees. According to Curran, Ben was not precise in outlining his difficulty and Curran asked him to go away and draft a submission, which he would then consider. Ben never took up the offer.

The trustees continued with their appeal and a hearing took place over three days in front of the Appeals Commissioner in September 1988. On 11 November the Appeals Commissioner found for the trustees, essentially deciding that the Trust had been extended lawfully and that no CGT liability existed. Revenue decided not to appeal to the High Court upon the advice of its lawyers, who warned that it would probably lose the case. Ben had shown his mettle and won a decisive battle.

While the company's value was the subject of disagreement and debate, it was certainly the case that Dunnes Stores was a vastly wealthy company, both in cash and assets, and the management of that wealth took various forms. Ben Snr took a dim view of restrictions on business and wealth generation, and Ben had learned from his father how to 'cook the books', to move money around to avoid, or to evade, tax. Tax avoidance is legal, whereas tax evasion is illegal and punishable by both fines and prison sentences at individual and corporate levels.

At the end of each financial year, a number of cheque-books were taken from an old leather briefcase in Ben's office, a practice inherited from his father. Bowen, a Dunnes trustee who was a senior member at Deloitte & Touche, which carried out audits on some of the Dunnes Stores companies in the overall group, would usually prepare cheques on Ben's behalf, or sometimes the task fell to Fox. Cheques were written out to 'bearer' rather than to named individuals or companies. Anyone who presented these 'bearer' cheques to a bank would receive cash while keeping their identity secret. Up to 40 cheques each year would be made out to 'bearer', for sums between £3,000 and £6,000, and given to senior executives. They were essentially tax-free cash bonuses. There were also bigger payments for other associates whose identities remained secret.

As the Dunnes Stores Group was owned by a trust, it meant that money belonging to the Group should not be used for non-Group or non-Trust purposes. That put limits on what the beneficiaries of the Trust could receive, unless the trustees simply gave them whatever they wanted. Ben was to allege later that his siblings wanted a different way to get money, without requiring the favour of the trustees. A method was devised to route money via countries in Asia, and to Switzerland, the Isle of Man and the Channel Islands, essentially diverting Group funds so they wouldn't be controlled by the Trust. It gave the siblings extra, unfettered cash to spend.

The reopening of Asia to international trade in the 1970s provided myriad opportunities, for the business itself and for personal enrichment, once diversions had been put in place out of sight of the authorities. Dunnes could order and purchase enormous amounts of cheaply produced clothing stock, manufactured to its own design specifications, that it could sell cheaply but at great profit when imported to Ireland. This was very bad news for Irish clothing suppliers but, as far as Dunnes was concerned, it was up to suppliers to get their prices down to global market levels.

There were financial opportunities beyond purchasing stock, however. Ben oversaw the establishment of a procurement agent, or trading operation, in Hong Kong, ostensibly to purchase and ship goods. Wytrex was not part of the Dunnes Stores Group, but the finances of it were under Ben's control, even though a Hong Kong national called Tse Kam Ming, also known as Laurence Tse, was its legally named owner.

Financial sleight of hand was employed: Dunnes would pay approximately 5% more than what was due for the goods sourced by Wytrex (or another company called Carica, put in place for the same purpose). This would constitute Wytrex's 'profits', for the enjoyment of the Dunne siblings when distributed. Every 12–18 months, Ben travelled to Hong Kong to collect bank drafts for between £100,000 and £200,000, made out in fictitious names but – according to allegations he would make but later withdraw as part of a legal claim – given to his siblings. Meanwhile, a new trust, called Equifex, was established in Switzerland, into which more money was poured, and another later in the Isle of Man, called Tutbury.

Coincidentally, Margaret also travelled regularly to Hong Kong for legitimate personal and business reasons before it became part of China in 1997 and enjoyed the comforts of The Peninsula, the colony's oldest upscale hotel and one of its most luxurious.

Through all this time, Margaret was keeping a close eye on Ben's actions, something I knew at the time. In the summer of 1991 *The Sunday Business Post*, which began publication in November 1989, was in deep financial trouble, struggling for cash as advertising revenues could not cover weekly costs. One of its founders, James Morrissey, moved temporarily to running the commercial department and sought to persuade some of his contacts to advertise in the paper.

Ben was sympathetic to Morrissey's plight and offered to buy full-page advertisements for four weeks, at the very generous price of £5,000 per page. It was essentially charity, as readers of the newspaper were considered unlikely to be Dunnes customers. On the Monday morning after the first advert appeared, Morrissey entered the office to be told by the receptionist that Margaret had called and wanted to speak to him. He delayed a while before responding, but when he did Margaret told him that she wanted to meet him urgently about the advertisements. Morrissey agreed to meet her at the Conrad Hotel that afternoon, praying that the £5,000 cheque Ben had given him the previous week had cleared. Fortunately, it had, but an icy Margaret demanded the return of the three other post-dated cheques. When Morrissey attempted to demur, Margaret insisted that Ben had acted without authorisation and that the newspaper was to run no further ads.

Journalist Rory Godson recalls a similar experience from his time editing the *Dublin Tribune*. He had a long-standing professional relationship with Ben, but with the newspaper in financial trouble in 1990, he went to Ben for advertising support. When he got the money, Margaret raised merry hell with Ben about the spending, even though it involved small sums.

It is clear that between 1987 and early 1992, Ben was operating brilliantly as a businessman and the Dunnes' wealth was growing exponentially, yet simultaneously he was unravelling personally. The biggest example of that was about to make front-page news and kick off one of the most remarkable sequences of events to ever have rocked Irish public life.

PART 4

The Blowout and the Fallout

1990–1994

21.

Crossing the Rubicon

AFTER HIS KIDNAP BEN RETURNED to working hard, but played that way too. In the absence of any counselling he kept busy, as if that would keep the demons at bay. He wanted to prove that he had not been affected adversely by his traumatic experience, that it was business (and life) as normal. He was lying to himself as much as everyone else.

He spent money freely. It was a thing with the Dunne family to buy expensive Mercedes cars – and to change them annually – but Ben went one better in November 1991. It was reported that he and Michael Smurfit were the first Irish buyers of the new Mercedes 600 SEL saloon car, at a price of £141,000. It would have been possible to buy two new three-bed houses in South Dublin at the time for that amount. The car was used mainly for around-town driving. If he went any further in Ireland, he called upon Celtic Helicopters for a lift. If he was going overseas, he had secured the use of a Cessna private aircraft, using Dunnes money to purchase it.

Ben bought one course-side mansion at The K Club in Kildare, a golf club and American-style country club resort, as an investment after Smurfit opened it in 1991. The 3,500 sq.ft home at Number 2 Churchfields was part of a small development of 20 individually designed and lavishly decorated homes overlooking the golf course. Although the two-storey house had just three bedrooms, it had a large viewing veranda on the first floor and the curved glass design of the south golf-course-facing side meant that when Ben decided to sell in 2006, just after the Ryder Cup had attracted enormous crowds to the location, he got €4m.

Golf was his main leisure activity, playing out of the men-only and restricted membership Portmarnock links course on the northside of Dublin, regarded as one of Ireland's best courses and certainly one that appealed to the monied classes. (It did not lift its restriction on female members until 2023.) If he wasn't playing there, Ben had the option of Luttrelstown, near his home, or from early 1991 The K Club.

Ben's gambling on the golf course became an issue for members of some of the clubs he frequented. He liked to play a '10-10-20' – a reference to advertising for a particularly well-known fertiliser. In Ben's case, it meant that playing partners would be required to wager £10,000 on who would win the first nine holes (the front nine), the same again on the second nine (the back nine) and £20,000 on the overall outcome. It limited the numbers of those who could afford to play for such stakes. Stories circulated of the bets on games reaching the almost unbelievable amount of £500,000 ... and of Ben losing.

He liked his few beers in the clubhouse afterwards and occasional foreign trips with the lads – to Spain or the United States – where daily golf would be followed by clubhouse pints and lunch or dinner. He was never regarded as an aggressive drunk, merely an amiable one, albeit a bit loud. His socialising led to regular disagreements with Mary, however, who tired of his late-night returns home and regular absences. They would go out together, especially to the cabaret dinner dances that were popular with executives of the time, but their relationship was strained by his behaviour. If Ben found it difficult to cope with the aftermath of his kidnap, others close to him had their own issues in trying to deal with his carry-on.

'The only thing I would have had in my mind was that my dad is a big boozer, he enjoys his drink,' his son Rob told Niamh Horan of the *Sunday Independent* in a 2024 interview. 'And that would have been the source of many an argument because my mother doesn't drink much and hates pubs. I don't know how they got together. But my dad would have been a real 19th-hole kind of guy, a big pub fella. He would have a feed of drink, go to the bar, drink a solid three hours, get home and be shower-fresh at 7am.

'When he got drunk, he was having a sing-song and telling jokes. He was never aggressive. There was never a problem in that sense. It was more that he would be out gallivanting until the late hours and that would lead to the usual barney. "Where were you? Were you out with so-and-so? I know you were out with so-and-so".

'I do have a memory of sneaking out of my room and sitting on the stairs to listen if they were having an argument, and that wasn't nice. From 10, 11, 12 [years] onwards. It wasn't every night, but every now and then there would be a barney and a shouting match. It never got out of hand. My dad would never lay a hand on my mother, so we didn't have to deal with anything like that. It was the kind of shouting that you could chat to your buddies about.'

Florida golf trips with the lads had become a thing in the late 1980s and the trip to Orlando in February 1992 was the fourth Ben had organised for a large group. They had been to Tarpon Springs on Florida's Gulf Coast, but Ben had heard that Orlando – better known as a family destination for the likes of Disneyworld and the Universal Studios theme park – might make for more fun. A travel agent booked eleven first-class seats on a British Airways flight from London on Saturday, 15 February, with 10 single rooms and a deluxe suite in Stouffer's Resort Hotel. Noel Fox was part of the group. The others were not so well-known or significant, other than John Mulholland, a future mayor of Galway. Ten of the party travelled from Ireland via London, but there was a late addition. Ben, for reasons never explained, had been playing golf in Jersey, the Channel Island well known for facilitating offshore banking. He took a liking to the taxi driver who ferried him around the island and, in quite the tip, invited him to come to Florida, all expenses paid.

What happened over the following days was recounted multiple times by Ben in the immediate aftermath and again afterwards, but also by police officers, lawyers and some of the women involved. It also appeared in detailed court documents. It is a story that has lost none of its drama in the telling.

Ben's deluxe suite at Stouffer's cost $500 per night, and it was known by the hotel staff that he was paying for 10 other rooms. Big spenders get the attention of the concierges at top hotels, and a staff member was able to procure more than the best tables at booked-out restaurants – he procured Ben female company and a very big bag of cocaine, believed to be at least 40 grammes in size.

Ben's first guest was Cindy Mitchell, a 32-year-old woman who wore a blonde wig and a purple spandex mini-dress. She later recalled that her first impression of Ben was provoked by his large Rolex watch, which she didn't reckon was fake. When she arrived, he was wearing a white toweling robe embossed with the hotel's logo. For security, she asked to see his passport, and noticed that it said his given name was Bernard and that it had many entry stamps to the USA. He told her, incorrectly, that he had arrived on his private Lear jet. They 'had fun' and Ben asked her to return two days later with a friend for a party.

Cindy came back with Andrea Nathanson, another 32-year-old in a blonde wig. They said that Ben was talkative and told many stories. Anyone Irish would have known the details of those stories was misleading and exaggerated, albeit with a grain of truth, although their memories may have been faulty given the drink and drugs involved. He told them that he had inherited Ireland's largest manufacturing business and was a billionaire. He spoke about his kidnapping as 'a horrible experience', the Catholic Church and confession, and how 'people cheat you in business'. In between stories he took more lines of cocaine, paced the room and displayed symptoms of paranoia. 'Watch the dimes and the dollars will look after themselves,' he said several times. Both the women left eventually, but when Mitchell returned again the following night, she met a strange man, whose name she didn't get and whose behaviour made her suspicious, so she left. She kept the credit card receipt for her $300 engagement, signed 'Bernard M Dunne'.

Ben got bored with Stouffer's – and the inconvenience of a daily mini-bus to travel to local golf courses – and decided to move everyone to the Hyatt (Marriot) Grand Cypress Hotel, which had two golf courses. He charged all the costs for the group to his Bank of Ireland credit card. Ben's 17th-floor suite was charged at $1,200 per night basic plus taxes; it was to cost him a hell of a lot more.

Ben declined invites from the golf party for dinner on Wednesday evening. Instead, he went to his split-level suite alone, watched television and then an in-house movie. To find company he went through the yellow pages of the Orlando telephone directory, where he found a full-page advert for a service called 'Escorts In A Flash – We Can Be With You In An Hour'. He called the agency and negotiated a $300 payment for two hours' company with a female escort. He was told the women employed could also offer 'extra services', free of any arrangement with the agency. A pimp called to his hotel room and collected the cash. The agency contacted Denise Wojcik, who shared a trailer in Powhatan Trail with her friend, Delta Rittenhouse, and the latter's nine-month-old baby. Wojcik was a recent addition to the agency after losing her job as a librarian six months earlier and would get just $90 of the fee. She would have to 'work' for tips. This was to be an encounter that would change her life, too.

It was 1am when Dunne greeted her with a glass of Dom Perignon and an immediate $400 tip. 'I just walked into the lobby of his suite and he was like, "Hello, would you like a drink?" We had champagne. He offered me coke. I hadn't done it in two weeks. He was pouring the coke out of his big bag. I was chopping it into lines. I was really wrecked after two or three lines, but I just kept going. I was thinking, "They must have very good coke in Ireland." It was a mutual agreement to get into the bath. I just wanted to get a bath. It was such a nice big bathtub. It was a very different night. The bath was OK.'

Wojcik later estimated they inhaled at least 16 lines of cocaine each over the next seven hours, taken from a cellophane bag Ben had on the nightstand beside his bed. In the bathwater Ben cut more lines along the edge of the tub, using his plastic membership card for The K Club, and they snorted it through a rolled-up $100 bill until they switched to a $20 bill after the first note became too wet. They raided the mini-bar, drinking everything from Michelob beer to a mix of Kahlua and Bailey's Irish Cream. Ben talked erratically about business, his wife, and his sexual fantasies. Around 5am Ben rang Rittenhouse – Denise had given him the number for her trailer-mate – and asked her to join them. She said she would have to get a babysitter but soon after she rang another woman, Cherie Rudulski, and told her to get to the suite immediately to earn $300 for just two hours' work. Neither woman would get there in time before Ben reached a tipping-point, and the party would go horribly wrong.

Denise would later say that he went 'berserk'. This wasn't surprising as police statements later recorded Ben 'had done 50 lines of cocaine. Denise said that he had done more cocaine than was humanly possible to her mind'. He wanted to recover cash from the room safe, to pay the intended new arrivals, but couldn't get the combination to work. When the safe wouldn't open he panicked, pacing the room. When Denise moved to reassure him, he shouted, 'Leave me alone, leave me alone'. He rang reception to complain about the safe and then jumped on the bed and roared at her to get out. She returned to the bedroom to get dressed but Ben followed, swinging a piece of wood over his head 'like some crazed King Kong, jumping up and down and swinging this object over his head'.

A man from reception arrived at the suite. When Ben opened the door, dressed in only his boxer shorts, he saw the security man, dressed in a black boilersuit, and he shouted, 'Help, get the police, get the police, I've been robbed' and moved to a corner of the balcony, near a window, but dangerously close to the edge and a 17-storey fall to the lobby below. A maid cleaning an adjoining suite rang reception seeking further assistance.

It had just passed 8am and the lobby, a tropical rainforest-themed space with live speaking parrots providing day-round entertainment, was busy with guests, including, in yet another 'you couldn't make it up' twist, the Irish rock group U2. Its members were heading to rehearsals for a US tour starting the following Saturday. Bono didn't recognise Ben at the distance. 'It wasn't at all noisy or aggravated,' Bono would say later. 'It was ugly and eerie. Everybody was hoping this guy would be okay.'

Rick de Treville, the hotel's security manager, wrongly assumed that someone from the band's entourage was causing the fuss. Wojcik arrived in the lobby and shouted, 'He's gone crazy, he's screaming and yelling. You need to do something. You need to get up there.' As de Treville waited for the elevator, he saw two bodyguards hired from a New York firm to protect U2, 'very large men, very physically competent looking, not very sophisticated but sophisticated in a sense of decorum within a hotel'. When he asked for their help, they agreed.

Up on the 17th floor de Treville moved cautiously towards Ben. 'I tried very hard to approach him in an extremely relaxed manner, non-threatening, with a smile and a cheery hello.' Then he made a mistake: he introduced the two men with him, thinking Ben would recognise them and be reassured. 'I was assuming at that point he was an official with the band,' said de Treville. 'He didn't look like a rocker. I expected to encounter some emaciated musician that was tripped out on drugs and these guys would pick him up and toss him in his room in his shower and we would all go away.' De Trevillle suddenly worried that he had opened the hotel to a legal liability by asking the two external security men to join him 'on a narrow balcony with an apparent lunatic . . . so I asked them if they wanted to assist officially. They said, "Yes, we haven't got anything better to do and we are having a good time".'

Three police patrol cars arrived. Orange County Deputy Sam Spanich tried to calm Ben. He assumed it was a suicide attempt. 'As I approached, he was screaming, "Stay away. I am surrounded". Mr. Dunne was very paranoid and kept looking around him,' Spanich wrote in his police report.

Orange County Sheriff's Office sent two specialist negotiators, Captain Le Fort and Major Marcus. 'Then I saw them clearing the floors below me and I thought they were going to do me in,' Ben recalled later in an interview with Rory Godson for the *Sunday Tribune*. 'The Rodney King episode where a black guy had been beaten up by the LA police had been on the TV recently and I thought the same thing was going to happen to me. I thought they were clearing the place to make sure that nobody would get a video of it. I was on the balcony and the police said that Major Marcus wanted to speak to me. I said there were no majors in the police. I was calling for my friends, wondering where they were. They never came. I wanted to stay out in the public view where they couldn't touch me. I didn't trust the police and I wanted to bring my pals along. I wasn't suicidal. I was fighting to stay alive.'

Spanich was the hero. 'The way he was acting, I thought he would go and take me with him. He said to me, "I'll do what I have to do, I'll take you with me if I have to," and he was really paranoid, but we built a bond, and I never left his side.' Ben asked for Fox and another friend, Declan O'Callaghan, but the police couldn't find them. Spanich knelt in front of Ben, asking him to sit down. 'I was looking at Ben, and Ben and I were on the ledge. I got into a position where he was closer to the window, and I was closer to the edge of the balcony.' Eventually, he manoeuvred Ben so he couldn't see any of the 15 policemen who were now on the 17th floor. Five of them pounced. Ben was overpowered, handcuffed and hog-tied to a poll at the wrists and ankles. The policemen carried his considerable weight first to the elevator and then through the lobby, trussed like a beast prepared for a barbeque.

Ben continued to struggle and roar in the police car all the way to Sand Lake Hospital. He had another panic attack in the hospital and had to be further restrained. 'In the hospital when anyone comes near me, they put on rubber gloves,' Ben explained to Godson. 'I know now that they were worried about AIDS, but I thought they were trying not to leave fingerprints on me. I was in a blind fucking panic over those rubber gloves, wondering if this is a real hospital, why is nobody coming to see me? Why is no one telephoning me?'

At 11am he was discharged and taken to Orange County jail, where he was ordered to wear a prison uniform, visible later in what became an infamous mugshot. He had the legal right to make phone calls. The first person he called was Haughey, at his private number in Abbeville. Haughey, ousted as Taoiseach just weeks earlier, apparently said he would do what he could. Typically, it appears that he did little to save Ben from utter humiliation, although by this stage it was probably too late. It was notable that Ben did not choose to ring any of his siblings or friends back in Ireland in his hour of most desperate need, but it was also understandable: just how would he explain this?

In an untimely coincidence, Mary phoned the hotel just as her husband was on the edge of the balcony. Her call, in the time before Irish people abroad carried mobile phones, was transferred to an assistant manager, Courtney Torreyson. 'We have a very unique situation on our hands with your husband,' Torreyson recalled saying. 'Mr. Dunne is not in his room right now, but he is in the hallway.' She went on to tell Mary, 'something is obviously wrong with him, he is being very paranoid, he is asking for the police, we don't know what is wrong'. Later, a senior police officer rang Mary and told her everything, including details of the presence of cocaine and a woman in his room.

Meanwhile, the rest of Ben's golfing party headed off. Some of them had looked at what was happening as they went to breakfast or to their golf carts, but like Bono they didn't recognise it was Ben. Once they found out, most of them hightailed it back to Ireland at speed, some getting flights as early as that evening, the others the following morning, ahead of their intended departure dates.

Fox – who has never spoken publicly about what happened – was on the hotel's golf course when he heard the news. He returned to his room and, among other calls, contacted the Irish embassy in Washington seeking assistance. It recommended Holland & Knight, an Ivy League firm of corporate lawyers, to represent Ben, but wisely that firm passed the brief on to Slaughter and Leventhal, specialist criminal defense lawyers in Florida. It was run by Bill Duane and Harrison 'Butch' Slaughter, and the latter headed to Orange County jail to meet his new client and arrange bail.

Ben was released after a $25,000 bail was provided by a local bondsman. He headed to another hotel. Ben later told Godson: 'I hadn't slept for two days. It was 6pm, then they said they were taking me to see my lawyer. I go into a room and this guy walks in, chewing gum, and says, "I'm your lawyer, my name is Slaughter, Butch Slaughter". Jesus Christ.'

Slaughter told Ben to repay the bondsman immediately to regain possession of his passport, taken as security. This was important because Ben wanted to get home, even though that no doubt meant a new and different set of difficult and humiliating problems.

First, he had to talk to Mary. His son Rob, in that interview with Horan in April 2024, gave the most detailed account of what happened, although if Rob's recollections of the timings are correct it seems that Ben may have delayed before summoning the courage to make the call.

'It was a Friday night, and I heard the worst shouting match I had ever heard, but I could only hear one side because it was on the phone. Dad was breaking the news to Mum about what happened, so I could hear it from the room. I thought, "What the f**k did Dad do?" It was a real humdinger, but I had no idea what had happened.

'My mum said to him, "Do you know what you are saddling me with? Telling the kids this. You're telling them." And so, she summoned Mark to her bedroom, and he had a conversation on the phone with Dad. I was outside thinking, "What the fuck is going on?" Mark came out looking pretty pale and I thought, "Jesus". Mum said, "Rob, come in." I took the phone and said, "Hey, Dad". And he said, "Look, Rob. I'm in big trouble. I've gotten in trouble for having drugs." I asked him what type of drugs, and he said cocaine. I was aware of cocaine, but I hadn't even smoked a joint. I would drink pints. I asked him what was going to happen. He said, "There's going to be an article and unfortunately, it's out of my control but it's going to be in the newspaper. They are going to say certain things that are true, but certain things that aren't."

'I didn't know what that meant, so I'm very worried. He said, "Look, Rob, they're going to say I had cocaine – and I did. I am just going to have to deal with that. There might be some other embarrassing stuff because there was an escort in the room. But one thing they are going to say, and it's not true, is this issue of trafficking."

'My feeling was, Dad, you bastard for humiliating Mum like this.'

The following day, the *Sunday Tribune* published the story. A New York-based contributor for the newspaper heard of the arrest from a source in Washington and phoned Godson in Dublin. Diarmuid Doyle, a young reporter in the newsroom (and now series producer for *The Last Word* on Today FM), was told to track down the tip-off. To his amazement it was correct, confirmed quickly by the authorities in Florida, who even helpfully supplied the police mugshot of Ben taken only a couple of days previously. He phoned Ben's home, seeking a comment, and the phone was answered by Mary. She asked what his inquiry was about. 'His drug-trafficking arrest,' he told her. She politely declined to say anything. Doyle remembers her being very softly spoken, almost whispering. 'I wasn't sure if she was surprised that I knew or whether she was finding out for the first time. She must have called Ben immediately though because he rang me back very quickly. He was all hail and hearty when he came on the line but still tried to control what would appear. "Be very careful about what you write," he said to me. But crucially, he didn't deny it.'

That Sunday morning the front-page headline on the *Sunday Tribune* screamed: 'Ben Dunne on U.S. drug trafficking charge.' It was quite the scoop. But to Doyle's surprise elements of the story were removed by his editors. He learnt later that Ben had phoned Michael Hand, a former editor of the *Sunday Independent* who now worked with the *Sunday Tribune,* and persuaded him to get Vincent Browne, the editor, to remove the information about Wojcik. It was wishful thinking if Ben believed this would prevent it from becoming public, but it was understandable why he tried, if less forgivable that the information was withheld.

On 22 February, just over a day after being released from custody, Ben flew to London and then on to Dublin, somehow apparently travelling under an assumed name in case he was met by the media at the airport. He arrived early on Sunday morning to see the newspaper as written confirmation of his humiliation.

'I came home and laid down in the bed, thinking about it. I told Mary all the details. Five minutes later the press arrived, and I had to deal with it.'

22.

Weathering the storm

THE 'FIVE MINUTES' WAS very much a figure of speech. Ben turned to Noel Smyth, who was on a fishing holiday at Loughrea in county Galway. After he got a call to tell him of the newspaper story, Smyth rang Ben's house to be greeted by, 'Where the fuck are you? Get back up here quick.' The media arrived at the house before Smyth did, but were made to wait outside the gates. When Smyth arrived the two men quickly agreed a plan, although stories vary as to who should take the credit for it. One has it that Smyth immediately advised Ben to prostrate himself at the feet of the Irish public, to apologise fully, no matter how embarrassing it would be, in the hope of getting forgiveness. Importantly, he said Ben had to do it himself, not use a spokesman on his behalf as others most likely would have done. Another said that Ben had already decided on that approach and Smyth merely concurred. Whoever was responsible, it was a risk, given a degree of media hostility towards Dunnes Stores because of its consistent rejection of media engagement and the apartheid strike.

Ben held a press conference for the print media and recorded a television interview with RTÉ in his house. He didn't spruce himself up – appearing somewhat unkempt as well as hangdog in demeanour – and he spoke quietly. 'I can blame no one but myself,' he said.

He deliberately misled the media about his ongoing cocaine abuse. No first-time user could have survived the quantity of cocaine he had consumed in Florida, especially given its purity, but only later would he admit it had not been his first time.

'No, I'm not a cocaine user,' he lied. 'In a weak moment I took the goddamn stuff and in no way am I looking for pity. I took it, I shouldn't have taken it. Just the same way, I'm not an alcoholic. I took cocaine and I won't be taking it again. It was hard to be arrested as a dealer, but it is something I will overcome. I was weak and that is why I took it. If the situation arose where it came up again, I wouldn't do it again. I'm admitting that nobody put a gun to my head to make me take cocaine. I had a free choice about whether to break the law or not. I am not addicted to any drugs, legal or otherwise. There is an awful lot of prescribed drugs that I wouldn't take. I don't drink shorts. I drink beer. I'm not interested in drinking shorts because I'm afraid to. I have caused a lot of hardship to my wife and kids.' He said the incident had 'cost me dear. I have hurt a lot of people, including myself. I would prefer to go to jail and tell the truth, than stay out of jail and tell lies.'

Hosting a press conference was never going to end the media interest in one of the most sensational stories of late 20th-century Ireland. In Florida, US Chief Assistant State Attorney Bill Vose said he had fielded more than 200 calls looking for information: 'I received more phone calls in this one case than in any case in my twenty years here.' The British tabloid newspaper *The Sun* paid Wojcik $1,000 for her tales of 'My night with Ben'. Far more controversially, two weeks after his return RTÉ paid Wojcik $500 – about £300 at the time – for an interview that was broadcast on its *Today Tonight* current affairs programme. This was about five times the normal RTÉ interview fee of the time and was justified on the basis of the three meetings required to set up the interview. However, RTÉ did not broadcast additional revelations to those already in the public domain 'because we were looking to avoid the hurt that might be done to Mrs Dunne and the children', its head of current affairs Peter Feeney said. Wojcik described specifically the nature of the sexual encounter with Ben in the unused footage.

'There are two sides to this,' Ben said. 'One is, some people near to me criticised the media for printing everything that they could find out about me. Nobody has any trouble dealing with the media when they're talking about how good you are or how nice you are or how much money you're worth. But when they say you're a bad boy, they say they've been unfair to you . . . I made the headlines, so the media were entitled to print them.'

Wojcik told the *Sunday Tribune* the publicity had another price: her parents, who thought she worked in a restaurant, learned about her escort job. Wojcik went into hiding and disconnected her telephone. Godson, sent by the *Sunday Tribune* to follow up on its initial revelations, found Wojcik and Rittenhouse at their trailer-park home and, more than

30 years on in an interview for this book, recalled 'two likeable women, struggling with life, somewhat baffled by the extraordinary story they found themselves part of'. There might have been subsequent opportunities to cash in further, but Wojcik managed to disappear.

If dealing with the media turned out to be relatively straightforward for Ben, the legal situation had to be resolved, as it was essential to keep him out of prison.

Noel Smyth flew to Orlando, where he was appointed attorney-in-fact, giving him the authority to make an agreement in Ben's name. Smyth was horrified by what he saw in the county prison in Orlando, knowing that Ben would not survive the confinement, not after his kidnap, and as a wealthy white Irishman he would be at high risk of intimidation and violence. The charges would have to be pleaded down and then the judge, Dorothy J. Russell, would have to be persuaded to give a lenient sentence for a guilty plea to lesser charges.

Smyth was helped by the botched nature of the initial investigation. Detective Chris Ford, promoted to plainclothes duties just six months earlier, made major mistakes in the hour after Ben was removed from the hotel. Detained in the hotel lobby, Wojcik was treated for cocaine overdose but was also asked to talk with the police urgently. She was canny enough to offer to tell them what was in the room only if guaranteed that she would not face any charges. The police agreed, if the information was good enough. She gave a statement, complaining that she was 'ripped off' by Dunne for her services, which she later withdrew. More pertinently, however, she told them Ben had a big black bag in the room containing lots of cash and cocaine. Ford immediately asked the hotel manager to open the door of Ben's suite, without first obtaining a search warrant. He found the black hold-all and inside a plastic bag with 32.5 grammes of cocaine. Separately, he found more than an ounce of cocaine in a trouser pocket. This was more cocaine than had been seized in the whole of Ireland in 1991. At Ford's request, the hotel security detail opened the safe. Inside were credit cards, Ben's passport, his driver's license and $9,738 in $20, $50 and $100 bills and 80 Irish £50 notes.

In Florida, anyone caught with 28 grammes of cocaine can be charged with trafficking even if they say the drug was solely for personal use. It appeared a conviction was inevitable given that Ben was in custody already. But the Orange County police realised they had a problem. Deputy Howard Wright, the arresting officer, refused to charge Ben with trafficking, even when more senior officers said the huge quantity justified it. Aware of the circumstances in which Ford had searched the room, Wright was worried. However, Sergeant Barbara Lewis directly ordered Wright to charge Ben with trafficking. Conviction would mean a mandatory prison sentence of three years minimum, with no time off for good behaviour or prison crowding.

The legal process in the USA works faster than in Ireland and the first court hearing was scheduled for 12 March. Slaughter indicated that he would challenge whether the police had legal cause to search Ben's room without a warrant and claimed too many people had been in and out of the room for the police to determine the cocaine belonged to Ben. Although the safe was unlocked, it was closed, so he argued its opening and searching were contentious.

Quickly, the prosecutors conceded. 'There were certain reasons they could go into the room,' said Randy Means, spokesman for the State Attorney's Office in Orlando. 'One of the reasons was to find out who he is. They knew that before they went in the room. They also can go in to find out if any crime is taking place in there. They were told there wasn't anybody in there so no crime could be going on in there. An ideal situation is they would have just stopped, got a search warrant, then went into the room and then they would have been able to charge him. But that didn't occur.'

Ironically, Ben later agreed, at least when it was safe for him to say so. 'I don't think the police done anything illegal. They were doing a job,' he said.

The prosecutors wanted Ben to stand trial in June. This created its own Catch-22: Ben could not get a visa to return to the US to face drug charges because he was facing those charges. In May, over a telephone conference, the charge of trafficking cocaine was dropped in favour of the more minor one of possession of the amount in Ben's trousers pocket. He pledged to plead guilty to possession of the lesser amount.

It was now merely a question of sentencing. Smyth blitzed the court with testimonials to Ben's good character, submitting 84 endorsements from friends, employees and charity organisers, in which Ben was described as 'fair-minded', 'humble', and 'generous to a fault', among many other things. Colleagues in the retail trade referred to his sense of 'fair play', 'honesty', and 'sense of humour', allied to his personal integrity and extraordinary business acumen.

One friend, Sydney Cooper of the distribution company of the same name, went so far as to say he was only alive because of Ben: 'I'm a non-swimmer and while boating in Spain I got in trouble in the water. Ben, without hesitation or regard for his own life, jumped in the sea and assisted me ashore. Without his prompt actions I would most certainly have drowned. I will always love Ben Dunne and I am proud to call him my best friend.'

An unnamed London-based property investor told of the time when a young man from a deprived area and background asked Ben if he would be a godparent to his illegitimate child and 'typical of Ben he readily agreed and both he and his wife Mary attended the christening. Ben also arranged when that child came to a certain age, he had something to look forward to.'

Testimonials regarding five-figure contributions to Saint Joseph's Hospital in Dublin, the Irish Grocers Benevolent Fund, the hardship fund at Galway RTC, the Irish Cancer Society, Kilkenny Civic Trust, Saint Patrick's College in Maynooth, Belvedere Youth Club in Dublin and Galway Hospice, amongst others, were deposited with the court. Sean Flanagan, a leukaemia sufferer from Sligo, said he had met Ben at a golf tournament and told him that because of his illness he had difficulty using the bath in his hotel room, where there was no shower. Ben paid for him to move to a better hotel. 'From that day on he has been a great supporter of the bone marrow leukaemia trust,' Flanagan said.

All the character witnesses said the Florida incident was totally out of character for Ben and cited his son's kidney disorder combined with the stress of his lifestyle as possible causes.

Mulholland, a bookie and a former Mayor of Galway who was one of the Orlando golfing group, said: 'I have not seen Ben since but have spoken with him many times on the phone. His remorse is total, and he has told me of counselling he has been having. He has stopped drinking and is spending much of his time at home with his family. This activity I think is by way of restitution for all the dignity taken from them and the shame he has brought on his family. He has told me that he allows himself to be tested for drugs on regular intervals to allay the fears of family and wife. I have no doubt that he is completely sincere in his rehabilitation.'

Feargal Quinn of Superquinn supported Ben generously: 'The grocery business is aggressively competitive in Ireland yet the fact that I hold Mr. Dunne in high esteem is in itself evidence of his integrity and his fair mindedness. Although we compete for the same customers' loyalty, I have never failed to regard Mr. Dunne as a man of principle and honour in his trading practice and on the basis of such honest business methods he has built his family business into the biggest in Ireland. Since we are competitors, we tend not to meet socially too often. Ben is a family man of the traditional kind and the incident in Florida would appear to be totally out of character for him.'

One of the most interesting depositions, from somebody described as a 'senior banker', said Ben had often taken responsibility for the debts of others who could no longer afford to repay them. Ben had said 'they worked hard, and the failure of their business is not their fault, and they gave me excellent service when times were good'.

The campaign succeeded. The court accepted Ben's guilty plea and he was fined $5,000. He undertook to enter residential evaluation for no less than 28 days and remain under the supervision of Dr Jeffrey A. Danziger for over a year. Both Danziger and Smith were required to report to the court about his progress. He would be blocked from entering the US again. Ben would enter the Charter Clinic in England on 1 June, where he would stay for most of the month.

Ben subsequently claimed that he was encouraged to sue the hotel for permitting the search: 'I told them to get stuffed. I am not criticising them, but there was no injustice done to me. You get the smart boys who'll tell you . . . the hotel allowed an illegal search so that means you can have a claim off the hotel. My attitude is very simple. I was very lucky that the search was illegal because if it hadn't been suppressed I was mandatory three years [sentence]. So, I was lucky.'

He was contrite in subsequent interviews: 'They've done less to me than what I was expecting. Yeah, I was expecting worse. So, that's more than fair, isn't it? Sometimes people are expecting too much. I was very unfair to the state of Florida. I showed disrespect to them, you know. When somebody shows disrespect, you get what you deserve.'

His sister Margaret didn't believe he had got what he deserved – she believed he hadn't suffered half enough.

23.

Seeking forgiveness

BEN SNR HAD LEFT his business to children who, even in adulthood, continued to behave like screaming children in violent competition with each other but who always had presented a united front to the world, at least until now. His protective structure, the Trust, could not and did not ensure their continued involvement and cooperation: some worked harder than others for the same rewards. Some siblings needed to be top dog or believed that they alone knew best what to do. The Dunnes had long been the most private of families, Dunnes Stores the most secretive of companies, but Ben's antics in Florida opened up a dangerous seam and then the war of the siblings in 1993 blew it all apart.

Just as with the aftermath of the kidnap, efforts were made to return to normal as quickly as possible. The day after his return from Orlando – the morning after the RTÉ interview – Ben went to Dunnes Stores headquarters to report for work. 'I went into work and apologised to each of my staff for the embarrassment I had caused them,' he said. Wisely, he made no public reference at this point to his siblings.

On his arrival his three sisters, Margaret, Therese and Elizabeth, absented themselves from headquarters on Stephen Street and went to their favourite hair salon. They took the escalator to the second floor of the Stephen's Green shopping centre and went into a Peter Mark premises, where they were well-known and discretion was assured. Justine McCarthy reported in the *Irish Independent* that 'there were tears streaming down their faces. They were shown to a private room on the mezzanine level of the salon, served coffee and discreetly left alone to comfort each other in their grief.'

At home, Mary insisted on sending the children to school to face the inevitable slagging and judgement. As she saw it, there was nothing to be gained by delaying things. 'It was really tough to go in,' said Rob. 'Everyone I knew was laughing at it. Within minutes of going on to the corridor, I overheard someone say, "Where can you find the jumpers in Dunnes Stores? On the 17th floor." I guess it's kind of clever. At the time, I didn't appreciate the humour.'

There were other jokes. At the time the Ford Escort was one of Ireland's best-selling cars. 'How do you get a Volvo into a bathroom?' was the starting line of a joke. The punchline: 'Ask Ben Dunne. He got an escort into his bath.' Part of Ben's own defence mechanism over time was to tell these jokes against himself.

'I just had this sick feeling – you were the laughing-stock and people got extra enjoyment from seeing this big powerful business mogul fall,' said Rob. 'I remember the school principal, Fr O'Shea, being really kind. He took me into the office and said, "This is going to be a difficult time, but I am looking out for you." He showed a lot of humanity, even though he was very strict. And I had buddies whose parents must have said not to give me a hard time. Everything was very, very tense. Dad gave us a hug and said sorry, but he was also very pragmatic. He said, "Look, I'm going to have to take care of some things. Maybe you won't like the way I do it, but it is what it is. I'm sorry for what I have done, but now I have to play the cards I've been dealt. Let's try our best not to make things worse. Let's try our best to be a team".'

Rob remembered spending a lot of time with his mother and 'deferring to her for decisions'. He said the relentless coverage of the event was 'completely understandable', despite it being so painful for the family. According to Horan in her telling of her encounter with him, 'his anger at the humiliation of his mother is still palpable'. She quoted him saying, 'My feeling was, "Dad, you bastard for humiliating Mum like this. Whatever you are doing in private gallivanting, don't have such a massive fucking fiasco".'

'She was a team player,' Rob said of his mother. 'She didn't abandon him, because that would have affected him, which in turn would badly affect all of us. It couldn't have been worse. Everything was just so sordid, the escort and the trafficking charge, and it was just so clichéd.'

The joke in business and banking circles was that whatever about facing a judge at trial or his wife, the worst punishment for Ben was the wrath of his elder sister. In an *Irish Independent* profile, Angela Phelan described Margaret as 'a devout Catholic: those who knew her didn't know whether Ben's involvement with a prostitute or the use of cocaine upset her the most'. That didn't consider the multiplier effect.

When she met with company employees, and any of them was brave enough to ask how she was, Margaret said that the family was supporting Ben. Travelling around the country she spoke to customers and, while admitting her upset, expressed her admiration for Ben's family and the support they were giving him. It was a performance. 'It was the best thing that has ever happened to him and he has turned it into something very positive,' she said at one stage. 'It's no secret that we have had our differences. I suppose the problem is that we are too alike.' It was an interesting comment: outsiders might have seen their behaviours as entirely different, but beneath that both were hot-headed and convinced they were in the right.

However, according to Phelan, Margaret told close friends that she'd struggled to cope. 'If my father knew what was going on he would turn in his grave, but he would turn in his grave much quicker if he felt the family would fall out over this. Ben has been incredibly stupid but he's my brother and I will stand by him and continue to give him whatever support he needs,' she said. That sangfroid soon evaporated.

Prior to entering the Charter Clinic, Ben had given one of his now characteristically frank interviews to Godson at the *Sunday Tribune*. 'I believe that potentially I would be a drug addict or drug user and that I would have to be on my guard all the time,' he said, in his now commonly heard declamatory style. 'There is a weakness in every business and in everybody. If it isn't controlled, there's a weakness in all of us that will destroy us. Greed will destroy us, age will destroy us, addiction will destroy us. I think my marriage is strong, but even before this not a day goes by that I don't get a flash that I'm going to die, that my business is going to fail, that my marriage is going to end. I think anyone in this world who gets too secure is heading for a disaster. I don't like the word security. I've given up cigarettes four times and gone back on them because of feeling secure.

'That's one of the signs of addiction when you think you're OK, somewhere at the back of the mind you know you are not. Talk to anyone who's addicted to anything and they think they're OK. An awful lot of fellows think they're just drunk but they are going down a slippery slope. Sometimes we run away from things a long time. When we're caught, it's not easy to stop running. And everybody that I know runs away from situations.

'I describe myself as an ordinary Joe Blow with too much money. It was only a few hours, but it has damaged a relatively clean and good record in business and in life. I made a terrible, bloody blunder. I was weak and stupid. I have fallen a long way, in front of my wife, in front of my kids, in front of myself.' But he also said of his family: 'I love them and they love me, I think.'

In Galway, the local Rotary Club persuaded him to accept an award for his large contribution to building a centre for the mentally disabled. In his brief speech he took issue with Irish author George Bernard Shaw, who said 'lack of money is the root of all evil'. Ben had his own theory: 'Money is like manure. It's of no use unless it is spread.'

Ben received both sympathetic and angry letters from parents whose children were addicted to drugs. 'I appreciate everybody's support, but at the end of the day the person that motivates you must be yourself. If I was to take notice of all the nice letters I got, and they meant well, I could really have thought I've done nothing wrong. But I know I did, and I told the judge that.'

Ben was focused on owning his mistake and not ducking away from judgement – official and personal. But he also wanted to put the incident behind him and refocus on the business and all he wanted to achieve with Dunnes Stores. For that, he needed others to forgive and forget, or at least move on from it. He told Godson: 'I learned to try and stop hurting people that mean a lot to me. I believe that if you try hard enough, you can achieve most things, and forgiveness is in everybody. Some people are a little slower to respond.'

Ben might have been holding out the olive branch, but not all of his siblings were willing to take it. In fact, they were arming themselves to do battle.

24.

The war of the siblings

MARGARET WAS DEEPLY UNIMPRESSED by the punishment meted out to Ben of 28 days' rehab at the Charter Clinic. Although it was a highly reputable private mental health hospital dedicated to helping adults with addictions, Margaret regarded it as a 'soft' punishment. Shortly after Ben's plea deal, a friend of mine was sitting beside Margaret at a business dinner. He hadn't met her before and didn't know Ben either but, wishing to be polite, he said to her that the media coverage over the previous months had been somewhat excessive and prurient. She replied witheringly: 'It wasn't bad enough for him. He should have gone to prison.' My friend was stunned by the ferociousness of her comment, but it meant that what happened over the next year did not surprise him.

It was not a one-off. A random individual operating a radio scanner in the Phoenix Park picked up a telephone call between Margaret and Noel Smyth as one of them drove through the park and the contents were leaked. Margaret was heard berating Smyth that the clinic was a holiday home and 'that little bastard' could have done with six months in prison. She told the solicitor that he was a bad influence on her brother. She might well have had a point about Charter, because Ben was able to continue to work from there. He stayed in regular contact with his financial controller, Michael Irwin. Ben was worried when Irwin told him that Margaret was asking for various pieces of financial information to be sent by fax to her house, which was unusual. Ben told him to tell her the information couldn't leave the premises.

Margaret had her work cut out for her because Ben took an even more hands-on approach at Dunnes after his return from the clinic. He seemed filled with new energy, focus and determination. This suggested that the experience of the clinic had not left him feeling chastised or introspective but instead emboldened. He declared himself sole chairman, regarding it as formal recognition of what he believed was the de facto situation. He told his siblings they would have to work full-time if they wanted full pay and not limit themselves to occasional attendance at frequently disruptive meetings, a non-too-veiled reference to Frank.

'If I learned anything last year, it was the difference between right and wrong. Previously, I was like a man caged by my own family. One thing I knew was wrong was to have directors who were not fully involved in the business,' he said in yet another interview. Ben had a new suite developed on the ground floor, with a staircase leading to his old office on Stephen Street, and he finally hired a personal secretary. He conducted a review of the entire business. From this, he decided the loss-making UK chain was his biggest problem – costing as much as stg£20m to date – and that he had to admit the investment, made at the height of the late 1980s property boom, was largely his fault. Now he set about fixing it. Dunnes shut stores in Middlesborough, Sheffield, Blackburn and Southampton during the year, leaving it with just five stores in England. Margaret took control of this. She flew to the UK several times a week, and most Saturday afternoons she was to be found behind the checkout at its Liverpool store.

She wasn't taking Ben's assertiveness lying down. At her insistence, Frank returned to regular attendance at HQ, and this angered Ben greatly, even if it was partly prompted by his ultimatum. As far as Ben was concerned, Frank had left and needed to stay gone. Frank attended a board meeting in June 1992, his first time to do so in two years, while Ben was in Charter, saying that he was seeking to 're-establish family unity'. He proposed a new set of company rules and announced that he was resuming his role as joint managing director. Margaret and Therese supported him to provide a majority on the board. Ben, who only two months previously had said in an interview that 'the only time I will step aside is if I am put in jail', was suddenly vulnerable. He should not have been surprised: he had anticipated it, admitting in one interview prior to entering the clinic that his job was 'in jeopardy'. He understood how his siblings might be thinking and feeling: 'If there were similar people around me, it would take time before I had confidence enough that those people were stable. I have fallen a long way. I will just have to crawl back up the slippery slope.'

Ben fought back. He alleged that Frank and Margaret 'purported to convene a meeting of the board without notice to him' and had passed resolutions with the effect of 'undermining in a significant and radical way' how the business of the group was carried out. He called another board meeting to render that previous meeting and its outcome void and was restored as executive chairman on a 3–2 vote; Liz and Therese sided with him. But Therese was vacillating, and the stress and strain were affecting her personal behaviour, as would become clear later. For now, Ben had a slim margin holding him in place.

Relations deteriorated further between the siblings. The back-to-school sale in the autumn of 1992 was a disappointment and Ben blamed Margaret for that, even though spending power in the economy had fallen sharply. Ben thought the company needed to 'get back to basics' by offering cheap stock that would get customers through the doors – just as Ben Snr had advocated. He bought an enormous consignment of shirts and jeans from the UK and introduced this bargain range to the Irish stores as the basis of a pre-Christmas '20 per cent off' sale. In a rare public comment Margaret told Ursula Halligan of the *Sunday Tribune* in December 1992 that the decision had been an enormous success: 'We are talking about a lot of money. We beat our best figures since the company was founded in 1944. We got very, very, very large increases. The name of the game is to be first, and we pride ourselves as being leaders in the retail business. If we're going to stay leaders, we've got to be the first with the ideas. The people who are in first are the people who win. It is totally and absolutely a cut-throat business.' Margaret's public endorsement of a strategy with which she disagreed profoundly appeared motivated by the desire on her part not to air company disputes publicly. The new lines doubled turnover in some outlets but impacted enormously on the viability of competitors, who couldn't compete with the prices.

When supplies ran short, Ben and Smyth flew first-class to Singapore in November, where they spent six days at the Shangri-La Hotel meeting suppliers and visiting factories. They spent four days at the Hyatt Hotel in Bali. By the time they had finished their tour, Ben had ordered £20m worth of goods, an enormous commitment.

In January 1993, Ben showed samples to the board and, he claimed, Margaret proposed a vote of thanks for his enterprise. Later, she would describe these discount purchases as a 'disaster', and it was widely reported that this was the reason she moved against Ben. It wasn't. That power move had happened long before, when Frank had returned in the summer of 1992. It just took time to play out. Margaret was playing the long game, patiently but unrelentingly, but Ben did a lot while she prepared her next move.

Ben had returned to his price-cutting obsession in the supermarkets. Late in 1992 he knocked another 10p off the price of own-brand white sliced pan. He publicly stated that the 150 top selling items in his supermarkets would come down in price if he was able to obtain enough stock to ensure every store could take part in the cuts. It promised to be a bonanza for shoppers. He said he would consider going north of the border for goods if negotiations with suppliers in the Republic failed and prevented Dunnes from lowering prices. He said there was no question of below-cost selling and that Dunnes would abide by the law.

In November 1992, Ben gave an interview to the *Sunday Tribune* that must have caused consternation among the siblings. Indeed, it is hard to understand what purpose it would have served other than that. He said that Dunnes was part of a price-fixing cartel designed to keep the price of milk and other foodstuffs artificially high and that if he tried to break the alleged cartel, suppliers would refuse to deliver to him. 'Look at milk. A two litre pack is 112p in Dunnes, Quinnsworth, Crazy Prices and Superquinn. I could sell 2 litres of milk at 99p and still make a profit but my suppliers will cut me off. I am part of a cartel.' Willie Fagan, the Director of Consumer Affairs, said he could not act unless Ben or another person signed an affidavit setting out a complaint.

Ben made these comments after a separate High Court injunction had ended a Dunnes Stores discount voucher scheme that gave customers £5 for every £40 spent. Fagan argued that coupon schemes were effectively forms of below-cost selling and therefore banned under the Groceries Order, and he threatened High Court action. Ben said: 'I'm not doing anything wrong. I am pissed off. I'm trying to give the housewife what she deserves. Dunnes Stores does not need new business, we are doing this for the consumer.'

During 1992, Ben managed to increase market share for the supermarket division in Ireland substantially. He was helped when the value of sterling on international markets collapsed, giving Dunnes greater purchasing power for its imports. Ben saw the opportunity to increase volume at lower prices, but became angry at the reluctance of suppliers and importers to pass on the benefits of an effective 20% devaluation in sterling. He also concentrated on drapery, cutting prices by 20% in a pre-Christmas sale the day after Bertie Ahern, as Minister for Finance, increased VAT on adult clothes and shoes to 21%. There was uproar among Irish suppliers who couldn't drop their prices in what they sold to Dunnes. Ben didn't care; he bought even more from various countries in Asia. Competitors complained bitterly too and over the next six months many smaller clothes retailers shut down as consumer spending tumbled and more of what money was being spent headed to Dunnes.

Ben raged against what he saw as restrictions on his business practices: 'If you can't sell below cost, you might as well hand the business over to accountants, there would be no skill left in retailing. Every retailer has to sell below cost. If you buy a line of clothes that doesn't work, you have to sell below cost. It's not a question of what it's costing Dunnes Stores, it's a question of what it's costing the consumer.'

The price cuts were largely moved from normal groceries to fresh perishable goods, which were exempted from below-cost-selling legislation. As far as Ben was concerned, he was in control of the business, a leader who was delivering on all fronts and steering the company towards ever greater success.

To the outsider it may have seemed aggressive and ruthless, but successful. As far as Margaret and Frank were concerned, Ben was running amok, his actions explained by unresolved addictions which, despite his subsequent denials, included a predilection for gambling. Doing it on the golf course with his own money was one thing, risking the business with company money another. They needed to convince their siblings of this so they could oust him.

Margaret had competing demands on her attention in late 1992 and into early 1993. This was a time of considerable turmoil for her personally as well. When it was reported in the newspapers that Margaret was buying Stackallen House in county Meath, it was widely regarded as a wedding present for her daughter Anne, and her husband Charles O'Brien, now starting his own career. Stackallen is one of Ireland's few surviving great country homes, a Williamite mansion with a 275-acre stud, built in 1710 and located halfway between Slane and Navan in the Boyne Valley. Margaret was set to buy it for £1.6m – at the time the highest price ever achieved for a residential property in Ireland. Margaret said she wanted a country home where her husband could pursue his passionate hobby of breeding horses and training point-to-pointers. But speculation mounted that it was a gift for Anne and Charles. It was the biggest private house transaction of the era and the details appealed to the nosy, so the newspapers obliged.

Mother and daughter were on a trip to Hong Kong in 1992 when Anne, 24, revealed that she was three months' pregnant. Margaret, who was highly conscious of the mores of the era and wedded to her Catholicism, believed that babies should be born to married couples. On their return, Margaret immediately organised a quiet, quick wedding for the young couple. Only immediate members of both families were informed or invited and the ceremony was attended by 14 people. A wedding-day feast was held at Kilkee Castle, followed by a day's racing in Leopardstown. The next morning Charles was on his way to the yearling sales in Newmarket, while Anne returned to duty as a first-year intern at Beaumont Hospital. Only then did Margaret inform her siblings and their families.

The story went around Dublin quickly, mainly because Ben glee-fully told as many people as possible. In the end, Martin Naughton of Glen Dimplex purchased Stackallen. Margaret told the *Irish Independent* that 'having done the sums I decided I couldn't afford the upkeep costs and right now my attention cannot be diverted from work.' Nobody believed the first part of that statement, and while she was devoted to work, other things were going on in her life that were upsetting her. Separately, she told the *Sunday Tribune*: 'People read a lot of nonsense in the *Independent* about a Dallas lifestyle but all we have is paper money. The only money I have is the salary cheque at the end of the month, I am just a PAYE worker.'

The issues in their private lives and the differences of opinion about corporate issues meant tensions between Ben and Margaret were simmering further. Frank, despite his reputation for indecision, had picked his side, and this time his decision was final. That was two against one, and they needed to persuade just one of the other two to turn against Ben to remove him and take control. Liz was regarded as less likely, her loyalty to Ben running deep, but Therese could, perhaps, be persuadable.

25.

The coup

BEN MAY HAVE BEEN ERRATIC and volatile, but he was not blind to the potential threats to his position. He had Smyth in his ear – his solicitor was almost always available and present to issue warnings and suggest courses of actions. While he believed that he had Ben's best interests at heart and acted accordingly, Margaret came to regard him as manipulative and damaging. She made this known privately to Ben during their increasingly fractious interactions, which Ben reported back to Smyth.

They decided that they would force the issue. At the 2 February 1993 board meeting, Ben read a long statement into the minutes detailing numerous allegations made against him and his responses. He denied that he had used the board as a rubberstamp for decisions he had already taken and implemented. He rejected allegations that Dunnes was offered inducements to locate stores in certain developments, implying that Ben was getting kickbacks from developers and that he wanted cover by getting the family to join him. Specifically, it had been claimed that property developers close to Ben had offered him a £3m bribe to have Dunnes invest in a county Dublin site. Frank complained that Ben had been negligent in agreeing the terms of a lease in Cork and this would prevent the firm from ever joining the stock exchange as a way of raising cash. Ben was also accused of bribing senior managers to not cooperate with his siblings while he was being treated in the London clinic.

Ben forced a vote of confidence in his actions and, to his enormous relief, Elizabeth and Therese sided with him again.

A week later, on 8 February, at another board meeting, he made what was a tactical mistake, one that implied stress was impairing his judgement, because it was a move that made no sense and could only have been made on impulse. He offered to sell his shares to Frank, at a price to be agreed by an independent third party. Frank allegedly agreed to buy them on 22 February, but on 1 March the deal, such as it was, was cancelled. And by that time the single most dramatic act in the saga to date had taken place.

Ben arrived at a regular board meeting in Stephen Street on 23 February. Once seated, Margaret told him that she was proposing his removal as chairman. It hadn't been on the agenda but can't have come as too much of a surprise to Ben. He asked why. When told the reasons were 'numerous', he challenged his siblings to examine the records of the previous board meetings taken by Fox. They refused.

Unknown to him, Therese had turned sides, having been lobbied assiduously by Margaret in the preceding weeks. The vote to remove Ben was carried by 3 to 2; Ben's only supporter was Elizabeth. Ben asked who was to take over his position. He was told the chairman would be elected on a weekly basis. He said, 'This is crazy. Who are we supposed to report to? You can't have a team without a captain.'

Ben had been ousted by his own flesh and blood, despite building the company's sales revenues in a decade from about £150m to £1bn and annual profitability from less than £10m to nearly £100m. Past results hadn't saved him: three siblings were too worried about the present and future. Typically, no statement was made, either to staff or to the public.

Ben didn't attend board meetings for the next four weeks but received detailed memoranda after each one. After that, he decided that the time had come to go public. On 28 March 1993, *The Sunday Business Post*'s story on Ben's removal as chairman was published. It was light on detail beyond that basic fact and contained no quotes from any source.

On that Sunday I travelled speculatively to Ben's house in Porterstown, hoping to secure an interview with him for the *Irish Independent* (which I had joined in January as its Business Editor). I arrived at the same time as Jim Dunne from *The Irish Times*. Ben asked which one of us wanted to go first and I said I would wait. Ben ushered me into the front room, where Rob was sitting in front of the largest TV screen I'd ever seen, playing a video game. 'Don't ask him anything about this,' Ben warned me before striding out. We chatted about his pending Leaving Cert, an exam I'd done just a decade previously. Not long after that Jim left, and I was summoned to Ben's handsomely appointed home office.

He let rip about his siblings, giving me quote after quote that I doubted would make it past the newspaper's lawyers, but still there was enough for the front-page splash my editor Vinnie Doyle wanted. The vitriol that Ben displayed towards Frank was one of the most memorable parts of the interview. Ben was blunt and emphatic in declaring Frank an alcoholic, incapable of running the business and unqualified to decide to remove him. His anger was visceral. He was entirely unsympathetic to Frank's alcoholism. Ben was insistent that Frank had no ability to contribute to the management of the company, having absented himself for more than a decade. The dramatic upscaling of the business had happened under Ben's direction, so for Frank to return now and say that he would do it better was a bitter insult to the younger brother.

The personal comments about Frank did not feature in the piece that appeared in the following day's *Irish Independent*. What I wrote was: '"Ben Dunne has changed," the ousted executive chairman said of himself yesterday. "I know now the difference between right and wrong and it is wrong to sweep things like this under the carpet. It is a free society, and I am a free man and I will say what I like unless the board instructs me to make no more comments. If they do, I'll let you know that I've been asked to say no more. I'm not letting any secrets out".'

I wrote that he said his siblings hadn't told him of any charges serious enough to warrant his removal. 'If I was firing a man, I'd tell him why,' he declared. The reality was that he knew he hadn't been forgiven for Orlando and he wasn't trusted with the reputation of the family business because of his behaviour then and since.

'When Ben Dunne isn't the boss there's a different way of running Dunnes Stores. I am always worried about the future because I don't know what it holds. Certainly, if the board was to leave this company continue without leadership, I would be worried. A ship needs a captain, someone on board to take the decisions, and the board of Dunnes Stores must have a strong leader who will make strong, decisive and intelligent decisions.

'Dunnes is still my first love. Over the past 10 years I've built shopping centres, I've built stores, I bought textiles, I bought food, I retailed textiles, I retailed food and I manufactured bread and beef burgers. I have wide experience of the industries I'm talking about. Ben Dunne stands for Dunnes Stores and better value. I have a saying that it's not how far you fall but how much you bounce back. The board will have to take the consequences of this decision.'

By speaking so publicly Ben, still only 44 years old, was making it far more difficult for himself to continue in his new, lesser position at Dunnes, defined only in that he was no longer the boss, even if the board said it wanted him to remain as a director albeit with tighter controls imposed upon him. By talking about himself in the third person, I suspected he was showing signs of the stress he was clearly feeling, despite his expressions of optimism and strength. That said, psychologists sometimes say a person talking about themselves in the third person is showing a degree of self-awareness and the removal of emotion from their statements.

As we spoke, the phone on the desk in his study rang. He answered it, then said, 'Hello Boss' in a cheery and respectful fashion. Immediately I suspected it was Charlie Haughey, because many of his acolytes loved to call him The Boss. 'I'm okay, I'm fine,' Ben said, before continuing, 'you have nothing to worry about, it's all under control. It's fine, don't worry.' He then said he had a reporter from the *Irish Independent* with him and he would call back later to talk more freely. He put the phone down, looked at me and confirmed: 'Charlie. Just checking to see how I am.' As I was to realise later, it was more likely Haughey checking to see what damage might be caused to him by certain revelations that would take another few years to emerge. But that was a different storm, and it wasn't breaking over Ben's head just yet.

In response to his siblings' moves against him, Ben came up with a plan, in conjunction with Smyth. He had to convince his brother and sisters that he had options that would suit him, if not necessarily them.

He moved quickly. Dunloe House was a small company with its shares traded on the Irish stock market and its major shareholder, a British property developer, was easily persuaded to sell its 75% holding in the company for £900,000. From that, Ben transferred shares to Smyth, to his wife Mary, and to the man chosen as Dunloe's managing

The first Dunnes Stores opens on Patrick Street, Cork, 1944

Ben Dunne Snr and his wife Nora in 1976

© RollingNews.ie

Margaret Heffernan in 1991

© Irish Independent

Elizabeth McMahon (centre) with her daughter Sharon on the left, and
Theresa Dunne in the background (centre) with Mary Dunne, Ben Jnr's wife,
on the right, 1986

Ben Dunne at home in Castleknock, Dublin in 1993

Frank Dunne at a horse race in 1983

Margaret Heffernan being awarded an honorary doctorate from the National University of Ireland in 2007

Above: Ben Dunne with his wife Mary and Fr Dermod McCarthy in October 1981 following his release by the IRA

Left: Ben Dunne with a plaque containing the bullets that were handed to him by his IRA kidnappers

Bishop Desmond Tutu meeting Dunnes Stores strikers Mary Manning (left) and Karen Gearon in 1984

Dunnes Stores workers protest over working conditions in Dublin, 2015

Ben Dunne shakes hands with Fianna Fail leader Charles Haughey, 1986

Ben Dunne with his solicitor Noel Smyth at the Moriarty Tribunal in
Dublin Castle, 2000

The funeral of Ben Dunne, November 2023

Dunnes Stores on Patrick Street today

director, his friend Michael Cosgrove, an accountant from Mayo. His sister Elizabeth was also persuaded to join the board, to the considerable upset of the other siblings who felt she was supporting Ben in his disloyalty. In an effort to assuage them, Elizabeth declined his offer of shares in the company.

Ownership of this company gave Ben access to capital, if he wanted to raise it for new business ventures, or shares, as a currency to use in buying the assets of other companies. Ben was threatening implicitly to become a rival to Dunnes, even though he was still a shareholder and director. His main strategy seemed to be to keep his siblings guessing, although he tried to keep a door open for a possible return to control of Dunnes on his own terms, unlikely as that might have been. It was a bizarre situation, made worse for his siblings by his willingness to court the media, something anathema to them and especially to Margaret given her veneration of her father's wishes.

Ben gave more interviews, raising the temperature further but showing signs of the inconsistency and erraticism that had been apparent to his siblings. A week after the *Business Post* published the short report that he had been removed as chairman, heightening speculation that he was the source even if not quoted, he gave another interview to its deputy editor, Aileen O'Toole. 'It's not a case of civil war, or anything like that.' He said his removal as chairman was 'good for me, and if it's good for me, it's good for Dunnes Stores'. However, he added: 'I will not put up with things that I used to put up with, such as asking a question and not getting an answer ... I may never get the answer to the question now because they have removed me as chairman. At least I got to the stage where they did remove me ... Maybe some other person who would be removed as chairman would sulk but not me. It's a fact of life that I have been removed as chairman. My attitude is don't sulk, deal with it, deal with the situation and prove to yourself that you are still a good operator. That's what makes me happy and if you prove it to yourself, others will recognise it.

'Keep myself happy and if I am happy, then people around me will be happy. Doing the right thing makes me happy. Admitting to my weaknesses makes me happy. Turning my weaknesses into strengths makes me happy.

'I enjoy the company of myself today. I enjoy being with my wife and children. I enjoy explaining to them that if you have all the money in the world, if you break the law and get into trouble as I did, then you have to face the consequences.'

He also showed a degree of self-awareness that had seemed lacking. 'I've been listening to myself doing interviews and I have a knack of talking about myself in the third person. It's wrong. That's why I haven't used it in this interview. That's another thing I've learnt about myself. There's no third person, there's just me.'

Few believed he had bought Dunloe House for the bricks-and-mortar assets it owned. It was its stock market listing that was valuable. It gave him the ability to issue new shares to raise money from outside investors to grow a business, potentially providing him with more cash than he had ready access to at the time, given that his wealth was largely tied up in Dunnes. An offer of shares to the general public might have brought in lots of money from those prepared to gamble on backing his name as much as a business plan. However, investors from pension and insurance funds, who would have larger sums of money available, were likely to be more cautious given the publicity Ben's behaviour had attracted. 'If I put into Dunloe the time I put into playing golf, Dunloe will be very successful,' he told O'Toole. 'I put very little time into golf now but I was an avid golfer and spent a lot of time on the golf course while still running Dunnes Stores. If I convert the time I was playing golf, even less of it, into Dunloe, Dunloe will be successful.'

Of course, there had to be a real business in which to invest. Mary spent £300,000 buying units in the Janelle Shopping Centre in Finglas from Monarch Properties, a company owned by property speculator Phil Monahan, who was very close to Noel Smyth. She was going to open a new clothes shop, called Buy Right Stores, with the possibility of more to follow. She also registered the name 'Ben's Boutique'. Given that he was still employed as a director of Dunnes, Ben could not be involved in the business, but said he was just 'helping and advising' his wife. Yet everyone believed that he, not Mary, would be running things, even if he denied it.

Was there potential for a new clothes retailer, presumably following the preferred Ben model of buying very cheap and selling at low profit margins, especially if it would take time to gain market share? Starting from scratch would have proved difficult, but not impossible: after all, his own father had done it in Cork in 1944. But whereas established businesses often ignore scrappy upstarts only to find they grow faster than expected, nobody at Dunnes or other competitors was likely to take a new Ben-led challenger lightly.

He would need locations from which to trade, as well as stock. The deal with Monarch led to speculation that it might sell property assets to Dunloe, such as its half share in The Square in Tallaght, where Dunnes was the anchor tenant. Smyth was also in control of other properties that could have been easily transferred or rented to Dunloe. When I asked him about his plans Ben responded, 'How could it be seen as a threat to Dunnes Stores until they see what the strategy is?'

Ben said little, possibly because he wanted to say nothing that might be of benefit to his potential competitors or, more likely, because he didn't really know what he was going to do because he was engaged in a bluff against the family. It was provocation, however, and in April the board, at a meeting he didn't attend, stripped him of his remaining responsibility for the men's wear and footwear divisions. Ben went to the media to suggest he might sue for constructive dismissal and said Margaret and Frank had acted because of Mary opening her store in Finglas, which they saw as a conflict of interest. The *Sunday Tribune* persuaded trustee Eddie Montgomery – the old lunch pal of Ben Snr – to make a comment: 'I am a bit out on a limb,' he said. 'The trustees have nothing to do with this. It is a family fight. But there is no conflict of interest, not in the very least. We are all working for the good of the community.' Whatever about the good of the community, Montgomery's comment highlighted the powerless of everyone else connected to the family to get them to see sense and to act appropriately.

There was a further complication in May, when Ben instituted proceedings to stop 'family members and others' transferring his 190 preference shares in the Dunnes Holding Company to Frank. This was Frank trying to execute the deal that Ben had suggested in February but then resiled from in March. On 13 May, the family gave a voluntary undertaking not to put through the share transfer until the matter was dealt with in the courts. In his affidavit, Ben claimed that the family tried to force him to sell at the nominal price of £1 each, for a total of just £190. Ben said he would sell, but only at an independently determined price. Godson reported in the *Sunday Tribune* that Margaret had sought intermediaries to broker a peace deal, but she had imposed a condition: it was prerequisite that Ben had to sever all links with Smyth. He wouldn't do that. At a July 1993 board meeting the directors resolved that Ben wished to leave and to reach a settlement with him on a friendly rather than hostile basis.

And then Elizabeth Dunne died.

26.

The slow unravelling

THE PRESSURE OF THE PUBLIC scrutiny on the family brought about by Ben's travails weighed heavily on Therese and Elizabeth. As the youngest child, Therese didn't see much of her parents when she was growing up in Cork. She went to school at the Ursuline Convent, where she became an enthusiastic hockey player; she continued into adulthood, playing with Pembroke Wanderers in Ballsbridge, Dublin 4, very close to the penthouse apartment at Merrion Village that became her home. She, like her other siblings, learnt the retail trade at the Patrick Street branch, where she became known for barking orders at travelling salesmen. When she moved to Dublin, she was given more responsibility in textiles. She also ran children's wear for a time and developed a reputation as a hard task-master. According to a number of insiders, who worked for Dunnes at the time or as consultants and who helped provide material for the book on condition of anonymity, she may have been the most naturally talented retailer of the family, the one with the best eye for what would sell.

By the 1990s, however, Therese didn't spend as much time working as she did drinking, being the latest Dunne family member to fall foul of the illness of alcoholism. She arguably had too much money, more than was good for her, and from an early age: she had a wardrobe of designer clothes even as a teenager in Cork. It didn't bring her happiness or many deep friendships, despite her ability to tell a story and a love of company. She became a regular in the Berkeley Court Hotel, like her parents before her, drinking heavily, thickly made-up and dressed in the most expensive couture, bought in Richard Allen's boutique on Grafton Street, before she became a customer of Ian Galvin in Brown Thomas in her final years. Angela Phelan commented that 'Therese Dunne wore her wealth', wearing expensive diamonds as if they were an everyday accessory, from retailers such as Cartier and Asprey. Snobs were dismissive of her heavy make-up and occasional loudness and her very dark tan, which she topped up regularly on trips to Barbados or Asia.

She changed her top-of-the-range Mercedes convertible every year. She owned a string of racehorses and was a regular at Irish race meetings as well as travelling to Royal Ascot and the Prix de l'Arc in Paris. Her long-time companion was Gerry McPadden, although they did not live together. He was a businessman a couple of decades older who socialised regularly on the horse racing circuit and was a particularly close friend of John Mulhern's. Therese socialised mainly within the family. She spent her Christmas holidays with her sisters and their families in Barbados, 'where she was the life and soul of the many parties', a phrase often used as a euphemism.

On 14 May 1993 – three months after Ben's removal from his top role at Dunnes – Therese crashed her Mercedes into a van at Pembroke Cottages, at the junction of Nutley Lane and Merrion Road, outside St Vincent's Hospital. The van in turn hit the car in front. The arresting Garda told the court that, when he arrived at the scene, Therese was still behind the wheel of her car. 'Her speech was incoherent, and I couldn't make out what she was saying. She was also crying.' She was unsteady on her feet when he asked her to step out – which she was only able to do with his help – and there was a strong smell of alcohol. She was arrested under Section 49 of the Road Traffic Act because the Garda had formed the opinion that she had consumed intoxicants to such an extent as to make her incapable of driving. She gave a sample at Donnybrook Garda Station to Dr Conal Hooper and it registered a blood/alcohol level of 364 mg/100 ml. This meant she was very drunk, not something to which a blind eye could be turned.

Her sister Elizabeth was said to have stopped drinking years earlier. Elizabeth Dunne first featured in the newspapers during the 1960s when she turned up at a racecourse, as a 16-year-old, wearing a white chinchilla fur coat. She attended several Dunnes Stores fashion events in the 1960s and 1970s but her profile dropped as she juggled rearing young children – and a disintegrating marriage – with responsibilities for managing the Cassidy's chain. She repositioned the brand to cater for somewhat more affluent but still price-conscious customers, in competition largely with A-Wear, run at the time by former Dunnes executive Paul Kelly. She too was known by staff as a tough task-master.

She married young, to Brian McMahon, and they moved into an expensive house on the Merrion Road in Dublin 4. He owned Blue Balloon, a confectionery company, that he renamed first as McMahon Confectionery and then as Cleeves Toffee, with both Elizabeth and Ben as directors and shareholders. The marriage became strained, however, not helped by her growing dependence on alcohol, and it came to an end bitterly, to be resolved in the courts.

In one case, heard *in camera*, he issued proceedings against her, claiming custody of their four children and an order of divorce *a mensa et thoro*. This Latin term refers to a legal separation between a husband and wife where they live apart but are not divorced. They may have separate homes and finances, but are still legally married and cannot remarry until they obtain a divorce. Civil divorce was not allowed in Ireland until 1995, but courts did put in place certain provisions to allow for the reality of marriage breakdown.

This family law case only became known because of a commercial dispute that reached the High Court in October 1986, one that signalled the financial ruin of Brian McMahon, apparently brought about by the loss of financial support from the Dunne family. Ben resigned his directorship of Cleeves in December 1983, a move clearly related to his standing by his sister as her marriage broke down. On 12 July 1985, there was a High Court petition to wind up the business and McMahon subsequently alleged that the Dunne family had conspired with banks to demand immediate repayment of loans of £300,000. McMahon claimed AIB was under pressure from the Dunne family and was an active part of the conspiracy to inflict financial ruin on him. He alleged that this was to prevent him from bringing his High Court proceedings against his wife to a conclusion. In October 1986, the master of the High Court found in favour of AIB on the basis that McMahon had given written guarantees to cover the indebtedness of Cleeves Toffee. Without money from the Dunnes, he couldn't do that.

After the separation Elizabeth moved to a big new house on nearby but even more expensive and exclusive Ailesbury Road, where she parked her silver Mercedes sports car. The support Elizabeth received from Ben during this difficult period meant that she remained his loyal supporter when he was at war with their siblings.

But Elizabeth was somewhat fragile. At the time of her death it was said that she had not consumed alcohol in years but, such is the nature of the addiction, a return to alcohol is always possible, especially at times of great stress. She had failed to give up cigarettes, despite a few efforts, and tried to keep fit by swimming each day. Given her experiences of the effects of marriage breakdown, she was appalled now by the confrontation between her siblings. At a board meeting in mid-July, which Ben did not attend, the other four learned that Elizabeth was about to holiday with Ben – flying to Portugal to join Ben and Mary on their yacht before sailing to Spain and then to Greece. The meeting wasn't acrimonious, but she came under pressure to use her access to dissuade him from attacking the family Trust.

The sibling board members may have wanted to try to resolve things in an amicable manner with Ben, as much to restore family unity as to protect the business, but he was increasingly wild in his approach, taking his fight much further. He contacted trustee Bernard Uniacke in Cork and told him that he possessed an affidavit sworn by an internal accountant in Dunnes that detailed the widespread dissipation of company funds. He alleged that his siblings knew of and engaged in the taking of funds from beyond the trust's reach, which would lead to issues of both a civil and criminal nature. 'If they are taking me out, I will take them out,' Ben told Uniacke. He threatened to seek the appointment of an inspector. Then he made a dramatic threat: to disclose 'the payment of £1m paid to a member of the previous government to influence legislation affecting the Trust'. This was a red flag.

The pressure intensified in the following days, with the need to stop Ben doing something that would alert the authorities, such as applying to court for the appointment of an inspector, being paramount. Elizabeth was regarded by her siblings as the only one who could talk sense with Ben. There were phone calls that distressed Elizabeth so much she cancelled appointments over the weekend before her planned Monday departure for the holiday with Ben and Mary. Her children worried that she had become somewhat incoherent. She took to bed on the Sunday, asking her children to check on her regularly. On their second visit to her room, at 1am, they found her unresponsive. An ambulance was summoned, and she was removed promptly to St Vincent's Hospital. She was pronounced dead soon after arrival, a heart attack the attributed cause. Friends said it was the stress that broke her heart, aged just 46.

Former Taoisigh Charlie Haughey and Jack Lynch were among the mourners at the Church of the Sacred Heart in Donnybrook on 28 July and many Fine Gael TDs and ministers attended, too. The funeral was sombre, bereft of music. Her daughter Sharon and sons Brian, Paul and John sat on the right-hand side of the church alongside their mother's siblings, including Anne and Ben, who was on crutches after another mishap, and all their various children. Her estranged husband sat on the left-hand side and his son Brian, then a 20-year-old medical student, spoke: 'Our mother was a peacemaker at home with Frank, Margaret, Ben and Therese. She was also the peacemaker in Dunnes Stores. We intend to continue that legacy.' Sharon revealed that her mother demurred when the family urged her to accept public recognition for her charity work. 'She never wanted to be remembered or talked about for her giving, she truly gave of herself,' said Fr William Bradley. 'Liz died at an early age, but she packed so much into those years. Very few of us will be able to do as much.' Although she and Brian were separated, her wedding and engagement rings remained on her hand for the cremation; her Catholicism meant that she regarded her sacramental marriage as unbreakable.

After the funeral Ben didn't go to the Berkeley Court Hotel, where the family gathered with close friends. 'I was on the boat in Portugal at about 1am on Monday when Mark [his son] called to say Brian (her son) had called him to say Liz had died. I was devastated,' he told the *Sunday Tribune*. The newspaper printed a tribute to Elizabeth from Ben, one that read as if dictated over the phone: 'There were two people in my family who supported me, my father and my sister Liz. My two biggest supporters for the past year have been Liz and Noel Smyth. Before she died, she told me she felt ostracised. I was always very close to her. Liz had had her problems, but she had her life under control. She was a really good person; she supported me publicly when a lot of people would only support me privately. She was a woman who knew her own mind. She knew the best of me and the worst of me, that's why our relationship was strong.

'Liz was of great assistance to me when I came back from Florida. She was forthright and we told each other everything, personal things. I pledged to her that I was clean of drugs. I said to her that if she ever doubted me, she was to ask me to be tested. She must have had her doubts about me and I'd love her to have asked me once to prove myself.

'Liz visited me a lot in hospital. The two of us were very close friends. We had the connection, when a friend is in trouble you don't call for them, you're there with them.'

Ben said that, had he been asked to give a eulogy, he would have said that he was lonely without her. He described her as bright, honest and generous, 'she was no freewheeling supporter, she was like my best pal. She told me when I was right and when I was wrong.'

No pictures were carried in any of the daily newspapers of the funeral and very little was written. Peter Owens, who ran an advertising agency that had a contract with Dunnes for an advertising spend worth over £1m per annum, contacted the newspapers 'in a personal capacity' and asked them to respect the family's privacy. This angered Ben. 'Peter Owens is not a personal friend of this Dunne family,' Ben said within days to the *Sunday Tribune*. 'He came up to me at my sister's funeral and introduced himself, but I had not met him previously, to the best of my knowledge.' Ben said that he had phoned Owens and demanded that he contact all recipients of the correspondence and tell them it was not sent at his behest.

Owens responded to queries from the *Sunday Tribune*, which had not just ignored his request but made it a story in itself: 'If Ben Dunne wants to cause trouble that is his problem. I was instructed quite clearly. I was asked to do a favour. Ben Dunne is trying to stir it up. I'm merely telling you that I, as a longtime friend of the family going back to the grandfather of the Dunnes, was asked to do a charitable act, I was instructed by the whole Dunne family. He, for his own good reason, is complaining. I did precisely what I was asked to do.'

It seemed that Elizabeth's death had brought any chances of concili- ation to an end, as she was the bridge between the warring siblings.

'I just want what's legally right for me, what is just. If I got the money, I'd go,' Ben said. 'I have no interest in going back as chairman. They removed me as chairman, then they removed me as an executive director. As a director I want Dunnes Stores to succeed but I have very little to do with it now. The position is that Liz is gone as a director of Dunnes Stores. She has gone to the next world. I didn't resign from anything. I was sacked.'

In that interview Ben denied suggestions, which he said had been made by members of his family, that he had taken drugs after his arrest in Florida. 'If anyone has any doubts about me at any time, I just want them to say it. There is an undercurrent to all this that I was ripping off the company. All that will be cleared up. That is the great thing about a company: there are minutes of every board meeting. Liz's word is there. And everyone else's. The business when I ran it was well run and honestly run. Look at my track record and you'll see the vast majority of my deals were good deals.'

He might have been correct about his business achievements, but he was lying about the drugs. He was using cocaine. The crutches had been explained in the newspapers by a story that he had broken both his ankles jumping into the shallow end of a swimming pool; journalists who reported it could not prove otherwise. In fact, Ben had been drinking heavily and using cocaine, and he knew well that the public disclosure of this would cause legal complications with the terms of his release by the US courts following his arrest in Orlando.

At one of our meetings, I asked how he really broke his ankles. Ben told me how he had struggled over the years to cope with the aftermath of the IRA kidnap and how the memories often resurfaced. He described how he had been drinking and using cocaine on his own at home – Mary was away – when he had suffered a panic attack, brought on by combination of the alcohol, the cocaine and lack of sleep. He explicitly linked his panic directly to his kidnapping. He had a permanent team of security at his home to provide protection, but in his panic he believed these men were from the IRA and had come to kidnap him again. He told me how he tried to escape from them and how, with the electrically controlled entrance gates closed, he climbed the perimeter wall as his minders chased him in a vain effort to prevent him from doing harm to himself. He jumped off the wall. It was about a 12-foot drop, and he suffered his injuries as his considerable weight crushed his ankles when he landed. I did not write the story at the time because he asked me not to do so. He told the story partially years later in a TV interview with Eamon Dunphy, during the period when he became something of a media personality.

The truth was that Ben never stopped drinking and never properly addressed his issues with alcohol, always believing he had it under control, despite plenty of evidence to the contrary. The stress was telling on him, too – just as it was on Therese and as it had on Elizabeth. When I had my dealings with Ben in the 1990s, his favourite tipple was pints of Heineken that he diluted with large ice cubes in an effort to moderate his intake. He told me on one occasion how he would also drink through the night with friends and head for 'early houses' – pubs that had special license to open at 7.30am – in areas such as Smithfield, near the old fruit markets. Even while he was attending at the Mater Private for treatment for his broken ankles, he often slipped out to nearby pubs on Dorset Street in a wheelchair for pints. He also headed on one occasion for lunch with Haughey at the latter's home, Abbeville at Kinsealy. That would be a visit with extraordinary consequences. Indeed, it was later reported that Haughey had pushed Ben in his wheelchair around the perimeter of the lake outside the mansion – an image somewhat hard to believe given the disparity in size and Haughey's haughtiness. Haughey said that if he knew what was to follow, he would have pushed Ben into the lake.

27.

Bad blood

MICHAEL IRWIN WAS BEN'S 'eyes and ears' within the Dunnes Stores organisation and that made him a marked man as far as Margaret was concerned. An accountant, he was seconded to Dunnes from Oliver Freaney's practice in 1984 and given the task of implementing new management systems and chairing an IT development group. He reported to Ben and Fox and was belatedly given the title of chief accountant when, worried about what has happening during 1992, he sought confirmation of his position. After Ben's departure, Irwin was told to report to Margaret and Frank, but he remained in contact with his former boss.

The day after Elizabeth's funeral, Margaret asked Irwin to help her 'get Ben back'. Irwin refused, saying that shouldn't be his responsibility. This confirmed for Margaret where his loyalties lay, although she also made no further efforts to try to persuade Ben to return to the fold. Irwin alleged that Margaret deliberately made his life difficult after that, phoning him at meetings, asking him where he was, what he was doing, and who he was with.

Margaret wasn't wrong to believe that he continued to give Ben information, which Ben demanded as a shareholder. On 20 September 1993, Margaret told Irwin he was no longer to talk to Ben about the company or provide financial information to him, but she refused Irwin's request to put that in writing. Ben was told not to contact Irwin, that he was to receive information only from the board or Pat O'Donoghue, the latest accountant to have arrived from Oliver Freaney but who Ben believed was essentially Margaret's personal accountant.

On Monday, 27 September 1993 there was a dinner at the annual outing of the St Bernard Golf Society, where senior managers and key suppliers were invited for a day's sport with the money raised given to charity. Ben and his nephew, Brian McMahon, Elizabeth's son, were the only family attendees. Ben made a short speech in which he said business was about more than management, it was about leadership. It struck those attending as a public challenge ... and those who weren't there and heard about it afterwards.

In early October, O'Donoghue refused to give Ben sales figures. Within days, Margaret and Frank moved against Irwin and Niall Walsh, the grocery division's chief accountant, who was regarded also as remaining loyal to Ben. Frank refused to tell Irwin why they were sacking him and told him to leave the premises immediately. When Irwin came back to work the following day, he found the locks to his office had been changed, as had Walsh's. He received a legal letter telling him he had not carried out instructions from the directors, a charge he rejected. He began his own legal proceedings. Irwin accused Margaret and Frank of sacking him in order to exclude Ben from involvement in the company and not because of any 'bona fide belief' that it would be good for Dunnes. He claimed his dismissal was unlawful and unjustified.

Simultaneously, Margaret and Frank had to deal with the prospect of an external legal challenge. Willie Fagan, director of Consumer Affairs, informed the company that he had received information that required him to investigate Dunnes' treatment of suppliers on their credit terms. The 1987 Groceries Order required suppliers to have fixed credit terms, with which the multiples had to comply. Dunnes was taking about £50m of groceries from suppliers each month. If it took an extra 15 days' credit, this would mean it was £25m overdue in payments to suppliers, money on which Dunnes could earn interest in the bank. It wasn't clear if creditors were being strung out or the management controls at the company had failed as senior accountants left, but either way it was another headache for Margaret and Frank because it struck to the heart of how Dunnes made much of its profits.

Then a big legal action came from Ben. After Irwin and Walsh's dismissals, he secured two High Court temporary injunctions to prevent Dunnes from dismissing any further key executives and to stop the group from spending more than £500,000 without first getting a valid board resolution. He claimed the dismissals were motivated by 'ill-will and malice' towards him by Margaret and Frank and had not followed correct procedures. He claimed they had sought repeatedly to undermine his position as a director and that Margaret had removed the key to his personal office in front of him and two independent witnesses. He did not believe Margaret and Frank's actions 'had been motivated by any consideration or desire for the company's well-being but had been prompted by ill-will and malice towards him in securing his lawful entitlements'.

He further claimed that profits of Dunnes during 1993 to that point had fallen £13m and there had been a significant decline in its market share. He said the group had committed to £30m in capital expenditure without a proper resolution of the directors, which he called 'questionable and foolhardy in the extreme'. He also raised a technical point about board approval being required for any staff appointment at an annual rate of pay of more than £30,000.

Ben gilded the lily somewhat in his claims regarding the profits. Interest rates collapsed during 1993 from the extraordinary double-digit highs they had reached during the 'currency crisis' of 1992, prior to a devaluation of the pound in early 1993. Much of Dunnes' profit in 1992 was earned by the overnight interest rates paid by the banks on the enormous cash reserves of the business.

Margaret responded by accusing Ben of actions 'calculated to cause extreme damage to the business', something Ben had always denied he would do, and said that his actions were intolerable.

Ben's original injunction was secured on as an *ex parte* basis, whereby the judge reaches a decision without the other party present in court to argue against the claims. There was nothing unusual in this mechanism, it was simply to prevent actions happening that would be of disadvantage to the claimant before a full hearing took place. The denials and counter-allegations issued by Margaret and Dunnes Stores were headline-grabbers that dominated newspaper headlines for days.

In a statement to the court that made for extraordinary headlines when disclosed, Margaret related a story of how Ben had charged, uninvited, into a meeting she was hosting with milk suppliers from Waterford Foods. She alleged that Ben 'burst' into the room and announced that, as a 20% shareholder, he was there to see what was going on. Margaret said she was gravely embarrassed, apologised to her guests, and told them that the meeting would have to pause. Ben sat down and extinguished his cigarette in Margaret's glass of mineral water. He told his sister, 'I am here, and I am going to do more of this, and you had better get used to it.' So much for him being terrified of her.

O'Donoghue's own statement, in support of Margaret, claimed he had never experienced 'such vile and offensive personal abuse' as he was subjected to by Ben. He related that he was in a meeting with Irwin and Walsh when he took a call from Ben. The phrase 'you fucking bollocks' was roared a number of times by Ben. After O'Donoghue hung up, Ben then entered the room, 'disrupted the meeting and proceeded to direct extremely vile abuse' and 'generally ranted on in an extremely agitated manner'. Ben apparently shouted at other managers to affirm their support for Irwin and Walsh 'and referred in an incoherent way to court proceedings and affidavits'. He threatened to 'destroy' O'Donoghue in the witness-box and suggested that he 'think hard' about how Ben was a 'street fighter' and would not lose any battle. After about 30 minutes of this tirade, Ben left. Margaret let fly in her affidavit, making the possibility of reconciliation less likely than ever. 'I regret to say however that far from building up its commercial strength, the actions of the plaintiff within the past two years or so were calculated to cause extreme damage to the business,' she alleged. In relation to Ben's claim about the £30,000 salaries, she said this had been ignored for years and that Ben had made staff appointments of this rate many times without consulting the board. She said the injunction was obtained on an entirely false basis. She claimed it was untrue for Ben to allege that seven capital expenditure proposals had not been discussed adequately at the board level. The minutes showed he had attended some of the meetings and had received minutes of the others. She said she did not challenge Ben's account of 'his regrettable behaviour' in the US except to point out 'that the personal trauma was not limited to himself but reflected adversely on the rest of the family and on the company.' This may have been her most revealing comment. She complained, too, that Ben had failed to mention that, when he'd finished rehab treatment, he had submitted a statement via Noel Smyth that he had 'stepped down' as joint managing director. She accused him of furnishing the court with 'an entirely false picture'.

Margaret also made an issue of his Asian buying spree of late 1992, despite having praised him publicly at the time. She claimed it was 'a form of discount buying which was inconsistent with the company policy of improving quality' involving 'serious and damaging commitments' for the company. She said she had tried to cancel the contracts, but when a supplier came to Dublin for meetings, Ben had failed to show up. While Frank and Therese did not file documents, they didn't have to; Margaret was doing so on their behalf. This tit-for-tat of allegations steadily upped the ante and set the siblings against each other in a grim fight for succession. One can only imagine what their parents would have made of it all.

In retrospect, not enough attention was being paid by all parties to the stress under which they were operating, particularly the impact of Elizabeth's death, Therese's drinking and Ben's erraticism, fuelled by continued use of alcohol and cocaine. There doesn't appear to have been enough effort made at mediation. It was difficult for outsiders – such as lawyers and accountants – and inside managers to advise caution and restraint when emotions were so high. Measured advice wasn't always heeded and it would have been a brave person who would have told their clients or bosses that they needed to cop themselves on. If there was a family trait that everyone shared, it was stubbornness.

While the family were making headlines for their legal spat, Therese had her own issue to face in the courts, criminal not civil. Therese's drink-driving case still had to be heard and that would be another public embarrassment. Remarkably, however, when her case was due to come to trial, evidence required for the prosecution disappeared from a Garda station. It took three attempts to prosecute the case before Garda James McElroy went into the District Court and complained that 'summonses keep disappearing in connection with these charges. Somebody has been interfering with this case internally'. This was an extraordinary statement, essentially implying that someone within the force was attempting to pervert the course of justice at the behest of someone from outside it.

Garda Commissioner Patrick Culligan, under pressure from politicians who realised the gravity of McElroy's allegation, ordered an inquiry, although the findings were never disclosed. Eventually, in early February 1994, Therese was disqualified from driving for a year and fined £100 by Dublin District Court. Her licence was endorsed. Therese didn't attend the court. She was represented by Eamon de Valera SC, who pleaded guilty on her behalf – after an initial indication that she would plead not guilty – and her guilty plea was accepted by the Director of Public Prosecutions (DPP). By this stage Therese already had a driver – she resented having one, believing it removed her independence and she blamed Ben for forcing the driver on her instead of taking responsibility for her own behaviour – but now she needed security as well. Nine months after her arrest she was subjected to a terrifying robbery and assault at her home that further badly damaged her confidence. Masked intruders smashed in the door of her apartment, pinned her to her bed and ripped rings off her fingers. They found more jewellery in the apartment, worth over £80,000, before they left. The trauma of that experience, on top of what was going on within the family, may have contributed to what followed for her a year later.

28.

Courtroom drama

BEN HAD BECOME CONSISTENT in his inconsistency. In August 1993 he told the *Sunday Tribune:* 'I want them to buy me out and start my own operations. I think this would be good for me and my family. Often in a marriage or business when people are not getting on, when they separate things improve and their relationship is normal.' However, his siblings believed that, as with Catholic marriage, the family owner-ship of the business was indissoluble and that going into competition with Dunnes Stores would be a sin. That's what made Ben's next feint most unlikely to succeed.

In late December 1993, he made an offer to his siblings to buy the entire business from them for £320 million, in what he claimed was a tax-efficient manner. The Fianna Fáil/Labour government and its Minister for Finance Bertie Ahern had announced a highly controver-sial amnesty for anyone who had undeclared income and not paid tax on it. Those who decided to make an unpaid tax declaration would only have to pay a flat 15% tax initially, and then whatever tax might apply in the future now that Revenue knew of the existence of the hidden money. Pertinently, it did not apply just to income tax but to capital gains as well. This was a way to break up the Trust that would give money to everyone without having to pay much tax on it. He made the offer 'without prejudice' to the ongoing legal actions.

Ben's offer was rejected by Margaret and Frank. Margaret, in particular, was worried about protecting the family legacy and she didn't trust Ben to run the business properly, along the lines their father had. She didn't want her brother's money. But Ben still harboured ambitions to complete the deal and spoke about it with a widening circle of people.

I became aware of Ben's attempts to buy out his siblings early in 1994 and was able to write about the structure of the deal for the

Irish Independent. Even with the tax benefit closed because too much time had passed, Ben was prepared to offer £320m for the 80% of Dunnes he didn't own, which implied he valued his own share at £80m. It appeared an undervaluation of the entire business, an offer perhaps priced according to his ability to raise money. Two English venture capital funds were willing to provide €120m in equity for about 40% ownership of the company. For his 60%, Ben would borrow another £210m, with about £10m to cover costs. To prove his bona fides to potential investors, he let it be known that his corporate finance team was led by Nigel Boardman, a partner in solicitors Slaughter and May, Chris Beresford, a management buyout specialist at Peat Marwick in London, Sean Mooney, a partner at KPMG in Dublin, and Noel Smyth. Bernard Somers and Laurence Crowley, two of the most well-known and respected figures in Irish corporate circles, also had roles.

His potential new co-investors had insisted on inserting severe penalty clauses into any agreement in the event of his behaviour not matching his promises and their stated expectations. This would include a requirement to sell his shareholding to the other investors at a discounted price in certain circumstances. While he would hold the position of chief executive, it was proposed that a full-time executive chairman would be appointed as well, along with a board packed with reputable non-executive directors.

Ben didn't want to just buy the assets of the Trust, he wanted to include Ringmahon in the deal. Ringmahon owned a chain of stores trading under the Dunnes name but held separately to the Trust, including Neville Bakeries and Newbridge Foods, a frozen food company that supplied frozen burgers, pies and pizzas to Dunnes following a £9m investment. Ringmahon allowed the family members to pay themselves generous dividends without seeking the approval of the trustees. In 1991 it made profits of around £6m on sales of close to £90m.

Margaret and Frank decided they needed as much information as possible to confirm or rebut a series of allegations made by Ben over the previous year, but particularly the claims made to Uniacke and, as would later emerge in public, to Irwin and which both had reported to Margaret and Frank. They also wanted to know what had happened within the company without their knowledge. Margaret contacted Tom Grace – a former rugby international – at one of the country's biggest accountancy practices, Price Waterhouse, and asked him to investigate. What was later to become famous as the Price Waterhouse report began its life with the innocuous formal title, *A report on cheques drawn on Dunnes Stores Ulster Bank No 7 Trade Overheads Account*. The accountants examined the books as presented to them, conducted interviews and found a number of questionable payments.

Ben could have accepted his exile at that point and taken an income from the Trust (and Ringmahon and other ventures he co-owned with siblings), but that might not have been enough to fund his lifestyle, not when he charged much of it, such as private planes and helicopters, to the business and had become used to the additional cash from the side ventures to the Trust where he had lost control over their distributions. He was also aged just 44 and wanted to run a business because it was all he knew how to do, and better this established one than a new one, if possible. He was caught in a bind. If he couldn't negotiate the purchase of the company from the family, he faced the possibility of owning shares that he couldn't sell, leaving him without the money to fund his lifestyle and to invest in a new business. He had to introduce some leverage, to force the situation to deliver a better outcome. He decided once again to go the legal route, but this time he did so with a gamble that was even bigger than those he made on the golf course and with far more than money at stake, now that reputations were on the line too. What Ben did next was quite unlike anything seen before or since in a major Irish business.

Law often has little to do with justice. Instead, the legal process allows one party to enforce their position over another, not just because the law is on their side but because they have greater stomach for the fight or the resources to conduct it. Both sides had enormous financial reserves, so Ben had to persuade his siblings that he was willing to do or say things they wouldn't to win the fight. He had to persuade them of the seriousness of his craziness, that he was willing to be a corporate suicide-bomber. Then his siblings would have to decide if they could call his bluff.

Ben retained some of the country's most eminent trial and commercial lawyers, including Dermot Gleeson, Peter Kelly, Paul Gallagher and John Trainor, to make his case, or rather cases, because there were a number of legal avenues to be explored.

His first case was against the trustees. The second involved a claim for damages from his fellow directors because of alleged oppression of his rights as a minority shareholder. The expectation was that the dirt would not be thrown in the first case but in the second. In the first, he alleged the establishment of the Trust in 1964 was a 'sham' and its extension in 1985 was improper and had no legal effect; that it failed to operate as a genuine discretionary trust; that the trustees failed to maintain control over the Trust and its assets, allowing him and other family members to use its assets; that it was set up to keep assets out of the reach of the Revenue Commissioners; that there was a serious conflict of interest because the trustees acted as personal and professional advisers to some members of the family. In his oppression proceedings, he alleged a complete breakdown in trust that had resulted in his exclusion from the affairs of Dunnes Stores. He alleged that he had been removed as chairman without notice.

He anticipated that victory in a court case would bring either an order that his siblings buy his shares or pay him damages. Defeat would be expensive – costs incurred and sibling relationships damaged further. But, crucially, he would remain a part-owner of Dunnes Stores even if the actions failed.

In April 1994, the High Court ordered that the legal action being taken by Ben be split into two separate trials: the first to deal with his allegation that the Trust fund holding the Dunnes assets was null and void; the second to hear his allegations that he was oppressed as a shareholder and seeking relief and damages. The date for the first trial was set for 15 November 1994.

In taking his legal action Ben had assembled a Pandora's box and keeping a lid on it after he had stuffed it with serious allegations would prove impossible. The whole process was meant to be confidential, known only to the court, but the circle of knowledge spread too widely. Margaret and Frank had rarely had problems keeping confidential information in a tightly sealed circle, but the problem was that Ben, in his wildness, might make the contents public if it suited him, assuming, of course, that he got his hands on the Price Waterhouse report, something that would have backed up his most sensational allegations. In October 1994 that came to pass when a judge decided that the report's contents would be available to both plaintiffs and defendants in the legal actions due to be heard the following month. All of this was done away from the glare of the media.

Once he had possession of the Price Waterhouse report, Ben decided it wasn't enough and that he had to up the ante. It was now that he gambled, much as he did on the golf course except this time with much greater jeopardy and appalling potential consequences. He decided to add allegations about major payments to former Taoiseach Charles Haughey. But that in itself was not enough. He needed to emphasise in any threat of court action that he had not acted alone in making cheque payments to Haughey from company funds, that he had the full authority of the board to make whatever payments he believed were necessary to further the interests of Dunnes Stores or the family Trust.

He alleged that four separate payments were made from Dunnes Stores accounts to foreign accounts and that Haughey was the ultimate beneficiary once the money had washed through. He alleged that: in July 1988 stg£471,000 was paid from a Swiss account into an account in Barclays Bank in Knightsbridge, payable to a Mr John A. Furze; in 1988/89 stg£250,000 was paid from Dunnes Stores in Bangor to Furze; in May 1989 stg£150,000 was paid into an account in the Royal Bank of Scotland in Threadneedle Street in London in the name of another bank, Henry Ansbacher & Co; in 1990/91 stg£200,000 was paid from an Isle of Man account into an account in Henry Ansbacher & Co in London.

The total payments came to stg£1.071 million, or more than IR£1.1 million. Ben said he had executed three of the four payments and that the fourth payment – the one initiated in Northern Ireland – was undertaken on his instructions by a Dublin accountant.

But that wasn't all that Ben did as he tried to exert maximum pressure on his siblings to settle with him.

In the statement of claim to the High Court in September 1994, which was not disclosed to the public in advance of any trial, Ben also alleged his siblings instructed him to pay money into overseas bank accounts, which was then transferred into accounts beneficially owned by some of the directors but held in fictitious names. He alleged that

Frank had instructed him to pay £650,000 from a Hong Kong-registered company into an account in an unnamed Swiss bank and that Frank had received regular payments from two Dunnes Stores accounts held at the Ulster Bank, College Green in Dublin. He alleged that Margaret had instructed him on occasion to make payments to her from Wytrex in Hong Kong and that the bank drafts were made out in fictitious names lodged from an account held by her in the Bank of Ireland branch in O'Connell Street, Dublin. He alleged she had used the name Caroline Dunne and a special arrangement was made with the bank for the handling and processing of that account. He said Therese had instructed him to make payments from bank accounts held by Wytrex to accounts in her name. He claimed she had also received bank drafts and cheques made out in fictitious names, which were accounts in her name and an account controlled by Margaret, and transferred into an account of which the ultimate beneficiary was Therese. He also alleged that payment for Therese's American Express card account was discharged from the accounts of companies within the Dunnes Stores Group.

All allegations of financial impropriety were vigorously denied by Frank, Margaret and Therese in their responses. As far as they were concerned, the Price Waterhouse report made it look like Ben had been solely responsible for all the dodgy dealings at the company. In response, Ben had to make it clear that he had not acted alone. He did not draw the money for Des Traynor, Haughey's right-hand man, without the help of others, especially Noel Fox. And here was the key claim: others in the family knew of his payments to Haughey. That was his ace card, as he saw it, that the others knew and approved. Would they fold if the card was played, as it would be if a case went to trial?

In early November, as the public hearing of the case loomed, everyone saw sense. Armageddon had to be averted. A settlement had to be found. The lawyers negotiated. Margaret and Frank normally agonised over reaching decisions, and hated for things not to go their way, but they realised they had to settle and pay Ben. They agreed either £100m or £125m, depending on what reports were to be believed because it was never formally revealed in court. On Ben's behalf, senior counsel Dermot Gleeson stood up in the High Court in November 1994 and announced that he was withdrawing all claims and allegations to the effect that the trustees, or any of them, were at any time negligent or that they were in breach of their fiduciary duties. Significantly, his siblings did not disavow the content of their counter-claim against him, the fundamental plank of which was that Ben alone was responsible for every wrong that had been done and that only he among the siblings had knowledge of what he was doing.

The Trust wasn't broken up immediately by the settlement, which meant that a CAT bill did not come into play. Essentially, Ben was paid to give up his claim or entitlement to ownership of part of the Trust, and its benefits passed to the other existing members. Ben received his settlement over a number of years, allowing the family to fund it from the company cash flow. He may have received more money than almost anyone could dream of getting in a lifetime, and yet he settled cheaply, for a fraction of what the company would become worth.

After the case was settled, Ben spoke in metaphorical terms about the experience: 'If you had an operation, you get back to your good health, but the scars are always there. You could always look at them.' For the first time in four decades, Ben was not involved in Dunnes Stores. The company that he saw as his birthright, as his identity, as his direct link to his father and all he wanted as his legacy for his family was no longer part of his life. It was over for him. He had to make a new life, one in which he was estranged from his siblings, his power, status and, to an extent, his reason for living.

What Ben didn't know then was that the scars would be ripped open again and become heavy wounds. The claims and allegations in his threatened legal action, and the evidence assembled to support and rebut those claims, would all tumble into the public arena two years later, this time with extraordinary consequences.

PART 5

Power Plays

1995–1999

29.

More tragedy, more conflict

MARGARET WANTED TO SHOW that life went on without Ben and that she was now the boss. Alongside Therese, but without Frank, she hosted a 50th birthday celebration for Dunnes Stores on 20 April 1994, when the family's legal disputes were still raging. More than 1,000 people were brought to supper at the State Apartments of Dublin Castle – made available on the instruction of Taoiseach Albert Reynolds – having been first treated to a variety show by the Dunnes Stores' Tops of the Town at the Olympia Theatre.

In her speech, Margaret remembered only Elizabeth: 'She was too nice to be a Dunne.' It was a rare moment of public reflection and even emotion, a lament for her sister, but also perhaps a personal reprimand for what she felt she herself had become in running the business. Her other siblings didn't get a mention, not even Frank. She was defiant in her prediction: 'Have no fear, during the next 50 years Dunnes Stores will continue to go from strength to strength. It will continue to be an Irish company, despite anything you might have heard. There will be no takeover by English companies. We will continue to grow and we will, as always, continue to give the Irish people better value. I know that's what my father would have wanted.' She had many motivations, but that reference to her father was pointed, then and for the future.

She also had Dunnes sponsor the Horse Show Ball and a Hockey World Cup tournament, something Ben would have seen as utterly inappropriate to the market the company served. They may have played well in the circles in which Margaret moved though, and Therese, who retained her love of hockey, may have been involved in this too, as much as an effort by Margaret to give her sister something to keep her engaged as an expression of Therese's own interest.

If those might have been regarded as superficial displays, Margaret was implementing major changes in operations at Dunnes Stores. She and Frank were now joint managing directors, with Therese a director, but essentially it gave Margaret far more freedom in her decision-making, even if she ran everything by Frank and didn't proceed unless he approved.

She spent undisclosed sums on upgrading the stores, assumed to run into tens of millions of pounds, all paid with cash flow and no borrowings. She converted the Cassidy's women's clothing and fabric stores to Dunnes Stores' draperies, which in turn went more upmarket. She ran the risk of alienating existing customers while not attracting enough replacements, especially as the new customers were expected to spend more. It left open the speculation as to whether there would be room for a more traditional, old-style Dunnes.

'It's a question of whether you can run one Dunnes Stores in one area with more upmarket clothing and another in a different area with more traditional stock,' said one observer, 'but they have plenty of locations where it is possible to vary type of clothing. They could have a mix of newer, more upmarket clothing and some of the more tradi-tional stuff which they've always done.' There was some confusion as to what Dunnes offered, however. The clothing and food offerings did not necessarily match; those prepared to buy from the new, more expensive Dunnes clothing collections might not necessarily want to purchase St Bernard own-brand foods in a downmarket food store, the latter being one of Margaret's major innovations.

In Margaret's first year in charge, the Dunnes Stores' share of the grocery market fell from 24% to 20%, despite greater investment in advertising, which went up from £1.1m in 1992 to £1.8m in 1993 and was higher again the following year. 'Better quality, better value' replaced the old mantra, suggesting that Margaret wouldn't always stick slavishly to her late father's ways, although at the same time any change was careful and minimal. She introduced new products, such as St Bernard's Cola and Corn Flakes, and marketed them aggressively. Ben would have responded to an erosion in market share by targeted price-cutting instead of putting money into launching new brands that would have to go head-to-head with internationally established names. While Ben might have gone to court to secure cut-price milk supplies, it's unlikely he would have become embroiled in a legal dispute with Kellogg's about the use of the trade name 'pops' in cereals. Insiders said far more attention was given to the sourcing of goods for quality, with upgraded packaging in many lines adding to costs.

More pertinently, some insiders complained, *sotto voce* of course, of a sense of drift within the company. Margaret told remaining management there would be more delegation and consultation, but the opposite happened. Financial information was more tightly controlled. Direct telephone lines were removed; all calls had to go through the company switchboard. In Ben's time the business had been run to a simple formula backed up by a management information system that showed exact profit-and-loss breakdowns for every department of every store. Remaining Ben loyalists complained that the business was now run by obscurely worded memos that indicated a degree of distrust.

Frank got a lot of the blame. He was pedantically cost-conscious, but took ages to make a decision, and after his lengthy absence from day-to-day management many of his ideas were regarded as old-fashioned. He struggled, and then others did because of that. His inability to take on more than one problem at a time was a major handicap. The cliché 'paralysis by analysis' could have been invented for him. Frank 'presented as grumpy, but in reality, he was shy and didn't communicate well,' an associate from that era told me. 'He was somewhat neurotic. He behaved far older than he was, had that bearing, was very low on energy and seemed always weary.'

Margaret, in her desire not to fall out with Frank, indulged it. Insiders told a story, perhaps apocryphal, but believable, about the time Margaret and Frank were presented with a proposal and adjourned to the boardroom to deliberate. They eventually emerged with the news that they had decided to reject it, adding 'but we want it to be known that this was not a unanimous decision'. This was reported at the time as 'bizarre', but it actually made sense. Margaret had wanted to implement the proposal but when Frank wouldn't agree, she wouldn't force it. Margaret was very conscious of keeping Frank happy. 'I've lost one brother, I'm not losing the other,' she remarked to one colleague who had expressed frustration that Frank had stopped Margaret from doing something that everybody agreed was necessary.

The same associate described Margaret to me as '85 per cent brilliant, 15 per cent irrational' – the latter if she was distracted – 'but easily one of the most impressive businesspeople I've ever come across. Her nose for what was needed was almost always correct and her work ethic was extraordinary.'

Margaret and Frank shared a long, narrow office, with a single table at which they sat at opposite ends. On the table were up to six landline units and, to the amusement of some, an actual red phone with its own non-switchboard number to be used for what the duo would have considered corporate emergencies – as if they were going to deploy the nuclear codes. Margaret was regarded by her colleagues as very confident and self-assured, but she had to be persuaded gently to do something she mightn't have thought of herself: nobody, either internal or external to the organisation, was going to tell her what to do. Her father, from whom she had learnt everything in business since she was a teenager, seemed to be her touchstone. Whatever views he held, about unions for example, were often hers, as if by osmosis. A senior manager named Bill McGuinness was seen as something of a 'Margaret whisperer', his ability to remain calm in almost all circumstances regarded as vital in reassuring other managers as to her overall good intentions.

Margaret made important changes notwithstanding Frank's reluctance, such as hiring Andersen Consulting in 1995 to overhaul management systems. She realised that a proper information and point-of-sale system would yield big savings in ordering stock, storage and management of logistics. New tech like checkout scanning equipment had to be introduced, but this needed competent management, not consultants. Clearing out Ben's loyalists as management was one thing, finding replacements was another. Margaret and Frank went back to the future when they forgave a former rising star in the organisation for his defection to Quinnsworth, where he had risen to the position of chief executive, and brought him back.

Dick Reeves qualified as a barrister before joining Dunnes as a buyer, a position he held for 14 years. In 1983 he was poached by Don Tidey to join ABF's Quinnsworth, and he succeeded Tidey as chief executive. He was regarded as a big success in the job because ABF saw its 'share of stomach' (the trade's expression for market share) rise significantly under his direction. ABF sold quality goods at Quinnsworth, where he was credited with introducing premium brand labels, and sold at low prices at Crazy Prices, bringing market share for the sister stores to 25%.

Reeves had previously got on well with Frank. His mantras were quality and margin. Now in his early 50s, he brought with him knowledge of Dunnes' biggest competitor and of purchasing deals with suppliers. Frank acted upon the latter, phoning many to demand better terms along the lines he now knew were given to Quinnsworth. Aside from fresh food suppliers, there are about 40 main suppliers to the large retail multiples, making for a significant overlap. Speculation was that Reeves would be paid about £500,000 per annum on a five-year deal. He was not granted any shares or options, however: they were for family only.

Reeves came back to what appeared to be a lesser title than he had enjoyed at Quinnsworth: director of food. The key word was director. He was now part of the board, along with another new hire, Andrew Street, the former director of information systems at Boots in the UK, who was to fill the same role for Dunnes and for logistics too. Financial controller Margaret Davin arrived from the Kerry Group but was not given a board position (and departed in May 2001 for a position at Horse Racing Ireland). Nigel Reddy joined as the first ever marketing director from McConnell's advertising agency but left within a year to take up a new position as an executive with the Dimension agency. A while later Diarmuid Ryan joined from Pepsi-Cola International, where he had been director of international resourcing and development, although his time with the company would prove short-lived, too. He was one of a number of senior hires under Margaret's watch who would either leave or be let go within a year of arriving, an assessment as to their ability and loyalty made. His appointment meant that, for the first time, the members of the Dunne family were in a board minority, holding two family positions alongside three outsiders, not that in reality it made an enormous difference; in this family business, two votes would beat three.

These board appointments were still significant, being the first non-family members to formally join and get votes, even if others, such as Fox, continued to attend meetings. Both Frank and Margaret remained somewhat suspicious of outsiders. But at least they had made a commitment to share the burden with those not from the family gene pool, for now at least. Other managers who played a key role at the time and who gained Margaret's trust were Pat O'Donoghue as head of finance, Mary South as head of human resources, John McNiffe, Linda O'Keeffe and Darina Walsh.

Margaret oversaw all this while affected by yet another family tragedy. Therese's death, on 16 September 1995 at the age of 44, was a deeply distressing affair for her family and friends. The Dublin Coroner's Court was told that she had battled alcohol addiction but had finally 'come to terms' with her difficulty before her tragic death. Barrister Richard Nesbitt, representing her estate, said her body was found in her apartment. A post-mortem found no alcohol had been consumed, and that death was due to obstructive asphyxia caused by the inhalation of gastric contents. The vomiting was probably brought on by a severe fatty liver. Gerry McPadden, her long-time companion, recalled how he was unable to get an answer at her home, so he got in touch with housekeeper Sally McDonald and met her at the apartment. They found Therese in a slumped position and called an ambulance. She was removed to St Vincent's Hospital, where she was formally pronounced dead. A verdict of misadventure was returned.

After Therese's death, Angela Phelan wrote that 'many felt that Therese had a troubled life. She was devastated by her sister's death in 1993; some say a depression descended on her at that time from which she never recovered. While she didn't seem outwardly upset by the split between Ben and Margaret, in reality the feud affected her greatly.' Therese was buried in Glasnevin alongside her parents, after a funeral mass celebrated by Fr Gerry O'Brien and Fr Dermod McCarthy in front of just dozens of family and friends. To Ben's anger, and some surprise among others, Dunnes Stores remained open on the day of her funeral, breaking the precedent set to mark the funerals of their parents and Elizabeth.

Unfortunately, Therese's death did not bring her surviving siblings back to each other. When Therese's estate was disclosed in November 1995 it was given a valuation of £22.5m, but that didn't tell the full story. She left her 265 preference shares in Dunnes Stores to Margaret and Elizabeth, but had not updated her will after Elizabeth died, so all of those shares went to Margaret. There was nothing for her other sister, Anne, or her brothers, who received separate bequests from her property portfolio and who would have inherited the preference shares had Margaret pre-deceased them.

Ben had reason to challenge the will. Margaret, as executrix, had each share valued at £1, the par value when the Trust was established. However, in settling his own tax bill on the sale of his 230 preference shares, Ben had put a value of £75,000 per share on them, to reflect the passage of time and increased value of the business. This reduced his tax bill on the sale of the shares. Ben feared this lower valuation – if applied by Revenue to his own shares – might result in a much bigger CGT liability retrospectively for him. He sought Margaret's removal as executrix and corrections in her affidavit to the Revenue Commissioners claiming the value of her shares, accusing her of an 'intention to appropriate' the shares.

Ben had initial success in the High Court, when Mr Justice Smyth displaced Margaret as executrix on the grounds that otherwise it would be detrimental to the welfare of the estate and its beneficiaries. Smyth appointed an administrator, given what he described as the 'unspoken but clear antipathy' of the siblings towards each other and their propensity to litigate. He said he was not concerned with deciding the correct value of the shares. Margaret contended that the correct valuation had been returned to the Revenue but that, even if it was wrong, it was 'none of my brother's business'.

The five-judge Supreme Court unanimously reversed the High Court decision. On its behalf Mr Justice Lynch said there was no justification for Ben distrusting Margaret or losing faith or confidence in her ability to properly and fairly administer the estate. He said she had the advice and assistance of well-known and reputable solicitors, and 'no impropriety or wrongdoing had been shown in relation to the valuation of these shares' and that Ben's mistaken perception that she had done wrong could not alter the position that she had not: 'The alleged conflict of interest is flimsy in the extreme. It would be a strange state of affairs if a parent or a member of the family was not entitled to entrust the administration of their estate to a child or brother or sister just because of the nature and complications of the business enterprise.'

Lynch was correct in a general and legal sense, but this was no normal family.

Ben decided to keep busy after he settled his legal action with Dunnes in late 1994. It was probably wise: a bored Ben would have struggled to an even greater degree to deal with his addictions if his life was simply one of leisure, golf and living off the immense proceeds of the settlement.

In October 1995, he gave me an interview for the *Irish Independent* to discuss his new business plans. We sat for hours in the front room of his home and, as I recall, he was in fine fettle, although as time passed he revealed some very sensitive details about his life, without the need for too much prompting, which he asked me not to include in the article. I respected that request.

In the on-the-record part he ruled out the possibility of ever returning to food or drapery retailing: 'I have heard stories of people who sold out their interests in a business and then started out doing the same thing again and the failure rate in doing that can be very high. But I can apply the same principles in this new business as I did in the last: provide the customer with the best service possible at the best price, but I know that I'd be targeting a different customer with a different product and a different sector. If I provide quality and value for money, I believe I'll succeed.'

The new business venture was in fitness, something that was only coming into vogue at that time and for relatively small numbers of people. The interview showed, in retrospect, foresight on Ben's part about how Irish society was developing. 'People have relatively little choice in their leisure activities,' he told me. 'They go to the pub or nightclub, maybe go to a match or the cinema, but more and more people are concerned with living a healthy lifestyle and want to take exercise. There's a growing population of people in their 20s and 30s, they want to look good, feel good. There's a market there for that if you provide them with the right facilities. Look at the way the cinema business rescued itself when video became a threat to its numbers. It went out and built big, new, modern, comfortable facilities which have attracted more and more numbers. We intend doing the same in leisure.'

Ben was planning a major, 40,000 sq.ft leisure complex in west Dublin, the biggest of its kind in Ireland at the time. It was adjacent to the new Blanchardstown Town Centre – still under construction in 1995 – and he hoped to have it open within 15 months. He had already applied for planning permission to build a 25,000 sq.ft development in Kilkenny city, although that did not go ahead. He had travelled extensively with Denis McCoy, a former senior at the fruit distributors Fyffes, who had joined him as chief executive of a new company called BarkIsland, which would buy the properties and be the holding company for the gyms which traded under Ben's recognisable name. 'There may be a perception that I spent my time at the golf course but it's not true. We travelled thousands of miles throughout the country looking at possible sites. We visited centres throughout the UK and Europe looking at how it should be done. We worked regular 12- and 14-hour days. This is a full-time job. People will be expecting things of me. They know what Ben Dunne stands for: value for money and doing things properly on behalf of the customer. I want to do that again.

'I see a huge similarity with the retail business in the mid- to late 70s, when there were a lot of good smallish retail units of about 5,000–7,000 sq.ft in size serving the customer. There were plenty of supermarkets, but there weren't the superstores that the customer wanted. At Dunnes, we gave the same professional service but at much bigger stores and because of the volumes and scale we were generating we were able to provide better prices and a better range for the customer.' And make bigger profits.

He believed most existing leisure centres in Ireland weren't big enough to provide the level of service the customer wanted; too many of the large existing ones were just add-ons to hotels. Others contained too many low-yielding tennis courts, which took up too much space at the expense of other activities. Some were simply too small to allow unrestricted access to members. Ben intended to construct units of between 30,000 and 40,000 sq.ft, about twice the size of most existing premises. He believed he could pick locations with the eye and the skill he had developed with Dunnes, where he had developed more than 1 million sq.ft of property.

'We want a concept which is visually attractive and provides atmosphere. In Blanchardstown we will have a large gymnasium, a 25-metre swimming pool, a treatment room, beauty salon, coffee docks and the like, and once you pay your annual subscription that'll be it, there'll be no extra payments unless it's for things like aromatherapy,' he said, describing a model that has become commonplace. 'People won't be asked to pay extra each time they want to use the pool or get instruction and have a fitness test.' He implied the cost would be about £500 per year, per member. 'It'll cost the customer less than the price of five pints a week or two morning newspapers each day,' he said.

He was clear that he wouldn't look to maximise the numbers using his facilities. 'There must be strict control of numbers. You can't have members coming in to use the gym in the evening and then have them finding that they must wait for someone else to get off the treadmill. Members must always have the facilities available when they want them and if there are times of the day when the facilities are not being used, we won't be going after bringing corporate groups or anything like that.'

He believed that a combination of demographics and changing income patterns, as well as the facilities provided and the locations chosen, would allow him to attract the required numbers of customers. However, he made mistakes at the start, such as building expensive swimming pools that would lose money. But he had an insurance policy: purchased sites could be used for other property ventures, such as housing, even if bought primarily with leisure in mind.

'We were able to finance everything from our own resources,' he said. 'We won't need to borrow money from the bank, so we won't be under pressure to do things that we don't think are right. We won't rush in customers to start but build up our numbers gradually and reach our targets in our time. All I want is X return from my investment.' He would not say what X was. 'I could go for X + 20% but I would be cheating the customers if I did that. All I want is a fair return.'

He told me that Dunloe House had proved too restrictive a vehicle for financing his interests. Instead, Noel Smyth would take control of it for his own property ambitions. 'Stock exchange rules dictate that you can't use the shell to develop a new line of business without going to a great expense and trouble. I decided we were better off doing it in a private company.'

'This is my life now, I'm putting all my time and effort into it,' he said.

He was a salesman, and he was convincing, his confidence being somewhat infectious. McCoy joined us for the last half-hour or so of the conversation and then things took an uncomfortable turn. Ben asked me how Michael Lowry was getting on as a government minister, given that he was attracting a lot of publicity, not all of it positive. To my subsequent embarrassment, I wasn't aware of Lowry's business links to Dunnes Stores (not to mention what was to come later) and I told Ben a story of something that had happened between myself and Lowry a month previously. It was a funny story – or at least anyone else I had told privately thought that – and most certainly did not paint Lowry in a good light, but Ben's reaction surprised me at the time. He seemed almost angry about it. The atmosphere in the room changed, and the meeting did not carry on for much longer. It would be more than a year later before I would understand why.

30.

Zealous custodian and guardian

As far as Margaret was concerned, she didn't cause the strike that closed Dunnes Stores for three weeks in the summer of 1995 and she wasn't going to give way to those who had caused it, not least because her father would never have done so. Her father had managed largely, although not always, to avoid strikes, or to limit them to individual outlets, partly because he formed a good relationship with union leaders such as Owen Nulty, the head of IDATU, and was able, after arm-twisting, to reach agreements.

However, in 1994 IDATU merged with another union to form Mandate, which was headed up by Brendan Archbold. The enlarged leadership was determined to make a mark to justify the fees it was collecting from members. Controversially, it started a strike by Dublin bar workers in 1994, just as people were packing into pubs to watch Ireland play in the World Cup, the second time the country had qualified under the leadership of Jack Charlton. In 1995, Mandate wanted a new target. Nulty remained a level-headed negotiator who was respected by Dunnes, albeit from afar, but the company regarded Archbold as an abrasive character. He had wound up the family beyond leading the anti-apartheid strike, going back to an incident where he had staged a picket outside a family member's house, walking with his dog while carrying a placard that said: *This dog is treated better than a Dunnes Stores worker*. It wasn't clear if it was going to the house or the placard that caused the greater offence.

The strike in 1995 was caused by allegations of what came to be known as 'zero hours contracts', which meant part-time workers had to be available to work whenever called upon but were not guaranteed minimum employment hours. The working hours offered varied, at the discretion of management, from zero to 30 hours. Dunnes was portrayed for weeks in the extensive media coverage as a harsh employer continually squeezing its workers, totally out of step with modern, inclusive industrial relations. Margaret was both furious and disbelieving. As far as she was concerned the staff were very well paid and looked after, better than their rivals' staff, and there wasn't any more that she should be expected to give. Perhaps naively, she didn't think the public would support workers on strike, believing people would be more interested in the extended services she intended to offer.

Margaret wanted to introduce Sunday opening hours. In the UK, Sunday had become the second most popular trading day of the week after Saturday and she felt this would be replicated in Ireland. 'The attempt by Dunnes to go into Sunday trading is just an attempt to scoop up more trade, but if all the supermarkets do it, no one will be any better off they will be simply spreading six days' trade over seven,' said Michael Campbell of RGDATA. 'Sunday opening could well cause loss of business for the independents, many of whom are family stores and who have a higher proportion of full-time staff than the multiples.'

The Knights of Columbanus – a lay religious organisation that had limited, and declining, influence – issued a 'hands-off Sunday' warning and described as 'totally unacceptable' the drift by larger retailers towards the commercialisation of Sundays. Its supreme knight, William Roe, said that Sunday trading endangered the livelihood of small traders and undermined family life 'as large amoral companies worship at the shrine of their God, profit'. Bishop Brendan Comiskey – who less than a decade later would be forced by the Vatican to resign because of his part in covering up child sexual abuse by a priest in his diocese – was also to the forefront in moralising about Dunnes being open on a Sunday.

In the *Sunday Tribune* Frank Fitzgibbon argued that 'the issue of Sunday trading has become wrapped up in woolly arguments about keeping the Sabbath sacred. That notion has long since been devalued. Convenience stores have been trading on Sundays for years. So too have petrol stations, cinemas and a host of other specialist retailers. Buses run on Sunday, newspapers work on Sunday, and I understand that even the pubs are open on a Sunday. It is significant that the bishops and other groups who have managed to rouse themselves to object to

Sunday trading never sought to have the pubs closed on Sundays despite overwhelming evidence that many individuals like nothing better than to get legless on the Lord's Day. Any reasonable person would take the view that the controversy surrounding Sunday trading is a red herring. Once that point is accepted then the Dunnes issue can be brought down to a simple matter of pounds, shillings and pence, a relatively straight-forward matter.'

Margaret had followed her parents in their Catholic faith and must have taken notice of the comments from Comiskey, in particular, and Roe. It was a form of challenge to her adherence to her faith: God versus Mammon. The latter won, if only because she felt that if she lost, the entire business could be undermined. She decided to take the pain of a nationwide strike, with pickets outside every store, which only management passed, sometimes to their considerable upset.

On the question of the three-week strike, Fitzgibbon wrote: 'The Dunnes dispute is about preserving competitiveness. Secondly, it reflects the radical restructuring of the Irish employment market and, in that respect, is no different from the industrial upheavals that have taken place at Packard Electric or any other Irish company in recent years.' Fitzgibbon argued that 'the company is no worse and no better than its competitors but without a Maurice Pratt or Feargal Quinn to present its case the public is left with the impression that employment conditions in Dunnes are considerably worse than in competing companies. The personal publicity surrounding the lifestyle of the Dunnes is another factor in alienating the company from the public.'

It was a valid argument. Margaret could reply that Ben was gone, but she too was receiving vast sums of money, as he clearly had, and calling herself a simple PAYE worker would not wash. Margaret was following the example of her father – 'when you're explaining, you're losing' – but she may not have been confident enough in her abilities to convince the public, even if she emphasised that she would give them a better service at low prices. She did not want to lose control of the narrative.

What she and Dunnes was losing was market share because of increased competition, as Fitzgibbon explained: 'One of the weapons Dunnes requires to adjust this balance is increased worker flexibility and an agreement on Sunday trading. The company is seeking to change the way in which it runs this business because it believes that this better reflects the demands of its customers. Those demands have changed because the way in which people live and work has changed. Dunnes knows this and the company is prepared to offer its employees a deal in return for new agreements. The trade unions also know that things are changing but they want to be the ones to present the new package to their members. After all, if the management can go straight to the workforce, who needs a union in the first place? But that's another matter altogether.'

Industrial relations lecturer Tom Hayes called the strike 'probably the most important dispute in Irish industrial relations since the "infamous" 1969 maintenance craftsmen's strike'. Hayes described the 1969 strike as a 'watershed, ending the localised approach of industrial relations in the 1960s and ushering in, with the National Pay Agreements, the social partnership that has grown so strong in recent years. The Dunnes strike will have equally profound consequences.'

Hayes also described the issues surrounding the 'zero hours contracts' that had triggered the dispute: 'Dunnes with its very high proportion of part-time workers is almost a textbook definition of a firm with a flexible workforce. The company can call in and send home workers at a moment's notice. What Dunnes is doing is making its profits secure by making the jobs of its workers insecure. How can workers plan to take on ordinary everyday commitments if they don't know from day to day how many hours they are going to work? If Dunnes wins on these issues the unions rightly fear that it will open the floodgates to insecurity in the labour market generally, not just in the retail sector.

'The second key issue is trade union recognition. Not only does Dunnes refuse to negotiate with Mandate it also refuses to attend meetings arranged by the Labour Relations Commission and the Labour Court. The company gives the impression that the rules which we as a community have adopted for the conduct of industrial relations do not apply to it. The resolution of this dispute therefore is going to require radical new thinking on the part of the government. Dunnes is so big in terms of the Irish economy with so many people dependent on it that this dispute cannot be allowed to drag on.'

Margaret placed newspaper adverts arguing the Dunnes position, including an assertion that 'zero hours contracts have never existed.

All permanent part-time staff work regular hours and earn regular weekly incomes. The company has guaranteed basic minimum number of hours will be set.' It said there would be extra holidays and new full-time positions that would include working one Sunday in seven and every third weekend. Conditions would not change for full-time staff unless requested.

In a separate letter to Mandate, Margaret questioned the validity of the union claims, which she said were presented in a 'biased and detrimental way'. She alleged the union was engaged in an 'offensive and disdainful attempt' to diminish the Dunnes reputation and relationship with its staff. She said Dunnes always negotiated directly with staff: 'We will not passively stand by and allow a prejudiced attack go unnoticed. We remain the zealous custodian and guardian to protect the company's status and position that exists today.'

The strike became a major political issue. Since 1987 governments had sought a national consensus with unions, employers and government, with successive pacts urging wage restraint and industrial relations peace, all of which were now threatened. It wasn't just workers at Dunnes who were impacted by the strike either, suppliers and their staff were deeply affected too. As its own cashflow suffered, Dunnes delayed payments to suppliers, putting them under enormous pressure. ISME complained that businesses in the labour-intensive clothing trade would not survive a long closure because, it said, Dunnes left no margin for profit when buying from companies and small and medium firms supplying them had no reserves of capital. Controversially, the Department of Social Welfare, where the minister was socialist Proinsias de Rossa, allowed for payments to strikers under a rarely used section of the regulations. De Rossa arranged for workers to get social welfare on the basis that the strikers were unemployed, which was a stretch, but allowed by a decision that Dunnes had not observed 'normal industrial relations procedures', although they had not broken the law. It was unprecedented for the State to subsidise one side in an industrial dispute, to pay workers for not working. In addition, the union was topping up their strike pay with cash.

Margaret and Frank were in a corner. Reluctantly, Margaret turned to outside help, hiring PR consultant Pat Heneghan to deal with the media 'off-the-record'. Heneghan, in turn, told her to bring in consultants Leslie Buckley and Martin Walsh to deal with industrial relations, which she did. Buckley and Walsh opened an informal line of communication with the union.

John Douglas, who later became the leader at Mandate when Nulty retired, remembers days of informal talks taking place at the offices of Oliver Freaney in Ballsbridge, with Fox deeply involved for Dunnes and Frank often present in the background alongside Buckley and Walsh. Margaret never showed at these meetings. However, she did concede to a meeting with two senior ICTU leaders, Kevin Duffy, later to be chair of the Labour Court, and Phil Flynn, the man to whom Fox had turned at the start of Ben's kidnap ordeal 14 years earlier. Duffy and Flynn had their meeting with Margaret, then went straight to meet Douglas and Nulty at Jury's Hotel in Ballsbridge to deliver the message: 'You're fucked'. Douglas asked why, and he recalls Duffy telling him: 'We were in her boardroom and Margaret's sitting under this enormous painting of her Da. She listens to what we said and then she swiveled in her chair, turned to it and addressed it loudly, "Daddy, Daddy, what am I going to do?" I knew then you had no chance.'

On 4 July 1995, the deputy chairman of the Labour Court, Finbarr Flood, issued a peace formula, urging management and unions 'to consider carefully the recommendation, not in the context of what has been gained or lost, but rather in the context of what can be achieved, given proper working relations.' The union struggled to get members to agree as the first strike took place during a summer of record high temperatures, which added an extra complication. Many of the Dunnes staff were happy to be on strike, to have time to bask in the glorious weather, because many were earning more in strike pay and State benefits than they received from their employer. 'It was nearly impossible get them back,' recalled Douglas. The strike ended after three weeks, but crucially it left a 3% pay demand to be settled by further negotiation.

By October both sides were back at the Labour Court, looking for clarifications, and by Christmas they were in dispute once more. The company's outlets remained closed to pre-Christmas Sunday shoppers because, alone among the Republic's major retailers, Dunnes could not agree overtime rates. In January 1996 efforts to establish an independent tribunal failed after the chairman, the former ESB chief executive Paddy Moriarty, resigned, blaming the company's attitude.

Over the next eight months there was a succession of stalled talks, abortive peace initiatives and deferred strike ballots, to the frustration of almost everybody involved. Frank was given a lot of the blame, regarded by many as 'confrontational and dictatorial', although many shared that view of Margaret. The days when Margaret would assemble staff in a store and ask them to express their grievances – a measure that didn't necessarily achieve much other than make Margaret feel she was trying – were long gone. Margaret realised that she had to change and, albeit reluctantly, hired a new PR company, Drury Communications, to advise on both internal and external communications. Its founder, Fintan Drury, remembers her as 'a hoot. What a work ethic, and no time for anything other than straight talking. She asked me one day in the boardroom why I never wore a Dunnes Stores shirt or sweater. "I bet your knickers are Dunnes though, aren't they?"' Drury left his own company not long afterwards and handed the responsibility to his successor Padraig McKeon, who would work closely with Margaret for the next few years.

Dunnes sponsored the very popular Dublin Women's Mini Marathon in an effort to improve its public image, but Mandate countered by distributing 40,000 *Fair Play to the Dunnes Stores Workers* badges and union members ran in the race in T-shirts bearing the same slogan. Things came to a head in late August 1996 when staff voted by a nine-to-one margin to go on strike. Superquinn had become the first supermarket chain to introduce do-it-yourself scanning for customers, but Dunnes had not reached agreement with Mandate. The union offered to co-operate in return for a 3% annual productivity payment. Andrew Street joined the negotiations on behalf of the Dunnes board, a move seen as highly significant by the unions because of his seniority and position. The unions found that he listened carefully and spoke only when he had something of use to say. Street was someone they felt they could do a deal with, but the problem was whether it would be endorsed by Margaret and Frank.

At the end of August, the unions felt a deal had been struck with Street to avoid a strike. 'We had the best part of a deal,' said Douglas after a 16-hour negotiating session. 'We shook hands on two documents and believed that the two signed documents would emanate from Dunnes Stores later in the morning.' One document covered pay, jobs and conditions, the second procedures for referring disputes to third parties, such as the Labour Court. The board refused both documents, which Nulty saw as 'the rug was pulled' from under Street, undermining his credibility.

'The issue here is not a commercial one,' said one Mandate insider. 'It's pride, family pride.' Margaret and Frank did not want to give a formal role, or power, to any third party, such as the Labour Court or Labour Relations Commission. Peter Cassells, for the Irish Congress of Trade Unions (ICTU) executive council, condemned the Dunnes intransigence: 'Management's refusal to implement the agreement agreed last July marks a new low in industrial relations in this country.' He called on the public to show the same support for the workers in this dispute as they had shown in 1995.

A costly two-week strike started on 3 September 1996. Dunnes was believed to have lost £2m in turnover each day and market share that it would take years to recover. It was estimated that suppliers lost over £1m a day and 100 members of the Small Firms Association had to place nearly 1,000 employees on temporary lay-off.

Within two weeks a solution was found, and the unions probably made more of it than the company did. The terms provided for full backdating of a 3% productivity pay rise to 4 September 1995, provision for 400 full-time jobs and further talks on pensions, sick pay and other benefits. They also provided for a formal agreement between the company and its unions and a provision to refer problems that couldn't be solved 'in-house' to the Labour Relations Commission and the Labour Court. This met the key requirement of the three unions involved at Dunnes Stores that the company honour the substance of the previous year's Labour Court recommendations.

However, the unions – led by Nulty, Douglas and Maurice Sheehan – conceded that the company could recruit new full-time staff on the basis of a seven-day week instead of the existing six-day week. New full-time staff would have compulsory Sunday working and be paid only time-and-a-half for it. The change would apply even to existing long-serving part-time staff who received double time for Sunday work if they chose to work Sundays. This was very unpopular with many workers and meant that the deal was barely ratified. 'The closeness of the vote indicates a deep sense of unease among the workforce about the company's ability to honour agreements entered into with their staff,' Nulty said. Street said the company and the workers had come a long way in two weeks to resolve problems 'which have restricted the natural development of this company in recent times', a comment that could have been seen as a backhanded dig at Frank and Margaret. The Organisation of Working Time Act was implemented in 1997 by the government; many saw it as the legacy of the Dunnes dispute.

The circumstances of the dispute did not do the perception of the company and how it was managed any favours. Time has not diluted that impression. It was all not just unnecessary but counterproductive and damaging to the image of Dunnes Stores and its remaining principals, Frank and Margaret.

Frank essentially left the management team after the strikes were resolved, returning only occasionally for meetings and leaving Margaret to get on with it. He went back to his horses, where he was happier. At least he didn't return to alcohol, but he wasn't off the radar for long, however. From late 1996 onwards he and Margaret ended up intimately involved in dealing with an even bigger public crisis for the company, one that stemmed from Ben's antics in Orlando four years earlier, but which drew in much of what happened before and after that life-changing event.

31.

The Lowry affair

'YOU'VE GOT YOUR FUCKING ETHICS and I've got a business to run. I want it done that way', was Ben's emphatic response to accountant Michael Irwin when the latter queried a particularly large payment. Ben put £1.4m worth of reconstruction at his Porterstown home through the Dunnes books, invoicing it as if it was work done for Newbridge Foods, a company fully owned by the Dunnes family outside of the Trust. Irwin queried it – and got short shrift. The meeting lasted 'about one minute and 30 seconds,' Irwin told a subsequent court hearing in 2001. Ben, he said, 'always got his way' and 'Ben Dunne being Ben Dunne you certainly didn't argue with him'. Irwin said that Ben was 'a difficult man to deal with' and while what was being suggested was 'clearly wrong', he felt he had to do as instructed.

Irwin then went to Fox and Bowen and was instructed to reverse the payments and have them charged to Ben, who reluctantly paid up. According to Irwin, this meant there was 'no loss to the Revenue Commissioners and no fraud'. Faxhill Homes, the building company Ben had used, faced charges in Naas, county Kildare, in 2001, of failing to keep proper books of account and pleaded guilty to some. Ben faced no charges for authorising the misdescribing of the work.

Irwin's account provided an arresting insight into how business was conducted during Ben's time as head of Dunnes Stores. Sometimes he came up against someone like Irwin, with their 'fucking ethics', other times he engaged with more likeminded people. Ironically, Irwin was one of those closest to him, something Margaret detested.

Irwin was left to deal with Michael Lowry, a man who always had an eye for an opportunity. Lowry first became known to the public in Tipperary for voluntary work as a young man, raising money for the Tipperary county board of the GAA as it cleared debts on the redevelopment of Semple Stadium. Credit for organising major concerts staged at the venue was banked politically and when local Fine Gael TD David Moloney died suddenly, Lowry was nominated to replace him. A national political career beckoned, one that would make him a minister just seven years after he was first elected for Tipperary North in 1987 at the age of 33. His career has endured for nearly 40 years since, allowing him to play a key role as a broker in the formation of a coalition government in January 2025 between Fine Gael, Fianna Fáil and regional independents (of whom he was one), the same month he learnt that the DPP was reviewing a file about his relationships with Ben and others.

Lowry was also a businessman, if not quite a self-made man as he might have liked to portray himself. He apprenticed as a refrigeration engineer with Butler Refrigeration in Thurles as a 17-year-old. Much of that company's work was on behalf of Dunnes Stores. In 1988, at Ben's suggestion, as a side hustle Lowry set up a company called Garuda, trading as Streamline, enabling Ben to end the Dunnes contract with Butler and offer the work to the new TD. Dunnes was the only customer for Streamline and its books were kept by Oliver Freaney & Co, auditors to Dunnes. Ben provided the capital of £165,000 to set up the business, even though it was to be in Lowry's name. Essentially, Lowry was Ben's kept employee, and Dunnes would make more money this way than by outsourcing refrigeration work to a genuine third party. It was presented differently to the public, just as Nevilles and Newbridge were apparently independent entities, but in Lowry's case it was varied. A tribunal was told later that he worked personally as a 'consultant' to Dunnes' operations in Northern Ireland and Great Britain, although this seemed to be an attempt to explain Lowry's tax evasion.

Up until his removal from Dunnes in 1993, Ben had paid 'bonuses' to Lowry while Garuda showed small profits or losses, with Ben deciding what prices were paid for its work. It appeared that Lowry made substantial savings for Dunnes. During a meeting with Ben in the latter's office, he was told: 'You are doing an excellent job and Dunnes Stores will look after you.' In October 1990, Ben paid £25,000 to a new Lowry account in the Isle of Man from another account Ben owned in that location. In May 1992, Ben made payments of £50,000 and £40,000 to Lowry, lodged in Jersey and the Isle of Man. Lowry claimed subsequently that he was 'concerned' about the ad hoc, informal method of payment and went to Irwin at Dunnes to get it sorted. However, he went deeper into Ben's pocket when Dunnes paid for construction work at his recently purchased rural mansion.

In 1992 Lowry bought a large old house in its own grounds at Holycross, near Thurles, for £140,000. It needed renovations and Lowry wanted to extend it, giving him 'a modest house of good standard' as he would later describe it, almost hilariously. Dunnes paid for work worth £395,107 but there was nothing on company records to explain that the expenditure was for Lowry's benefit. Indeed, some of the bills were mis-recorded as covering costs for work at the ILAC shopping centre in Dublin. It more than resembled the manner of paying for the building work on Ben's own house.

Lowry had secured a key role within Fine Gael in reducing its debts. He was never shy in asking for something, particularly money, and he did it many times privately for Fine Gael. Pushy and desperate to impress, he became friendly with many of those in the horse-racing set with whom Margaret fraternised, including Michael Smurfit. He was deemed so successful that he became chairman of the parliamentary party and a year later was central to defending John Bruton from a heave to remove him as party leader. Late in 1994 he was an essential fixer for the creation of the rainbow coalition of Fine Gael, Labour and Democratic Left after the Fianna Fáil/Labour administration collapsed amid many recriminations. His reward was inclusion in the cabinet, as Minister for Transport, Energy and Communications, a position that gave him political responsibility for some major state-owned commercial entities and for regulation of privately owned ones. Before naming his cabinet, Bruton asked all his potential ministers if their tax affairs were in order. Lowry lied. He admitted privately to the new Taoiseach of availing of the controversial tax amnesty introduced by the 1993 government, but he did not admit that there were other issues outstanding. He had resigned his role as managing director of Streamline on becoming minister, putting his brother Peter in charge nominally, to create the appearance of concentrating on politics.

Sam Smyth followed Lowry's career assiduously, especially after he became a minister. When Sam and I worked in the *Irish Independent* we reported separately about Lowry but also combined to write stories about a minister who sought a high profile but who bridled when the publicity was not always positive. Lowry actively sought attention: it was not unusual to find the minister on the other end of my office phoneline, giving me stories about semi-state companies for which he had responsibility and demanding that his name appear in whatever I wrote in return for providing the information. He claimed to be on a mission to bust 'cosy cartels' in the public sector, but the suspicion was that he was not doing so out of ideological reasons but to benefit friends in the private sector. At one stage he created headlines when he complained that he was being followed by unknown figures 'in white hi-ace vans'. And on one occasion, in September 1995, he complained to me that our coverage of this was unfair, but as the explanation he offered to me was 'off-the-record' I cannot repeat it here, although I found it very hard to ever take him seriously again. (This was the story I had told Ben that he hadn't liked.)

Lowry became very upset in October 1996 when I was tipped off that he had bought an expensive house in Blackrock, Dublin, and asked Diarmuid Doyle in the *Sunday Tribune* – where I had become editor the previous month – to check out how Lowry could afford this. We were somewhat surprised by how angry Lowry was at the questions put to him, but years later the reason for his sensitivity would become very clear, although the source of the purchase money in this particular case was not Ben or Dunnes Stores.

In office, Lowry had ministerial oversight of the competition for the grant of a lucrative mobile-phone licence. In 1995 that was won unexpectedly by the Esat Digifone consortium led by Denis O'Brien. Two months later, O'Brien asked his Norwegian partners, Telenor, to facilitate a $50,000 donation to Fine Gael, via businessman David Austin, a key aide of Smurfit's and a member of the Dunne family's social set, as mentioned earlier. In October 1996, again to be disclosed only years later, £147,000 was lodged to an account opened in Lowry's name with Irish Nationwide in the Isle of Man, the money coming originally from O'Brien but routed through Austin. That money was advanced to help finance the refurbishment of the house in Blackrock about which I'd been asking questions. Lowry repaid the money in February 1997, the day a tribunal of inquiry to investigate his actions was set up, headed by Justice Brian McCracken. All of this would emerge later.

Lowry had gathered enemies because of his ministerial activities and there were those who were aware of his vulnerability. A man with access to the Price Waterhouse report regarding Dunnes Stores organised that a portion referring to Lowry found its way to Smyth via a third party, without incriminating anyone connected to the leak. Smyth's dramatic *Irish Independent* story – headlined, 'The Minister, A Tycoon, and his £208,000 House Extension' – caused a major political storm. The story was partial in its content, as would be disclosed later, but it had enough detail to derail Lowry. Crucially, Smyth revealed that one of the cheques to cover the bill was signed by Ben, bizarrely one of the very last he'd signed before he was removed as executive chairman by Frank and Margaret.

Initially, it looked as if Lowry might survive the Friday morning disclosure. Agents on his behalf tried desperately to convince journalists that the payments should be described as a form of loan – a 'credit facility', not income – and as a business arrangement that in no way influenced his political decision-making. They claimed this was a private matter of no interest to the public. If more extensive privacy laws had existed in the mid-1990s, Lowry most probably would have tried to obtain an injunction to prevent publication. Should Smyth have ignored it on the basis that the document was private and confidential, the property of Dunnes Stores, and was naming people who might struggle to answer questions at short notice? Of course not. The story was more important than the motives of the person supplying the information, or the method by which it came into his possession. Its disclosure was in the public interest, especially given what else would emerge.

The Labour party realised quickly the significance of what was going on and forced Bruton to seek Lowry's resignation, which he did reluctantly. Lowry resigned as minister on 30 November 1996. Unwisely, Bruton stood for a parting photograph with Lowry, who loudly described his party leader as 'my friend, my best friend forever', a phrase noted widely then and repeated many times subsequently. Lowry insisted, 'There was no impropriety on my part

in respect of any payments made for work carried out on my house.'
He said the payment was 'an entirely legitimate and normal commercial agreement' and entirely unrelated to his duties as a minister. Few believed him then, and subsequent disclosures made an absolute mockery of that.

32.

Investigating hidden payments

THE DAY AFTER MICHAEL LOWRY'S RESIGNATION I wrote in the *Sunday Tribune* that this would not be the end of the matter, which was not a particularly brave or insightful prediction: the nature of this resignation, a minister seemingly in the pocket of a businessman, was certain to raise questions as to whether he was alone in receiving money from Ben. I was confident in the assertion because late in the autumn of 1994 I had been told of payments to Haughey from the accounts of Dunnes Stores via Des Traynor. This was when I was working in the *Irish Independent* and not long before Ben's case against the family and Trust, with its allegations about those payments, was due to begin. I was told also of the Price Waterhouse report and was able to report in the *Sunday Tribune* the day after the Lowry resignation that other political figures, including a significant person in Fianna Fáil and his wife, had received payments and that these were listed. (The more substantial allegations were made in the court pleadings and were not in the report by the accountants.) But as in 1994, when I told my *Irish Independent* editor Vinnie Doyle about the information I had, I had no documentary proof and just a single source, albeit one excellently placed. It was not enough to allow me to name Haughey at either time.

Days after Lowry's resignation, Cliff Taylor reported in *The Irish Times* that an unnamed Fianna Fáil figure had received over £1m from Dunne. Everybody in political and business circles began talking about Haughey, without naming him publicly. After all, who else could it be? Even before he became leader of Fianna Fáil and Taoiseach in December 1979, Haughey's finances had been the subject of speculation. His lavish lifestyle included fine dining at the most expensive restaurants, wearing hand-crafted clothes and indulging the expensive hobby of riding to hounds. He bought an 18th-century period mansion, Abbeville, at

Kinsealy (designed by the celebrated architect James Gandon, the Englishman who designed the Four Courts and King's Inns), despite having no obvious means to do so as a serving politician with a relatively modest, publicly provided salary.

Haughey's critics and enemies had always believed him to be corrupt, and even some of his supporters suspected errant behaviour but excused it because of his supposed political achievements and 'charisma'. Haughey's defenders said he profited from so-called 'good investments', believed to centre around property speculation. The reality was that he lived largely on borrowed money that he didn't look to repay, spending as if it was his due. We were about to discover, although not for some months yet, that he had run up debts of about £1m by the time he first became Taoiseach in 1979. He was lucky that his friend and financial manager Des Traynor forced a deal with AIB to write off most of it and transfer the balance to a bank, Guinness & Mahon, where Traynor was a director. Over the years Traynor received money on Haughey's behalf from multiple donors that he shifted offshore to a bank called Ansbacher Cayman, presumably to avoid detection in the event of any Central Bank of Ireland audit and to make it almost impossible for the Revenue Commissioners to detect. However, money was returned secretly to Ireland to allow accountants acting on Haughey's behalf, led by Jack Stakelum, to pay his many big bills.

Back in early 1987, not long after Haughey had returned as Taoiseach following nearly five years in opposition, the new Japanese owners of Guinness & Mahon asked searching questions as to why Haughey had such large debts outstanding. His identity as Ireland's new prime minister did not impress them. Traynor decided this was not a problem that would go away easily, that a foreign-owned bank might call his bluff and demand full repayment. Haughey needed to clear the loans, but had no financial means to do so. Traynor apparently decided to do a 'whip-around', It was an extraordinary decision. Haughey would have been ruined politically had the bank moved publicly against him, and disclosure of the extent of his debts would have undermined his authority fatally. However, if news broke that he was canvassing cash, it would have been equally ruinous – although he could have claimed that Traynor was acting without his authority or knowledge. Not everyone would have accepted that and it would have raised questions as to what he or Traynor was selling in return, had it been known at the time. That was where Ben was to come in.

The libel laws prevented the naming of Haughey in late 1996 – he would not only deny but might take legal action to force his accusers to prove what they were saying. Hearsay would not do. Physical proof – and witnesses – would be required to defend any action. (One small publication, a magazine called *The Phoenix*, did put Haughey's name into print, but no bigger entity, more vulnerable to being sued by Haughey, was going to trust that as a reliable source.)

The following Sunday, 8 December, I decided to include Haughey's name in our front-page story after lengthy discussions with the *Sunday Tribune*'s legal adviser, Hugh Mohan. We devoted the front page to a large photograph of Haughey under the headline that his late accountant, Des Traynor, had received and managed almost £2m in bank accounts using money that had come from Ben. Dead men can't sue, but following Mohan's strong advice I wrote that we were not alleging that Haughey had received the money. It was a deliberate mistruth to provide us with protection, included much to my chagrin. It would not be until March 1997 that the Irish edition of *The Sunday Times* would definitively state that Haughey was under tribunal investigation for receipt of the payments, while also reporting his denials.

Meanwhile, Lowry continued to dominate the headlines. Just before Christmas 1996 he handed a gift-wrapped present to those who wanted further investigation. He made a lengthy statement to Dáil Éireann on 19 December, 'to set the record straight'. He did anything but. The lies he told would not be disclosed until later, but he gave hostages to fortune by reading his statement into the official Dáil record as he explained his relationship with Ben: 'Mr. Dunne said that I should leave it to my own judgement to make a decision on profits but clearly stated that he would put the company in profit and also remunerate me appropriately for my technical advice and for project management on various jobs. There would also be a performance bonus. It was agreed that the company's costs and outlays were recalculated annually and that there would be regular payments on account. At the end of the year auditors appointed by Dunnes Stores would check income against expenditure and any outstanding money would be paid by Dunnes. He gave me a commitment that he would personally review the performance and agree monies due on an annual basis. Unfortunately for me he never got around to doing that. As our negotiating positions were far from equal, I did not feel able to press the matter more strongly.'

He lied that he had not been trying to hide income from the Revenue Commissioners: 'If someone were trying to hide income, would he or she not be more likely to put it in an offshore account?' As would become apparent within months, he had multiple offshore accounts of long standing but also one opened just two months earlier, while serving as a minister. He showed little contrition. 'In taking up the offer of ministry I made the declaration to the Taoiseach to the effect that I had availed of the tax amnesty and insofar as I was aware all my tax affairs were up-to-date and paid.' That was another massive lie.

Within days of Lowry's resignation and following calls from Spring, Margaret gave the Price Waterhouse report to the Revenue Commissioners. The report outlined in full detail the cheques to builders, including one signed by Ben for Lowry, and other information that showed sleight of hand. The full report also included plenty of information that gave rise to other tax issues.

The government, under enormous pressure to act appropriately, appointed Judge Gerard Buchanan to investigate and report to the Dáil Committee on Procedures and Privileges. He was asked to establish what money was received and for what purpose, although limits were put on who he could name. Only four names would eventually be published: Lowry, and three members of the Haughey family, his wife (Maureen), son (Ciaran) and brother (Eoghan, a priest), but not Charlie himself. There was no direct reference in the report to the allegation that 'Mister You Know Who', as he had become known, received £1.1m.

Buchanan did not have it easy. Although Ben was co-operative, he declined to provide details of his controversial 1994 affidavit for the Trust case, saying this would constitute contempt of court. Buchanan recorded the explanation without comment. Ben suggested the company would be able to provide the judge with all information relating to the Price Waterhouse report, but Dunnes responded this was 'totally inaccurate and misleading'.

Buchanan was unable to establish the beneficiaries of £3.5m of the £5.6m in irregular payments. Money was made out to cash or paid into credit card accounts. A further £1m was paid to persons who were 'not relevant', and slightly more to 'identified or alleged beneficiaries' who were not named. The work on Lowry's house had cost Dunnes Stores £395,000, not £208,000.

Political parties scrambled to be transparent about money they'd received from either Ben or Dunnes Stores. Ruairi Quinn of Labour told of going to The Barge pub, beside Dublin's Grand Canal, to host a table quiz to raise £200–£300 for Mary Robinson's 1990 presidential election campaign. He joined a friend at the bar, who was with Ben. After a brief conversation about the cost of paying for campaign advertisements, Ben went to his car and returned with a cheque book. 'I'm a great admirer of that woman,' he told Quinn. 'My wife is very fond of her.' He borrowed Quinn's pen to write a cheque for £15,000, payable to the Labour Party. Quinn said he could keep the pen. Spring told of how he secured £50,000 from Ben on behalf of the Waterworld Aquadome project in Tralee in early 1993, a public facility from which Spring gained no personal benefit.

In October 1989, Ben met Fine Gael leader Alan Dukes for dinner in Barberstown Castle. Ben gave him a cheque for £30,000 and promised the same again for the next two years. In May 1991, Bruton, now leader of Fine Gael, called to Ben's home for a meeting arranged by Lowry. After an hour of chat he left with a cheque for £50,000. Ben sent another cheque for £100,000 to the party in May 1993, bringing the total to £180,000.

There were also individual donations, details of which were expanded upon in subsequent tribunal hearings. Michael Noonan received £3,900 from Ben towards expenses during the 1992 election campaign and was told of the contribution by Lowry. 'I was surprised as I hadn't asked Mr Dunne for anything,' Noonan later explained. He asked Lowry why Ben was giving him the money and was told, 'He has a lot of time for you as a politician.' Noonan was formally introduced to Ben in 1991. Lowry was giving him a lift one day and said he had to call to Ben's house on business. Lowry invited him in, and Noonan and Ben had a conversation that lasted five or six minutes. The next meeting was in 1993, when Ben was in the Mater Hospital and Lowry brought Noonan on a visit. The conversation was not about politics and didn't have anything to do with contributions.

Ivan Yates, without asking, received £5,700 from Ben towards his 1992 election campaign, more than half his costs, by far the biggest donation he ever received. It was organised by Lowry. Yates sent his sister to Dublin to collect the cash. Yates told Lowry he was very grateful and would like to meet Ben, which he did after the election in the Conrad Hotel in Dublin. Ben struck him as a very gregarious, larger-than-life type: 'It was the first time I'd seen a person drinking pints of Heineken with lots of ice in it. He didn't give me the impression he was a Fine Gael supporter or was very interested in politics.' Yates said the contribution did not buy any extra influence.

In the summer of 1988, Ben ran into Jim Mitchell, the Fine Gael justice minister at the time of his kidnap, in Myo's pub in Castleknock. After an affable couple of pints Ben gave Mitchell a cheque for £5,000, telling him to use half for his own constituency expenses and to give the other half to Bruton, which Mitchell did. 'It was completely unsolicited,' said Mitchell.

It can all be put down to Ben's impetuosity, his need for people to like him, as much as having favours to collect at a later date. The money, while relatively large amounts, at least for these payments was smaller than many of the golf bets he placed. All of which raised the question: why did Fianna Fáil get nothing?

The answer would draw Ben, Margaret, Frank and Dunnes Stores into a gripping and explosive tale of lies, allegations and counter-allegations and, eventually, shocking truths – all played out in the world of politics. If Lowry was already causing Fine Gael embarrassment and grief, it paled in comparison to what it would do to the reputation of Fianna Fáil's one-time hero: Haughey.

33.

The McCracken Tribunal and its revelations

THE BUCHANAN REPORT PROVIDED the necessary raw material and based on its findings the government started a sworn inquiry under the Tribunal of Inquiry (Evidence) Acts, 1921–79. It was to investigate the alleged payments made by Dunnes Stores between 1 January 1986 and 31 December 1996 and alleged payments to members of the Houses of the Oireachtas, their relatives or connected persons, and political parties. The inquiry was given the power to compel attendance of witnesses and to acquire documents, chaired by recently appointed High Court Justice Brian McCracken.

McCracken made a public promise: the hearings would not be 'adversarial' but 'inquisitorial'. He didn't add that they would be sensational, dominating media coverage and public conversation for months to come, causing outrage and undermining faith in politics, deepening suspicions that rich and powerful businesspeople had preferential access. Sadly, they were not televised despite media pressure.

A generation earlier – in 1970 – Haughey was at the centre of one of the State's most astounding court cases. After being fired as a government minister, he was acquitted in the Central Criminal Court on charges of gunrunning in the historically famous Arms Trial. Now, Haughey was again going to be the star attraction of a major event, more so than Lowry or Ben or Margaret or anyone else, even though they too got plenty of attention. But it wasn't clear at the first hearing if he would be required to attend and testify because the breakthrough in finding evidence hadn't yet been made. He wasn't even named by McCracken at the first public hearing in late February 1997.

The judge explained that the circumstances facing him were 'unusual'. Documentation was almost 'non-existent', apart from what he'd received in Buchanan's report. Investigative work would be needed before public hearings. Many of the country's leading and most expensive barristers were retained by those who faced investigation but there was nobody there for Haughey. McCracken promised findings and recommendations would be made, but that confidentiality would be respected. He assembled his own legal team, led by senior counsel Denis McCullough, with fellow barrister Michael Collins and solicitor John Lawless. The work they did was outstanding, although later discovered to be incomplete.

The lawyers searched a mountain of documents, bank statements, letters, copies of letters, cheques, covering notes and memoranda. The Buchanan document – and what was reported in the media – gave them the leads to uncover what became known as the 'Ansbacher deposits', a scheme established in the 1970s by Traynor that allowed rich Irish people, and many more besides Haughey, to hide money on a Caribbean island in the Ansbacher Cayman bank, yet still have ready access to it in Dublin at Guinness & Mahon Bank.

(McCracken's work would subsequently lead to a High Court-appointed inspector conducting his own investigation. When what became known as the Ansbacher Report was published in June 2002, it revealed that 190 Irish people, including senior politicians, bankers and other so-called pillars of society, put £38m into secret coded accounts. It caused outrage, only partially mitigated by the Revenue Commissioners subsequently recovering well over €100m in tax payments from the account holders. It is almost certain that none of this would have been uncovered had the McCracken team not first done its work.)

The tribunal lawyers had Haughey in their sights. They contacted him, but received the customary rebuff. On 7 March, Haughey wrote that 'neither I nor any connected person or relative' had received payments from Ben or Dunnes Stores. He included the letter he had sent two years earlier to solicitors for the Dunnes because, as we were soon to learn, Margaret had sought return of the money from him. 'As no such monies have been paid, no repayment arises,' he wrote.

The tribunal had documents that showed Ben's money was paid into Ansbacher, but the problem was proving that it then got to Haughey. The tribunal's lawyers travelled to the Cayman Islands to seek permission to compel witnesses to give evidence, but with limited success. There was a breakthrough, however, when they saw on one document a notation that led them to believe that Haughey was the beneficiary of two specific Ansbacher accounts, known as S8 and S9. One of the accountants who managed the money, Padraig Collery, who had taken over management of the accounts shortly before Traynor's death, cracked when presented with the evidence. Rather than perjure himself, he admitted his work and that of an accountant, Jack Stakelum, who used the repatriated money to discharge the Haughey household's living expenses.

On 21 April, to audible gasps in the public gallery, senior counsel Denis McCullough made an extraordinary statement. He detailed how Haughey received money from various banks outside the State to banks in London, and from there to an account in Guinness & Mahon in Dublin. McCullough set out, step-by-step and across a myriad of complex transactions, what the tribunal had learnt about transfers from Ben to Traynor and how this money had found its way to Haughey. That was jaw-dropping enough, but then came his revelation that Ben would give evidence that in addition to the £1.1m he had transferred to Traynor and the Ansbacher accounts, as detailed in his previous court pleadings, he now 'remembered' another £210,000 given to Haughey, in three £70,000 bank drafts, all personally handed to Haughey and all bearing the date 19 November 1991. McCullough was careful to say there was no evidence that Haughey had acted wrongly or improperly in receiving money and that Ben had not asked for or received any political or other favour in return, merely that he paid it because he 'admired and respected' Haughey and wished to help him in his financial difficulties. Haughey wrote to the tribunal to maintain 'neither he nor any other connected person or relative had received any money from Mr Dunne, other than what had already been revealed to the Buchanan inquiry.'

Ben made his first, eagerly anticipated tribunal appearance on 22 April. He told a story of how Noel Fox had come to him in 1987 to tell him that Haughey had financial problems and that Haughey's friend and financial manager Des Traynor was collecting money to pay his debts. Fox told him that Traynor was asking wealthy individuals to donate about £150,000 each, with the ambition of reaching £750,000 or £900,000. Ben was among those being approached because he had met Haughey in 1986, an introduction arranged for him by Fox, at just the same time that Dunnes had a big problem with the tax position of the Trust. Ben said he volunteered to pay the lot, even though he testified he didn't ask how or why Haughey was in this position. 'I think he's making a huge mistake trying to get six or seven people together,' Ben recalled telling Fox. 'Christ picked twelve apostles and one of them crucified him.' There was a mixture of gasps and laughs from those assembled in Dublin Castle.

Ben's evidence was that there was no doubt in his mind that Haughey was the beneficiary of the transactions between him and Traynor. He had only met Haughey once before 1987, and twice since November 1991, but '50 or 60 times' in total. Explaining his generosity, Ben said, 'I had tremendous respect for him and I continue in my own way to respect him . . . It would have crossed my mind on a personal basis it would not have been nice to see our prime minister in huge financial difficulties.' He said that on 'a good few occasions' in his life he had helped people in financial difficulties by giving them up to £400,000 or £500,000 and 'in no way did [I] feel they were indebted to me'.

What commanded the headlines was the detail of giving Haughey the drafts personally, because it was both the simplest transaction and the only one face-to-face. Ben told of how shortly after 13 November 1991 – he wasn't exactly sure of the date – he called to Abbeville 'for a cup of tea' after a round of golf at the County Louth Golf Club, better known as Baltray, a favourite of his near Drogheda. Ben felt Haughey was 'not himself . . . don't want this to sound the wrong way, but I felt sorry for him, he looked down, like a broken man, I couldn't put my finger on it'. This was surprising as Haughey had just managed to defeat an attempt by Albert Reynolds to remove him as Fianna Fáil party leader. Ben had three bank drafts for an Isle of Man account, with the names Scott, Montgomery and Blair on them, in the back pocket of his golf trousers. 'Look,' said Ben, 'that's something for yourself.' According to Ben, Haughey replied, 'Thank you, big fella'. It was a phrase that would be remembered for decades. While the money might have cheered up Haughey, it provided a short-lived respite. In late January 1992, former Minister for Justice Sean Doherty went on television and alleged that in 1982 Haughey had been aware that Doherty was tapping journalists' telephones. Within weeks Haughey was forced to resign as party leader and as Taoiseach.

Ben wasn't the only star attraction at the tribunal that week. Fox also gave evidence. Fox had become so important to Dunnes during Ben's time that he attended the daily 8am management meeting and even chaired it when Ben was unavailable. Apparently, Traynor – who died in 1994 before anyone could ask questions of him – told Fox that Haughey 'had a significant problem' and explained his plan. Fox could have said no, especially as he was a trustee to the family's fortune, but apparently he acted as a messenger boy, leaving it up to Ben to decide what he wanted to do and then facilitating it in full, without telling Ben's siblings.

Fox said he never had any doubt that cheques issued between 1987 and 1991 were for the benefit of Haughey. Asked for Traynor's reaction to the news that Ben was prepared to pay Haughey's debt in full, Fox replied, to laughter in the public gallery, 'He was quite pleased.' In his seat, Ben doubled over with mirth, shaking his head with disbelieving amusement – quite the reaction given that he had caused all of this. Fox said Traynor never suggested that Ben or Dunnes Stores might benefit in any way from the transactions, nor had Ben ever said he hoped or expected to get any benefit. Fox praised Ben's motives: 'I thought it was very generous, actually. It was in character. He was a very generous man and very compassionate.' It has never been revealed if Traynor did contact anyone else, if he was simply lucky that the recipient of his first call volunteered to pay the lot.

Irwin followed Fox into the witness-box. He described visiting Ben at his home in Porterstown in 1993, months after his removal as chairman and when he was in a wheelchair with broken ankles. 'He told me he had paid £1m to Charlie. I asked him if that meant Charles Haughey and he said yes, it did,' Irwin said. Irwin asked where the money came from and Ben told him not to worry about that.

'A lot of people would find it staggering. Knowing him as you do, were you surprised?' McCracken's lawyers asked.

'No. He is very generous,' Irwin said.

'Is Mr Dunne the kind of man who would give £1m to someone in financial difficulties and look for nothing in return?'

'Yes.'

Irwin contacted Fox the following day and arranged an urgent meeting. Fox's reaction was 'pretty muted'. Irwin then went to Frank's home in Dunboyne and related his discussion with Ben. Frank was 'taken aback' and he arranged to meet with Margaret and Therese, in Margaret's office. Irwin said: 'I think they were stunned.'

Margaret concurred when she took her turn in the witness-box that Friday, dressed in black as if in mourning. She had prepared meticulously. She had been in attendance each day, watching proceedings alongside her solicitor, Houghton Fry. Dunnes arranged to rent rooms in Dublin Castle to which she could retire for daily consultations with her team of heavy-hitting barristers. They were accompanied by McKeon from Drury Communications, who presented a daily review of the media coverage. They had transcripts of all evidence from each previous day to decide how to address any issues raised either in her evidence or to press queries. Her son, Michael, was brought to the meetings, regarded by some insiders as a sign that he was being prepared for a senior management position in Dunnes. There were regular phone calls to Frank, who didn't attend.

Asked if she was 'stunned', as Irwin had testified, Margaret said, 'Very much so. I was actually flabbergasted. I couldn't believe it. I didn't believe my brother would give £1m to anybody.'

She had 'heard rumours my brother had made payments to Mr Haughey' but when she asked Ben, he flatly denied it. Their arguments became heated. At one board meeting she told him, 'If you don't tell me, I'm going to keep digging.' He replied, 'You can look all you like. You'll never trace them.' She suspected, hoped, he was saying it just to annoy her. She mentioned the rumours to Fox 'in passing', which, given the importance she was attaching to the matter, seemed surprisingly offhand, as was the reply she said he gave her. Fox didn't 'pass any comment that I remembered. He didn't deny it, and said something like "Is that so?".'

Margaret told of heading to Abbeville to confront Haughey. 'Anyone who I was told had got £1.3m of Dunnes Stores' money I would have gone to meet them,' she said. According to Margaret, the wily former Taoiseach fended her confidently. 'I said it had come to my knowledge that my brother had given him £1.1m. He was totally relaxed about

it, and he said: "I can't be responsible for what your brother says".'
She felt confused. 'He neither confirmed nor denied it to me. He
actually avoided the question. He kept going back to the stability of
my brother . . . I think my brother had had an accident,' she recalled,
a reference to Ben's broken ankles.

She had tried to steer the conversation back on track, 'not very
successfully. He said he felt my brother was unstable. That was the
line of the conversation. I have to tell you, I left there having doubts
about the stability of my brother and whether he ever got payments.'
She went to Frank to discuss the encounter and, typically, Frank said
they 'needed to look into it more'. The Trust sent solicitors' letters to
Haughey, seeking the return of the money. He continued to deny he'd
received it. Margaret's lawyers dissuaded Dunnes from further action
as there would be 'evidential difficulties' in bringing the matter to a
successful conclusion, notwithstanding how much money was involved
and the desire to get it back.

If Ben had wanted to make payments to political parties on behalf
of the company, he would have brought it to the board, which he hadn't,
Margaret said. Asked if she had any idea what the purpose of such
payments was, she said she and her brother would have different views.
'I don't make donations to political parties or individuals for anything.'

Asked about her brother's friendship with Haughey, she replied, 'It
certainly would not have happened in my father's time.' Her brother
would not have discussed this friendship with her because he knew
she would not approve of it. 'I would not agree with being over-friendly
with politicians and certainly not with Mr Haughey. I don't want to
go into it, but there was something between my father and Mr
Haughey.' (This was likely a reference to that confrontation in New
York that she had neither forgiven nor forgotten.) However, she said
she knew her brother met Haughey regularly. 'He would have been
cautious on what he would say to me, but he would let things slip,
like "I was with Charlie Saturday morning" or something like that. I
think Bernard was impressed he was able to ring up the Taoiseach of
the country.' Asked if this relationship made it more likely he would
give Haughey a sizeable sum, she said: 'I would be suspicious, yes.'

Margaret had a second meeting with Haughey, at his request, late
in 1994, and she went despite Frank being worried about it. Margaret

said she veered away from discussions about the payments. 'I was of the strong impression that he was still in close contact with my brother. My own feeling was that there was nothing that Bernard was doing that Mr Haughey would not have been aware of. That was just my feeling, so I was very wary going to that meeting.' Haughey brought up the family litigation that was nearing its court hearing. He recommended that she settle with Ben. Margaret thought this was none of his business, 'and without wanting to be downright rude to the man that was the impression I gave him'. McCullough noted the tribunal had heard a lot about her brother's generosity and that Ben had said this was true of all the Dunnes. 'Not to the extent I'm reading this week, Sir,' Margaret replied drily.

She addressed the company's relationship with Lowry, testifying that she knew nothing about how Lowry was being paid, especially the money for his house. She had told Lowry – and he had accepted – that the arrangement between his company and Dunnes would have to be 'regularised'. Since Ben's departure things were done in a 'more professional manner', she said. A settlement, for a confidential amount, had been reached with the Revenue Commissioners and the company's tax affairs had been resolved.

Beginning his cross-examination, Ben's barrister, Seamus McKenna, asked if she, like Ben, did not wish to reopen 'old wounds'. Margaret replied: 'No, we're friends now. As brother and sister we have healed those differences. I don't want to revive these differences.'

34.

Haughey's evidence

It was Friday, 25 April, when Margaret stepped down from the witness-box and returned to her reserved seat. When she emerged to face the photographers, the grim face she had displayed in previous days was gone and she was smiling widely, clearly believing things had gone well for her. Justine McCarthy in the *Irish Independent* wrote: 'Gone were the red hair, the orange tan and the gaudy glad-rags. We hardly knew her, this svelte composed woman dressed for a funeral in head-to-toe black. She was elegant and serene, a Mona Lisa to her kid brother's impish Just William.'

Her time in the stand did not get the attention that might have been expected in the weekend newspapers. Instead, that went to the man who followed her to give evidence, the solicitor she despised so much, the man she held responsible for holding too much influence over her brother: Noel Smyth. He was about to blow up Haughey's denials in a scarcely believable fashion, with a plot twist few novelists would have dared.

To the surprise of the tribunal lawyers, because he had not put the information into his statement, Smyth revealed that he and Haughey had met five times after the Buchanan inquiry was established and before the tribunal was set up. He also revealed he had spoken with Haughey previously in 1994 about the likelihood of his receipt of Dunnes' money being disclosed if the Trust case went to open court.

The nature of the relationship between Smyth and Haughey was to prove crucial. Smyth was Dunnes' solicitor, but was he also Haughey's? If he was, then he would be bound by the rules of legal confidentiality. Smyth didn't claim confidentiality because he did not regard himself as Haughey's formal or paid legal adviser. Therefore, he said he would provide information about their meetings if the tribunal decided it was entitled to ask for it. However, he asked the tribunal to consider that Haughey might have regarded the contents of their contacts as something that would not be disclosed to third parties. But he implied the former Taoiseach could not claim privilege as Smyth had asked him the identity of those in his legal team to deal with the tribunal investigations. Haughey had told him that Ivor Fitzpatrick and Deirdre Courtney were his advisers, so there was no confusion as to Smyth's position. Michael Collins, on behalf of the tribunal, asked McCracken to rule no solicitor–client relationship existed and no privilege in law for things said in confidence in a conventional way. There were audible calls of 'Hear hear' from the public gallery, as lawyers for Dunnes Margaret and Frank weighed in to demand Smyth's evidence be heard in full.

There was another twist. Smyth had written a statement detailing his contacts and conversations with Haughey, put it in a sealed registered envelope, posted it to himself and, when he received it, left it unopened. This would prove his account predated what he would now present in evidence, if allowed. He offered it to the tribunal, but instead McCracken ordered that it be sent to Haughey to review for accuracy. McCracken would decide later what to do with it himself.

The document revealed that between March 1994 and January 1997, Smyth met Haughey eight times. There were many other phone calls, nearly all from Haughey to Smyth's office on Fitzwilliam Square, all which Smyth logged. In the first meeting, in 1994, Smyth told Haughey that he had followed the money trail and was satisfied that Haughey was the ultimate recipient of the money from Dunnes. 'I never received those payments,' said Haughey, who maintained his customary sang-froid, for now at least.

Haughey became 'very agitated' at the second meeting, however. He told Smyth that he had reflected upon their first meeting and thought the planned disclosure in the pending court action was an attempt to destroy him. He said he had been in public life for many years, and it would certainly be devastating were the claims in the legal proceedings heard in open court. Many phone calls followed, but in November 1994 Smyth had some very bad news for Haughey. Ben had confirmed his decision to include the information about the payments in his written pleadings, which meant many more people – barristers, solicitors, possibly others – would know, increasing the risk of a leak.

Haughey was 'very gracious' at the time, Smyth said, and offered to try to settle the dispute, which explained how and why Haughey lobbied Margaret on her second visit to Abbeville. Smyth said Haughey was 'worried, very worried' by the litigation, but 'did not anticipate the damage that was coming down the tracks'. After the case was settled out of court, Smyth visited Haughey and told him the outcome. Presumably, Haughey was greatly relieved, but only to a point: he had denied receiving payments in writing to the Dunnes' solicitors. There was a chance that Margaret and Frank and/or the trustees would take legal action to recover the money. Haughey wanted to know what attitude Ben would take if Dunnes sued. Smyth told him Ben would give truthful evidence. Over time, Haughey became more relaxed about the likelihood of disclosure – until the Lowry revelations changed everything again.

Smyth and Haughey met again after Buchanan began his work. Smyth was somewhat reassuring: he told Haughey the scope appeared limited to the Price Waterhouse report and as this report made no mention of the larger payments to Haughey, there was little or nothing to worry about.

In the next meeting, on 2 January 1997, Smyth brought the Price Waterhouse report and showed Haughey how the references to him were innocuous. A relieved Haughey was confident that Buchanan would be the end of the investigations. But then there was to be that dramatic moment of recall that shifted the parameters yet again.

What jogged Ben's memory was never established, but he told Smyth that he remembered extra payments to Haughey that he had delivered personally instead of through intermediaries. Ben had not referred to these payments in legal correspondence with other members of the family in 1994, when he had outlined the payments of more than £1m made to Haughey. It was an extraordinary omission. Smyth told Ben that by making a new allegation, it would seem 'we were switching horses in midstream'. He told Ben to keep quiet until 'we were satisfied about where they went'. Ben suggested Smyth should ask Haughey if he could recall the drafts, which Smyth did. Haughey denied any knowledge, yet asked for details. Showing Haughey copies of the bank drafts, Smyth asked if he had lodged them. Haughey said he had not, 'but they could be a source of some embarrassment to me'. Smyth enquired, 'Well if you did not lodge them to your account, whose account were they lodged to?' Haughey said he thought they had been lodged to one operated by Des Traynor in the Irish Intercontinental Bank. Smyth said this was very serious as it established a firm connection between Haughey and Ben. Haughey replied that this was 'a disaster'. Smyth felt that Haughey's demeanour was one of panic and he drove out of Abbeville with the impression that Haughey thought the bank drafts were 'lethal', although he hadn't explicitly acknowledged to Smyth their receipt from Ben.

Ben offered a further payment of £1m to Haughey in January 1997, a loan to clear tax liabilities that almost certainly would arise when the Revenue Commissioners got wind of what had gone on via public disclosure of the investigations underway. Smyth returned once more to Abbeville and urged Haughey to make a full voluntary disclosure to the McCracken tribunal before it came to him with the allegation. This would mitigate somewhat the impending damage. 'I pleaded with him to put his hands up. He felt that would be the wrong thing to do.' Ben then withdrew the loan offer, for reasons never explained, asking Smyth to call Haughey and make that clear. It was the last conversation between Smyth and Haughey before Smyth's dramatic evidence at the tribunal.

The tribunal's lawyers now embarked on a series of written communications with Haughey, who replied on 7 March 1997 that he, or any connected person or relative of his as defined in the Ethics in Public Office Act, 1995, had never received any payment in cash or in kind of the nature referred to in the terms of reference of the tribunal, other than contributions to his family. He enclosed a copy of the letter sent to Matheson Ormsby Prentice, solicitors to the Dunnes Stores group, in late 1994, which specifically denied the receipt of any monies from Ben.

The tribunal was not easily dissuaded. On 27 March, it asked him to furnish a statement about the transactions outlined by Ben. A week later Haughey replied: 'It is suggested that the accompanying documents support the said allegations and with respect to the tribunal I venture to suggest that a careful perusal of these documents on their own does not corroborate the allegations being made against me.'

Then Smyth made his remarkable declaration about their meetings. Haughey sought limited legal representation at the tribunal, solely to deal with the confidentiality of discussions he'd had with Smyth. It was only the decision in May to halt public hearings until after the 1997 general election had been concluded that slowed the arrival of his day of judgement.

On 30 June, Haughey eventually sought – and was granted – full legal representation, choosing senior counsel Eoin McGonigal as his main advocate. McGonigal told the tribunal his client would furnish a statement acknowledging that as 'a matter of probability' £1.3m was paid into accounts managed by Traynor on his behalf, but that he didn't know they came from Ben or Dunnes Stores. Haughey still denied receiving three bank drafts personally. He admitted knowledge of the payments since 1993 because Traynor had told him in a telephone conversation after Margaret's first visit. McGonigal said documents to be furnished by Haughey would show he was not aware the money had been given by Ben to Traynor for his benefit and would make it clear he did not personally receive three cheques made out by Ben to fictitious persons. A week later McCracken ruled Smyth should reveal the details of their conversations and Haughey's humiliation, which had been arriving slowly, suddenly came in a rush.

Haughey's lawyers were furious when they saw Smyth's statements, realising not just that they had been misled by Haughey but had been sent by him to mislead the tribunal. They threatened to quit their brief, but were prevailed upon to stay once they received a full apology from their client, who was now forced to write a different statement for the tribunal.

In Dublin Castle on 15 July, McCracken started proceedings by reading into the record Haughey's statement. It was a landmark occasion. A former Taoiseach had been forced to admit his wrongdoing and deceit. It was the tearing down of a reputation, a jaw-dropping exposure of the frailties and failings of a deeply flawed man. McCracken read:

'I accept that I have not co-operated with this tribunal in a manner which would have been expected of me . . . I deeply regret that I have allowed this situation to arise . . .

'I omitted to instruct my lawyers fully . . . I was concerned as to the effect that the publication of these payments would have for me in the public mind and in hindsight I accept that a lot of the problems and embarrassment that I have caused would have been avoided if I had been more forthcoming at each and every relevant period.'

But on that day it was *Hamlet* without the Prince. The humiliation of the former Taoiseach had to take place in public if the national anger was to be assuaged. That would come the following day.

On Tuesday, 15 July 1997, at 11am, Charles Haughey entered the witness-box in the King George's Hall of Dublin Castle to face examination. He had been allowed to bypass the massing crowds in the courtyard by entering through a private rear exit. Dressed expensively and impeccably, as always, the small-statured Haughey carried himself with his usual portentous bearing, although age, he was now 71, had diminished his ease of movement. The nasally-gravelly voice carried through the hall, but now without its previous authority. It was to diminish further over the course of the next two hours. Justine McCarthy in the *Irish Independent* wrote 'how the man who long perpetuated his own defied myth, who had been fabled for rising from the dead, was locked in the grip of the gods. A sudden shaft of watery sunlight illuminated the witness box where he sat upright and tense, the light falling at such a sharp angle through the skylight in the ceiling that it speared him, and him alone. Like a biblical painting depicting the ire of a wrathful God.'

Haughey told the tribunal that, when he walked out of Government Buildings on 11 February 1992, he was determined to leave public life behind and to detach himself permanently from it. McCullough said to him, 'You have done the State some service' – recalling the self-congratulatory manner in which Haughey had spoken of himself when stepping down as Taoiseach – before adding acidly, 'the State has paid you in respect of that service'. Haughey merely replied, 'Yes.' The former commander of detail now claimed his recollection of events became 'increasingly remote and diffused'. In endeavouring to recollect dates, times and sequences of events, details of meetings and conversations, he had been 'at this disadvantage'. He had 'omitted' to inform his lawyers fully. 'These letters and statements were unhelpful to the tribunal in the carrying out of its work,' he admitted.

McCullough pressed further. 'And would you accept now, Mr Haughey, that you sat outside the tribunal, in Abbeville, waiting to see whether or not the tribunal would gather sufficient evidence to make it incumbent upon you to make a statement? Would that be a fair summation?' Haughey replied: 'Well, it could be, but I suppose basically I was looking at the fact of the inevitable disclosure.' The audience laughed when Haughey admitted to being impressed by the assiduous investigative skills of the tribunal.

What Haughey tried to describe as 'incorrect', McCullough correctly characterised as 'untrue'. Haughey kept his composure for the most part, showed no flashes of anger, didn't appear particularly upset, and yet he unravelled. He took refuge behind a dead man. Traynor apparently told Haughey he had 'difficulties' in his personal finances but that he would 'take care' of them. Haughey, deliberately perhaps, didn't want to know the details of how he would do that and his claims now could not be contradicted. Haughey maintained he had not paid any attention to his financial affairs since the 1960s, that they were 'peripheral to my lifestyle', leaving them in the hands of Traynor so that he 'could get on with affairs of State . . . My work was my lifestyle. When I was in office I worked every day all day. There was no room for any sort of extravagant lifestyle.' The haughtiness and pomposity was breathtaking to most of us present, as was that particular lie: we knew full well, and would find out more in the future, of the nature of his extra-marital affair with the journalist Terry Keane, marked by intimate meals in the most exclusive restaurants, and of other activities, such as riding with hounds, rarely afforded to the ordinary people from whom Haughey had emerged. But it was entirely possible that he spent without regard to how much money was coming in, or from where, as if it was his due.

He said Ben was a very extraordinary man who had undertaken 'this extraordinary action out of generosity and perhaps out of public spirit'. He had no recollection of taking the drafts but 'on the facts presented I have no alternative but to accept it'.

Conor Cruise O'Brien, a former diplomat, government minister and journalist, and for many years the most prominent of Haughey's critics, was sitting in the body of the audience, perhaps enjoying the spectacle. He once wrote that it would take a string of garlic, a fistful of silver bullets and a stake through the heart at midnight to take out Haughey. Instead, it was three bank drafts that did it.

Smiling as he emerged through the entrance to the State apartments at 1pm to get into his car in the upper courtyard of Dublin Castle, Haughey waved to the largely silent crowd, seemingly assuming all of us assembled were his supporters. There was one, 78-year-old Frank Harrison, a waiter in the Trocadero restaurant, who raced forward to shake Haughey's hand, evading security. The silence broke at that point. The hissing and booing started, along with cries of 'liar' and 'lock him up'. Haughey was visibly startled. He quickly got into the front seat of his chauffeur-driven car and departed.

35.

Lowry's skewed perception of reality

IF HAUGHEY WAS THE FOCUS of attention for many, Lowry was not forgotten. The tribunal's work was suspended for the 1997 general election campaign in June and did not resume until the end of the month. Lowry had topped the poll in North Tipperary, exceeding the quota on the first count comfortably. The locals weren't allowing their hero to be torn down by the media and the establishment.

Lowry's opportunity to give evidence didn't come until Friday, 4 July. I wrote that Sunday how his perception of reality was skewed, that he seemed to believe that the value system he held was shared by many other people. When asked about having Dunnes complete work on his house as payment in lieu of income, he not only said that he saw nothing unusual in this arrangement but claimed that the vast majority of people present would have engaged in a similar 'cost-effective' manner of improving their accommodation if offered the chance. Given the level of tax evasion that took place in Ireland in the late 20th century, he mightn't have been entirely incorrect.

When questioned, Lowry denied that he was 'absolutely and completely in Ben's pocket', but admitted receiving almost £500,000 in various payments, in addition to the £390,000 for the extension to his house, all before he became a minister but while a serving TD. They had agreed a figure of £200,000 for the work on the house, later considerably exceeded. An architect, Peter Stevens, did the work, which included acquiring paintings, furniture and a custom-made bed, towards which Lowry paid just £31,000. Ben's evidence was that Lowry suggested that Ben pay for the house improvements, and that it was up to Lowry to account for his own tax.

Lowry was supposed to supply service to Dunnes Stores at cost price, and be paid a guaranteed £50,000 a year personally with a bonus based on performance, decided upon by Ben. Lowry hadn't told Buchanan of these payments. It was a significant omission, likely to be regarded as indicative of a continuing desire to deceive and hide.

Lowry maintained he 'had tried for years' to regularise the method of payments from Dunnes and failure to do so was the cause of the 'nightmare I have lived over six to eight months'. Lowry said he did not know at the time that he was the owner of a company in the Isle of Man. Asked about a payment of stg£25,000 into a Bank of Ireland account in the Isle of Man in October 1990, he said he 'didn't know' why it was made that way but all payments were 'strictly and solely' for refrigeration services. 'If you look at the situation, I wasn't the only one who was paid in that manner. The Price Waterhouse report identified in the region of £3.5m of such payments. I was the only one who was publicly identified with that kind of payment and I don't know why. I would much prefer if the payment was made directly to me.'

He claimed it was up to the company 'to decide on what fashion they were going to pay me', which was clearly nonsense. 'I did not ask for the money to be paid in that way and I was never comfortable with the monies being paid in that way and I asked (on) countless occasions that the matter would be regularised so that I could finalise my business with Dunnes Stores.' He was shown a letter from Noel Smyth to him that stated bluntly in its first line that the off-shore bank account had been set up 'at your request'. He was unable to explain why, if he disapproved of being paid into foreign accounts, he didn't bring the money back to Ireland immediately and declare it to the Revenue as he should have.

Lowry was asked to explain why Ben gave money to Fine Gael. 'Ben said to me that when the country is going well, Dunnes Stores is going well, and for that we need good government and to have that we need good opposition,' he replied.

Margaret and Frank were determined the company's good name should be upheld in the tribunal's report and the company's lawyer, Garrett Cooney SC, asked McCracken to exonerate the company, in specific terms, 'of all the charges and insinuations of wrong-doing'.

Cooney said Ben had engaged 'in business practices which were unorthodox to say the least and his distribution of largesse to politicians by the improper diversion of company funds was extremely ill-advised and, when discovered, caused outrage to his fellow directors.' Margaret and Frank were 'stunned', 'amazed' and 'shocked', he asserted. The board hadn't sanctioned or acknowledged the payments in advance and once they learnt details had immediately investigated. Finding out was 'all but impossible', he claimed.

Cooney emphasised the payments had four common characteristics: made by or at the direction of Ben; not authorised by the company; deliberately concealed from the other directors; almost all made from accounts outside the books and records of the company. The establishment of various companies and accounts in the Isle of Man by Noel Smyth were 'on Mr Bernard Dunne's sole instruction'.

Cooney said the others only became aware of the nature of the dealings with Lowry after Ben was removed from the board. Most payments were routed through off-shore companies established by Ben, or Smyth, or through accounts held by Ben at the Bank of Ireland in Marino. Cooney asserted that no benefit was sought or gained at the meeting between Ben and the Revenue Commissioners, which was 'clearly the product of Mr Bernard Dunne's modus operandi rather than a resolution of the company'.

Cooney took issue with the 'constant use on television of the company logo' when reports were being broadcast about tribunal hearings. It was understood, he said, that the pictures were motivated by 'considerations of convenience' rather than any desire to convey the impression that the company was at the heart of any perceived or real wrongdoing. 'Nonetheless, it illustrates the potential for grave harm and damage being done to the company's reputation and good name which could, in turn, have very grave consequences for its business activities and commercial success. For that reason, justice required that the tribunal's final report should exonerate the company in specific terms. The company had achieved its 'unparalleled success' without the assistance of any grant, subsidy or other form of payment or favour from any government or individual politician.

Ben's lawyers maintained that Ben had told the truth about all payments made to politicians and the circumstances in which they were made, that he saw it as his duty to be fully transparent and obliging. Seamus McKenna said it was 'unfortunate' that Cooney raised matters subject to separate family litigation. 'However, I would strongly urge you, on the totality of the evidence, that Mr Dunne is entitled to a finding that in making the payments he had neither the intention nor the expectation of obtaining political favour or other benefit of any kind.'

The court of public opinion made its verdict known in T-shirts bearing the legend: *Ben there, Dunne that, bought the Taoiseach*. It remained to be seen what conclusions would derive from McCracken's informed judgement.

In the tribunal report, published on 25 August 1997, McCracken declined to exonerate Dunnes Stores. He found it had knowingly colluded in tax evasion by making under-the-counter payments to employees. He criticised Ben's Bank of Ireland account in Marino as an example of how the board couldn't escape responsibility for Ben's actions by claiming ignorance. 'A curious feature of this account is that Mrs Margaret Heffernan's evidence is that this account was operated solely by Ben Dunne and that neither she nor her fellow directors knew anything about it. The fact that the account existed and that payments were made out of it without the knowledge of the board of the company shows the extent of the financial control which Ben Dunne had over the affairs of Dunnes Stores at the relevant time.' He noted that Ben could issue cheques at will, or have Irwin do so, without authority from anybody else. 'It is certainly strange that the financial affairs of one of the country's largest commercial enterprises should be controlled solely by one man . . . It was clearly unwise that one person should be given such unsupervised financial control of the affairs of a business the size of Dunnes Stores Group . . . at the very least the company must bear some blame for not having put any proper supervisory procedures in place.'

He did not accept Lowry's evidence that many payments received from Dunnes Stores were for personal consultancy work. He labelled him a tax evader, knowingly assisted by Ben. 'These accounts were opened and the monies paid in this way with the intention of allowing Mr Lowry to have money in an offshore account, contrary to the exchange control legislation then in being.' He noted Lowry 'was able to ignore, and indeed cynically evade, both the taxation and exchange control laws of the State with impunity . . . If such a person can behave in this way without serious sanctions being imposed it becomes very difficult to condemn others who similarly flout the law . . . While the tribunal accepts that Streamline Enterprises made large savings for the Dunnes Stores Group, it is unacceptable to make this a justification for Lowry's behaviour.'

Lowry's tax evasion made him vulnerable to all kinds of pressures from Dunnes Stores, even though there was no evidence of political favours granted in return for money. Should the existence of these accounts have become known to any third party, political or financial, favours could have been sought in return for silence. 'The possibility that political or financial favours could be sought in return for such gifts, or even given without being sought, is very high, and if such gifts are permissible, they would inevitably lead in some cases to bribery and corruption,' wrote McCracken. 'It is also not acceptable that any person or commercial enterprise should make such gifts in conditions of secrecy, no matter how well intentioned the motives may have been.'

McCracken condemned Lowry's 'apparent lack of candour' – a euphemism if ever there was one – in his 1996 Dáil statement implying he did not have offshore accounts.

The report went no softer on Haughey. McCracken found as 'unacceptable and untrue' Haughey's claims of knowing nothing of his personal finances, of never knowing about his account with Ansbacher Cayman, of not remembering Ben personally handing him bank drafts for £210,000, and of being unaware of the tax implications of the gifts. He rejected Haughey's evidence under 11 different headings, noting how even after admitting he had misled his lawyers, he gave evidence under oath that the judge regarded as incredible. Comments such as 'quite unbelievable', 'beyond all credibility', and 'factually incorrect' littered McCracken's written assessment. He said it was unacceptable for a Taoiseach's lifestyle to be supported by gifts, and for those then to be stored in secret offshore accounts to hide them from Revenue Commissioners.

McCracken concluded neither Dunnes Stores nor Ben ever requested Lowry to make personal or political interventions on foot of the gifts of money paid over to him. No such findings were laid against Haughey either. However, McCracken didn't have the full facts. It had painted only a partial picture. Another tribunal, steered by Mr Justice Michael Moriarty, would do all of that and more, and it would paint a very different picture not just of Haughey and Lowry, but of Ben too.

36.

Desperate people and desperate things – the Moriarty Tribunal

BERTIE AHERN, THE FIANNA FÁIL leader who became Taoiseach after the June 1997 general election, came under immediate pressure on the publication of the McCracken report to establish a new tribunal, with a wider brief, to investigate further. He did so reluctantly, anticipating correctly that he would not be able to control what was discovered. In establishing the new tribunal on 26 September 1997, he let rip at Haughey, despite being regarded by many as his protégé: 'It is sad for our democracy and our nation, that a leader who, after Lemass, put more of his stamp on the Ireland of the second half of the 20th century than possibly anyone else should have demeaned himself and political life by accepting such huge sums of money for his personal benefit from Ben Dunne.'

Worse was to come. Moriarty would disclose that Ben had told a materially incorrect story and concealed crucial evidence about additional payments to Haughey he claimed to have 'forgotten'. These were worth more than £600,000, an extraordinarily large sum to forget. That was bad enough, but more significant was that many of them predated the story Ben had told McCracken about making payments after Traynor's phone call to Fox.

The news came tumbling out in February 1999, after more than a year's investigation by the tribunal before it commenced public hearings. Ben took the witness stand for the first of 10 outings between then and 2005, having heard the outline of the Moriarty discovery. He 'accepted' that he must have paid the money although he claimed the first he knew of this was when Moriarty lawyers told him in 1998.

In summary, there were 'bearer' cheques in January 1987, signed by Ben, that amounted to £32,200 and ended up with Haughey. A cheque from Dunnes Stores Bangor for stg£282,500 went to a company called Tripleplan, where the directors were John Furze and John Collins, both officers of Ansbacher Cayman, and who controlled money for Haughey's benefit. This money cleared one of Haughey's bank overdrafts in Dublin in May 1987, long before what Ben and Fox had claimed at McCracken was the initial contact date between Traynor and Fox.

Remarkably, Fox, who would have six days in the witness stand, said he 'ceased to have a memory' of this payment and it did not 'resurface until the results of the company search against Tripleplan came to hand in January 1998', when Moriarty's work was underway. He claimed this despite the issue being a major one for auditor Kevin Drumgoole of Oliver Freaney (the firm that employed Fox) during the late 1980s. When asked why he didn't tell the auditors, he said he believed it was his 'duty to Ben to keep the payments highly confidential unless otherwise authorised by Ben'. When tribunal lawyer John Coughlan put it to Fox that his testimony was 'incredible', Fox replied that this was 'very unfair'. He had simply forgotten, but now his memory had been triggered.

Another payment of £200,000 was lodged to Ansbacher Cayman in November 1990: this was from Wytrex in Hong Kong. Another £180,000 went to Haughey in November 1992 (of which £100,000 went to Celtic Helicopters, co-owned by his son, Ciaran Haughey) and that came after Ben and Mary, and Smyth and his wife Anne-Marie, had dinner at Haughey's home.

Remarkably, a cheque for £20,000 in May 1993 was made from Ben's personal account directly to Haughey's account in National Irish Bank. This was when Ben was in hospital, recovering from his broken ankles. Haughey contacted him twice, asking him to lunch at Abbeville. On both occasions the wheelchair-bound Ben was driven there by an unnamed friend, probably his security detail, who joined the lunch party. The lunches were 'simple affairs' taken in the gardens. Although Ben said he had no recollection, he admitted it was probable he had given a cheque to Haughey on one of these two occasions. Ben thought it represented a direct payment, or may have related to some charitable cause to which Haughey had asked him to contribute. 'I have a vague memory, somewhere in the back of my head,' he told the tribunal. It was a personal cheque because Ben no longer had access to the Dunnes Stores' cheque book. The tribunal would find there was no doubt they were handed over personally. It was a remarkable conclusion given the fuss Haughey had caused in denying the receipt of three £70,000 drafts in late 1991, although those had been potentially more serious because it happened when he was still in office.

Moriarty commanded the headlines as its hearings went on, and many more key revelations were made. Ben, for example, said he never thought of his payments to Haughey as being his own money. 'I didn't see any difference between Dunnes Stores money and my money. I thought of it all as the one.' He also said he didn't have access to £700,000 personally and had always planned to use company money when the request from Haughey came. Fox, for his part, claimed he'd had 'every confidence that Ben would personally look after the payments', which is why he didn't tell the auditors. Remarkably, too, it emerged that far from pursuing repayment, as Margaret had said at McCracken, a decision was taken by Dunnes Stores, either in late 1993 or early 1994, to write off the debts and not seek repayment from Haughey – this at a time when Ben had been removed from any authority at the company but was still engaged in his legal action against the family.

Haughey stopped giving evidence at an early stage, citing ill-health. Margaret wasn't even called. Ben became more uncomfortable as his evidence unravelled and he sought to explain his behaviour by reference to mental fragility. He made a statement to the tribunal that pleaded publicly for understanding and mercy: 'I was very unbalanced to say the least, suicidal. I had the trouble in the US, I had nearly killed myself twice. I would like the tribunal to understand how broken and sick a man I was . . . The family said that I was mad and suicidal, and they were right.' He said that 'desperate people do desperate things, there was civil war going on in Dunnes Stores'.

Moriarty didn't accept the evidence from Ben and Fox when he issued his first report in December 2006, describing the payments to Haughey as 'covert and extremely difficult to detect'. Of the Tripleplan payment he concluded: 'It is inconceivable that either of them could have forgotten the fact of the payment in the circumstances in which it arose. It is all the more inconceivable that the Tripleplan payment could have slipped their minds when entirely proper and appropriate inquiries were being made year in year out by Mr. Drumgoole in the context of the annual audit. Those inquiries must have been the source of considerable discomfort for Dunne and Fox. Neither of them was willing to disclose the true purpose of the payment and it seems to the tribunal that each of them was seeking to visit the problem on the other . . . The only conclusion that could be drawn is that both Dunne and Fox deliberately concealed the fact of this payment from the Dunnes group from the Buchanan inquiry and from the McCracken tribunal. Had the connection not become apparent from the result of searches, the tribunal considers it probable that this concealment would have continued, and the payment would not have been revealed to this tribunal.' This was damning of both men.

The tribunal decided that the potential consequences of the payment becoming known would have been sufficient motivation for its exclusion from the particulars furnished to the court in the litigation between Ben and the trustees. Ben argued that if he had remembered it, he would have added it to the list, as it would have been in his interest to do so. Moriarty disagreed, suggesting that Ben had enough ammunition against his siblings with what he'd chosen to disclose without dragging in the contacts he'd had with the Revenue Commissioners. Its revelation would have caused too much additional trouble. There was only so far Ben was willing to go with his 'commercial terrorism', as he had called his own actions in taking legal action against his family in 1993 and 1994.

Moriarty noted how McCracken had decided there 'was no wrongful use of his position by Haughey', but Moriarty said 'in the light of the further payments identified, and the additional evidence it has heard, [I] cannot share that view'.

Ben hadn't told McCracken about his meetings with Seamus Pairceir, the head of the Revenue Commisioners, because he 'hadn't remembered it'. Tribunal lawyers put it to Ben that the true motivation for payments to Haughey 'that both exceeded and predated what had been conveyed to McCracken' was not admiration but was for purposes connected with the Trust and its tax. Ben replied that the money was for one purpose only: to discharge Haughey's debts.

Moriarty noted the payments began 'when the battle lines had been drawn in the large capital taxation issues between Revenue and Dunne's interests'. Moriarty said Pairceir had instituted discussions and calculations, and made decisions, which provided for a significantly more favourable CGT regime for the Dunnes trust, and that the connection was not coincidental. In approaching Revenue on behalf of Ben, 'Haughey sought to and did confer a benefit on Mr Dunne by way of actual and offered amelioration of those problems in subsequent dealings with Pairceir ... The terms of settlement offered by Pairceir to Dunne constituted a real and tangible benefit to Dunne, in that they conferred on him an option which he did not have previously.' Ben had the choice to allow the appeal to proceed, or he could settle for a lower assessment of £16 million. Moriarty said that when Haughey facilitated Ben's access, the then Taoiseach was signalling 'his support for a radical reduction in the amount of tax being demanded by the Revenue' from the Trust.

Moriarty decided Ben was 'at all times fully aware of all the payments that he made to Haughey and the tribunal cannot accept that he had any absence of recollection'. It accused him of being 'selective in the information that he provided to the McCracken tribunal and deliberately confined his disclosure to those payments which were discoverable by that tribunal. Mr. Dunne's approach to this tribunal was no different. He disclosed none of the payments to the tribunal. On each occasion the tribunal unearthed further payments, he pleaded ignorance through lack of recollection.'

The tribunal assessed the medical reports supplied on behalf of Ben, which argued his recollection and capacity were affected adversely by his kidnapping and other experiences. Moriarty said he 'cannot accept what has been conveyed to it ... to the effect that the several instances of further payments on his part discovered by the tribunal had eluded his memory ... From careful observation of Mr Dunne in evidence on several occasions, it appeared that he could be an astute and observant witness in respect of many matters and, given the high quality of assistance and advice at all times available to him, the tribunal cannot accept that all these successive transactions were matters in respect of which he had no actual recollection.'

Moriarty threw Ben a single bone: 'Notwithstanding adverse conclusions it should be recorded that both Mr. Dunne and his legal advisers were at all times prompt, courteous and cooperative in their dealings with the tribunal.' It was faint praise given everything else that had been found against him, albeit at a tribunal rather than in a court of law.

Ben was furious at being called a liar in all but name. He played the wounded victim twice on radio, seeking sympathy as well as understanding. On RTÉ's *News at One* he thundered: 'I have never been accused of being a liar before and I did not tell lies and the tribunal have called me a liar. I dispute and I refuse to accept that. I haven't hid behind smoke screens. If I didn't have a recollection of certain things, it's that I genuinely forgot . . .'

The findings were released after Haughey had died in June 2006. 'I admired him because I think he could read the future extraordinarily clear and well in lots of areas,' Ben said on radio. 'Some historians will find negatives all the time, but on balance the vast majority will look and I think the late Charles Haughey will come out with more pluses than minuses.'

'It's still a very sad time for me,' Ben said. 'Unfortunately for me some things affect me emotionally more than other things and some deaths have a profound effect on me and the death of Charlie Haughey affected me that way. I had a lot of contact with him over the years. Whether I like it or not, I feel that some of my behaviour in the past had an effect on Charlie's life, and a bad effect and that saddens me . . . One of my weaknesses unfortunately is my brain and some things, whether I've been responsible in a small way or a big way, can upset me very emotionally. What I am certainly sure of is that I caused him some hurt. That hurts me.'

There was much more to come. Moriarty's findings with regard to Ben and Lowry were equally, if not more damning. What emerged from the investigation was an exceptionally serious allegation for the tribunal to consider.

Mark FitzGerald, son of former Taoiseach Garret FitzGerald, founded and for years managed one of the country's most successful estate agencies, Sherry FitzGerald. He eschewed front-line politics but worked for Fine Gael in a voluntary capacity, acting as a trustee. He approached the tribunal with details of an extraordinary attempt by

Lowry to put pressure on him to act in a way to confer financial benefit upon Ben, at the expense of the State, potentially involving millions of pounds.

Ben bought Marlborough House for £5.4m in 1995, a year after a rent review had started. Just off O'Connell Street in central Dublin, it was known as Telephone House, and Telecom Éireann, still a fully owned State commercial body, paid an annual rent of £425,000. Ben sought to double the rent. When he was refused, an arbitrator from Sherry FitzGerald, Gordon Gill, was appointed to decide upon a figure.

Ben contacted Lowry and asked him to contact FitzGerald. Lowry approached Mark FitzGerald three times in one week, by phone and in a meeting over coffee in a hotel. In his evidence to Moriarty, FitzGerald said he told Lowry that he could not, and would not, influence the arbitration. Lowry may have been desperately pleading, or simply conniving to put pressure on, but he then asked: 'What are we going to do as Ben Dunne has contributed £170,000 to Fine Gael?'

Both Ben and Lowry gave evidence that all they had sought to do was expedite the decision in arbitration. Moriarty's lawyers asked Ben if he wished to 'modify' his evidence to McCracken, where he said he never asked any political favour from Lowry. He stuck to his story. Ben said that if Lowry had ministerial responsibility for Telecom, Ben's tenant, this was not 'at the forefront of my mind'. He said he understood the difference between his best recollection and being absolutely positive. He acknowledged that for someone reading his evidence it 'looks terrible', but that was the way he did business. Ben claimed his approach to Lowry had been 'spontaneous' and in a 'personal context', rather than as a minister.

Lowry denied trying to influence the level of rent or mentioning Ben's donation to Fine Gael. He claimed that if FitzGerald was correct in his evidence, it would certainly be improper, but that it didn't happen. All he did was try to speed things up, which was an everyday occurrence with politicians.

Moriarty accepted FitzGerald's evidence. He noted that if Lowry and Ben had got their way, Ben's company would have virtually doubled the original investment of €6.86m made just months earlier. Moriarty wrote: 'Not merely was this patently improper conduct on the part of Mr Lowry and Mr Dunne as private individuals, but it was, in addition, a particularly flagrant dereliction of duty on the part of Mr Lowry . . . What was contemplated and attempted on the part of Mr Dunne and Mr Lowry was profoundly corrupt to a degree that is nothing short of breathtaking. Further, had the increase been achieved, it would have been appreciably immune from scrutiny having been obtained through a quasi-judicial process.'

Lowry was the minister 'who in effect stood in the shoes of Telecom Éireann as tenant of Marlborough House, and for him to have sought to procure unwarranted rent increases that would have improperly enriched Mr Dunne over a seven-year period and therefore burdened public funds within his Ministerial remit amounts to a grave conflict of duty and interest.

'The evidence indicated the lengths to which Lowry was prepared to go in securing financial advantages for Mr Dunne, for whom he had reason to be grateful, for his contributions to Mr Lowry's own finances, and also for his contributions to the finances of the Fine Gael party. Secondly, it reflected Mr Lowry's contempt for the quasi-judicial process in which the arbitrator, who was in a position analogous to a judicial officer, was involved, and from whom Mr Lowry expected cooperation in what, had it succeeded, would have amounted to a gross impropriety in the discharge of the functions of an arbitrator.'

Lowry was foiled in his attempt to confer on Ben 'a benefit amounting to approximately £2.38m in the short term, and a potential capital value increase of £7.35 million'. Moriarty decided Lowry 'had sought to bring wrongful influence to bear' with 'a view to having the inflated rent imposed' and this was done 'at the behest of Mr Ben Dunne, who had previously made substantial payments both to Mr Lowry personally and Fine Gael'.

This was somewhat downplayed in media coverage of the tribunal's findings about Lowry, which concentrated more on Lowry's management of the 1995 award of a mobile phone licence to a company controlled by Denis O'Brien. The Moriarty tribunal eventually determined in 2011 that Lowry had 'secured the winning' of a major corporate competition for O'Brien by conveying substantial information to the businessman 'of significant value and assistance to him in securing the licence'. Payments by O'Brien to Lowry were 'demonstrably referable' to Lowry's interference in the licence competition, it said. There were plenty of other adverse comments. O'Brien rejected the findings of the tribunal as based on mere 'opinions' and not as findings of evidence, fact or law. Lowry alleged the tribunal's report was 'factually wrong and deliberately misleading'. Neither man took legal action, however, and the findings stand unchallenged.

On the release of Moriarty's final report in March 2011, Ben again went on Joe Duffy's *Liveline* to plead his innocence to the Irish public. 'I done absolutely nothing wrong in any of my dealings,' he declared. He added that if found guilty of the 'breathtaking' corruption of which Moriarty accused him, 'I should be put behind bars for a minimum of 10 years . . . I phoned Lowry . . . I knew he knew Mark FitzGerald and Sherry FitzGerald were doing the review. I said, "Michael, you know Mark FitzGerald. I don't know him. They're doing a rent review. Will you ever get it speeded up?"'

By way of example of how commonplace this was, Ben told Duffy about getting a brain scan for a friend: 'There was a long, long waiting list, but I was able to ring somebody who rang somebody . . . In the business world, there is an old saying: it's not what you know but who you know.' He tried to think of the word for it and came up with 'internetting'. Duffy suggested the word he was looking for was 'networking'. Ben agreed.

On 31 March 2011, the Dáil passed this motion without a vote: 'The Dáil believes the conduct of Michael Lowry set out in the [Moriarty] tribunal report was completely unacceptable, and calls on Deputy Lowry to resign voluntarily his membership of Dáil Éireann.'

Lowry did not resign. He was re-elected in three subsequent general elections, although he complained many times about the toll 'this Chinese torture' had taken on him. He argued the tribunal constituted 'intrusion, examination, scrutiny, interference, stress and vilification', but it was an expensive experience for him, although decades later he received repayment from the State of his legal costs of €2.9m. However, it still cost him, financially as well as emotionally. In September 2007, tax settlements totalling €1.45 million, more than two-thirds comprising interest and penalties, were made by Lowry and his company Garuda. He was the only person on the Price Waterhouse list drawn up by Dunnes Stores in the mid-1990s who had to pay his own tax bill.

Dunnes Stores had made a 'global settlement' with the Revenue Commissioners for everyone else but him. The amount remained confidential between the company and the Revenue. He remained on good terms with Ben and, in time, regained the working contract with Dunnes Stores which remains in place to this day.

PART 6

New roles for Ben and Margaret

2000s–2020s

37.

Rivals

As THE TRIBUNALS MEANDERED through the first decade of the new century, Margaret had other crises to consider. Already burdened by the process of managerial change, the public reaction to the strikes and now the allegations aired at the tribunal – all of which manifested in reduced market share in the supermarket business – Dunnes Stores faced possibly its biggest challenge of all: the most intense competition ever.

In 1997 Tesco, now one of the world's largest retailers and many times the size of Dunnes, returned to Ireland. Given his long-standing interest in Ireland – and his continued ownership of Brown Thomas – Galen Weston surprised everyone when he sold ABF's 78 Quinnsworth/Crazy Prices stores in the Republic and 34 stores belonging to the Stewarts Group in Northern Ireland to Tesco for £630m. It was a little more than a decade since Tesco had departed the market as a failure, but the company had transformed and had aggressive ambitions, and the ability to deliver. It also saw that Ireland, moving closer to the end of the IRA campaign of violence and terrorism, was becoming a far more prosperous place in which to trade.

The Celtic Tiger economy had been born, unemployment had tumbled, incomes were up, and consumption patterns had changed. According to academics Edmund O'Callaghan and Don O'Riordan, 'between 1991 and 1997, the value of goods consumed increased by 25 per cent' as we were eating and drinking more and spending more on fashion. Tesco's timing in re-entering a changing, more prosperous Ireland was perfect: consumer spending increased from £31bn in 1998 to an estimated £40bn in 2000. It was the era of the breakfast roll for those on their way to work and ready-to-cook fresh food for time-pressed people on their way home in the evening. Food retailers increased their offerings of high-margin, premium-priced organic, low-fat and low-sugar ranges as well as ethnic cuisine.

If Quinnsworth/Crazy Prices had advertised heavily, Tesco could afford to do even more. If Superquinn had placed an emphasis on customer service, Tesco could do more with its own loyalty card. It introduced a wider product range, including enormous selection of quality own-brand food products and clothing, mobile phones, CDs and DVDs. It believed it would prosper from lower purchasing costs (through being a bigger buyer) and better management systems. Conscious of its previous failure, Tesco promised the government it would continue buying goods from Irish suppliers and would provide Irish products to stores in the UK. Tesco Ireland, as the brand would be called, developed 90 own-brand Irish products within its first year.

Margaret consistently warned her staff of the threat of new competition and used Drury Communications for internal communications. It told hand-picked journalists what Margaret was telling staff. In early 1998 she said it was not a question of if, but when Sainsburys would enter the market in the Republic. Her focus was increasingly on improving the stores, continuing to introduce new technology, staff training, and marketing. A year later she warned her staff that competition would come in towns as well as cities, repeating her expectation that Sainsbury's would try to emulate its success north of the border. She worried margins would be squeezed, particularly in fresh food.

Margaret's concern about Sainsbury's was matched by worries about another supermarket giant, Safeway, especially when it spent £100m in 1997 in buying into the owner of the Wellworth chain in Northern Ireland. Wellworth had been purchased in the early 1990s by Tony O'Reilly's Fitzwilton company, which in turn prompted Dunnes to buy 9% of the Fitzwilton shares, although it never tried to take over the company and eventually sold the shares again. It looked as if Safeway and Fitzwilton might use the partnership as a bridgehead into the Republic, but they missed the chance when Aldi and Lidl arrived instead.

Dick Reeves, Andrew Street and John McNiffe, as directors, were crucial to the Dunnes response as they assisted Margaret in refurbishing the stores, upgrading the fresh food available, and bringing in a value card after years of refusing a loyalty scheme. Margaret recognised that developing customer loyalty was as important as enticing new customers. Dunnes had the advantage of value-added non-food products in its extensive household and clothing departments that acted as a draw to grocery customers.

In 1997, Dunnes finally entered the loyalty card market despite not having the technology to make the best use of it. But the information that could be gleaned from each card made them irresistible. Basic demographic information – age, marital status, number of children – could be added to detailed logging of consumption, and offers could then be tailored for individual customers. The joke was that a super-market might know before a father-to-be that his partner was pregnant, gleaned from her purchases. It would be years, though, before Dunnes made full use of the data. But there was an immediate marketing benefit: the loyalty card offered cash discounts to regular shoppers and they built up points that could be exchanged for vouchers that entitled them to cash discounts. It kept customers.

There was also greater competition from convenience stores run by independents, offering longer opening hours but on smaller sales volumes that were not attractive to Dunnes. Convenience stores did not take the cost-conscious weekly shopper away from the multiple entirely but were used increasingly for spur-of-the-moment shopping where price was of less consequence, especially for those breakfast rolls. Their smaller size made symbol convenience stores ideal for city-centre outlets, and as inner-city populations continued to grow, symbol stores (particularly Centra and Spar) began to proliferate. Larger-format symbols, like BWG's Eurospar and SuperValu, traded well in suburbia. As the number of independent grocers decreased, the number of symbol operators increased; between 1993 and 1998, their numbers went up by 13.5%. Petrol forecourts became popular as expanded shops, too. Everyone was muscling in for market share, but the overall market was growing, with greater prosperity in a growing population, where emigration was falling and immigration was a new phenomenon.

By the end of the 1990s, Tesco Ireland, Dunnes Stores and Superquinn controlled just under 50% of the entire grocery market, but even more competition was emerging from German 'limited range discounters' (LRDs). Aldi arrived in 1999, and Lidl a year later. The big three full-service food retailers would typically carry about 30,000 items in their major stores. The new entrants had a 'no frills' approach, extremely cost-conscious, employing minimal staff numbers, stocking mainly own-brand products and avoiding elaborate displays. They carried only about 1,000 lines. Their focus was ambient, chilled or frozen products.

They were underestimated on arrival, the belief being that their offering was too limited and cheap and not Irish. But the impact of a demographic phenomenon – immigration from mainland European countries – was underestimated. The 'new Irish' were familiar with Aldi and Lidl. Contrary to expectations, the discounters consistently gained market share, trading based on price and value, not customer service or well-known brands. Twice-weekly special offers in hardware and DIY, electrical and household goods created an entirely new shopping category and queues of eager customers. Encouraged, the new entrants invested heavily in own-brands and central distribution, as well as using Irish producers for fresh fruit and vegetables and certain categories of fresh meat. Over a decade they gained about 10.6% market share between them. Dunnes envied how the LRDs paid less than 5% of their sales in wages, whereas it paid about 10%. Aldi and Lidl were reckoned to operate on a profit margin of 3–4%, as against about 11% at many Dunnes outlets.

Dunnes had mixed views at the time about government action. Despite its lobbying, the Groceries Orders Act (1987) was renewed in 2000. The Competition Authority estimated in 2004 that the Groceries Order Act was costing individual Irish households €480 per annum by preventing the likes of Dunnes from selling items at below wholesale cost. Successful lobbying by RGDATA kept the Order in place until 2006, when its abolition was hailed as a breakthrough on behalf of consumers that would result in lower prices. It didn't work out that way. Prices continued to increase. Not only that, prices at many supermarkets were remarkably similar to each other, a process known as 'price-matching'. It may not have been done by way of consensus – which would have been 'price-fixing' and illegal under competition laws – but the supermarkets were obsessive about not being undercut by each other. Surveys by the CAI found that the difference in the combined price of a basket of goods from one chain to the next might be as little as 50 cent. On more than one occasion it discovered the price of a basket in Dunnes and Tesco to be identical. However, informal agreements were reached that there would be no races of mutual destruction, where prices were pulled down to a level that was unprofitable for all. Competition was brought only to a point, but no further.

More useful, however, was the legislative cap on supermarket size. The government wanted to prevent a repeat of the British and American experiences of building large suburban complexes outside city- and town-centre locations. It didn't stop the development of retail parks – which did some damage to traditional retailing – but Dunnes already owned stores ranging in size from 75,000 sq.ft to 110,000 sq.ft throughout Dublin and Cork, giving it a competitive advantage.

This made Dunnes a target for international retailers wanting to come to Ireland. In late November 1999, the London-based specialist magazine *Retail Week* reported that Allan Leighton, chief executive of Asda, had visited Dunnes and was conducting an unofficial due diligence examination. Asda was the UK-owned subsidiary of the American company Wal-Mart, the world's largest supermarket chain, one that aggressively discounted prices but also specialised in clothes and other merchandise. The suggestion was that Wal-Mart was some-what dissatisfied with the profitability of Asda and wanted to combine it with Dunnes in Ireland to maximise its buying power and profits, something that did not augur well for existing suppliers to Dunnes.

In the following days I wrote for the *Sunday Tribune* that there was almost no chance that Dunnes would be sold to Wal-Mart, that the rumours were untrue, confident that the information I was getting from good sources was accurate. That's not to say that Margaret had not considered the possibility of an outright sale, although only briefly and cursorily, or a stock market flotation to raise money by selling a portion of the existing shares, both for expansion and to make payments to shareholders as part of a restructuring. Margaret took an interest in what had happened at WM Morrison, a UK-based super-market group that remained under family control despite joining the stock market. But even this was most unlikely: ownership was linked to control and neither could be diluted. The Dunne family had to be in charge, assisted by well remunerated loyal servants, but never more than that. Managers and even directors were courtiers who would be paid for their service but at the family discretion, never as a right.

Dunnes Stores entered the 21st century catering, as ever, for the mass market, offering quality goods at reasonable prices. *Always better value* became the company slogan, and competitors noted that it was barely removed from Ben Snr's *Better value beats them all*. Consumer spending continued to increase, although greater wealth for many, if not all, did not reduce price-consciousness. Ireland became wary of being 'ripped off'. The introduction of the euro in 2002 made price comparisons across Europe easier, even if what really exercised some people was the sterling stickers on many clothes in UK-owned shops that emphasised how much more expensive those items were when priced in euro. Mintel research in 2003 found that 21% of shoppers favoured own-brands and that the most important shopping factors for Irish shoppers were price, quality, locality, helpfulness of staff and range of products. That emphasis on price had not been noticed before. Retailers argued that the costs of doing business in Ireland – rent, insurance and VAT – forced dearer prices. IBEC said wages in the retail sector were 28% higher than in Northern Ireland and 60% higher than in Spain. Many consumers responded by heading over the border, particularly to buy alcohol.

The appointment of Eoin McGettigan to the board in 2005 suggested to some that an external managing director was coming. McGettigan, after all, was chief executive of Co-op, a large retail group in England, but knew Ireland well from his time as a senior member of Musgrave's management, where he headed its UK operations. The initial gossip was that he would take over from Reeves as director of food, given that Reeves was near retirement age. But the incumbent did not want to go yet and McGettigan's role was never made public, although it was rumoured that he was charged with building a centralised distribution depot. A site was identified in Ashbourne, county Meath, but Margaret baulked at the €50m-plus estimated cost and was loath to remove the flexibility on what stock to carry at individual outlets. McGettigan became increasingly frustrated, finding, as others had before, that the family made the big decisions and didn't concede autonomy to managers. McGettigan didn't last a year before heading to Lifestyle Sports.

In 2005 Margaret watched with great interest as one of her oldest rivals, Feargal Quinn, sold Superquinn for €450m. This business would not stay in the family, even though his son, Eamon, had become deeply involved in running it. The property boom was both a frustration and an opportunity. Superquinn found itself being outbid regularly when it looked to purchase sites, either by rival retailers or those building housing. But there were others, caught up in the frenzy of the time, who were prepared to pay more for property than the cautious, experienced Quinn and who thought they could ride the economic wave to make more money than him out of shopping.

The 69-year-old Quinn decided to sell to a consortium called Select Retail Holdings (SRH). Its day-to-day management was overseen by Dubliner Simon Burke, the former chairman of London toy retailer Hamleys. At the time of purchase, Superquinn's market share was just below 9% and it had only 20 outlets. The new owners spoke of opening 10 new outlets over the following five years, keeping the branding and its positioning at the top end of the market. It said it would review Superquinn's existing property portfolio with a view to 'releasing cash' for the redevelopment of existing properties or the purchase of new sites. This was taken to mean building apartments overhead existing units. It bought the Montrose Hotel in Stillorgan from Jury's Doyle for €40m and planned to develop the site not much more than a stone's throw from Margaret's domestic compound as a supermarket and apartments.

Margaret could later conclude that her approach was justified. In 2007, in an example of hubris, and failing entirely to anticipate what was coming for the economy, Superquinn introduced a new luxury food collection that was priced 25% higher than existing branded stock. A year later Select rejected approaches to sell from foreign retailers. By July 2011, receivers were appointed, with banks owed €400m fearing they would not get their money back. Within days Musgrave bought the business, and by 2014 the Superquinn name was gone, all 24 units rebranded as SuperValu. The SuperQuinn brand was retained for its famous sausages but few other products. It was proof, if Margaret needed it, that success in retailing was not permanent. Dunnes would always have to fight its corner, but Margaret had the appetite and the aptitude to do battle.

38.

Legal combat

DUNNES STORES RELISHED A legal fight. It took part in an enormous number of court cases under Margaret's leadership, many hundreds, most often as a defendant, appealing on many occasions to the Supreme Court when subject to judgements it disliked, delaying on fulfilling court orders until the last possible moment, settling cases sometimes only because embarrassing details were at risk of coming to light. Dunnes engaged in legal warfare, as it was perfectly entitled to do, but it was a classic example of how going to court often has little to do with achieving justice, as people outside of the system might assume is its purpose. Court actions can be designed to establish or confirm a balance of power, often won by the people or companies with the deeper pocket or greater willingness to fight, and to extract a better financial outcome than might otherwise emerge without involving the lawyers. They are not necessarily fought on principle. Under Margaret's stewardship, Dunnes fought legally with government, State agencies, landlords, property developers, exiting employees and business rivals. The cases would fill a book in themselves – and can't all be listed here – but given the business's reluctance to show itself to the public via the media, many of the cases have been extremely revealing about the company's mindset, and particularly Margaret's.

The willingness to take on the State was noticeable. Even if she had co-operated fully with the tribunals – although she had no choice about that – Margaret initiated a decade-long legal campaign against the appointment by the Minister for Enterprise and Employment – initially Mary Harney before she handed the position over to others – of an authorised officer to investigate Dunnes Stores for possible breaches of the Companies Acts, based on information that emerged from the tribunals. Dunnes made appeal after appeal – tying the State in knots and frustrating its efforts – and was not slow to hurl accusations in what lawyers for the State called a campaign of 'non-compliance'.

At one case, State counsel Eoghan Fitzsimons asked if Dunnes' lawyer, Adrian Hardiman (later a Supreme Court justice), was accusing the minister of being 'effectively guilty of fraud'. Hardiman responded that he wasn't, but he was alleging 'bad faith'. Margaret swore an affidavit, that her barrister read in court, in which she alleged the RTÉ newsroom had been contacted by persons acting on behalf of the minister to alert it to judicial review proceedings instituted by Dunnes challenging the appointment of the authorised officer. She also claimed material was being routinely published in newspapers that could only have had its origin in investigations being undertaken by the minister's department. If the minister was not 'restrained' by the court, there was 'a manifest risk of further disclosure of inform-ation relating to Dunnes', a potential breach of the confidentiality of sensitive records.

Margaret's attitude was to harden further in the following years. In 2004, Donie Cassidy, chairman of the Oireachtas Committee on Enterprise and Small Business, complained that Dunnes refused to turn up to a public inquiry it was hosting into high supermarket prices in the Republic. Cassidy said its non-appearance was unacceptable, that the 17 days he had given was 'ample notice'. Dunnes said the notice was 'too short'. In Ben Snr's time the company would have appeared, but Margaret was frustrated now by what she saw as unwar-ranted intrusion by the State into how she ran Dunnes; her father had never had to put up with this level of scrutiny. It is not uncommon for big powerful businesses to somehow regard themselves as victims. Sometimes, however, the paranoia and willingness to fight may have some justification.

Dunnes became embroiled in an extraordinary row with the Revenue Commissioners over the plastic bag levy introduced in 2002. The government imposed an initial 15 cent levy on the use of each plastic bag in a shopping outlet (increased to 22 cents in 2007), to reduce their consumption and the adverse effects of dumping and to encourage people to bring their own bags for shopping. Dunnes decided that the lighter plastic 'pinch and pull' bags used in its stores for loose fresh food items, should not fall within the scope of levy. The Revenue

Commissioners disagreed and made an assessment for €36.4m for a five-year period to 2008. Dunnes appealed.

A lengthy set of court proceedings began, lasting more than 15 years. It paid off. The Revenue reduced its claim to €8.53m, but even then Dunnes continued its argument that it didn't owe any money. In November 2023 it finally lost the case at the Tax Appeals Commission, but at least only had to pay the lower amount. Ironically, given its regular battles with the Revenue Commissioners, it was discovered in 2012 that a company called Silverwood Developments, owned by trust companies operating out of Earlsfort Terrace and in charge of the Dunne family's property portfolio, was landlord to the Revenue for a premises on South Great George's Street, very close to the Dunnes headquarters: the rent was €1.8m per annum.

A 2011 case taken by its former head of finance, Larry Howard, also gained prominence. Howard alleged in court that Margaret froze him out with veiled threats to sack him, that he once heard her say that she wanted 'either fucking men or mice' [sic] to help run the business. He claimed she had a 'tempestuous' management style. He believed he was a marked man from the time Street departed for Superquinn in 2010 to become its chief executive because he was regarded as an 'Andrew man': 'I was treated differently and was excluded from many functions for reasons which I can only assume were based on some ill-conceived and unjustified presumption that I was going to leave and join Superquinn.'

At a meeting on 1 June 2010, with Fox, her daughter Anne and her niece Sharon present, Margaret challenged Howard about figures from a newly introduced software package and told him, 'If you don't get yourself up to speed on Oracle, you're wasting your time here'. Margaret and Fox had a side conversation in which Howard said he heard Margaret remark, 'He's not effective', to which Fox replied, 'He is effective – he is still holding money'. Howard took that to mean delaying payments to suppliers. Margaret told him 'we have account-ants coming out of our ears' and by her facial expression and tone of voice was inappropriately critical of him, he claimed. She called him a 'floater' and said she was paying him too much money 'to float'. Over the subsequent months, he was removed from responsibility for a significant number of functions.

When summonsed to Margaret's office in September, she 'told me not "to look so worried" as she was eating her lunch and "would not 'sack' me yet".' In December, Margaret phoned him about an error he had highlighted in a VAT return and had brought to Fox's attention. He told her that a repayment was 'the right thing to do' and Margaret became 'very animated' and told him: 'That is exactly why you have no future in Dunnes Stores.' Margaret told Howard to write down on a piece of paper the functions he was responsible for and to send it to her so she could 'discuss it with Frank Dunne'. This revelation was somewhat surprising as it was assumed widely that Frank was very much removed from the business by this stage; it appeared that Margaret still contacted him on some key issues.

After Howard's solicitors wrote to Margaret, he was asked to attend a meeting with Anne and Sharon, who were now in senior management and operating as Margaret's right-hand women. They asked him to go home while the issues his solicitors had raised were investigated. He was told it was not a disciplinary action. He attended work on 7 March and Anne told him she was directing him to go home and that his salary would be paid. The case was later settled out of court.

Similar allegations were levelled against Margaret in an unfair dismissal case at the Employment Appeals Tribunal. The company's security chief of ten years, Sean Cavanagh, a former senior Garda, alleged that he was almost reduced to tears when sacked by her. 'She [Heffernan] was slapping the desk. She was sitting opposite me across the table, her face as white as a sheet and black hair streaming across her face,' was how he later described the meeting that led to his dismissal. He said that Margaret was 'shouting, screaming and banging the desk . . . There I was across the table from a multimillionaire who was destroying my life,' he told the tribunal. The finding was that both had been aggressive.

An 'infringement' case taken by the Karen Millen fashion business took nearly 10 years of legal argument and went to the European Court of Justice (ECJ) where, in 2014, Dunnes lost again, having already failed in the Supreme Court. Karen Millen claimed Dunnes produced 'rip-off' copies of its designer clothes, in breach of its intellectual property rights. In its judgement the ECJ said Karen Millen had put a shirt and top on sale in Ireland in 2005 and the items were purchased by representatives of Dunnes which 'subsequently had copies of the garments manufactured outside Ireland and put them on sale in its Irish stores in late 2006'.

Margaret ignored complaints by Aldi alleging her company was carrying on a misleading comparative advertising campaign in 'flagrant' breach of the relevant laws. Aldi told the Commercial Court that Dunnes acted unlawfully in how it carried out a comparative advert-ising campaign aimed at trying to stem a 'haemorrhage' of customers to Aldi and Lidl. Aldi alleged Dunnes had put up banners and labels in several stores across the country conveying the 'completely misleading impression' that various Dunnes products were cheaper than equivalent Aldi ones. It alleged Dunnes compared a series of products, including oranges, cosmetic creams, shower gel, tomato ketchup and dog food, that were not comparable on grounds including that the weights or quality differed. Inferior products were compared with Aldi products and objective differences were not drawn to the attention of customers.

Margaret showed that in some respects she was no different from Ben in how she ran her business. Although Dunnes did not have a centralised warehouse of its own, it had used Whelan Frozen Foods for more than 25 years for some services and had always been the only client of the family-owned warehouse and distribution firm.

In February 2005, Whelan was given a year's notice that its chilled and frozen foods distribution business would lose its contract and six months' notice in relation to the textiles and non-chilled business. Whelan secured an interlocutory injunction against the retailer, alleging that Frank had told Whelan that Dunnes was 'unhappy' with the level of profits being made by the service provider and threatened to halve the business given to the distributor if it did not cut operating costs. Whelan claimed Dunnes was using 'economic duress' as a negotiating tool to obtain information about Whelan's accounts, in order to direct the company on how it should manage its business. It turned out the distributor reported turnover of almost €190m in the 12 months to January 2005 and an operating profit of €1.8m. Whelan claimed Dunnes had 'sensationalised' its profits and accused Dunnes of trying to put it out of business by squeezing its profit margins to unsustainable levels, and that the company was set up to supply Dunnes and terms and margins were agreed verbally between the two sides. 'I say and believe that it has always been the policy of Dunnes never to enter into written agreements,' Paddy Whelan Snr said during the legal battle.

At the injunction hearing, Dunnes claimed the directors of Whelan were getting excessive fees and that the company balance sheet indicated the company was making 'excessive profits'. In further contacts, Frank told Whelan Snr that he did not want to put Whelan out of business and was 'interested in fairness'. The case was eventually settled out of court, but only after it became known that Ben was willing to appear as a witness on behalf of Whelan, even though this was more than a decade after he left Dunnes.

The cost of all these legal actions has never been disclosed but they would not have been cheap, not with the retainers demanded and bills submitted by expensive lawyers. It doesn't seem to have always been about winning – there are times when warnings had to be given that the likelihood of success was low – but it may have been as much about discomfiting the opponent, an exercise of power when with the better hand, of stubbornness when holding the weaker cards, but having the financial wherewithal to bluff it out. In Margaret's world, supported by Frank, might was right.

39.

The Great Recession

MARGARET DID NOT SEE the property and banking crash looming in 2008. In the years running up to it, Dunnes actively purchased sites for new stores. Industry insiders believed many of the purchases were merely to block competitors, not for Dunnes to build on, but they cost tens of millions of euro to assemble. Margaret was far from alone in missing what should have been obvious: that a speculative bubble was inflating, and that it would burst. In 2007 she made a peak Celtic Tiger-era personal investment, buying a €4.3m three-bedroom apartment overlooking Government Buildings at Dunloe Hall on Merrion Street (which was sold in 2024 for just over €2m). She also committed Dunnes to multiple investments that implied she saw no threat to continued economic prosperity.

By the time the 'Great Recession' arrived, Dunnes had 114 outlets in the Republic, 23 in Northern Ireland, six in England, five in Scotland and five in Spain. If secrecy was paramount in the Republic, Dunnes allowed the accounts in the north to be visible. In 2008 it reported a pre-tax profit of stg£37.1m and retained profits of stg£245m, despite paying tens of millions in dividends to the family over the previous decade. The assumption was that the much larger division in the Republic was making massively bigger profits and paying the owners big dividends. But as far as Margaret was concerned, the recession would threaten that profitability if corrective measures were not taken to protect the business.

Following the 2008 crash, grocery retailers lowered prices, introducing special deals on main meal products. Sales of own-brand products benefitted from the downturn and discounters' market share rose. According to Kantar's *Worldwide Panel 2010 Report*, up to 2008 the Irish grocery market was still growing (it grew by 5.7% from 2007 to 2008), but experienced a value downturn in 2009 of 3.5%, which accelerated sharply to 6.1% in the final quarter. As deflation occurred, households spent less, but the volume of goods purchased rose as consumers responded to in-store branded promotions. They weren't going out, but people still had to eat.

It wasn't that Dunnes was facing an existential crisis, as so many other businesses were. It didn't have borrowings, and the valuation of its properties was moot essentially; other companies had borrowed against the value of properties and faced loan repayment demands when those plummeted. That was irrelevant to Dunnes. Nonetheless, Margaret decided to conserve cash by pulling back on capital expenditure and what she deemed as unnecessary current spending. Plans for several new stores were delayed and where Dunnes was a tenant, it sought cheaper rents. She had signed various contracts for expansion into new units but once she saw how quickly and adversely economic conditions changed, she reneged on deals with developers, exacerbating their financial difficulties while protecting Dunnes' position.

It created conflict with developers, but also with the State in the shape of the National Asset Management Agency (NAMA), formed as an emergency measure in 2010 to take responsibility for big debts away from the near-bankrupt banks. In essence, NAMA became the banker to the developers with whom Dunnes would get into dispute.

Harry Crosbie was one tough high-profile businessman who found it almost impossible to fight Dunnes. Best-known for development of the Point Depot as Ireland's leading indoor events arena, the building of the Bord Gáis Energy Theatre and part of the redevelopment of the Dublin docklands where he lived, Crosbie got into financial trouble during the Great Recession – and a fight with Margaret made it worse.

Crosbie planned a €850m Point Village development, to include a major Dunnes outlet. Agreement was reached in February 2008 for a Dunnes unit costing €46m plus VAT. But when he scrapped the landmark 102-metre, 31-storey, Watchtower apartment block, and what was to be called The U2 Experience as a major tourist venue, Margaret decided in May 2009 that she would also pull back, dashing his slim chances of raising enough money to clear his debts. Crosbie argued they were separate developments, unconnected to Dunnes, but also that Dunnes' alleged failure to proceed jeopardised the continued financing of the remainder of his project. Dunnes didn't make the first payment as due. Crosbie claimed 'it became apparent' that it wanted to delay things to extract 'a number of significant concessions' before it would proceed.

Crosbie met with Margaret, Noel Fox and Dunnes' property agent, Irwin Druker, and Margaret told him the project was 'two years too early' and that Dunnes could not honour its contract with changes 'reflecting new market conditions'. Crosbie alleged that Druker told him that 'Dunnes can break any contract' and that, with huge redundancies coming to the docklands, the homewares business 'is fucked'. Crosbie said Druker demanded a 20–30% discount on the original terms and 10 years to pay. Reluctantly, Crosbie agreed to reduce the price Dunnes would pay from €46m to €31m, of which €11.8m was paid in late 2010. But Dunnes reneged on paying the balance and when NAMA took control of Crosbie's debts and Point Village Development Ltd (PVDL), it decided to enforce agreements with Dunnes, including the release of €15.5m held in a suspense account. Cue more legal fights.

Dunnes said PVDL was in breach of the 2008 original agreement because the square at the Point was not of a 'first-class standard appropriate to a prestigious shopping centre'. It ignored a court mandate in 2016 to fit out the store and didn't start until seven years later, finally opening the unit in 2024. Along the way Justice Máire Whelan in the Court of Appeal accused Dunnes of looking for the courts to grant it an 'Alice in Wonderland' license to interpret words in the settlement as Dunnes wished, 'depending on the result they sought to achieve'.

Meanwhile, an equally bitter dispute erupted on the Kilkenny/Waterford county border, at the Ferrybank Shopping Centre. Dunnes signed an agreement in 2007 with the centre's developer – Holtglen, owned by Derry McPhillips in Kilkenny – to anchor the scheme, which was built. It then spent most of the following years trying to evade honouring the deal, leaving a major retail space unopened for more than 15 years, even though the larger centre became home to Kilkenny Library and Kilkenny County Council municipal offices.

Dunnes agreed to pay Holtglen over €37m for the development when completed. It only paid €18m and Holtglen defaulted on its loans to Bank of Ireland, which were transferred to NAMA. The State agency decided to confront Dunnes and encouraged Holtglen to secure an award at arbitration and then a judgement at the Commercial Court, where it succeeded in getting an order for payment. Dunnes ignored the judgements and didn't pay, so NAMA went nuclear. It wrote to Dunnes, giving it seven days to pay €21.6m or it would petition the court to have Dunnes liquidated on the basis that it was unable to pay its debts, and that it would be just and equitable to have it wound up. The plaintiffs argued that Dunnes deliberately didn't pay and that planning issues raised by Margaret were 'just thought up'.

Dunnes offered just €7.5m as a settlement and to transfer all its right in the property to NAMA, but the State refused. Margaret was livid. She wrote to NAMA chief executive Brendan McDonagh, describing the Ferrybank centre as 'an unmitigated disaster' and NAMA's winding-up petition as 'an abuse of process' and 'an extraordinary step' for anybody, particularly a public agency, to take. She accused NAMA of failing to address any of the 'substantial issues' raised by Dunnes and said a report prepared by a planning consultant expressed the view that the centre was not compliant with planning permission. NAMA chairman Frank Daly – a former head of the Revenue Commissioners – responded that he didn't agree the centre was not commercially viable, and that the Dunnes' failure as anchor tenant to fit out and open its store had adversely affected the reputation of the centre and Holtglen. Daly was 'disappointed' there were no 'meaningful proposals' from Dunnes. Eventually, Margaret caved and Dunnes paid, but only after Judge Peter Kelly scolded it in court: 'Why not pay the debt due? Dunnes Stores is no different to any other litigant. It must pay its debts. It cannot prevaricate, any more than any other litigant.' Margaret wasn't someone who cared about what anyone else did: her only motivation was to do what she thought best for her family business and to fight as hard as possible for that.

It didn't end there. In the commercial court in 2016, Justice Max Barrett, in making an award for costs against Dunnes over a case it took against An Bord Pleanála regarding Ferrybank, said the retailer had 'an ulterior motive' in seeking to overturn aspects of the centre's planning permission, to get out of its contractual obligations. The judge said Dunnes had abused the process of the court. In June 2025 locals noted a sign had been posted at the centre that Better Value Unlimited Company intended to apply for permission for development at this site.

NAMA also sued Dunnes over The Square shopping centre in Tallaght, alleging 'blocking tactics' to prevent a €40m extension. NAMA previously only backed its developer clients in disagreements with the company, rather than suing Dunnes itself. NAMA was financing the extension for The Square, one of its prime remaining retail assets. Dunnes argued that the redevelopment would disadvantage its anchor store at the back of the atrium in the original shopping centre. Dunnes delayed expansion by securing a judicial review of an extension, which would add 200,000 sq.ft of new retail space and a six-storey car park. Eventually, Dunnes lost the case.

Dunnes took the approach that nobody would tell it what it could do with its land or property and that, if necessary, it would leave premises vacant, derelict or unused rather than be forced to do something with them. It was so wealthy it could afford to do that. There are many examples throughout the country of what could be best described as waste or, at worst, as acting contrary to the public good.

Dunnes built the Fair Green Plaza on the site of the old Neville's Bakery in Macroom in 2005 and fitted out 20 apartments above the shopping centre to a very high standard. Over the following 20 years those apartments never had tenants, despite the housing crisis and despite being fully fitted. Dunnes refused engagement with local politicians about their potential use. It was a decision that baffled almost everyone in the area; it made no commercial or indeed moral sense. In October 2024 then Minister for Housing Darragh O'Brien appealed for the units to be used, either by the local council or an approved housing body, but in saying 'the door is always open for Dunnes to talk to me directly' he did nothing that would provoke real engagement.

A former Dunnes Stores premises at 26–29 Upper George's Street in the centre of Dún Laoghaire remained vacant for the best part of 20 years and was the subject of a petition initiated by local councillor Lorraine Hall, who called it 'a blight on our town centre'. Despite the presence of prominent 'To Let' signage on the buildings, Hall said the buildings hadn't had tenants for a considerable number of years, while the planning registry at Dún Laoghaire Rathdown County

Council (DRCC) showed planning applications over 16 years that weren't acted upon. She accused Dunnes of 'land hoarding', which she said was 'completely at odds with what local residents and businesses want and detracts considerably from the vibrancy of our town'. Hall relied upon the Derelict Sites Act, which defined a derelict site as any land that 'detracts, or is likely to detract, to a material degree from the amenity, character or appearance of land in the neighbourhood'. Owners of derelict sites listed on the register must pay an annual levy of 7% of the property value to the local authority. However, Paul Kennedy, director of infrastructure at DRCC, said while parts of the site have been vacant for 20 years, the owners were doing 'just enough' to avoid the inspectors deeming it eligible for the Derelict Sites Register.

Dunnes appealed a vacant-site levy in relation to a newly constructed property in the Sarsfield Street Shopping Centre in Limerick, which lay idle for more than a decade before Dunnes successfully offloaded the premises to the University of Limerick (UL) in what later proved to be a highly controversial deal: UL was accused by the Comptroller and Auditor General of vastly overpaying for the vacant property, although fault for that did not lie with Dunnes. Fine Gael senator Martin Conway criticised Dunnes for leaving 'a large unit in Tralee town centre' empty. 'The existence of this vacant unit in the centre of Tralee is choking development in the area.' Retail Excellence chief executive David Fitzsimons said that Dunnes undermined trade in town centres by sitting on vacant shops around the country. Vacancy in a central area tends to decrease footfall to it.

Dunnes also engaged in rows where it was a tenant. It failed to overturn an award of €45,000 made against Dunnes because of its closure of doors that provided an important public walk-through between two Galway city shopping centres. It had been served with potential sequestration of assets and jailing of directors over its failure to comply with a Supreme Court order to pay a €384,000 judgement against it for unpaid rent to Camiveo, operators of the Edward Square Shopping Centre; Dunnes refused to honour a contract for a rent increase. When that judgement was handed down, Margaret reacted within 11 minutes, phoning a local store manager and ordering him to close the doors.

The Court of Appeal held the action was an extraordinarily swift 'retaliatory measure'. In 2019 the Court of Appeal found that the Galway chief fire officer had directed the doors be reopened for safety reasons and that Dunnes, in failing to comply, had breached its planning permission. The company owns most of the properties in which its stores are located, which is probably a mercy for landlords who don't have to deal with Dunnes, if a test for those who might be tenants of subsidiary units at centres Dunnes owns. It's the Dunnes' way or no way at all.

40.

Fitness test

IN EARLY FEBRUARY 2002 I phoned Ben at his office in the Westpoint Gym in Blanchardstown and requested an interview to mark 10 years since Orlando. Initially reluctant, he agreed, so he could tell other journalists he'd done one and that was it, no more. Two hours later I was seated in his office and we agreed we wouldn't talk about Moriarty while its work was still ongoing – or the Orlando incident itself – but instead about almost everything else. He laughed as he said, 'Who would have thought a decade ago that I would now own and run a health and fitness business. Isn't that funny given what I was doing with cocaine?'

His office was almost immediately inside the front door, with a large glass window with the blinds open, meaning anyone could look in at him; reception was at the far end of the long corridor. Customers could pop into him as first port of call, which appealed to him. He was literally the front-of-house man.

He admitted that after he left Dunnes he'd felt a bit lonely: 'I remember days when I was in Dunnes and if I decided that I wanted to play a round of golf there were any of 30 people I could ring and ask to play a round that day. Now I find it difficult to make up a fourball. I always had a small circle of friends, but I now have a much smaller circle of acquaintances. The phone stopped ringing and there were times when I used to pick it up to check it was still working. It took me a good while to accept what was happening. You learn a lot from it. But I'm not complaining because it happens to loads of people, at all levels in life. I was no different from the guy who retires and who doesn't know what to do, or the guy who is struck down by ill-health, or the guy who loses his job. At the time you think it's the worst thing possible that could happen to you but when you look back afterwards you find that you've been given a bit of space. You then use it.'

What made him different from the retiree or the unemployed was his money . . . and his realisation that having money, or the need to do business with him, had bought him company over the years. It wasn't that people didn't want to be seen with him – although maybe some shunned him from disapproval – but that they no longer had a need to suck up to him.

Although he had made various commitments to the US authorities after his conviction, he was unable to go 'cold turkey', such was the nature of his addictions. He continued to drink. 'Nobody stops me from doing anything but me. Any other way, or any attempt to control me simply wouldn't work. I have a few pints every now and again like everyone else. I know how to enjoy myself.' It was more that he was a bit more discreet apparently, and a little more sensible now.

He believed some stories about him were exaggerated, particularly in relation to his gambling. 'I can do nothing about the stories, and I do still gamble but in nothing like the way that was suggested.' This comment suggested that he was either in denial as to the extent of his gambling or too embarrassed to admit to it.

'The changes in my life came at different times in my life. There were two changes really, one of my personal life, the other in my business life. I changed my personal life after some great advice that to survive and be happier I had to change because to continue as I was going, I was going to remain unhappy. Following the initial publicity it largely happened privately. It took time.'

Those close to him suffered a lot, he conceded, and that Mary suffered greatly from the public exposure of these actions was something he regretted deeply. He wouldn't say anything more about his wife because he didn't want to talk on her behalf. 'She is a private person by nature. If she wants to make comments, she can do so for herself.'

His relationship with Margaret and with her children was not close, but it was not closed: 'If I meet them on the street or in a hotel lobby, we'd stop and talk about things, but we don't go out of our way to seek each other out and we've never really been much for family functions. I don't like weddings, for example. In any case I'm somewhat out of circulation because of where I am, so the opportunities to bump into them don't arise often.' He only went into the city centre two or three times a month.

'If I cause trouble for other people, I always regret it, but it would only have been because it turned out that way, not because something I did was meant to cause trouble. I would never do anything deliberately to cause anyone trouble in life. I think of the consequences of actions before I do most things now. I understand myself a lot more than I used to. I enjoy my own company. There was a period in my life there, and lots of areas of it, I didn't know what I wanted. Everyone goes through it to one degree or another. Some people go through their lives without enough contentment and happiness. I think there are a lot of people who don't know what they want out of life except something material. Don't get me wrong, I'm still a capitalist and enjoy making money, but there's a lot more to life than money.'

He conceded it might be easier for him to say that when he had so much money, but he still believed the proper use of time was more important: 'I can now understand the phrase that people are given time in jail. You can't buy time, but you can take it, you can spend it, and you can waste it. There are so many people who say that only if they won the lottery, they would be happy. Well, I'm not saying that it's not important, but it's only an ingredient in life. When I got into my troubles, I had to set myself goals to deal with my problems. To achieve these goals, they had to be realistic. I realised that you have to train yourself and you have to be shown how to do it. For example, you can only get good at golf through practice, but it must be shown to you how to do it. It's the same in life. You need good advisors and good teachers. I was lucky to have good people around me to help me through what I was going through although what I thought worked for me might not work for anyone else.'

Ben did not dwell on the past but said he was aware of it 'because you can't walk away from it. I've learned from it, but I think about today and tomorrow. I was extremely lucky to have a second chance, while still young enough, to start a new career.' He told me he relied greatly on his own common sense. 'If it was counselling it would work with everybody. It needs to come from someone with experience who genuinely cares for you.'

If leaving Dunnes had been a necessity for his health, I wondered if he ever regretted the price at which he'd sold his shares, now that they were worth so much more. His payment was regarded – correctly – as an enormous amount at the time, but it may have underestimated the potential value of the business. 'It was a fantastic deal, and it still is,' he told me, and he seemed genuine in that. He could have made more money, but he had much more than anyone would ever need for the rest of his life, if he didn't waste it on reckless investments.

Among the art on the walls of his office there was a particularly large painting hanging directly behind his desk entitled 'Guilty or Not Guilty?' It was by Sir Robert Ponsonby Staples, one of Northern Ireland's best-known artists of the early 20th century. It was an inexpensive piece from his collection but appeared to have been selected for its content. It featured several bewigged gentlemen arguing in a courtroom. When I asked him if the painting symbolised his personal position and, if so, what the verdict would be, he laughed and said, 'The jury doesn't seem to have been picked yet.' Anyone entering the room could not have failed to notice it: they would have to wonder what message it was meant to imply given what was known of Ben's travails.

Two of his sons, Mark and Nicholas, had joined him in the gym business. Robert lived in Washington DC and was studying to be called to the New York bar. (He later practised.) Caroline had graduated at UCD before studying for a Master's in fashion journalism at the London School of Fashion. She ran a children's clothing boutique.

It was six years since I'd interviewed him about his plans for the fitness and leisure business. He admitted it hadn't gone as expected. 'It started badly, as any business will if you don't understand it. And at first I didn't know how to run it. We had only 600 members and although we put on a brave face we were doing very badly. It took me nearly four years to learn the business but now we're doing very well.'

He cited Ryanair as an inspiration for keeping costs down although he could have as easily cited Dunnes Stores. He was prescient about changing consumer habits. 'In 10 years' time there will be three times as many people working out in these centres as there are now. The secret will be to drive down the annual subscription fee. You used to have to pay £500 a year here. Now it is £600. My ambition is to drive it down to £400. Then I'll look to drive it down again. We'll be like Ryanair, we'll be dropping prices to get more people in.' It was a clear contradiction of the plan he had set six years earlier but a good businessperson does not resist changing their mind. Plans to add medical facilities to the fitness centres, which he had spoken of two years earlier, seemed to have been abandoned, although the idea was a good one. He had just purchased an eight-acre site at Crumlin, Dublin 12, on the former Carlisle sports grounds on which he had spent £4m. It was to become one of his most important locations for the next two decades. But within a few years he did away with the expensive swimming pools and saunas and moved to a 'dry' club model, as he had seen in Germany.

He employed a small number, just 33, at Westpoint. 'I have cut out all the unnecessary functions, all the unnecessary jobs. People can design their own training programmes, they have their own cards for themselves. Ryanair succeeded in the airline industry because the rest of them were all copying each other in offering services whereas Ryanair did it differently by offering cheap seats. It's going to be the same in the fitness industry and believe me if you manage your costs, you will make good money.'

He still had a hatred for 'red tape', as he called regulations. 'Nobody smokes in here but there isn't a single No Smoking sign in the building. If you have one, people start asking where the smoking area is. Then, who regulates it? You only create work for yourself. There's no customer complaints department. I deal with complaints or Mark does. If people have a major problem I just refund their money, just as I did at Dunnes Stores.'

His ambitions had shifted, too. 'I'd like to have maybe five or six of them nationwide, no more, and I'm not interested in going overseas. When I was in Dunnes in the mid-1980s, I used to think that the organisation would be better with fewer stores but bigger stores. It took as much effort to manage Mallow as it did Cabinteely but the profits were much bigger in the Dublin store. This business is also like retail in that you have times when we are really busy and others when the stores are quiet. Just like we had to entice people to change their shopping patterns, we need to persuade people to change the times of engaging in their fitness habit.'

He advertised heavily on Dublin local radio, doing his own scripts and voiceovers, loving to compare his prices to those of perceived rivals. 'Take that, Jackie Skelly!' was a favourite line, or 'Here's something that Jackie Skelly won't like', focusing on a bemused smaller operator who had to suck it up on the basis there was no such thing as bad publicity. 'The Irish public won't tolerate a rip-off,' he intoned in other ads, mentioning the admittedly expensive David Lloyd Riverview club.

'I have nothing against Jackie Skelly at all,' he told the journalist Conor Pope. 'I don't even really know her, but in business it helps if you have an enemy and if you don't actually have an enemy, you just make one up and then go after them.' When Skelly left the business in 2010, Ben instead used FlyFit as his punching bag.

He was keen to expand the business, but it was difficult to get development sites. 'If Ryanair wants to expand, it can buy a plane and expand, but getting sites is not that easy.' He opened his Kimmage centre, but his plans for many others went astray. He failed to build on a 4.6-acre site in Drumcondra, but benefited from the increase in value on the €7.2m he paid for it. He did a deal to invest €2m in Shamrock Rovers to build a 2,000-seater stand at one end of the Tallaght ground, in return for an adjacent site on which he would build a fitness complex. He gave the club €200,000 as a deposit, but didn't follow through on the deal.

Ben estimated the cost of opening each new outlet at close to €15m, excluding site-acquisition costs, and he was cautious. In April 2005, he paid £3m for a 21-acre site in South London that had housed BBC sports facilities. His first idea was a fitness and leisure centre but instead of applying for planning permission for that, Barkisland sought a change of use to a cemetery. Local residents complained bitterly, including the Mayor of London, and by October 2008 Ben had withdrawn the idea. He had 12 outlets at its peak, reduced to five at the time of his death. The company was profitable. Ben Dunne Gyms posted an operating profit of €3m in 2022 in the first full year after the Covid-19 pandemic.

The gyms weren't his only focus. Ben was a scattergun of ideas, some of them good, some not so good, but he often lacked the time or inclination to follow through on them or the willingness to risk large amounts of capital. He was not a natural entrepreneur. He had joined an established family business and learnt how it was done, but he had expanded instead of innovated. He didn't necessarily have the hunger either: he was financially comfortable and didn't have the drive to keep himself reasonably busy. He essentially worked off one big idea: cut prices and drive up volumes. But things in business are often more complex.

He spotted the potential for the internet to revolutionise retailing, but failed to follow through. In March 2008 he announced bendunnedirect.com, promising to have the website in operation by September, selling discounted products from suits to bed linen, to jewellery and toys, household and kitchen items, stocked from a large warehouse. Bendunnedirect.com would not sell food items, only products where he perceived there were large profit margins.

He intended taking so-called guerilla marketing to a new level. 'When you're buying online, you'll always wonder, "will the jacket fit?" My sizes will be very similar to Dunnes, so you can go into Dunnes and try it on, get your size, and buy it online from me. I'm the only online retailer with a fitting room in every town in Ireland. That's the way I'm thinking and there's no law against it.'

He said the site would undercut traditional retailers and should have a similar effect to the way Ryanair had changed the aviation market. 'At the minute, the only reason people go online is for convenience. But if the customer gets value, it will take off like wildfire. And if it fails, well, I was never afraid of failure. At the beginning, the investment is no more than €1m, but there are all sorts of opportunities after that. Somebody might want to link into me, or we might get into the UK market as a discounter. I'd be known by the Irish community in the UK.'

Ben hired an Irish web development firm, but some of the work on the site was to be outsourced to India. His enthusiasm didn't last long. 'I'm not going ahead with it,' he told an interviewer later in the year. 'I did about eight weeks of exploratory work and it was of no interest to me. I looked at the pros and cons and decided it wasn't the kind of business I wanted to get into.'

He said his decision had nothing to do with the deteriorating economic climate as consumer spending starting to fall dramatically. 'There's never a bad time to start a good business. Online works for ticket sales, concerts, cinema and theatre, it works for very specific things. For supermarkets, it's a no-go area. You have a 2,000-to-one chance at hitting the jackpot with online retail of textiles, and the odds are worse for food. In online sales, 40pc of what you sell is returned. About 3pc of your sales are fraudulent because it's all credit card payment. If they are doing it, they would want to get a lot more brains into their organisation.' Ben admitted that selling online was 'not retail the way I'm used to in retail'.

He may have been spooked by Dunnes Stores' decision to react to him. At almost the same time Ben bought and registered online domain names like dunnesdirect.com, Dunnes bought almost identical addresses – the only difference being the .com was replaced with .ie. Ben's response was to tell his old company not to bother: 'If I was Dunnes Stores I would be far more worried about Aldi and Lidl than I would be about competing online.' Indeed, Dunnes was very slow to move much of its business online.

He returned in 2009 with another idea, an online marketplace, BenDunne.com, to compete with Buy & Sell, DoneDeal and Adverts.ie. Following a so-called soft launch, the website was unable to handle sufficient traffic without crashing. Its official launch was cancelled and the website taken offline. It was relaunched in 2010, but failed within a year. Ben admitted that 'the internet is one of my failures. I can't work it out. I can't get people to advertise on BenDunne.com for nothing and I can't get them to pay €3.' The site was supposed to be a simple online trading facility, allowing users to upload photos of the product they wanted to sell, available for inspection by potential buyers for 14 days. 'It's as simple as booking an airline ticket,' it boasted. Users would pay €1.50 to place an advertisement for two weeks. It would advertise jobs, holidays and homes to rent.

Ben explained: 'It just didn't perform at all. Even with a small bit of flow it was stalling. If you have it wrong, you've got to stop it. It would be like Aer Lingus saying they could beat Ryanair on prices but then having no seats. There was no point.'

Ben's mind seemed to work differently from most people's, always inventive when it came to business, taking ideas like a corporate magpie and talking about them imaginatively, but not having the discipline or interest for follow-through. He had been schooled in traditional retailing and that was where he was at his best.

41.

Attention-seeking

ONE OF BEN'S ADDICTIONS was a need for attention. Like his grandfather Barney Dunn a century earlier, he loved to perform. If his grandfather was restricted to the stage in Rostrevor, his grandson had access to radio, television and newspapers. At one stage he agreed to write a weekly consumer column for the *Irish Sun* every Saturday. The publisher, News International, called him part of its 'Value Campaign' to help Irish consumers. Ben found a niche as the plain-talking, commonsense campaigner on consumer issues. He was indulged as some sort of national character to be enjoyed. His willingness to admit to his addictions and flaws apparently endeared him to the large parts of the public. He was on *Liveline* so often that after he died the programme was able to play a lengthy montage of his many contributions over the years, including a prayer he had recited once.

He played the mystery Santa on the Christmas Eve 2003 edition of *Liveline* broadcast live from Grafton Street. Brendan O'Connor in the *Sunday Independent* condemned how 'he and Joe Duffy proceeded to have a great laugh about how Benny stole money from the family business to give it to a corrupt old Taoiseach who didn't pay any tax on it, who considered it his due to be a kept man – a man who shouldn't have the inconvenience of financial limitations of his own, because that allowed him to work for the national interest. "Thanks a million, big fellah," Joe chortled. "That should be, thanks 1.8 million," laughs Benny back. All hail St Bernard, the patron saint of Christmas. Sure he did some awful things but he really is great craic. And, after all, from "ho ho ho" in Florida to "ho ho ho" on Grafton Street isn't that a big leap.'

Duffy first became aware of Ben when working as a probation officer in Dublin's inner city. 'It was known that if you had a very sick child and were really stuck for medical treatment that you might have to get abroad, then Ben was the person who would organise and pay for it. He was known as very generous, but he never sought to get any publicity for it,' said Duffy. He recalled a campaign that *Liveline* organised to raise money for the Mater Hospital when it faced an A&E queues crisis. 'We heard lots of complaints about conditions in the waiting rooms so we organised for three fully equipped portacabins,' said Duffy. 'Ben chipped in thirty grand and another businessman did the same and we bought them all and the Mater wouldn't take them, but we gave them to drug rehab clinics instead.'

Duffy was central to Ben's short-lived TV career. Almost incredibly, given that he had been the subject of the damning first tranche of Moriarty findings less than a year previously, RTÉ cast him as a judge in November 2007 on a new prime-time Sunday evening show *Highly Recommended*, presented by Duffy. The concept was that members of the public would compete to convince a panel of consumer experts that their deal ought to be 'Highly Recommended'. The panel, comprising Ben and two journalists, freelance Barbara McCarthy and *Irish Times* staffer Conor Pope, debated the deals and then Duffy canvassed the studio audience for opinions and the public voted via online polls. The 'winning' idea received a prize of between €1,000 and €2,000. The show, described by Pope as being 'like *Dragon's Den* for penny-pinchers' lasted just six episodes.

'My fellow judge was always affable behind the scenes, but more so before the cameras,' wrote Pope. 'A contestant's notion had to be truly terrible for him not to give it the thumbs-up, and at all times he was playing to the gallery. While he feigned tough talking in the early discussions about the ideas brought to the table, he loved nothing more than giving a money-saving plan the green light to the cheers of the studio audience.'

Duffy recalls 'a decent man who was never convicted of anything'. He described Ben as a hard worker, 'affable and low maintenance, never complained about the long hours during recording, no airs and graces, and very straight'. Their relationship became a friendship: they shared an interest in graveyards and occasionally swapped books about the histories of cemeteries. Duffy agreed that, in retrospect, this might have been explained in Ben's case by his experience of hiding in an open grave after his release from kidnap.

In July 2008 Ben seemingly flirted with entering politics. Although he insisted it was not a publicity stunt, few took the prospect seriously. It started, as so many things did with Ben, when he spoke to Joe on *Liveline*. He declared that he would contest the following year's elections for the European Parliament, if a second referendum on the Lisbon Treaty of the EU was held before that date. The Irish electorate had just rejected the treaty in a referendum, causing consternation across Europe. Without all nation states agreeing, the treaty would fall. French President Nicolas Sarkozy said Ireland would have to vote again to get the required approval. 'He [Sarkozy] is entitled to his free speech but he mightn't like the answers he's going to get back and I think he's got a hell of a cheek,' Ben said. 'We've only just had a referendum and the "No" side won and we shouldn't be putting it back to the country as quickly as he's attempting to do it.'

He said he would run as an independent, probably in the three-seater Dublin constituency. 'I didn't run away as a taxpayer to save money and I didn't run away after I was kidnapped. I'm an Irishman to my fingertips and I believe in democracy, and Europe is not democratic enough for me the way it's going at the moment, and if I have to stand to fight my little corner for this little island, I'm prepared to do it.' Ben said the EU was undemocratic and European neighbours bullied Ireland. 'Europe is being run by a load of bureaucrats who are making rules and regulations for us, some of which are quite good but some of which are terrible, and they are not elected,' he said. He pledged to take on the establishment figures who tried to 'make dirt' of ordinary people, apparently oblivious to the findings of the Moriarty tribunal.

It was typical of the language being used by Nigel Farage and other 'little Englanders' of the time, culminating in the disastrous Brexit referendum of 2016 and departure of the UK from the EU in 2020, and was akin to the message Donald Trump would sell in the US of 'draining the swamp'.

A year later a second referendum was called and Ben had changed his tune somewhat. He now insisted he was pro-European and would not do anything to jeopardise Ireland's place within the EU. 'I know we must vote Yes this time because I know it's the right thing for the country. My position the last time was that if you didn't know, vote No, but I don't want to be in any way involved with the No campaign now. I am a pro-European.'

Years later he went on a programme on Classic Hits Radio – a small Dublin station – and explained what had changed his mind. He said he'd received assurances from unnamed 'senior people in politics' that The Angelus was not going to be abolished, as he had alleged the EU wanted. In his tirade he alleged that 'it's now got worse, they want us to do away with crucifixions, they want to deny we are Christians publicly.' It was a classic Ben malapropism: kindly, the newspapers reporting it the following day changed 'crucifixions' to crucifixes, which is what he had meant.

Ben said that he would never 'let down' his saviour Jesus Christ and vowed to fight to keep The Angelus on RTÉ. 'The Lord saved me from getting in a lot of trouble and the politicians, if they – for one moment – think that they can get away with taking Jesus Christ out of our lives, they are sadly mistaken. I am disgusted to hear what is being said in parliament in Europe about taking Christianity out of our lives. We are a Christian country and there is nobody going to take that out of me or the vast majority of people in this country.' His belief in God, inherited from his parents, was genuine, not something he said for effect. Ben said that he prayed every day because 'sometimes there is nobody else to talk to except your maker, and sometimes He's busy talking to someone else, so you have got to talk to yourself'.

He knew how to make headlines, presumably to boost business as much as give him his broadcast adrenaline fix. One of the more amusing stunts was when he claimed to have removed hair-dryers from the male changing-rooms at all his gyms after seeing members using them on their private parts; he claimed this was unhygienic for other users. 'When you see people using a hairdryer on other parts of their bodies and then putting it back, there is no way you can allow that to go on in any business. I will not allow that to go on in my business.' He dismissed suggestions the decision was a Ryanair-style cost-cutting measure, saying 'if it was to save electricity, I would take the plugs out so they could not plug in their dryers', but most saw it as a successful O'Leary-style way of getting free publicity for his business.

There was always a sense, though, that he protested too much about being happy to be gone from Dunnes Stores. He was always keen to share his knowledge and understanding of the retail world and, according to Pope, had total recall of every triumph and every slight. 'He used to marvel at how the German discounters Aldi and Lidl had been allowed to establish a presence in the Republic,' wrote Pope. 'He admired their laser sharp focus on the 80/20 rule of retailing: 80% of sales come from 20% of the products.' Pope recalled him saying, 'Hey, stock the basics and cut the daylights out of them.' He was also of the view that, had he remained in charge of the family business, the Germans would never have got a foothold in Ireland. 'I would never have let them get a look in,' he said. 'I would have driven them out before they got started.'

If Ben wasn't talking about business, consumer issues and politics, or God, he was talking publicly about his siblings, being noticeably more reticent about his wife and children. Frank and Margaret had made an 'absolute decision' that neither they nor their children would ever talk publicly about their business or private lives. Ben did exactly the opposite.

When Eamon Dunphy launched *The Dunphy Show* on TV3 in an effort to take on the *Late Late Show* on RTÉ, Ben was one of the first big-name guests. He said to Dunphy: 'People talk about Margaret and myself, but one of the great favours Margaret done me was firing me from Dunnes because there were three in our family at the time who was addicted and two of them are dead. I believe if I hadn't been fired from Dunnes, I really believe heart and soul that I would have gone the same route. I couldn't have taken all that pressure. It takes a long time to destroy yourself and the unfortunate thing – the road back – it takes just as long to get back.'

In a revealing interview with Patricia Devine of the *Sunday Independent* in 2004, Ben expressed regret that he hadn't been able to do more for his two sisters. 'I mean that I should have tried to help them more. I lost my two sisters to alcoholism, which had an impact on my life. They didn't survive. They both died and I was in the middle of all my turmoil. They played a big role in helping me to sort myself out. I really loved the two of them. I was very close to them. I don't think anybody sets out to be an addict. I think that's the thing a lot of people don't understand. When I look at my parental family it's well documented about me and then of course my two sisters who didn't survive it. I was addicted to drugs but never an alcoholic. That's not to say I couldn't become one.

'I would say things are very normal between myself and my sister Margaret now. From literally living in each other's ear and seeing one another at work having formal meetings on a daily basis, sometimes a couple a day, I would say that was abnormal. But we have today this normal brother and sister relationship.'

This was true, and it actually ran deeper than Ben let on. Margaret was determined to be charitable to her little brother. Knowing how much he cared about the business, she spoke to Ben regularly about it, what she was doing and why, allowing him to express his opinions, even if never giving him hope of a way back in. She realised that Ben struggled without the business he had grown up in, that everything else he did professionally was limited by comparison. She was kind to him and with that many of Ben's tensions eased, even if they didn't disappear.

Ben even joked with Gerry Adams and Martin McGuinness over his kidnapping. Invited to a charity event by Sinn Féin's Mary Lou McDonald, he found himself face-to-face with two of the most prominent IRA commanders (although Adams continues to deny IRA membership). 'I was sitting at the top table with Martin McGuinness and Gerry Adams and they didn't look comfortable at all. I wasn't too comfortable myself. So I turned around and said, "Listen fellas, if this is a fundraising lunch, it is a refund I'll be looking for." They broke their hearts laughing and we had a fantastic lunch.'

Counselling had helped him deal with his many demons. 'If you have a gammy heart, you see a heart specialist once a year. If you know that your brain is a bit suspect, you go and see a psychiatrist. Anybody who knows me will say I'm half-mad but I never denied it. For a fella who is half-mad, I've done well.'

There was nearly considerable embarrassment in 2015 when newspapers were furnished with a video of Ben engaging in actions that would have caused humiliation if written about. Ben provided confirmation to one newspaper that he was one of the people in the video. The newspaper, which had seen the footage, decided not to publish, on the basis there was no public interest involved in causing Ben and his family further discomfiture. He believed other newspapers had come to the same judgement. I was aware of the video at the time, friends of mine, not in the media, having received it on a WhatsApp group.

Ben also paid more serious attention to his physical health, including dealing with his sixty-a-day cigarette habit. 'He tried from his mid-thirties,' said his son, Rob. 'He tried the patches; he tried the gum. He tried something they put in his ear. It was the fear that he wouldn't live to see his grandchildren that ultimately worked.' Conquering that habit led to significant weight gain. 'He had a major problem with food when he first gave up the cigs, put on a load of weight and then that became the focus,' said Rob. 'He would be using the treadmill every day. Up until the time he died, he would walk the Phoenix Park every other day. He was probably a little overweight, but at one point he would have been verging on obese. He cut out a lot of the stuff that was bad for him. He loved rasher sandwiches and toffees and he would devour them. Everything was always in excess. That was one of the things about him.

'I didn't make any moral judgements about Dad's behaviour. My main grievance was the huge public humiliation of my mum. She had always been very private – not in a snobby way. She has no airs or graces. She knew she was marrying the guy who was going to be head of Dunnes Stores. If she wanted a completely private life, she married the wrong guy. She knew his personality, but there is a threshold.'

Mary stayed loyal to him, married for over 50 years. She insisted on regular random drug-testing but also allowed him to head on holidays to Dubai, sometimes with Mark in tow. Mark was diagnosed with a series kidney condition in his late teens, about two years after the Florida escapade, and required dialysis every three days for five hours until he was the successful recipient of a kidney transplant.

Although Rob spent much of his time in the US, he remained close to Ben. However, he said Ben had not spoken to or seen Frank for years. Ben contacted his older brother by letter and Frank responded by phone. 'They had a phone conversation in which Dad suggested they try and meet up,' said Rob. 'And that was declined. That was the final conversation they ever had. It was an awful thing.' Rob said that his father was 'deeply affected' by the snub but never mentioned it again.

The brothers never found a way back after all that had happened in their lives and in Dunnes Stores. 'I can do nothing about it,' Ben said. If he wants to meet me, he knows where I am. I would happily meet him. But I have no grievances.'

42.

Frank's legacy

FRANK'S FINAL YEARS WERE not easy. He spent little time with
Dunnes Stores from 2000 on. Even though he remained on the board,
he limited his attendance at meetings. Margaret had established
control and spent the subsequent decades training the next generation of family members. He suffered from agoraphobia – the fear of
open spaces – and found it difficult to leave his home. This was
deeply ironic as Frank arguably loved nothing more than the company
of horses, the freedom of the open field. His last winner was Highland
Fling in Ballinrobe in 2016. He ceased training that year, but his
colours remained prominent on the track through his partner, Ann
Marshall, who had horses in training with Jack Davison, Jessica
Harrington and Johnny Murtagh. Sadly, he could not attend races
to watch.

He became a near recluse in his final decade, living with Ann on
their stud farm. 'I visited him a couple of times and he was in the
house, in a fog of smoke from all the cigarettes, poorly shaven and
not looking well,' said one associate who spoke on condition of
anonymity. 'It was sad, because he was a very good businessman, but
he was a product of the harsh family upbringing and it haunted him.'

There had been some adversarial contact with his first wife, Ann
Achmann, years after their separation. In 1990 they reached a settlement
for the payment of extra money to Achmann. Frank brought Noel Fox
and his legal team of three solicitors and a barrister to a meeting in a
solicitor's office in London at which his estranged wife outlined the
various problems in their marriage (detailed in an earlier chapter). She
claimed that Frank was worth between £20m and £30m, but Fox
insisted Frank's assets were worth less. Fox listed them as Hanwood
Stud, valued at £2m, house contents and machinery worth £350,000,

a property company called Bloomfield worth £200,000, a shareholding in Vouch Grace Property which owned his London flat worth £200,000, 26% of the preference shares in Dunnes, three bank accounts totalling £113,000, and a gross salary in the region of £300,000. Achmann's legal team countered that she was in serious financial difficulties and had a bank overdraft of £2,000. After 12 hours of negotiations she agreed to accept a settlement for just £275,000.

Frank purchased Hamwood stud farm on the Kildare/Meath border in 2017 and expanded further by buying the 294-acre Ballymacoll Stud, the birthplace of Arkle, one of Ireland's most famous racehorses, for €8.15m. His property at Dunboyne, county Meath, was adjacent to Hamwood. Peter Reynolds, manager at Ballymacoll, always spoke fondly of Frank. 'Frank and I were friends for years,' he told *The Irish Field*. 'We used to foal his mares at Ballymacoll and he bought the dams of Youmzain from us. He was very reclusive and didn't go racing for many years but he knew exactly what was going on and loved discussing stallions and matings. I often travelled to Coolmore and Newmarket with him to inspect stallions. I was extremely happy when he bought Ballymacoll as I knew he would look after the place.' The last time in his life that Frank came to public attention was when he, Ann Marshall and Hamwood Stud launched a legal action against the refurbishment of a major 22km electricity line that crossed their land. They claimed it would have a 'significant effect' on their prize blood-stock and breeding operations as the ESB and Eirgrid required access to their lands. Frank and Ann feared a risk of foetal loss among their mares and cows if works with machinery took place on-site. They argued that any disruption to operations might damage Hamwood Stud's worldwide reputation.

They failed partly because they left it so late to appeal. Typically of Frank, the necessary papers were presented at the High Court's central office just 12 minutes before closing time on the final day of the statutory period, leaving 'absolutely no margin for error if anything went wrong, which of course it did,' Judge Richard Humphreys said. The legal papers were not stamped as required, resulting in the application being made to the court a day late. 'Human error rarely qualifies as good and sufficient reason for the late commencement of proceedings in a context where certainty is particularly important,' the judge said.

Frank died in November 2022, aged 79. His funeral was a private affair, with reportedly no more than 50 people present. 'It was so sad that Frank became a recluse,' said accountant Paschal Taggart, 'because he was engaging and brilliant. I don't buy that he wasn't a businessman, as some people said.'

In his last will and testament, dated 4 August 2022, just three months before he died, Frank left an estate valued at nearly €276m. The will ran for eight pages. Frank bequeathed half of his Approved Retirement Fund to Ann Marshall, the remainder equally between his children. His shares in Dunnes Holding Company went to his children, Ben and Annie, making them two of the largest shareholders. His interest in 6% preference shares in the capital of Dunnes Holding Company went to Margaret. He left his 'shares and securities' at Hamwood Stud together with all his land and property and principal dwelling-house to Ann Marshall. She also got 'all the livestock, bloodstock, cars and farm machinery' as well as 'furniture, paintings, soft furniture and articles of domestic, household or garden use or ornament'. Frank left his interest in the company Lovely Lee Limited to Annie, and his interest in property at Stephen Street Upper and at South Great George's Street, Dublin 2, the Dunnes Stores headquarters, to Annie and Ben.

Frank's adult children have kept a low profile, in keeping with the rest of the family, but have completed spells working with Dunnes. Annie spent 2014 as a fashion stylist with the company, specialising in organising fashion shows. She worked for Paul Costelloe, a key Dunnes designer, as an assistant brand manager in London from May 2015 to September 2016. She now has a creative event design company in Dublin, AD Event Design. She also works as a liaison partner with Soho House in London, a private members' club that has been looking to establish in Ireland. But she has ambitions in homeware, too. Recently she launched a new tableware brand called Acquerello Home, specialising in ceramics. Its website claims that Annie 'recognised an unmet gap in the market: beautifully designed, high quality tableware that remains accessible', emphasising artisanal craftsmanship. Essentially, she is in competition with Dunnes Stores.

Having graduated from the University of Warwick in 2011, Ben was employed as a project manager at Dunnes from October 2011 to May 2014, working with senior management 'to design and implement an end-to-end e-commerce solution for fashion and homewares'. He was responsible for its project-managing, according to a LinkedIn profile that is markedly more detailed than any of his cousins'. He moved from there to various consultancy roles before becoming managing director and partner, strategy and consulting, with Accenture in Dublin. He was a member of Accenture's global retail leadership team and for a period the global lead for its ai.Retail initiative. In that role he gave interviews to tech publications, outlining his ideas for using AI to change retailer logistics and home deliveries: these brought to mind the confidence his father had shown at a similar age in engaging with the media.

His time at Accenture – after nearly six years – ended in September 2024. Former colleagues there remember someone who was 'very smart, very capable'. Should he want to take a major role in the future of Dunnes, it would seem he has some of the relevant experience required, but there is no obvious sign of that happening. He has not updated his LinkedIn profile between September 2024 and the completion of this book, other than announcing in May 2025 that he had become a non-executive director at an IT services and consulting company called Sryve, headquartered in Carlow town. It describes itself as offering 'bespoke private cloud solutions underpinned by cyber security advice and technical support to support your business data'. He may well have a career to watch.

43.

Ben's death

BEN DIED SUDDENLY IN DUBAI, in the United Arab Emirates, on 18 November 2023, just five months shy of his 75th birthday. He was on a golfing break with his son Mark and others and suffered a heart attack while sitting poolside at the five-star Jumeirah Beach Hotel. There was a doctor present as part of the travelling party, but he was unable to do anything to save Ben.

The news of his death was a considerable shock to the family. Although he'd had stents fitted, he was regarded as being in good health and had apparently received encouraging confirmation of that in his most recent medical assessment. It took some effort on the part of the Department of Foreign Affairs to repatriate his body relatively quickly, but Ben had been a regular in Dubai, and was well-known, and his family's wishes were accommodated without delay. Wealth buys that, especially in places like Dubai.

His death notice described him as the 'beloved husband' of Mary, the 'dear father' of Mark, Robert, Caroline and Nicholas, and the 'beloved grandfather' of Ben, Katie, Pearl and Joseph. It also referenced his surviving sisters, Margaret and Ann, extended family, relatives and 'a large circle of friends'. His funeral took place on Tuesday, 28 November 2023, with a requiem mass at the small St Mochta's church in Porterstown.

As Ben's pallbearers carried his wicker coffin up the narrow centre aisle, his son Rob, following with the family, noticed Mary Lou McDonald, the leader of Sinn Féin, standing at the end of the third last pew. McDonald had caught considerable flak when she – or someone on her behalf – took to social media to post her sympathies on news of Ben's death 10 days earlier. Many responded by accusing her of hypocrisy, recalling his kidnap by the IRA. Rob replied on

X (formerly Twitter), thanking her for her public message of condolence. Now, limping slowly behind those carrying the coffin, Rob saw her and stopped for a split-second to shake her hand and thank her, before continuing up the church as part of the family procession.

It was Mark, not Rob, who took to the altar to deliver a pre-Mass eulogy. Within minutes he referred to the kidnap in what was an emotional but composed, impressive and quite moving oration. 'His kidnapping in 1981 was hugely traumatic on him, and it was the source of much of his personal troubles throughout the years that followed, but time is a great healer and he held no ill feeling toward his captors. He did the Christian thing and forgave.'

Mark told some good stories to bring cheer to the church, to create an air of celebration of a life lived fully, albeit not always happily. He explained to mourners that his father 'never liked going to funerals' but would always insist on a 'full report' from those his son attended. 'This is a funeral he must attend and even though he didn't like funerals, he would be glad to see how many people are here today.' He spoke of his father's love of a sociable drink, and how in recent years the pints had been replaced by Bombay Sapphire gin. Mark joked that his father bought by family-pack size, 'a measure of wholesale proportions', to qualify for discounts. Deliberately mixing up slogans attributed to Dunnes and its great rival Tesco, Mark recalled that his father used to say, 'It might not be better value, but every little helps'.

Mark recalled how his parents had celebrated their 50th wedding anniversary earlier that year and that 'no matter what life has thrown at us, Dad would be the first to say our mother was our rock.' He recalled how his father loved nothing more than holidays with his family and 'was at his happiest' on his boat 'enjoying a drink and watching the sun set'. He was 'a brilliant and a loving father and grandfather' who rang his children daily.

He revealed that his father was dyslexic and had boasted that he'd never failed an exam because he'd never sat one. He said he was given to sometimes hilarious malapropisms. On one occasion, he implored a man not to park his car in a disabled bay, to which the man replied, 'But I have a prosthetic', to which Ben roared, 'I have a prostate too and I'm not parking there.'

Mark told how his family had received many messages of condolences, detailing Ben's 'generosity'. His father was 'humble in his generosity' and never looked for public acknowledgement or sought to 'use it as any kind of public redemption', perhaps unaware of the deliberate testimonials during the Florida sentencing hearing. He said his father's 'openness and willingness to lay out his flaws was a major part of what people found so appealing about him and his personality. He had his vices, as we all do, but I can assure you he's earned his ticket to walk through those pearly white gates today.'

Mark made many serious points about his father that referenced his colourful and controversial past, admitting that his actions had caused great difficulties and embarrassment. He navigated skilfully the specifics of the more notable and headline-making antics in which Ben had participated. One thing was very clear from everything Mark said, and his siblings too in their contributions: Ben was very much loved by them. They understood his demons and his behaviour and did not judge him too harshly for that.

Mark recalled some of their happiest times on family holidays in Spain and said each of his siblings would miss the daily phone calls from their father 'to check in'. He described Ben as an 'ambitious and driven' businessman who was 'razor sharp with numbers'. He told how his father 'recreated his working life' to found Ben Dunne Gyms and said his father 'loved' the fitness industry, often travelling the world with his son. 'Many of you know just how difficult running a business can be and being part of a family business is even more difficult, as you can well imagine.' A nod to the circumstances in which his father was exiled from Dunnes. 'My father endured many things with his siblings, some private and some unfortunately very public. However at the core of any family business is that word 'family' and family always finds a way of going back to its roots.' He said his father spoke to Margaret 'almost daily' and the pair 'loved each other dearly' and were 'a great source of strength to each other over the years'.

Mark recalled a conversation over dinner about the prayer his father recited every night. 'This was the prayer: So far, all my nights have been followed by more days, but in this world of mine a night will come when there will be no more day for me. Lord, look after me today.'

Mark's ex-wife, an actress and former model Vivienne Connolly, was there with his two children. Their marriage in December 2005, with the reception at Ashford Castle, had attracted plenty of media attention because of her celebrity. It was a sign of the times that nobody bothered that their first child, not far short of two years old, was at their wedding. Ben and Mary certainly weren't going to object.

The mourners included few politicians other than McDonald. Conor Lenihan, a former junior minister from Fianna Fáil, and, of course, Michael Lowry were the only ones I recognised from my position in the pew directly behind McDonald. An Taoiseach Leo Varadkar, a local TD for Fine Gael, sent his aide-de-camp Cmmdt Claire Mortimer. This move attracted some comment subsequently as to its appropriateness given the tribunal findings. Larry Goodman, the 'beef baron' and a billionaire from that and property investments – and in his time equally as controversial a figure as Ben for his own links to Haughey – was the most prominent of the wealthy who paid their respects in person. Now aged 86, Goodman walked with a visible limp and after searching for a seat was given one in the very back row of the church by a sympathetic mourner who gave it up to one of the most elderly people without a seat.

The church was a sea of grey hair as most of the mourners, other than family members, were as old as or older than Ben. There were a few well-known sporting figures, such as former Ryder Cup golfer Des Smyth, a long-time friend of Ben's, who sat just behind the family pews. Those who couldn't gain access to the small church were facilitated in the adjacent parish hall in front of a large screen, and the service was also streamed live.

'No one was more aware of his human weaknesses and frailties than Ben,' Canon Damian O'Reilly said in an overly long sermon that didn't match Mark's for insight. He described Ben as 'a wonderful character with personality and charm' who would be remembered as a 'good, decent, generous and loving man'. After the mass ended, the wicker coffin was carried out of the church to the strains of a recording of 'The Lonesome Boatman' by Finbar Furey, ahead of Ben's burial in Castleknock cemetery.

In his will, Ben left more than €30m, an enormous amount but only a fraction of what he'd received for his shares in Dunnes 30 years earlier and of what Frank left in his will. The economic crash of 2008 may have impacted on his fortune. He sold 39 major pieces from his art collection, worth millions, including paintings by Jack B. Yeats and Sir John Lavery – his favourite was *Pro-Cathedral, Dublin 1922* (*The Requiem Mass for Michael Collins*), which he'd bought from a London dealer in February 1995. 'Anything that was costing money and wasting money I got rid of,' he said. 'The yacht and the helicopter went very quickly. All the people I know have taken a hit and I think it has done nobody any harm. It has done me no harm.'

Much of his wealth may have been transferred prior to his death to his children. He cancelled €4m in loans provided to Mark – who invested heavily in an EdTech start-up, Classhub, and stipulated that Robert, Caroline and Nicholas would be released 'from any legal liability to repay any debt which may be due from them' on the event of his death. The 'rest, residue and remainder' of his €30m estate 'of every nature and kind' as well as 'any property' was left to his wife, Mary. This included Ben's shares in the gyms. Rob got a property in Enniscrone, county Sligo, and Ben bequeathed all his shares in Stoney Way Properties Ltd to Caroline.

Mary, as his widow, retained ownership of the family home. Ben and Mary had left Winterwood some years earlier. It had become too big for them once their children had left. Two years after his death, a property development company applied for planning permission to knock down the house and replace it with 30 houses and 145 apartments, the largest building to be six storeys in height. The developers also sought a crèche facility, 111 car-parking spaces and 387 bicycle spaces in their application, made with Mary's express authorisation. The nature of how the profits on the development would be split was not disclosed, but the directors of the newly formed company Winterwood had done a similar deal previously with Larry Goodman. More than 120 objections were lodged to Fingal County Council, so the outcome of the plan at the time of writing remains unknown.

In early August 2025 Rob Dunne's death was announced. His death notice said that he had died peacefully in New York on 1 August. His body was returned to Dublin and he was buried on 11 August, the funeral ceremony taking place in the same church as his father's had less than two years previously. Rob had suffered the loss of Ben greatly, having been close to him despite living for decades in the United States, working as a lawyer in New York. His candid and honest interview with the *Sunday Independent* after Ben's death had caused consternation in the wider family, especially his claim that he had recorded 20 hours of interviews with Ben for future use. It is now almost certain that they will never be made publicly available.

Ben had been a man who never shied away from the limelight. The performer and pseudo-philosopher in him meant he once read a poem on *The Late Late Show*. It was 'The Indispensable Man' by Saxon White Kessinger, and he explained its words as saying there is no such thing as an 'indispensable man', that life will go on as it did before any individual passed, so you may as well do 'the best you can'. Ben and Frank were gone, Therese and Elizabeth were gone, the family hollowed out by loss. The question now became, how indispensable was the woman who had forced Ben out of the family business: his sister, Margaret?

PART 7

The 21st-century Dunnes Stores

44.

At your service

THE MODERNISATION AND REPOSITIONING of the Dunnes Stores brand during the 21st century may be Margaret's finest strategic business achievement, even if her greatest overall result was keeping the company in family ownership and management. The latter might not have happened had the first not succeeded. That she did it at a time in life when others would have retired and that it involved such a major gamble as changing a pillar of the company's long-standing way of doing business is even more remarkable, a tribute to her intuition, judgement and execution. Many executives of her age (83 years in 2025) would have stuck to the tried-and-trusted, believing that what had always worked always would work, perhaps not having the energy or determination to countenance change. It helped, though, that two people emerged from the family, the all-important flesh-and-blood, who were willing to commit and who had the ability to do it (as proven by their academic qualifications, by which she set great store), when other family members either weren't willing or weren't able. Her daughter Anne and her niece Sharon (McMahon) took up senior positions, and as they prospered, they also become enormous influences who changed Margaret as a retailer and made her simply better.

Margaret chose to perform the transition in clothing and food, but perhaps underappreciated is how well she also created essentially a highly profitable third leg to the Dunnes retail empire during the 21st century: homeware. Dunnes now has a collection of standalone homeware stores but sells a range of its products in many of its all-in-one stores, as well as online, depending on the footfall to the location. Industry commentators suggested Dunnes had gone upmarket, but if that was true it was because it was serving the changing demands of Irish consumers, who wanted a taste of luxury and better lifestyle products at affordable prices. In developing homeware, Margaret embraced creative people and worked with them to build sub-brands for Dunnes Stores (which she would also do for clothing). Margaret has been described as one of Ireland's 'great champions of design', a patron to designers who otherwise might struggle to reach a large audience. She has brought Irish-designed homeware to people across the country who might not have thought of buying it if they hadn't seen it in Dunnes Stores.

Many of the creatives she hired had interesting back-stories that made them grateful for the opportunity to work with Dunnes. Designer Paul Costelloe is well-known for his clothing – he was a favourite of Britain's Princess Diana and, now in his 80s, he still exhibits at London Fashion Week. But his first collaboration with Dunnes was in homeware. He watched how Debenhams had launched a Designers at Debenhams brand, introducing Jasper Conran and John Rocha. He brought the idea to Margaret, and the Paul Costelloe Living brand was born. Costelloe credits Margaret with helping him through a difficult time when his business was struggling financially. The Irish distributor of his jewellery line went into receivership in 2009 and two years later the company that made and sold his womenswear collection went into administration.

Costelloe has spoken about what it's like working with Margaret: 'a businesswoman one moment, and the next she's deciding if the sleeves should be two inches shorter. Ninety per cent of the time, we have a good working relationship, based on mutual respect. Women are so versatile compared to men. She's very good to anyone on her staff who gets ill or has family problems. She looks after her staff incredibly well. If they have sadness in the family, she knows. She has a strong Catholic ethos. Above all, she's very human. We've got similar values – family values – and she understands my sense of design. She believes in me.'

Helen James was hired as creative director of homewares, setting up a design department for homewares before creating her own range, Considered. A graduate from the National College of Art & Design (NCAD) who specialised in texture and weave, she worked with the designer Donna Karan for over a decade before returning to Ireland. James has been with Dunnes Stores for well over 10 years. She spoke about bringing 'texture, smell and quality natural materials' to a wide audience and credits Dunnes with providing her with a 'platform to access so many people at a fantastic price-point', although in her many interviews promoting the brand she talks about herself and her experiences but not about her relationships with Dunnes management.

Dunnes also partners with 'brand ambassadors'. Margaret had been a guest at the five-star Park Hotel in Kenmare and became friendly with its flamboyant co-owner Francis Brennan, who had become a favourite on RTÉ television for his hotel inspector programme, *At Your Service*. She kept asking him to endorse product lines and eventually he agreed. Linen sheets and bedding became a particular favourite, but this expanded over time into lamps, fine china, crockery, towels, pillows and duvet covers, rugs, and then pyjamas, dressing gowns and robes. Brennan also began doing branded Dunnes exhibitions at industry events, as did Neven Maguire, a highly popular and very personable TV chef, who also became exceptionally important to the Dunnes brand. Cook with Neven Maguire – a range of excellent kitchen items – was launched in 2019, with perfect pre-pandemic timing as it turned out. The products were not as high in quality as those Brennan used at his hotel, or Maguire at his boutique restaurant MacNean in Blacklion, county Cavan, but they resembled them in look and feel and at affordable prices.

In clothing, Dunnes could have remained at the lower end of the market, competing with the likes of Penneys. Unlike Penneys, Margaret decided to concentrate on what she knew in Ireland, rather than risking expansion in the UK or elsewhere. She wanted to maintain the popularity of the stores in Ireland, and the value of its long-term investment in real estate, but sticking to the same 'cheap and cheerful' segment of the market would perhaps have been as much of a risk as she took in going upmarket.

Designer Carolyn Donnelly was originally brought into homewares in 2011 – for which she still works – but then moved into clothing, offering products under Carolyn Donnelly Eclectic and serving the company as creative director. 'The essence of Dunnes is that people go in regularly and they want to see something new,' Donnelly explained. 'Otherwise they get bored. I'll put a few new products out there every month. They're there for a couple of weeks and then they're gone.'

It's a model that works for both Dunnes and Donnelly. 'Dunnes don't like to talk about what they are doing, but I am very proud of what we have achieved in eight years,' said Donnelly in one interview in 2019. 'The backbone of Dunnes is the main collection – the designers are the icing on the cake. It is all about having a solid base. We are catering for different women's taste, but the same women are shopping across all brands and fit – absolutely critical for us, particularly with online – is the same across them all.'

Donnelly declared herself proud that Dunnes's manufacturing strength allowed for value from high-quality essentials to fashion-led pieces: 'I feel I am doing something that appeals to a discerning customer who appreciates quality and workmanship. That we are a design-driven business is a message I want to spread. I travel a huge amount, and I believe our fashion collections could hold their own anywhere. Margaret Heffernan had the confidence in me, gave me all the opportunities to do my own ranges, and then allowed me to oversee other areas of the business. The relationship with the designers is incredibly important to Mrs Heffernan. It's a passion. She allows designers have huge creativity, and to maintain their autonomy. In this way Mrs Heffernan and Dunnes Stores are providing a platform for Irish designers that would otherwise not exist, and that's a very important thing, in my view.'

Dunnes put in place its own main ranges – Gallery, Savida and The Edit – all designed in-house and a long way from the days of St Bernard and the relabelling of Marks & Spencer cast-offs. Costelloe designed for women, then men, and then highly popular communion dresses. Leigh Tucker arrived with the Willow children's wear range. Joanne Hynes was regarded as edgy, avant-garde, and a favourite of style-bloggers. Helen Steele's highly colourful and modern designs have become one of the most successful sub-brands, offering comfortable, enduring women's clothing for active lifestyles at lower prices.

Top-end 1980s fashion designer Michael Mortell re-emerged with trench coats (and expensive furniture), although his relationship with the company did not endure. Nor did that of Peter O'Brien, the first haute couturier to join the stable of Irish designers. Neither did a clothing line called Lennon Courtney – which subsequently moved to Kilkenny Design – put together by stylist Sonia Lennon and broadcaster Brendan Courtney. Dunnes has found that working with identifiably Irish designers works best. The collaborations with 1960s

British fashion model Twiggy and Scottish businesswoman Michelle Mone were not so enduring, but Baroness Mone – later to be embroiled in political controversy in the UK – later said that her lingerie range would not have succeeded without Margaret's early encouragement.

There were surprise additions to the portfolio. If the signing of golfer Pádraig Harrington – a three-time Major winner – to endorse a range of golf wear made obvious sense, the signing of Paul Galvin as a designer was unexpected. A former Kerry Gaelic footballer, Galvin was a fiery character on the football pitch but hard-working and highly successful, winning multiple All-Ireland championships. He was an individual who stood out as unusual in his environment because he cared about how he presented himself visually and vocally, which wasn't what people expected of a rural footballer, especially when he wrote a book about it.

'I walked into Dunnes Stores's head office with a copy of the book for Margaret Heffernan, who then invited me in to show the samples I had made,' he explained. He arrived with 'an effort of clothing I would call it', around 10 pieces he had made for himself over the previous few years, illustrating his vision or his 'point of view'. Galvin wrote a note commenting on the progress Dunnes had made in fashion generally and, in particular, menswear. 'From there, I agreed a contract to start a clothing label.' The relationship has endured for over a decade.

One of the more surprising collaborations was with celebrity TV gardener Diarmuid Gavin, who went to Anne with a plan for Diarmuid Gavin's Outer Spaces, a range of easy-to-care-for but attractive plants at relatively cheap prices. Anne liked his suggestion that younger adults who couldn't afford houses with big gardens, or even any gardens, might be interested in keeping plants on their balconies or indoors.

Dunnes allowed Gavin to give interviews. 'Mrs Heffernan makes every decision and is on top of everything that's going on,' he revealed. 'I might get an email at 4.30am with a suggestion or two and her instincts are always right. Mrs Heffernan, like a lot of people in Dunnes, is driven to make this perfect, so I don't think I have any option but to get it absolutely right.' The relationship continued at the time of writing, but perhaps did not develop to be quite as big as both parties might have anticipated.

Journalist Anne Harris wrote that Margaret 'understood the changing face of Ireland through consumers. She proved prescient in the face of economic adversity. The crash in 2008 squeezed the middle market out. Those department stores that didn't go by the wayside, re-grouped, re-strategised, and struggled. Because Middle Ireland, which could no longer afford to shop in the stores they used to love, defected to Dunnes. Here, instead of feeling poor after the crash, they discovered a new world – affordable handbags and lovely clothes. And in spite of the austerity, they felt good about themselves.'

In refurbishing its main stores, Dunnes moved away from the old pile 'em high strategy and dedicated less space in store to the display of goods. It realised earlier than many competitors that modern customers searched online first to see the range and pricing and if they didn't buy online, they would want a better 'experience' in store as they checked out items in person. In 2015, the Dunnes' flagship store in Cornelscourt was refurbished, according to the company's website to 'reimagine' the shopping experience. The transformation in the clothing and homeware areas was extraordinary, the space brightened enormously, and everything given an upmarket aesthetic refreshment. The task was given to the Italian international store design company Schweitzer, known to Margaret for its work with high-profile clients including Armani and MaxMara in Italy, Carrefour and Galeries Lafayette in France, Burberry and Ralph Lauren. This was not a cheap touch-up job. It wasn't the only major refurbishment that took place. The St Stephen's Green shopping centre units in Dublin got a similar makeover, as did the empire's birthplace on St Patrick's Street in Cork, completed only in early 2025, the second major upgrading in less than two decades. Possibly even more impressive is what was done on the outskirts of Cork city, on the junction between the Bandon Road and the southern by-pass motorway of the city: here is a development arguably bigger and better than Cornelscourt, a draw for shoppers from all over Cork and beyond.

'Dunnes is a mass-market retailer,' said one unnamed competitor to *The Sunday Times* in December 2006. 'You can't be mass-market and [at the same time] be a niche retailer of upmarket goods. It's a confusing proposition for the consumer.' Whoever said that, Margaret was to prove them wrong.

45.

Simply better

As the Irish operations switched tack in 2015 there was speculation, emanating from retail estate agents in England, that Dunnes was considering 40 more stores, perhaps by acquiring a job-lot of properties to be divested by one of the big UK retailers, such as Marks & Spencer or BHS. This move would double the size of its UK business in total. Margaret waited and watched and instead, after the 2016 Brexit vote, decided that Dunnes would close its British interests, correctly anticipating a major downturn in its economy. The concentration would be on shoring up interests on the island of Ireland without risky overseas distractions.

Dunnes found itself behind SuperValu and Tesco for market share in the food retailing sector, and being challenged more aggressively from behind by Aldi and Lidl, which between them were moving towards having one-fifth of the market and had the resources to undercut Dunnes on price. Margaret decided on a pivot for the supermarket division, one that leaned strongly on the experiences of clothing and homeware and on her appreciation of the strength of the economic recovery – which canny retailers see before anyone else – and changing consumer demands. While SuperValu outdid Dunnes in the regions outside Dublin, Margaret's business remained dominant in the capital where disposable income was higher for many and there was a greater willingness to indulge in more expensive food items. She decided to introduce upscale Irish food brands and to emphasise quality and food provenance.

In 2013, Dunnes began the introduction of a range of higher-priced but seemingly better-quality food products, under the *Simply Better* branding. It was a very brave step in a country that was only just emerging from the deepest recession in a generation, but Dunnes had the information from the spending patterns of its customers to give it a guide.

More than a decade later the company's website describes it as a 'premium food collection with over 350 products, 270 of which are produced right here in Ireland'. The change was accompanied by a subtle change in the advertising tagline. The *Simply Better Value* that had replaced *Dunnes Stores, Better Value beats them all* was now replaced by *Simply Better*. To drop the word *value,* one of the main-stays of Ben Snr's beliefs, was highly significant. It emphasised that Margaret was willing to change.

Dunnes decided to do many more things as well, radically over-hauling its supermarket business. It bought several small Irish luxury food businesses and did partnership deals with others. It signed part-nership deals for in-store concessions, for example with Sheridans cheesemongers, offering more than 120 cheeses, olives, house-made pesto and hummus and charcuterie from Ireland, France, Spain and Italy. Sheridans has opened in 25 Dunnes outlets, 14 in Dublin, but the concessions are fully staffed by its own employees. Dunnes did a similar deal with the Nourish chain of health-food stores, set up in the mid-1980s by Derek and Yvonne Kelly, which Derek still runs with two of their children, and with K O'Connell Fishmongers for its Cork stores. Dunnes made an approach to buy the Base Wood Fired Pizza restaurant group but couldn't strike a deal.

It created Baxter & Greene food halls in several locations, having bought the brand name and business, allowing diners to get salads or sandwiches that could be eaten at dining areas in the supermarket or taken away to eat elsewhere. Accompanying coffees could be purchased from Café Sol, the coffee chain brand. Shopping at Dunnes Stores was becoming more of an 'experience'; these were destination locations to visit instead of doing a boring shop online. To achieve this, Dunnes also had to pull off the remarkable trick of selling these more expensive products alongside the cheaper ones that some loyal shoppers still wanted. It was as if there were two stores in one: an old-style family value grocery store and a would-be epicurean dining destination. It worked.

Margaret also looked at a second wave of expansion, but not under the Dunnes Stores name. She tried to buy Avoca Handweavers – an upmarket store selling expensive food products, clothing and home-ware and now with 15 stores, mainly in Leinster – but was beaten to a deal in 2015 by multinational caterer Aramark, who made the surprise purchase from the founding Pratt family. She also missed out on buying Donnybrook Fair in 2018. The industry talk was that Margaret wrecked her daughter's deal, that Anne had agreed a purchase price and the vendors walked away when Margaret, in typical style, tried to chisel it. Donnybrook Fair, owned by Joe Doyle and his wife, built a chain of five well-regarded epicurean food outlets as well as a food production facility. Dunnes offered the Doyles well over €20m, as well as taking on its debt, after it completed a due diligence examination of the books. But when Margaret bluffed once too often on reducing the price, the Doyles sold to Musgrave instead.

Margaret also offered to buy Fallon & Byrne, yet another upmarket food retailer, when it opened a large unit in the Swan Centre in Rathmines adjacent to her Dunnes homeware unit and along the corridor from her supermarket and clothing outlet. When the owners rejected her offer Dunnes began selling a suspiciously similar range of products at notably cheaper prices. Fallon & Byrne in Rathmines subsequently closed, unable to deal with the competition from Dunnes.

If she missed out on something she wanted, Margaret found other ways to get it. Having missed out on buying Avoca, Dunnes turned its focus instead to its meat concessionaire, James Whelan Butchers, a mainstay of Avoca's luxury food markets. It was known for carcasses hanging behind glass and spot-lit pedestal butcher blocks, the normally back-of-house preparation performed visibly behind a glass screen, almost as if an entertainment. Within eight weeks of losing Avoca, Dunnes bought the retail operation of the butcher chain, while Pat Whelan retained the slaughterhouse and farm in Clonmel, county Tipperary, he had inherited from his father. Whelan also joined Dunnes Stores as a manager and in interviews revealed that Dunnes has its own unique supply chain for meat: 'No other Irish grocer controls its own meat factory, but Dunnes employs 150 butchers at its facility in Clondalkin.' When Dunnes buys a food brand, it takes on the company's existing management who continue to run the brand but who step away from the board of directors, to be replaced by Dunnes nominees. Some get promoted: Emmet Daly from Café Sol became head of Dunnes' Group hospitality division a decade ago.

Dunnes finished the year before the Covid-19 outbreak as the State's largest grocery supermarket player, holding a 22.8% market share and growing strongly outside Dublin. Things improved again in the aftermath of Covid, but it wasn't all down to the products in the shops. Price still played its part. Damian O'Reilly, retail lecturer at Technological University of Dublin (TUI), said Dunnes' €10 off €50 promotion, and more recently its €5 off €25, has been important in maintaining customer loyalty and market share. But how does the company make its profit margins if it is offering up to 20% off prices? 'The margins on the more expensive goods are very high and they essentially subsidise the overall price discounts,' he suggested.

As Margaret undertook an overhaul in what Dunnes offered its customers, she tried to maintain the status quo in industrial relations, which meant continuing to exclude the unions.

There was a series of extraordinary cases, many of which hit the headlines. In December 2001, William O'Byrne, who had worn a goatee-style beard for many years, was told he had to remove his beard or face dismissal. The Dunnes' staff handbook states male employees must be clean-shaven. After several meetings, it was suggested he wear a hygiene mask at work. He did so for a week, but encountered derogatory comments from customers. He stopped wearing the mask. He was dismissed in April 2002. The court upheld O'Byrne's claim that he had been discriminated against on the basis of gender, had been unfairly dismissed and should be reinstated.

In late 2005, Dunnes sacked 22-year-old shop worker Joanne Delaney from the Ashleaf Centre in Crumlin for wearing a union badge on her uniform and refusing to remove it when told to do so. Mandate claimed a disciplinary meeting was later cancelled when Delaney turned up in the presence of a union official. Dunnes was told by the Labour Court to change its disciplinary procedures to allow staff the right to union representation. Dunnes said it did not negotiate with unions. With echoes of the South African dispute, the dismissal was condemned in the Dáil and the House of Commons in London before Dunnes eventually succumbed and reinstated Delaney early in 2006.

The unions believed that Margaret was central to the hard line displayed by the management on every issue. There was a series of disputes across the mid-2010s and a one-day stoppage in April 2015 that brought back memories of 20 years earlier, with rows continuing about secure hours and earnings, pay, and the right to union representation.

Ben had suggested in his 2002 interview with me that 'there were many people who worked in Dunnes who gave their lives to it and on retirement did not really get a lot out of Dunnes Stores.' When Margaret took control in 1993, approximately 80% of Dunnes staff were full-time. By 2015, the same percentage of Dunnes' predominantly young and female staff were on part-time contracts, only guaranteeing 15 hours per week. More than 1,200 Dunnes staff received casual jobseeker's allowance or family income supplement payments, more than from any other employer in the country.

'These workers have no security in their life,' said John Douglas, general secretary of Mandate. 'Child-minding is a serious problem and forget about looking for a mortgage.' He said workers 'do not know what hours they'll have on a week-to-week basis and consequently their income can fluctuate from approximately €144 per week to €400 per week . . . There are many Dunnes workers who have been with the company for up to 10 years doing 35 hours per week, only to have their hours slashed overnight and the company then hires new staff on lower wages. This is a complete abuse of power, and it must be stopped. This is not about the inability of Dunnes to treat their workers fairly, it's about their unwillingness to do so . . .' Mandate said Dunnes was 'the most difficult' retailer it has ever dealt with; whenever Mandate took grievances to the Labour Court or Labour Relations Commission hearings, Dunnes failed to show. Countless more cases were heard, again one-sided, at the Employment Appeals Tribunal.

In early 2015 Mandate moved towards a strike action. Dunnes responded by writing to each staff member directly. It warned of possible layoffs and redundancies if 'harm' was inflicted on the company by industrial action. It accused Mandate of 'engineering a row on issues that did not exist' to pursue an agenda of securing union representation rights. Dunnes said it did not engage directly with trade unions and that staff had received two pay increases in recent years.

Mandate's Gerry Light said: 'All Dunnes had to do was pick up the phone and agree to meaningfully engage. Sadly, they've chosen the route of conflict rather than behaving in a responsible manner. This is not how any employer should behave in 21st-century Ireland.' The trade union accused the retailer of intimidation ahead of the strike. 'Similar disputes in the retail trade have been solved long before they ever got to this point. But Dunnes is a family business and it only answers to itself. They have no outside shareholders shouting about the loss of revenue, the poor staff relations and the bad publicity. There is a fortress mentality of Dunnes against the world.'

After the strike took place, the union said it had received complaints 'from all over the country' of management calling in workers who were on pickets on Holy Thursday and telling them their hours had been reduced or they were being moved from long-held positions. Dismissals of strikers and changes to their shift patterns were also alleged. 'If those workers do not comply with those demands, they threaten disciplinary action or reassignment and they deny those workers trade union representation,' said Patricia King of ICTU.

Even though he was no longer involved in the company, Ben accused the media and Mandate of unfairly targeting Dunnes. He claimed Dunnes ensured its employees had 'the same, if not better' terms and conditions than its main rivals in the grocery sector, a business he described as 'a rat race'. He said he was not defending the stance being taken by Margaret, but he argued other companies that did not deal with unions were not being vilified in the newspapers.

Again, the politicians sided with the workers, especially when Dunnes attempted a new form of 'strike busting'. Instead of expecting shoppers to pass pickets, it offered 20% discounts on its website. Taoiseach Enda Kenny publicly supported the right of Dunnes workers to 'clarity in their working lives'. The Industrial Relations Amendment Act 2015 provides employees with the ability to have the Labour Court issue recommendations that are enforceable through the Circuit Court. While Dunnes said it had a constitutional right not to engage directly with trade unions, this legislation was prompted by its behaviour more than any other company's.

Now retired, John Douglas said Dunnes has gone through a recent transformation in its relationship with unions, and that he would go so far as to suggest 'that it is now possibly the best employer in the sector'. In December 2024, after negotiations with Mandate, it agreed an 8% pay increase and the lifting of the ceiling on the staff discount card from €1,000 to €1,500. There was only so far it would go, however. The union alleged some workers were on higher pay than others for doing exactly the same job, but Dunnes would not accede to a union demand for a unified pay scale for all workers. The change in Dunnes' stance is attributed by some to the influence of Anne and Sharon on Margaret. Others say it is a function of the labour market, that Dunnes has to pay this money to attract and retain staff. If that's the case and unemployment rises again, and people are looking for work, Dunnes may not continue with its new-found relative generosity. It will do what suits its bottom-line at the time.

46.

Market leader

DUNNES STORES ENTERED 2025 in fine fettle. The company now had 138 stores: 118 in the Republic, 15 in Northern Ireland and five in Spain. It employed 18,000-plus people and is estimated to spend over €10m annually on various forms of advertising. At the end of January 2025 the monthly survey by Kantar Worldpanel – the industry benchmark – estimated its grocery market share at 25%, making it the market leader ahead of Tesco (24.1%) and SuperValu (20.3%). Nobody knows the profitability of the group, but it is not unreasonable to estimate annual turnover up to €5bn. It may operate off profit margins of high single digits in the food business, and as much as a third in drapery and household products. But who knows the truth other than a small select group? It's all kept deeply private. All that can be said with confidence is that Dunnes Stores has little or no debt and that the enterprise is worth many billions of euro, making its owners among the richest people in Ireland.

How will that be maintained? Dunnes has been cautious about opening new supermarkets over the previous decade and yet has maintained its market lead over those establishing new units. It bought JC Savage Supermarket in Swords in 2019 and Condron's SuperValu in Clane, county Kildare, in 2023, which it rebranded. Late in 2024 it joined Maxol to trial the sale of Dunnes' *Simply Better* range in Maxol petrol stations. The choice of partner is instructive. The McMullans set up the Maxol business more than a century ago and it is the largest family-owned convenience forecourt retailer on the island of Ireland, with a network of 242 branded service stations. The idea of hooking up with another Irish family-owned business would appeal to Margaret's values. Dunnes doesn't want to be a petrol retailer, but it is a means by which it can get a share of the lucrative trade that has developed in shops at stations all over the country.

Dunnes also opened a home and clothing store in Dundrum Town Centre, at an estimated annual rent of €2m. It closed its shop in Stillorgan, where it had been since the 1960s, and bought the former Union Café in nearby Mount Merrion from Paddy McKillen Jr's Oakmount, presumably with the intention of putting in place a modern replacement. It spent €38m buying Lucan Shopping Centre, where it had been a tenant.

It finally moved to deal with some of the property dereliction for which it was responsible, in places like Enniscorthy and Wexford town, either by selling the units or finding tenants. In late 2024 it let its Grafton Street store on a 15-year lease to Alo Yoga, a California-based athletic wear retailer, for a reported annual rent of €625,000. That this unit had been left closed for years without any tenant on Dublin's main shopping street, when that much money could have been earned from renting it, was baffling. Dunnes finally opened a Café Sol on South Great George's Street, at the entrance to its headquarters, the site where it had reneged on a deal for a Starbucks as far back as 2008.

Much of its Crumlin shopping centre development was left in near-dereliction for over a decade, an eyesore in an area of increasing social deprivation, but in May 2024 Dunnes received planning permission to demolish the centre and build a shopping centre with a café, medical centre and food market. Demolition work has started and if Dunnes goes ahead with the development, it could be a godsend for the regeneration of the area. That's what's sometimes forgotten about the impact of shopping centres: they can act as a social hub, which is another reason why Dunnes has been so important over its 80-plus years, as a place for people to go and meet as much as to shop.

It has been cautious about embracing the internet for online food retailing but a strategy has now been put in place, based around the acquisition of an app called Buymie developed by entrepreneur Devan Hughes. It allows users to do their online shopping and, for a delivery fee, have it brought to their home or place of work within a relatively short timeframe. Hughes ran short of money as he tried to scale the business and when he looked for new investment, Dunnes became the only likely buyer. Margaret was deeply involved in the negotiations and drove the purchase price down to a very low level. The consolation for Hughes was that he became chief digital officer at the company.

Moves such as this will be necessary to stave off competition. There are always ebbs and flows to market share in groceries. Dunnes has fallen to second and third place at times, leading to talk of crisis and potential sale, and yet has always worked its way back to the top. Lidl, Aldi and Tesco are aggressive operators with the financial resources to open new stores to suit the expanding population. If the Republic's population grows as expected, it will reach six million people by 2050, about double what it was when Dunnes began its expansion into groceries in the 1960s. The opportunities will be enormous. A note in its annual accounts for Dunnes Stores (Bangor) in the north, the one arm of the business that provides visibility, states that the company sees 'things in the longer term' and makes 'key business decisions accordingly'. Competitors – Roches Stores and Superquinn come to mind in this century, and many others from earlier – were not able to fulfil such ambitions.

But an increasing population is no guarantee of success. Much of it depends on immigration, and newcomers will have no sense of the Dunnes heritage. More people – wherever they are from originally – have moved online for clothes and homeware shopping. The prices being paid by investors to buy shopping centres – even the busiest ones like Blanchardstown and The Square in Tallaght – have collapsed, a sign of footfall and buying in physical stores being in decline. In early 2025 fashion retailer New Look closed its 26 Irish stores and Ted Baker shut its doors the previous year. Dunnes has always held Marks & Spencer in the highest regard, but the UK giant has had more than its share of difficulties. However, Dunnes continues to innovate its offer to new generations. In 2024 it entered partnerships with newcomers such as Belle Brush, a Galway hairstyling brand, and Aimee Connolly, the highly impressive young Dublin businesswoman who started her Sculpted By Aimee beauty product business in her early twenties and made it a sensational success in profitably taking on bigger international brands with enormous marketing budgets. Sculpted By Aimee is not exclusive to Dunnes, but is still stocked. These moves show that Dunnes continues to spot the modern trends and adapt accordingly. That is one of its main strengths that has allowed it to endure.

Loyalty is another reason for Dunnes' enduring success – both staff and customer – and loyalty is a big issue for the Dunne family. Noel Fox became almost a permanent fixture after retiring as senior partner from Oliver Freaney's in 1999 at the age of 60. In 2003, Fox was given a hands-on executive role in the day-to-day running of Dunnes on top of managing the family Trust. At one stage he became seriously ill, apparently a stroke, and his time with the company seemed over. Margaret waited for him to recover and then insisted he return, such was her trust in him and her dependence on him. His continued presence is extraordinary. Fox remains the key consigliore to Margaret, despite being present in Florida for Ben's humiliation and being the key conduit for Haughey's money and apparently not revealing to the family what was going on. (Fox's relationship with Ben had never recovered: Ben reserved withering contempt for his old friend.) Similarly, Irwin Druker, the property expert, remains a key adviser, advancing age not seen as an impediment.

These are Margaret's people, however. They have been in place a long time and that time will naturally come to an end. If Dunnes is to maintain its position and market share into the coming decades, it will need the loyalty of a new set of leaders, staff and customers. The future of the Dunnes dynasty will be shaped and defined by those chosen – or indeed those who fight and win the prize – to carry on the legacy.

Epilogue: The dynasty endures for now . . .

The ownership structure of Dunnes remains largely masked from the public eye. This remains the most private of companies. The 'unlimited' status for the main Dunnes Stores Holding Company – and most of its subsidiaries – is a legal construct that means it does not have to report turnover, profits and dividend payments publicly, and that provides a degree of cover in disclosing ownership. There have been at least two major restructuring events in the 21st century. In 2016, Dunnes merged at least 16 parts of its corporate structure into one entity, Dunnes Stores Ireland Company (DSIC), which now owns all 115 stores in the State. Ownership of its business ultimately flows, via an Isle of Man company Benlettery, to the Irish-registered Dunnes Stores Holding Company. It, in turn, is owned by a trust company operated by the Dublin law firm William Fry. It appears there were three classes of ordinary shares in the Holding Company. One-third of the shares – an entire class – was owned by Frank Dunne and his family. Most of another one-third class shares are owned by Margaret and her family. The ownership of the remaining third is with a nominee company on behalf of an unknown third party. It's assumed that this belongs to Elizabeth's children, although there has been speculation that Sharon has purchased as least some of the holdings of her three brothers.

Ownership has little to do with leadership. Viewers of the recent hit TV show *Succession* may remember how four children – a daughter and three sons – of the patriarch Logan Roy vied for the right to succeed him. The fictionalised series was allegedly based on Rupert Murdoch's global media empire and the desire of his adult children to succeed him. Although there is no suggestion that any of Margaret's children in any way resemble the misfits depicted in *Succession*, some parallels could be drawn with the situation in which they found themselves had they wanted to take control of the company from their mother. The use of the past tense is deliberate: among the Heffernans the daughter, Anne, has won the war, if there even was a war between this generation of siblings.

For years Michael, the eldest son, looked to outsiders as if he was the preferred successor. He ascended to the role of director by his mid-thirties, received an early endowment of his mother's shares – a transfer said to be worth about €30m in the early years of the 21st century – and racked up experience in a few roles, such as head of textiles, head of international operations and in property, seemingly to groom him for the top position. He spoke once to the media in 2008 to assure everyone that Dunnes would remain in family control in the next generation. For years, he was the only member of his generation to sit on the board and was a director of several subsidiary companies. But suddenly, in 2010, he was gone, just shy of 40 years old, without explanation to the public or staff. Rumour had it that Margaret had decided he simply didn't meet her exacting standards. She expected a lot of anyone who worked for Dunnes, and arguably more of a family member, and put her love for her son to the side in coming to what she saw as the correct business decision.

'Michael was a lovely fellow, not spoilt, never one to let it be known that he was a member of the family and should be treated accordingly,' said one interviewee under condition of anonymity. 'But equally he wasn't a leader, and he didn't have the work ethic required by his mother. He went around the country to various stores and the feedback Margaret got from people she trusted was that he wasn't solving anything for them.'

Another former senior executive disagreed: 'I think Michael worked very hard and was able. What handicapped him was that he didn't have the academic smarts of two of his siblings.' When I suggested that was surprising given Ben Snr's scepticism about the value of education and Margaret's own early departure from school, I was told that Margaret's husband Andrew's influence was to the fore given his own involvement in academia as well as medicine.

Michael invested widely after he received his €30m endowment. For eight years, until September 2008, his wife Maureen Dolan, a former model, ran Modi, an upmarket fashion boutique in Dublin.

She became co-director with Michael of Drisca, described on LinkedIn as 'a collection of online fashion websites including Dresses.ie, OnTrend.eu, and MyKindofDress.com'. The site is heavily influenced by celebrity fashion looks and promotes itself via Instagram, claiming over 150,000 monthly users and selling clothing and shoes all over the world. Michael invested in a fashion agency and distribution operation called TCA Showroom, with offices in Dublin, London and Manchester, which distributes a range of clothing labels in the US and Europe.

There were other retail-related interests and an organic food retail venture, Hives Natural. He invested $300,000 into sandollarswim, a UV protective range of swimwear for children, founded by Maureen in 2013 and in which she still works. He put money into several coast hotels in Rosslare Strand and Kilmore Quay in county Wexford and the Wilde Hotel in Ballybunion, county Kerry, which traded as the H&H collection, before selling them in 2022. Michael is chairman and a main shareholder, holding over 50%, in the established jewellery retailer Dinny Hall, which has five London stores and sells to Liberty and Harvey Nichols. Its annual sales are around £10m. It confirms that his career is well away from Dunnes Stores.

Andrew Jnr never got too involved in Dunnes, despite doing the traditional student stints working in the family store, and a little more after he graduated. Academically very highly qualified, it seemed at first as if he would enter his father's profession when he qualified as a doctor, coming first in his year. But after a brief spell in medicine he decided to enter business and went to a job in investment banking with elite Wall Street outfit Goldman Sachs, before going to Harvard to complete his MBA in 2006. From there he went to Amsterdam to work as a consultant for the giant US investment firm Bain Capital. He told the Harvard Alumni website for an article published in 2014 that this didn't provide the satisfaction he envisioned and he longed to return to his family roots in retailing. 'I always dreamed of being in the branding and fashion business,' he said. But his choice was that it would not be with Dunnes.

In September 2009 he enrolled in a fashion-marketing programme at the Parsons School of Fashion, where he met Anna Lundberg, a former Ralph Lauren marketeer from Sweden, with whom he now has four children. Since he finished that programme Andrew has divided his time between angel investing and consulting with small clothing and retail brands. Milan in Italy, a key location for the fashion industry, is their home.

The youngest sibling, Bernard, never showed any inclination to become involved in the retail business, preferring to work with the family's private property portfolio, the extent of which is not known publicly. Married to Caroline Moloney, with four children, he has a small coffee shop company, Hustle Coffee. He was an early investor in Cainthus, an Irish agtech firm set up in 2016 that developed proprietary facial recognition technology for cows that alerts farmers to changes in a cow's health, both physical and mental. A Texas company bought Cainthus in 2022, presumably providing Bernard with a big return. In October 2023 he registered the company Raynor Lifestyle Clothing. He is a keen regular golfer.

As the sons exited, it was a daughter and a niece who worked their way to the fore. Anne Heffernan graduated from Royal College of Surgeons in June 1992 and practised medicine for the next seven years, specialising in nephrology at St Vincent's Hospital. She left medicine in June 1999 and completed the full-time MBA programme at the Michael Smurfit School of Business in UCD, graduating in November 2000. She joined Dunnes in January 2001 and, according to a biography supplied to UCD when she later became a member of the emeritus board, started her retail career in the food buying office. She moved to human resources in November 2003 and became a full director in 2005.

Anne does not just resemble her mother physically, she has much of Margaret's presence and attitude, although there are various views as to how similar she is to her mother and if she quite reaches the same level, an admittedly near-impossible task. Anne had two children from her marriage to Charles O'Brien, but they later separated. She entered a new relationship with a design consultant from Northern Ireland, Iain Slater, who did some work on Dunnes Stores' packaging. He moved his business south after their daughter, Anne's third child, was born. Anne lives in the house adjacent to her mother's, in a private compound in Stillorgan, just off the N11, a sign of just how close the pair are.

Anne may be the heiress-apparent to her mother, but if so it may be in conjunction with her cousin Sharon, daughter of Elizabeth. Anne and Sharon have formed a leadership triumvirate with Margaret for well over a decade now, but with the common perception that the final call remains with the older woman and that Anne holds more influence over her thinking than Sharon. This is where the issue of succession gets tricky, and it appears to be another reason why Margaret remains so engaged: Anne has become the de facto successor, and is regarded by some insiders and contractors as the real boss, but to hold the overall family together Sharon must be accommodated, so that the Heffernan family, with the same one-third share as Elizabeth's inheritors and Frank's, isn't seen to be taking control at the expense of other members of the Dunne family.

Some long-time insiders said Sharon reminds them of her mother Elizabeth in her occasional iciness. Others say that is simply how she has to be at times in the business, the same as any manager, and that she is a very likeable and personable individual who is determined to have the lowest profile possible. A fully qualified solicitor, she worked with the Irish law giant Matheson Ormsby Prentice for five years before leaving in 1999 to do the same MBA course as her cousin at UCD, graduating at the same time. She then joined Dunnes in a full-time capacity and went through the same 'learning on the job' process as Anne. She is said to be involved in Dunnes' property and investment interests, although that might underplay her involvement in clothing and homeware. She was married in 1995 to Brian Kennedy, who works in the family construction company Sheelin Homes, which owns the Herbert Park Hotel in Ballsbridge and has built homes around Dublin for many decades. Having grown up on Ailesbury Road, in Dublin 4, Sharon still lives there with Brian. Both eschew alcohol but are regarded as highly sociable, with much of their activity revolving around their children's school activities, although many of them are now adults. Sharon inherited her mother's stake in the business alongside her brothers Brian, Paul and John, but the three boys are not involved in running the business.

This, then, would seem to be the future of Dunnes Stores: Margaret leading with Anne and Sharon for now, until the two younger women step fully into the leadership role, with Anne essentially senior to Sharon, if not nominally so. They will need a good personal relationship to make it work, which might be awkward if Sharon owns a bigger holding of shares than Anne once Margaret passes.

Even if Anne, 57 at the time of writing, and Sharon, two years younger, carry things on, for how long will they be able? How many of their own children, in turn, or maybe Frank's son Ben, if he was to return, will be willing to put in the work when so many family members have fallen by the wayside? Will dispersed ownership, with many descendants taking dividends but not contributing to the running of the business, continue without some people getting greedy or envious? How will this wealth affect future generations, especially as it has not provided an insulation to date for some members of the family against the various vicissitudes of life and an addictive nature that runs through the family?

At 83 years of age, Margaret shows no signs to stepping back. It seems that Margaret Heffernan has her own addiction: Dunnes Stores. She can't let it go. Every time it looks as if she might retire, hand things over to the next generation, something happens that, to her mind, makes her continued presence essential. She may have been able to give up alcohol, which she did as a young woman seeing what it was doing to those she loved, but she cannot give up Dunnes Stores.

It looked, in September 2007, as if she might be taking a lap of honour in advance of departure. In presenting her with an honorary degree from the NUI, Professor Michael Murphy said while the award was 'more than amply justified by her tremendous success in the world of business, it would have been merited otherwise by her contribution to Irish society through personal philanthropy, and the promotion of philanthropy among the Irish business community'. After receiving the honour, Margaret went on Joe Duffy's *Liveline* in an extremely rare media appearance and enjoyed 20 minutes of the presenter's company and a flurry of complimentary texts. She said the award was fantastic for 'the company and its workers' and that a lot of Dunnes' success was down to the staff. She was undoubtedly sincere and modest, but it was also true that the lion's share of the proceeds went to the owners.

There would have been a nice symmetry had she chosen the reopening of the St Patrick's Street store in Cork in 2009 as a time to announce she was stepping down. She was accompanied there by her children Anne and Michael, her niece Sharon and her nephew Brian McMahon, and by Frank's children, Ben and Annie. Margaret made a brief speech to those assembled, including some reporters who were granted admission:

> 'Our aim is to keep it as a family-run company and I am confident that the next generation will be able to do that with the support and dedication and loyalty of a fantastic workforce. With the support we have had from all our customers all over Ireland, and above all the people who work with us, I'm confident that we will go from strength to strength and I'm also confident that we will stay in Irish hands and continue to give value to the Irish people. I've worked in the store from the very beginning. I never wanted to do anything except work in Dunnes Stores with my father. I still work as hard as I can, I know that we will go from strength to strength with the support of the Irish people.'

Some commentators over the decades have suggested that what Dunnes does is not too difficult and that the rewards the family has drawn from its business have been excessive. The latter point is one for debate – we have a tax system that can redistribute wealth fairly and Margaret has also given back by way of philanthropy – but the first is fatuous. Economic history is littered with examples of complacent businesses expecting the future to be exactly as the past was, of not realising the new trends in consumer behaviour, the changes being wrought by technology, the willingness of competitors to fight harder. That Dunnes Stores is still intact after the family in-fighting, the many personal traumas and tragedies, and the harsh light of deserved public scrutiny (because it could not be as big and important as it is in Irish society and carry on without supervision) is an extraordinary achievement. That is largely due to Margaret, a woman of resilience and drive, who may well be Ireland's most successful and influential businesswoman since the creation of the State in 1922. Name another woman who has done more in Irish business.

Even if many of the senior management and advisor roles are held by men, women play a stronger part than in most companies. The World Economic Forum's 2022 *Gender Gap Report* demonstrated that the biggest disparity, across a range of sectors, between overall female representation and representation in leadership roles was in the retail sector: 51% of all retail positions are held by women, while female leadership stands at only 32%. That isn't a problem for the Dunnes triumvirate of women, which is a strength given that estimates are that at least 75% of all shopping decisions are made by women. The men may have made most of the headlines, but what started with a Margaret is unlikely to finish with one.

That brings us to the future, one without Margaret, which must come at some time. Fintan Drury described Margaret to me as a 'one-off', an assessment shared by others who didn't want to be quoted in the book. Anne Heffernan and Sharon McMahon may be formidable women in their own rights, essential to the success of the enterprise over the last decade and who have shown their commitment in full, but neither of them is Margaret, a woman who is unique. It will be very hard for any succeeding generation to have the same attitude, or the same success. Retirement doesn't seem an option. Margaret continues to provide support for her sister, Anne, who remains in an institution in Cork. Margaret visits Anne regularly and, at the same time, she checks in on how things are doing at the stores in Cork city. The family and the business are intertwined, inseparable, always.

Dunnes Stores and its owning family have been written off, incorrectly, so many times that nobody should do so again. But the longer things go on, the more difficult the trick gets to pull off. The intention is clear, though. It lies in the statement made on the company website: 'We continue to be run by Ben Dunne's family. Dunnes Stores is not merely a name above the door, it is his legacy.'

Sources cited

Chambers, Anne, *T.K. Whitaker: Portrait of a Patriot* (Doubleday Ireland, 2014)

Ferriter, Diarmaid, *The Revelation of Ireland, 1995–2020* (Profile Books, 2024)

Findlater, Alex, *Findlaters: The Story of a Dublin Merchant Family* (A&A Farmar, 2001)

Garvin, Tom, *Preventing the Future: Why was Ireland So Poor for So Long?* (Gill & Macmillan, 2005)

Harnden, Toby, *Bandit Country: The IRA and South Armagh* (Biteback Publishing, 2024)

Manning, Mary with Sinéad O'Brien, *Striking Back: The Untold Story of an Anti-Apartheid Striker* (The Collins Press, 2017)

McGowan, J.B., Clearing the Hurdles (Liberties Press, 2019)

Murphy, Professor John A., *Ireland in the Twentieth Century*, (Gill & Macmillan, 1975)

Murtagh, Peter and Joyce, Joe, *The Boss: Charles J. Haughey in Government* (Poolbeg, 1983)

O'Callaghan, Edmund and Don O'Riordan (eds), *Retailing in Ireland: Contemporary Perspectives* (Gill & Macmillan, 2012)

Ó Gráda, Cormac and O'Rourke, Kevin Hjortshøj, *The Irish economy during the century after partition* (UCD Centre for Economic Research Working Paper Series, No. WP21/08, University College Dublin, UCD Centre for Economic Research, Dublin, 2021); available at: https://hdl.handle.net/10197/12104

O'Toole, Fintan, *We Don't Know Ourselves: A Personal History of Ireland Since 1958* (Apollo, 2022)

Smyth, Sam, *Thanks a Million, Big Fella* (Blackwater Press, 1997)

Acknowledgements

Acknowledgements must start with my family, my wife Aileen and our children, for putting up with the time I spend in my home office away from them, the times I make myself unavailable because I'm busy researching and writing. The children are adults now, so they have their own lives to lead, but we still see a lot of each other daily and socialise together and the interest they take in my projects, such as this, is greatly encouraging to me. My thanks as ever to them and to my friends also for the support.

My editor Rachel Pierce is central to my books. She is incredibly patient, helps me organise my editorial structures and ideas, probes why I'm taking angles, makes valuable suggestions as to what's needed and that I've ignored or omitted, or simply haven't thought of including. This is the fifth book on which we have collaborated, and she is essential to my work.

From Bonnier Books UK, I'd like to thank Deirdre Nolan, the publishing director of Eriu, Lisa Gilmour, the assistant editor with Eriu, and everyone in the sales and marketing team at Bonnier. At Gill Hess, Simon Hess, Declan Heeney, Helen McKean and Jacq Murphy played key roles. For legal support, a big thanks to Kieran Kelly.

My agent Niamh Tyndall at NKM (along with Noel Kelly and Niamh McCormack) has also been essential in getting the book started and to this point. This is also an opportunity to thank all my Path to Power colleagues at NKM, including Aidan Power for overseeing production and my co-presenter Ivan Yates, for indulging me in the podcast project.

My daily work colleagues have also showed great patience with me as I go about other things. *The Last Word* at Today FM is a show I've edited and presented since January 2003 and it remains the centre piece of each day for me, incredibly important to get right for the listener. I could not do it without the core team of Diarmuid Doyle,

Liz O'Neill, Orla Carney and Aoibhean Meghan, and others who help produce on a freelance basis. There are a host of regular contributors to the programme as well, too many to name here but who are all greatly appreciated.

My newspaper editors – Conor O'Donnell at the *Irish Daily Mail* and Daniel McConnell at the *Business Post* – are also very tolerant of me as I brush up against deadlines regularly as I juggle commitments. My thanks again to them for their encouragement and tolerance.

This book has been one of the most interesting and exciting projects I've carried out in my career, now over 35 years long. It is a story that has almost everything, of a family that has owns a company that has interacted with the public for over 80 years, and which has grown with Ireland. Thank you to the many people who spoke to me for this book, many of whom are quoted in the text. A lot of them aren't identified however, with many interviews conducted "off-the-record" because of their sensitivity about publicly discussing the subject matter. I understand the reticence, but I hope they will feel that the information they provided has been treated in a considered and sensitive fashion.

Index

A
ABF 115, 218–19, 283
AD Event Design 323
Adams, Gerry 318
ADM/Londis 109, 310
advertising 13, 19, 28–9, 68, 114,
    149, 216, 284
Ahern, Bertie 179, 205
AIB 193
Ainsworth, Assistant Commissioner
    Joe 84
alcohol/alcoholism 2–3, 7, 50, 70,
    71–2, 95, 117, 185, 191–3,
    197–8, 220, 317–18
Aldi 284, 285–6, 295, 317
Andersen Consulting 218
Andersons, Drogheda 9, 23
'Ansbacher deposits' 250, 251
apartheid, South African 125–31
Archbold, Brendan 126–7, 139, 227
Argos 68
Arms Trial (1970) 249
Army, British 59, 92
Army, Irish 85
Asda 287
Asmal, Louise 127–8
Associated British Foods (ABF) 32, 60
Assumption Sisters, South Africa 130
Attorney General 40–1
Austin, David 240
Aviette 112

B
Báinne, Bord 123
bakery closures 135–6, 137–8

BarkIsland 223
Barrett, Dan 52
Baxter & Green food-halls 340
Ben Dunne Gyms 308–10
bendunnedirect.co.uk 311–12
Beresford, Chris 206
Boardman, Nigel 206
Bolger, Jeanne 61–2
Bolger, John 61–2
Bolger Stores Group 61–2
Bono 158
Bord Fáilte 22
Bourke, John 46–7, 141
Bowen, Frank 143–4, 145, 147
Bradley, Fr William 195
branded goods 19, 24, 115, 216–17
bread wars 133–9
Brennan and McGowan 65–6
Brennan, Francis 335
Brennan, Seamus 112
Bri-Nylon 22
British Land (BL) 141–2
Brown Thomas 60–1, 191, 283
Browne, Vincent 162
Bruton, John 128–9, 239, 241–2
Buchanan, Judge Gerard 246–8, 249,
    250, 259
Buckley, Leslie 232
Burke, Ray 137–8
Burke, Simon 289
Business & Finance 99–101, 137
Business Post 187–8
Buy Right Stores 188–9
BWG 68
Byrne, Gay 100, 123

C

Cameron's drapery shop, Longford
9–10
Camiveo 302
Campbell, Michael 228
Casey, Eamonn 128
'cash-and-carry' operations 68–9
cash only terms 13
Cassels, Peter 234
Cassidy, Donie 292
Cassidy's clothing change 61–3, 106,
107, 192–3, 216
Catholicism 14, 30, 48, 81–2, 101,
173, 180, 195, 229
Catholics, Northern Irish 59
Cavanagh, Sean 294
Celtic Tiger economy 283–4
charity work/fundraising 120–4,
169, 195
Charleton, Joseph 104–5
Charter Clinic rehab 170, 173,
175, 314
Cleeves Toffee 193
clothing
affordable versions of latest
fashions 62–3
Bri-Nylon 22
'cut, make, and trim' (CMT)
garment production 24–5
designer Carolyn Donnelly 335–6
designer Paul Costelloe 323,
334, 336
imported ideas 20
Margaret in control of 117–18
mini-skirts 45
modernised manufacturing 19
nylon stockings 17, 25–6, 45
Orlon wool substitute 46
clothing and hosiery factories 14
cocaine addiction, Ben Jr's 3, 95,
165–6, 170, 173–4, 175
Collery, Padraig 251

Collins, Michael 250, 258
Comiskey, Bishop Brendan 228, 229
competitors 2
1980s price wars 109–15
British and European supermarkets
283–4, 285–9, 317
clothing retail 60–2
food retail 31–6, 60, 67–9, 136,
178–9, 283–4, 285–9, 317, 339–40
Connolly, Vivienne 328
Consumers Association of Ireland 133
Conway, Martin 302
Cooney SC, Garret 266–7, 268
Cooper, Sydney 169
Corcoran, John 113
Cork Corporation 75
Cornelscourt Shopping Centre
27–30, 47, 338
Cosgrove, Michael 187
Costelloe, Paul 323, 334, 336
Coughlan, John 272
Covid-19 global pandemic 342
Crazy Prices 114–15, 219, 283, 284
Creachadoir 71
Crosbie, Harry 298–9
Crowley, Laurence 206
Crumlin Shopping Centre 65
Culligan, Garda Commissioner
Patrick 203
Culloty, Sergeant Dennis 37–42
Curragh racecourse 119–20
Curran, Philip 146–7

D

Daly, Emmet 341–2
Daly, Frank 300
Danker, Trevor 120–1
Danziger, Dr Jeffrey 170
Darrer, Des 11, 14, 19
Davin, Margaret 219
de Rossa, Proinsias 231
de Treville, Rick 158–9

Dee, Frank 111
Delaney, Joanne 342–3
Derelict Sites Act 302
Desmond, Dermot 123
Devine, Patricia 317–18
Dillon, Elizabeth 38–9, 40, 41–422
Discretionary Trust Tax (DTT) 145
Doherty, Justice Sean 252–3
Dolan, Maureen 352–3
Donnelly, Carolyn 335–6
Donnybrook Fair 341
Donoughmore, Earl and Duchess 82
Douglas, John 232, 233–4, 343,
    344–5
Doyle, Diarmuid 162, 240
Doyle, Joe 341
Doyle, PV 119
Doyle, Vinnie 185, 243
drapery businesses 8, 9, 13, 14, 24
Druker, Irwin 141, 299, 350
Druker, Ivan 66–7
Drumgoole, Kevin 272, 274
Drury Communications 233, 284
Drury, Fintan 233, 358
Duane, Bill 161
Dublin
    Castle 84, 215
    first Dunnes store in 18
    Jury's Hotel 76
    loyalist bombings in 59
    Shelbourne Hotel 70
    St Bernard's House superstore 23,
        37, 39
    Women's Mini Marathon 233
Dublin District Court 39
Dublin Tribune 149
Duffy, Joe 279, 313–15, 356
Duffy, Kevin 232
Dugdale, Rose 82
Dukes, Alan 144, 247
Dunguaire Castle, county Galway 70
Dunloe House 186–8, 224

Dunn, Annie 7
Dunn, Barney 7, 51
Dunn, John 'Dennis' 7, 8, 54
Dunn (née Byrne), Margaret 7, 51
Dunne (née Achmann), Ann 70, 72,
    321–2
Dunne, Anne 11, 23–4, 105, 143,
    145, 195
Dunne (Frank's daughter), Annie 323
Dunne (Frank's son), Ben 323–4
Dunne (Ben Jr's sister), Caroline 308
Dunne, Frank 11, 23, 27–9, 38, 51,
    107, 109, 319–20
    1970s business expansion 66–7,
        68–9
    alcohol dependence 70, 71–2,
        185
    Ben Jr's allegations of financial
        impropriety 209–11
    business expansion in Northern
        Ireland 60
    business networks and social
        circles 69–70
    death and funeral 323
    Green Property 113
    Hamwood Stud Farm 322–3
    horses and horseracing 70–1, 76,
        321, 322
    in joint chairman role with
        Margaret 217–19, 232, 233, 235
    last will and testament 323
    marriage 70, 72, 321–2
    mocks Ben Jr's affair confession 95
    National Prices Commission
        (1971) 33–6
    reclusive lifestyle 321
    removal of Ben Jr as chairman
        183–4, 185, 189–90
    sibling business disputes 176–7,
        179, 180–1, 185, 189–90, 194,
        200–1, 205, 206, 210–11
Dunne, Jim 184–5

Dunne Jr, Bernard 'Ben' 3, 4, 11, 23, 76, 107, 237, 319–20
  1980s bread wars and bakery closures 134–9
  1980s supermarket price wars 109–13
  1990s price-cutting 178–9
  1992 Florida golf trip – drugs and escorts scandal 155–63
  facing the media 165–6
  legal proceedings and charges 167–70
  post-trial home life in Ireland 171, 172
  2002 interview with author 305–10
  alcohol and drug addiction 3, 95, 165–6, 170, 173–4, 175, 197–8, 203, 306
  and apartheid strikers 128, 129–31
  arranges kidnap of adversary 95
  attempt to buy-out siblings 205–6
  Ben Sr's funeral 105–6
  bendunnedirect.co.uk 311–12
  business conflict with siblings 176–7, 179, 180–1, 183–90, 194, 196–7, 199, 200–3, 205–6, 207–11
  Buy Right Stores 188–9
  character 113, 168–9, 313, 314–15
  and Charles Haughey 138, 186, 198, 209, 210, 243, 245, 250–6, 259–63, 271–6
  Charter Clinic rehab 170, 173, 175
  consumer column 313
  contests Therese's will 221–2
  Cornelscourt SC fire (1970) 30
  damages claim to siblings for violation of shareholder rights 208–11
  death and funeral 325–9
  death of sister, Elizabeth 195–6
  the EU and European Parliament 315–16
  fitness and leisure business 222–5, 308–10, 316
  golf, gambling and excess 153–4, 155
  High Court injunction against siblings 200–1
  Highly Recommended TV show 314
  Buchanan investigations into hidden payments 243, 245, 246–8
  kidnapped by the IRA 79–87, 318
  the rescue 89–93
  resulting trauma 93–5, 153, 197, 318
  last will and testament 328–9
  and lawyers give evidence at the McCracken Tribunal 250–3, 267–8
  Liveline radio 130, 279, 313
  marriage 76–7
  and Michael Lowry 225, 238–9, 241, 245–8, 265–6, 268–70, 276–7
  Moriarty Tribunal 271–9
  ownership of Dunloe House 186–8, 224
  Presentation Brothers College (Pres) 73
  Price Waterhouse report 207, 209, 243, 246, 266, 279–80
  removal as chairman 183–7, 189–90, 196–7
  renewed friendship with Margaret 318
  school and early career 74–5, 76
  'sham' Trust allegations 208–11, 246
  Stephen's Green Shopping Centre 141–3
  talks about sisters in the media 317–18

'The Indispensable Man' (S.W.
  Kessinger) 330
the Trust and taxation 144–8
working with Ben Sr 74
Dunne, Margaret *see* Heffernan
  (née Dunne), Margaret
Dunne (Ben Jr's son), Mark 76, 94,
  161, 308, 319, 325, 326, 329
Dunne (née Godwin), Mary 76–7,
  85, 89–91, 93, 94, 95, 154, 160,
  161–2, 171–2, 186, 188, 319,
  325, 329
Dunne (Ben Jr's son), Nicholas 308
Dunne (née Maloney), Nora 4,
  10–11, 23, 30, 51, 70, 76–7, 99,
  101, 105, 106–7, 118
Dunne (Ben Jr's son), Rob 93, 94–5,
  154, 161–2, 172, 184–5, 308,
  319–20, 325, 329
Dunne Sr, Bernard 'Ben' 4, 67, 70,
  76–7, 118
  1970s expansion 65
  Ben Jr's kidnap and ransom 82,
    90, 91–2, 93
  business expansion in Northern
    Ireland 59
  Business & Finance interview
    99–101
  business meetings with John
    Bourke 46–7
  character 45–7, 74, 75, 100, 102,
    103–4, 105
  and Charles Haughey 22, 105, 106
  childhood and youth 7–8
  Cornelscourt Shopping Centre
    27–30, 47
  court case against employees 40–1
  death and funeral 99, 101, 102–6
  early entrepreneurship 8–9
  employee's civil action against and
    Supreme Court appeal 41–3
  estate's worth at death 106

expansion plans (1963) 23
Fair-Trade Commission (1961)
  25–6
family business ownership and
  inheritance 52–3
family property upgrades 51–2
first shop 13–15
food retailing 31, 32
foreign travel and importing ideas
  20, 21, 27
Irish Times interview 47–50, 52
Irish trade fair, New York
  (1968) 22
Jury's Hotel, Dublin 76
marries Nora 11
Mitchelstown Stud Farm 69, 71,
  75–6, 106
NRMAA 22
press conferences 45
on Public companies 52–3
purchases Andersons 23
Ringmahon House, Cork 51, 75
at Roches Stores 10
settlement Trust 53–5
Shelbourne Hotel, Dublin 70,
  76
St Bernard branded goods 24–5
store security 37–8
suppliers 18–19, 23, 24–5
working for Anderson 9
Dunne, Therese 11, 23, 62, 107,
  109, 117, 145, 171, 177, 181,
  183, 184, 191–2, 203–4, 210,
  220–1
Dunnes Holding Company 54
Dunnes Stores 1–2
  50th birthday celebrations 215
  1980s growth of market share 110
  1980s prices wars 109–15
  1990s price-cutting 178–9
  annual turnover and profits 2, 24,
    297, 347

Dunnes Stores (*cont.*)
branded goods 19, 24, 115,
216–17
bread wars 133–9
cash flow 13, 18, 36
Cassidy's clothing chain 61–3, 106,
107, 192–3, 216
Cornelscourt Shopping Centre
27–30, 338
current ownership 351–2
dismissed employee public
grievances 342
Dublin HQ, St Bernard House 23
employees charged with larceny
38–41
employee's civil action against and
Supreme Court appeal 41–3
English outlets closed 176
expansion in Northern Ireland
59–60
extended opening hours 29
family ownership 2, 23, 52–3, 143,
205, 287–8, 357–8
firebomb in Dublin store 59
first shop, Cork 13–15
food retailing established 31, 32
homewares 334–5
improved treatment of staff 345
industrial disputes 99–100,
125–31, 227–8, 229, 230–4, 344
introduction of loyalty cards 285
introduction of security tags 37
modernisation and expansion
333–8, 347–50
National Prices Commission
enquiry (1971) 33–6
number of outlets 2, 24, 106,
297, 347
online food retailing 349–50
post-WWII expansion 18
shop security 37–8
Simply Better food range 339–40

sports sponsorship 215, 233
trade with Asia 148, 177–8,
179, 203
value of business 2
zero hours contracts 227–8
Dunnes Stores Ireland Company
(DSIC) 351
Durnin, Padraig 127–8
Dury, Fintan 233

E
economy, Irish
1950s 20
1960s 21
1970s 63–4
1980s 109
ban on low-cost selling 134,
136–8
bread wars 133–9
Celtic Tiger 283–4, 297
Global Recession (2008) 297–8
post-Emergency 17–18
the Emergency 11, 14, 17
emigration 8, 9, 20, 21, 109
employment, Irish 14, 21, 229, 283
Equifex Trust, Switzerland 148
European Economic Community
(EEC) 49
European Union (EU) 49, 315
Eurospar 285
Evening Echo 13

F
Fagan, Willie 200
Fair-Trade Commission (1961) 25–6
Fallon & Byrne 341
Fanning, Aengus 102–3, 104
Feeney, Peter 166
Ferriter, Diarmaid 63
Fianna Fáil 63, 91, 205, 243, 248
Finance Act (1984) 145
Findlater, Alex 17

Fine Gael 112, 128–9, 195, 239, 240, 248, 266, 277, 278
fire at Cornelscourt Shopping Centre (1970) 30
FitzGerald, Garret 83, 92, 105, 129
FitzGerald, Mark 276–7, 279
Fitzgibbon, Frank 99–101, 228–30
Fitzsimons, Eoghan 292
Fitzwilton 284
Five Star 67
Flanagan, Sean 169
Flood, Finbarr 232
Flynn, Phil 82–3, 232
Ford, Detective Chris 167
Ford, Henry 18
Fox, Noel 82–3, 155, 159, 161, 232, 251–2, 253–4, 272, 273–4, 293–4, 299, 321–2, 350
Freaney, Oliver 143–4
Freyne, Hilary 60
Fry, Houghton 254
Fuengirola hyperstore, Dunnes 118–19
Fundraiser and Latin Quarter racehorses 120

G
Gallagher, Eddie 82
Gallagher, Matt 69
Gallagher, Patrick 69, 91
Gallagher, Paul 207–8
Galvin, Paul 337
Galway Blazers 70
Gardaí 13, 37–42
    kidnap and ransom of Ben Jr 80, 83–6, 87, 90–1, 92
    post-kidnap Dunne family security detail 94
    responses to apartheid strikers 127
    Therese's drink-driving charges 203–4
Garvin, Professor Tom 20, 21

Gavin, Diarmuid 337
Gilmore, Brendan 112
Giobbe, Marcello 106
Gleeson, Dermot 207–8, 210–11
Global Recession (2008) 297
Godson, Rory 134, 149, 159, 161, 162, 166–7, 173–4, 190
Goodman, Larry 328
government, British 82–3
government, Irish 19
    Ben Jr's kidnap and ransom 82–3, 92
    bread wars and Irish bakeries 134, 136–9
    Department of Industry and Commerce 112
    First Programme for Economic Expansion 8
    Groceries Order Act (1987) 200, 286
    Industrial Relations Amendment Act (2015) 344
    National Prices Commission 33–4
    South African apartheid 128–9
    VAT increases 134, 179
Grace, Tom 207
Green Property 113
Green Shield Stamps 68
Groceries Order Act (1987) 200, 286
Gubay, Albert 67
Guinness, Arthur 1
Guinness & Mahon 244

H
H Williams 110–13, 137
Hall, Lorraine 301–2
Halligan, Ursula 177
Hand, Michael 162
Hardiman, Adrian 292
Harrington, Pádraig 337
Harris, Anne 338
Harrison, Frank 264

Haughey, Charles 22, 63, 91, 105,
106, 120, 138, 146, 160, 186,
195, 198, 209, 210, 243–5
McCracken Tribunal 249–56,
257–64, 274
Moriarty Tribunal 271–6
Hayes, Tom 230
Heaney, Seamus 127
Hederman, Carmencita 123
Heffernan (Margaret's son), Andrew
118, 353–4
Heffernan, Anne 118, 119, 179–80,
293, 333, 345, 352, 354–6, 358
Heffernan (Margaret's son), Bernard
119, 354
Heffernan, Dr Andrew 118, 352
Heffernan (née Dunne), Margaret 2,
4, 11, 32, 51, 73, 76, 107, 109,
148–9, 170, 357–8
21st century staff grievances and
industrial action 342–4
apartheid strikers 129
Ben Jr's allegations of financial
impropriety 208–11
Ben Jr's High Court injunction
against 200–3
business disputes with Ben Jr 149,
176, 177, 179, 180–1, 183–4,
189–90, 194, 199, 200–3, 205,
206–7, 208–11
character 123–4, 218, 233, 358
charity work and fundraising
120–4, 357
and Charles Haughey 22, 106, 120
control of Dunne's clothing 117–19
court cases against employees 37–41
death of sister, Therese 220–1
designers and collaborators 334–8
Dublin Lord Mayor's Awards 122
Dunnes Store homeware 334–5
Dunnes Stores 50th birthday
celebrations 215

Dunne's Stores industrial action
(1995–96) 227–8, 229, 230–5
the Dunne's Trust 145
employee's civil action against and
Supreme Court appeal 41–3
empty properties and land
hoarding allegations 301–2
failed property development at
Fair Green Plaza 301
father's funeral 106
food retailing expansion 339–40
Fuengirola hyperstore 118–19
Global Recession (2008) 297–8
horses and horseracing 119–20,
180
in joint chairman role with Frank
215–20
marriage and children 118
McCracken Tribunal 254–6, 257,
266–8
and the media 120–1, 123, 177,
180, 356
modernisation of Dunnes Stores
333–8
plastic bag levy 292–3
potential purchase of Stackallen
House 179–80
reaction to Ben Jr's Florida
scandal 170, 171, 173, 175, 202
removal of Ben Jr as chairman
183–4, 189–90
renewed friendship with Ben Jr 318
reopening of the St Patrick's Street
store 356–7
share-price dispute with Ben Jr 221
as sole chairman of Dunnes Stores
284–9, 333–8
legal battles 291–6, 298–302
Sunday trading proposal 228–9
Supreme Court rent increase
dispute 302
working with Ben Sr 22

Heffernan (Margaret's son), Michael 119, 254, 352–3

Hely-Hutchinson, John and Dorothy 82

Hemphill, Lord 70

Heneghan, Pat 231–2

Herrema, Tiede 82

Highly Recommended TV show 314

Holland, Finbarr 110–11

Holtglen 299–300

Hong Kong 148

Horan, Niamh 93, 154, 161, 172

Horgan, Liam 144

horses and horse-racing 51, 70–1, 119–20

Horseshoe Bar, Shelbourne Hotel, Dublin 70

Hospice Foundation 122

House of Cassidy 62

Howard, Larry 293–4

Hughes, Devan 348–9

Humphreys, Judge Richard 322

Hyatt (Marriot) Grand Cypress Hotel, Florida 156–9

Hynes, Joanne 336

I

ICTU 232, 234, 344

IDATU 128, 129–30, 227

independence, Irish Republic 8

independent retailer alliance 33–5

independent wholesalers 68

industrial action, Dunnes Stores 99–100, 125–31, 227–8, 229, 230–4, 343–4

Intelligence and Security Branch (ISB), Gardaí 84

Irish Anti-Apartheid Movement (IAAM) 127–8

Irish Bread Bakers Association 138

Irish Farmers Association 136

Irish Field 322

Irish Independent 102–3, 110, 119–20, 121, 171, 173, 184–5, 206, 222–5, 241, 257, 268

Irish Press 40, 104–5

Irish Republican Army (IRA) 79–87, 92, 283, 318

Irish Sugar 18

Irish Sun 313

Irish Times 9, 23, 24, 28, 32, 39, 45, 65–7, 90, 91, 99, 103, 105, 106, 111–12, 130–1, 243, 314

Irish trade fair, New York (1968) 22

Irwin, Michael 175, 199, 200–1, 206, 237, 253–4

J

James, Helen 334–5

James Whelan Butchers 341

Janelle Shopping Centre 188

Jordan, Paddy 137

Jury's Hotel, Dublin 76

K

K Security 37

Kader, 127

Karen Millen 294–5

Keane, Denis 69–70

Keane Mahony Smith Estate Agents 69–70

Keatinge, Richard 32

Kelly, Judge Peter 300

Kelly, Paul 193

Kelly, Peter 207–8

Kennedy, Brian 255

Kennedy, Ted 70

Kenny, Charles 123

Kenny, Enda 344–5

kidnap and ransom, Ben Dunne Jr's 3, 79–87, 318

the rescue 89–93

resulting trauma 93–4, 153, 197, 318

Kilroy, Norman 123
King, Patricia 126, 127
Knights of Columbanus 228

L
Labour Court 128–9, 230, 232, 234, 343, 344
Labour Party 128–9, 205, 241, 247
Labour Relations Commission 230, 234, 343
Lalor, Paddy 33
The Late Late Show TV show 100, 329
Lawless, John 250
legal battles, Dunne family
  An Bord Pleanála and the Ferrybank centre planning permissions 300–1
  Ben Jr's damages claim 208–11
  Ben Jr's Forida trial and charges 168–70
  Ben Jr's High Court injunctions against siblings 200–3
  Ben Jr's 'sham' Trust allegations 208–11
  and developer Harry Crosbie 298–9
  dismissed employee grievances 342–3
  Dunnes Stores vs the State 291–2
  Elizabeth's divorce *a mensa et thoro* 193
  employees charged with larceny 38–41
  and Holtglen developers 299–300
  Karen Millen clothing allegations 294–5
  Larry Howard allegations against company 293–4
  and National Asset Management Agency (NAMA) 298–301
  protecting Hamwood Stud Farm 322–3

Sean Cavanagh unfair dismissal tribunal 294
Therese's drink-driving charges 203–4
Trust share price dispute 221
Whelan Frozen Foods 295–6
see also McCracken (and McCracken Tribunal), Justice Brian; Moriarty (and the Moriarty Tribunal), Mr Justice Michael
Leighton, Allan 287
Lemass, Kathleen 28
Lemass, Seán 20, 21
Lewis, Sergeant Barbara 168
Lidl 284, 285–6, 295, 317
Light, Gerry 344
Liptons 67
Lisbon Treaty 315
Liveline radio 130, 279, 313, 315, 356
Londis 68
Lord Mayor of Dublin 122–3
Lowry, Michael 225, 237–42, 245–8, 256, 265–6, 268–70, 276–80, 328
Lowry, Peter 239
Luke Burkes 13
Lundberg, Anna 353–4
Lynch, Jack 41, 105, 195

M
MacDonald, Mary Lou 318, 325–6
McCarthy, Barbara 314
McCarthy, Fr Dermod 76, 85–6, 89–90, 92–3, 101, 220
McCarthy, Justine 171, 257, 268
McCoy, Denis 223, 225
McCracken (and McCracken Tribunal), Justice Brian 241, 249–56, 257–64, 265–70, 274
McCullough, Denis 250, 256, 262–3
McDonagh, Brendan 300
McElroy, Garda James 203

McGettigan, Eoin 288
McGonigal, Eoin 261
McGowan, Joe 66, 69–70, 138
McGuinness, Bill 218
McGuinness, Martin 318
McKenna, Seamus 256, 268
McKeon, Padraig 233, 254
McLaughlin, Commissioner Patrick 84
McLaughlin, Mr Justice 42
McMahon (née Dunne), Elizabeth
    11, 23, 107, 109, 145, 171,
    177, 181, 183, 184, 187, 190,
    192–5, 355
McMahon (Elizabeth's son), John 195
McMahon Jr (Elizabeth's son), Brian
    195, 200
McMahon (Elizabeth's son), Paul 195
McMahon (Elizabeth's daughter),
    Sharon 195, 333, 345, 354–6, 358
McMahon Sr, Brian 193, 195
McNiffe, John 220, 284
McNulty, Matt 123
McPadden, Gerry 192
McPhillips, Derry 299
MacSharry, Ray134
Mace 68
Magnier, John and Susan 119
Maguire, Neven 335
Maher, Fionnuala 129–30
Mallie, Eamonn 89, 90, 91
Maloney, Mary Ellen 10
Maloney, Pat 10–11
Mandate 227, 230, 233–4, 343–4
Mandela, Nelson 127, 130
Manning, Mary 125, 126, 127, 130
Marks & Spencer 24, 46–7
Marshall, Ann 321
Mater Hospital 314
Means, Randy 168
Metliss, Cyril 142
Mitchell, Cindy 155–6
Mitchell, Jim 92–3, 248

Mitchelstown Stud Farm 69, 71,
    75–6, 106
Mohan, Hugh 245
Molloy, Jerry 38–42
Monahan, Phil 188
Monarch Properties 188, 189
Montgomery, Edward 144, 189
Mooney, Sean 206
Moore, Christy 127
Moriarty (and the Moriarty Tribunal),
    Mr Justice Michael 271–9
Moriarty, Paddy 233
Morrisey, James 110–11, 112–13, 149
Mulhern, Eimear 120
Mulhern, John 70, 120
Mulholland, John 155, 169
Murphy, Dr Michael 121–2
Murphy, Gary 106
Murphy, Professor John 14
Musgrave 68
Musgrave/Supervalu 137

N
Nairac, Captain Robert 80
Nathanson, Andrea 156
National Asset Management Agency
    (NAMA) 298–301
National Prices Commission (1971)
    33–4
National Prices Commission (1973)
    67–8
National Retail Merchants
    Association of America
    (NRMAA) 22
networks, business 69–70
Neville's Bakeries 136–7, 206
Newbridge Foods 206
News at One radio program 276
News of The World 100
Niedermayer, Thomas 83
Night of Thunder (racehorse) 71
Noonan, Michael 247–8

Northern Ireland 284
  Ben Jr held for ransom 79–87
  Dunnes Stores in 59–60, 106, 297
  trade from the Republic 133–4
Nulty, Owen 227, 234, 235
'Nutting Squad,' IRA 92

O
Ó Dálaigh, Chief Justice Cearbhall 42
O'Brien, Charles 119, 180, 354
O'Brien, Conal 46–7
O'Brien, Conor Cruise 263
O'Brien, Darragh 301
O'Brien, Denis 240
O'Brien, Vincent 119, 180
O'Callaghan, Declan 159
O'Callaghan, Miriam 91–2
O'Connor, Brendan 313
O'Donoghue, Pat 199–200, 202, 220
O'Halloran, Brian 66
oil crises 63
O'Keefe, Linda 220
Oliver Freaney & Co. 82, 143, 199,
  232, 238, 272
O'Neill, Fr Hugh 89
Orange County Sheriff's Office
  159–60, 161, 167–8
O'Reilly, Canon Damian 328
O'Reilly, Damian 342
O'Reilly, Tony 284
Organisation of Working Time Act
  (1997) 235
O'Shea, Fr 172
O'Toole, Aileen 187–8
O'Toole, Fintan 62–3, 74–5, 135,
  138–9
Our Lady's Hospice, Dublin 121
Owens, Peter 196

P
Paircéir, Séamus 144–5, 146, 274, 275
Parr, Johnny 8–9

Penneys 60
People in Need 122–4
Phelan, Angela 120, 121, 123, 124,
  173, 220
Phoenix Park Racecourse 120
The Phoenix 245
Point Village Development Ltd
  (PVDL) 298–9
Pope, Conor 310, 314, 317
Portmarnock links 153–4
poverty 7, 14
Power, Robin 141
Power Supermarkets 32, 105
Pratt, Maurice 113–14, 115
press conferences 45
price wars, 1980s 109–15
Price Waterhouse report 207, 209,
  210, 241, 243, 246, 259, 266,
  279–80
Primark 60
Protestants 14
Provisional IRA 83
Purcell, Seamus 119

Q
Quinn, Feargal 33, 105, 170
Quinn, Pat 31–2, 105
Quinn, Ruairi 128–9, 247
Quinn's 33
Quinnsworth 31–2, 67, 105, 110,
  111, 112, 113–14, 115, 137,
  218–19, 283, 284

R
Racing Promotions Group 120
Reddy, Nigel 219
Reeves, Dick 105, 110, 114, 218–19,
  284, 288
Restrictive Practices (Groceries) Act
  (1987) 137
Retail News 69
Retail Week 287

Revenue, Irish 36, 143–6, 208, 221, 237, 244, 246, 250, 256, 260, 267, 269, 274, 280, 292–3
Reynolds, Albert 134, 215, 252
Reynolds, Peter 322, 71
RGDATA 228, 286
Ringmahon 113, 143, 206
Ringmahon House, Cork 51, 75
Rittenhouse, Delta 157, 166–7
road infrastructure development, Irish 27
Robinson, Mary 247
Roche, Stephen 121
Roches Stores 10, 11, 137
Roe, William 228, 229
Ronan, John 15
Ronan, Johnny 15
Ross family 8
Rowes, Dublin 24
Royal Ulster Constabulary (RUC) 80, 84–5, 92
RTÉ 21, 86, 91–2, 100, 123, 130, 165, 171, 314
Russell, Dorothy J. 167
Ryan, Arthur 60
Ryan, Chris 71
Ryan, Diarmuid 219
Ryan, Richie 113

S
Safeway 284
Sainsbury's 284
St Bernard brand 24, 115, 216–17
St Bernard House, Dublin 23, 37, 39
St Vincent's Hospital 120–2, 195, 220, 354
Sarkozy, President Nicolas 315
Scappaticci, Freddie 'Stakeknife' 92
Scargill, Arthur 127
Second World War 11, 14, 17
security, shop 37–8
Sejake, Nimrod 126

Select Retail Holdings (SRH) 289
self-service model 13, 29
Shaw, George Bernard 174
Sheehan, Maurice 234
Shelbourne Hotel, Dublin 70, 76, 100, 101–2, 106
Sheridan, Kathy 32
Sherry FitzGerald estate agents 276–7, 279
shipping agency 8
shopping centres, early 27–30, 47, 65–6
Sinn Féin 82, 92, 127, 318, 325–6
Skelly, Jack 310
Slater, Iain 355
Slaughter and Leventhal lawyers 161
Slaughter, Harrison 'Butch' 161, 168
Smurfit, Jefferson 123
Smurfit, Michael 2, 119, 120, 153, 239, 240
Smyth, Mr Justice 221
Smyth, Noel 112, 165, 167, 168–70, 175, 177, 183, 188, 189, 206, 224, 257–60, 267
Smyth, Richard 110
Smyth, Sam 27–8, 30, 52, 76, 100, 101–2, 103, 240, 241
social circles, Dunne family 69–70
Somers, Bernard 206
South Armagh, Northern Ireland 80
South, Mary 220
Spanich, Sam 159
Spar 68
Special Air Service (SAS), British 85
Special Branch, British 82
Spillane, John 54
Spring, Dick 138
Stafford 105
Stakelum, Jack 244
Stanerra (race horse) 71
Steele, Helen 336

Stephen's Green Shopping Centre 141–3

Stewarts Cash Stores 60

Stouffer's Resort Hotel, Florida 155–6

Streamline 238–9, 269

Street, Andrew 219, 233, 235, 284

The Sun 166

Sunbeam textiles 19

Sunday Business Post 149, 184

Sunday Independent 71, 93, 114, 120, 154, 313, 317–18

Sunday Times 245, 338

Sunday trading 228–9, 234–5

Sunday Tribune 159, 162, 166–7, 173–4, 177, 178, 180, 189, 190, 195–7, 205, 228–30, 240, 243, 245, 287

supermarkets, growth of Irish 32

Superquinn 33, 105, 111, 137, 141–2, 170, 233, 284, 289

SuperValu 109, 113, 137, 285, 289, 339

suppliers 18–19, 23, 24–5, 33
   Asian 148, 177–8, 179, 203
   'long-term agreements' 109
   merchandiser shelf-loading 34–5
   Neville's bakery 136–7
   overdue payments to 200

Supreme Court 42–3

Swinburn, Wally 71

Switzers 61

T

Taggart, Paschal 112–13, 323

Tallaght Shopping Centre 66–7

Taylor, Cliff 243–4

Telenor 240

telethons, People in Need 123

terrorists, loyalist 59

Tesco 67, 110, 111–12, 283–4, 286, 339

'The Indispensable Man' (S.W. Kessinger) 329–30

3 Guys supermarkets 67

Tidey, Don 114, 218

Today Tonight TV show 90, 166

Tompkins, Richard 68

Torreyson, Courtney 160

Trainor, John 208

Travers, Jack 33–5

Traynor, Des 210, 243, 244–5, 251–2, 253, 260

Trócaire 128

the Troubles 59, 109

Trust, Dunne's settlement 53–5, 113, 194, 207, 211, 350
   and taxation 143–8, 205, 211, 275

Tse, Laurence 148

Tucker, Leigh 336

turnover tax 36

Tutu, Bishop Desmond 127

U

U2 124, 158

Uniacke, Bernard 143–4, 194, 206

unionists, NI 59

University College Dublin (UCD) 122

V

VAT payments, Irish republic 133, 179

Vose, Bill 166

W

Wal-Mart 287

Wall, Ken 119

Walsh, Brendan 17–18

Walsh, Darina 220

Walsh, Martin 232

Walsh, Niall 200–1

Watkins, Kathleen 123

Wellworth 284

Weston, Galen 32, 48, 60–1, 62, 283

Whelan Frozen Foods 295–6

Whelan, Pat 341
Whitaker, Edward 9
Whitaker, Sister Attracta 129–30
Whitaker, T.K. 8, 9, 18, 20, 37, 63–4, 74, 103–4, 105, 107, 130
Whittaker, Andrew 47–50, 52–3
WM Morrison 287
Wojcik, Denis 157–8, 162, 166–7
Woodside Restaurant Temperance Refreshment Rooms 7
Wren, Senior Deputy Commissioner Larry 83–4
Wright, Deputy Howard 168
Wright, Paddy 123

Wymes, Michael 41
Wytrex 148–9

X
X (formerly Twitter) 326

Y
Yates, Ivan 112, 248
Yellow Pack products 115
Youmzain 71
Yves Saint Laurent 117–18

Z
zero hours contracts 227–8, 230–1